# IRISH ARTS REVIEW

# IRISH ARTS REVIEW

## YEARBOOK 1993

SPONSORED BY GPA

COVER ILLUSTRATION
Jack B Yeats, *My Beautiful, My Beautiful*, 1953 (detail). Oil on canvas, 102 x 153 cm.
Private collection.

TITLE PAGE ILLUSTRATION

Mainie Jellett, *Achill Horses*, 1939. Oil on canvas, 61 x 91 cm. National Gallery of Ireland, Dublin.

© *Eton Enterprises Limited, 1992*
*Published for Ann Reihill by Eton Enterprises Limited, 22 Crofton Road, Dun Laoghaire, Co. Dublin, Ireland.*

*Irish Arts Review is sponsored by GPA Group plc, Shannon, Ireland.*
*The publishers also received a grant from the Arts Council of Northern Ireland and a grant from the Arts Council / An Chomhairle Ealaion.*

ISBN 0 — 9513722 — 6 — 2 (hardback)  0 — 9513722 — 7 — 0 (softback)  ISSN 0791 — 3540

*Editor: Alistair Smith. Assistant Editor: Elizabeth Mayes. Managing Director: Ann Reihill.*
*Advertising Manager: Vera Finnegan. Administrator: Anne Skelly.*

*Office:* Irish Arts Review, 22 Crofton Road, Dun Laoghaire, Co. Dublin, Ireland.
Telephone 01-2808415, Fax 01-2808309

*Design:* Q Design, 4 Strand Road, Sandymount, Dublin 4. Telephone 01-2839336

*Typeset in Ireland by Design and Art Facilities Limited, Dublin, Ireland.*

*Printed in Singapore by C S Graphics Private Limited.*

*All rights reserved, including the right to reproduce this book or portion thereof, in any form.*

# CONTENTS

## IRISH ARTS REVIEW 1993 VOLUME 9

# FOREWORD

GPA is delighted to maintain its support for the Irish Arts Review, a sponsorship we first undertook in 1986. Our association with the review is a key element of our comprehensive programme of support for the arts and cultural events in Ireland generally.

The Irish Arts Review has a well-established reputation as an authoritative, attractive and accessible record of activity and achievement across a broad spectrum of artistic endeavour in Ireland. The 1992/93 edition of the review maintains the high standards of previous years in the breadth and depth of its coverage and in the quality of production and design.

I compliment Alistair Smith and his editorial colleagues for their work and I commend the review to its readers in the knowledge that it will be a rich source of enjoyment to them.

T A RYAN
EXECUTIVE CHAIRMAN
GPA GROUP PLC

# PREFACE

The *Irish Arts Review* aims to bring to its readers the best studies on Irish Art, art events taking place in Ireland, and also the work of Irish scholars whose interests extend to the visual arts of other countries. This year in order to chronicle something of the extraordinary vitality and activity of Ireland's cultural life, we have instituted a *Calendar of the Year*. Allied with our expanding section of book reviews and saleroom reports, this will result in the *Review* becoming an ever more valuable work of reference for the future.

While this reflects the keen interest of the readers in Ireland *now*, we also seek to illuminate Ireland *then*. Indeed, the core of our enterprise is the publication of art historical research which constantly re-examines and re-defines the art of the past.

Accordingly, we have placed emphasis, this year, on Jack B Yeats whose reputation has been recently enhanced by a number of publications and exhibitions. With our high standard of reproduction, we seek to present our readers with something close to the experience of seeing Yeats' work 'in the flesh'; and through the research and insight of our authors, we seek to give the reader entry to the mind within that flesh.

Works of art, and their creators, are admired, loved, coveted, but little understood. It is the purpose of the *Irish Arts Review* to foster that understanding and to help our readers thereby to maintain intelligent contact with the force of art. In our efforts, we are principally supported by a most understanding GPA, who aid so many facets of the arts in Ireland, and by the Arts Council of Ireland and the Arts Council of Northern Ireland. To these generous agencies, we, and our readers, are grateful.

ALISTAIR SMITH
EDITOR

# ROYAL HIBERNIAN
# ACADEMY OF ARTS

EST 1823

RHA GALLAGHER GALLERY
ELY PLACE · DUBLIN 2
TELEPHONE 612558

# KERLIN GALLERY

## D U B L I N

38 Dawson Street    Telephone 779179    Facsimile 779652

# THE PAPER CONSERVATION STUDIO

Preserves and conserves all examples of works of art on paper including documents, prints, drawings and watercolours.

The studio offers advice on the proper care, storage, handling and display of images in this medium.

We are experienced in the treatment of large collections.

THE TOWER COMPLEX · PEARSE STREET · DUBLIN 2 · TELEPHONE 775655 EXTENSION 251
PATRICK McBRIDE

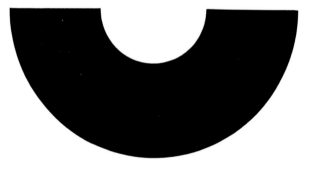

### Sterling Silver Collectables

Decorated with handpainted bone china pansies including two baby gift items with pink or blue bone china bows. Prices: photoframe £35; napkin ring £30; spoon £21; perfume bottles glass-lined £35 and £45; all boxes £30 each.

### The Classic Thoroughbred

Patinated pure bronze horse on a veined grey marble base. Standing 10" H x 9½"L, this study is one of a range of four equestrian pieces: The Rearing Stallion; Dressage, with extended foreleg; The Poser, with typically curved foreleg. Each piece £400, each presented in polished wooden crate.

### The Siren

In cold cast bronze with burnished golden limbs perched on a 'coral' base, 13½" high. Price £240. This piece is one of a range of stylish sea nymphs ranging in price from £155 to £250 each.

### In Full Sail

Sterling silver sailing ship complete with tiny dingy on polished narrow mahogany base. Size 6"H x 6½"L. Price £250.

These illustrations represent a selection from a wide variety of studies of literary, theatrical, equestrian, seafaring pieces, and studies of children in 'pure' bronze, cold cast bronze, and stone. Additionally, there is an unusual range of silver collectables and jewellery; 9ct gold celtic jewellery; solid brass travel alarm clocks, leather and corporate gifts may be viewed at our showrooms. We specialise in corporate and commemorative gifts.

**THE IRISH TIMES**

C·O·L·L·E·C·T·I·O·N     **16 D'Olier Street Dublin 2 Ireland  Tel: 01-6792022  Fax: 01-6797991**

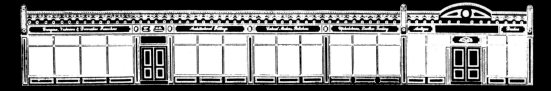

# COOKE ANTIQUES

Pair of Regency Consol Tables, Egyptian Revival, circa 1820

# G. C. Faulkner & Son Ltd

*(ESB Museum House)*

*Est 1950*

SOFT FURNISHING SPECIALISTS

FABRICS & TRIMMINGS FROM THE WORLD'S FINEST FURNISHING HOUSES.

● Curtains ● Blinds ● Bedcovers ●
● Wall Coverings ● Tenting ● Upholstery ●
● Conservatory Canopies ●

REAR LANDSCAPE HOUSE, LANDSCAPE ROAD, CHURCHTOWN, DUBLIN 14. PHONE/FAX: 2987317.
OPEN MON–FRI 8.30 A.M. – 5 P.M.

# Pyms Gallery, London
## FINE PAINTINGS

**Specializing in Nineteenth and Twentieth Century Irish paintings, also British post-Impressionist and French Nineteenth Century works of Art.**

RIGHT
JACK B YEATS, RHA (1871–1957)
*The Politician*
Oil on panel,  14 x 19 inches
Signed lower left JACK B YEATS

BELOW
SIR WILLIAM ORPEN RA, RHA (1878 – 1931)
*The Courtyard, Cany, 1901*
Oil on canvas, 21¹/₂ x  25¹/₂ inches

# Pyms Gallery, London
FINE PAINTINGS

Gallery Proprietors: Alan and Mary Hobart
## 13 Motcomb Street, Belgravia, London SW1X 8LB
Telephone 071-235 3050 Facsimile 071-235 1002
Hours: Monday to Friday 10am to 6pm  Other times, by appointment

# De Búrca Rare Books
## Antiquarian Booksellers
SELECTION FOR EVERY PALATE

Eamonn de Búrca and Charles J Haughey at the launching of
the *Annals of the Four Masters* at the Royal Irish Academy

This company specialises in fine books relating to Ireland. At any one time there is a stock of 10,000 volumes on Irish History, Genealogy, Topography, Biography, Literature etc.

You may feel free to browse in a friendly relaxed atmosphere where you can ramble back through the pages of Irish History.

Recently published
'THE ANNALS OF THE KINGDOM OF IRELAND BY THE FOUR MASTERS'

## The Book of Kells – Limited Edition

Just published is the Fine Art Facsimile Edition of: **The Most Beautiful** book in the world – The Book of Kells, 9th century.

Giraldus Cambrensis, the Norman Chronicler writing in the the twelfth century describes it so, "If you look closely and penetrate the Art, you will discover such delicate subtle lines, so closely wrought, so finely curved, so beautifully adorned with colours that are

still so fresh that you will acknowledge that all this is the work of an angelic, rather than a human hand", and he concludes, "I am always astounded afresh, and always find more and more to admire in it."

This latest limited edition was published in Switzerland and has all the folios in colour. It is in fact almost a replica in every detail of the original manuscript. Further details on request.

## Maamtrasna – Bestseller

Our latest publication, *Maamtrasna – The Murders and the Mystery* by Jarlath Waldron, is a runaway success. The first edition was out of print in two weeks and it has topped the Irish Bestsellers List for the past nine weeks..

The story concerns a horrific and apparently motiveless murder in the Joyce Country of Connemara, with the extraordinary aftermath both political and judicial. Robert Kee in his introduction states "At the centre of this book is one of the most blatant miscarriages of justice in British legal history." Perhaps the greatest statement that has come down to

us is that of Myles Joyce who, protesting his innocence in his only language, Irish, to the last on the scaffold in Galway Jail, stated "I am not guilty. I had neither hand nor foot in the killing. I never knew anything at all about it. May God forgive those people that swore against me. May God have mercy on my wife and her five orphans. But my priest is with me. I am as innocent as the child in the cradle." (translated from the Irish)

Published by Eamonn de Búrca - Edmund Burke Publisher

**LIBRARIES AND SINGLE ITEMS WANTED**

**WORLDWIDE MAIL-ORDER SERVICE**

## CATALOGUES AND FREE BOOK-SEARCH ON REQUEST

'Cloonagashel', 27 Priory Drive, Blackrock, Co Dublin, Telephone 01 288 2159, Fax 01 283 4080

# Gerald Kenyon

## FINE ART AND ANTIQUES

*A fine late 18th century mahogany double breakfront bookcase
of elegant proportions and a superb colour. The upper doors having
the original gilded brass 'chicken wire'. Circa 1790.
Width 11'6", height 8'4", Depth 1'10".*

# House of James Gallery

ELIZABETH COPE, *Garden Chair*, oil on board, 48 x 36 inches. IR£2,700

We have continuous exhibitions of contemporary
Irish artists as well as visiting exhibitions of work from all over the world.

We also have a good selection of 19th and 20th century paintings
and drawings for sale at all times. Ask for details.

Visits our craft shops for Ireland's best in pottery, hand blown glass,
furniture, wood carvings and sculpture.

HOUSE OF JAMES GALLERY · CASTLE STREET · GALWAY
TELEPHONE 091 67776    FAX 091 68271

# House of James Gallery

RAMIE LEAHY, *Wild Flowers at Deerpark*, oil on canvas, 36 x 36 inches. IR£2,500

### Gallery Restaurant

When visiting our gallery, arrange to have lunch in our bustling gallery restaurant
or a candlelight romantic evening meal where you can enjoy the very best of Irish food.
Seafood is our speciality at night. Book the famous *Algonquin Round Table* and meet
new friends or enjoy a quiet table in Galway's most exciting restaurant.

HOUSE OF JAMES GALLERY · CASTLE STREET · GALWAY
TELEPHONE 091 67776   FAX 091 68271

# A National Treasure

Dublin Castle - now restored to its former glory - is the home for a superb collection of paintings, fine art and historic artefacts. It's all part of a heritage of which we can be justly proud.

Together with our national parks and monuments, waterways and wildlife, this heritage is cared for and preserved by the Office of Public Works.

## THE OFFICE OF PUBLIC WORKS
*-caring for our heritage*

# Kilcroney Furniture Ltd

*The Quality Continental Furniture Store*

# THE
# IRISH
# MUSEUM
# OF
# MODERN
# ART

**Open Tuesday - Saturday**

**10AM - 5.30PM**

**Sunday 12PM - 5.30PM**

THE IRISH MUSEUM OF MODERN ART

ROYAL HOSPITAL KILMAINHAM

DUBLIN 8

TELEPHONE 01·718666

FACSIMILE 01·718695

**LEE JAFFE** Colored Nigger Extravaganza (1990)

*The Conjuror* Nathaniel Hone the Elder (1718-1784)

# OLD MASTERS ~ IRISH MASTERS
## The National Collection

# THE NATIONAL GALLERY OF IRELAND

Merrion Square Dublin 2 ~ Telephone 01-615133 Fax 01-615372

Open Mon. to Sat. 10a.m. ~ 6p.m.
Thurs. 10a.m. ~ 9p.m.
Sun. 2p.m. ~ 5p.m.

Restaurant and bookshop open
during Gallery hours.

**ADMISSION FREE**

# NEW APOLLO GALLERY

## PAINTINGS OF IRELAND

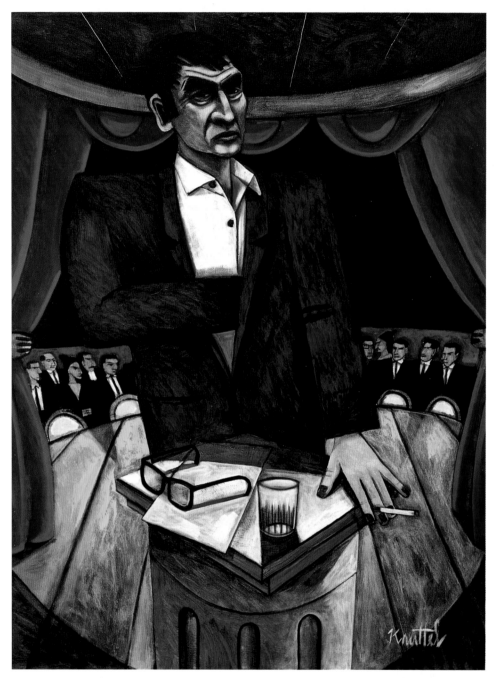

GRAHAM KNUTTEL, *Portrait of Michael Hartnett (Version 2)*, 36 x 48ins.

18 DUKE STREET (OFF GRAFTON STREET) · DUBLIN 2 · IRELAND
TELEPHONE 712609 OR 288 0748  FAX 679 7558

*7 days a week*

# THE TAYLOR GALLERY, LONDON
## Fine Paintings

Specialising in Nineteenth and Twentieth Century Fine Irish paintings,
also Modern British and Nineteenth Century paintings.

*The Blue Shop, Quimperlé,*

William John Leech

Oil on canvas, signed

24 x 16ins

Circa 1917

*The Blue Shop, Quimperlé* was painted circa 1917 on one of Leech's frequent
return visits to Brittany. The large areas of vivid blue and whites applied in
thick abbreviated brushstrokes convey a feeling of strong sunlight which in
turn creates an independent sense of space and depth within the picture.

Whilst undoubtedly Fauve in influence, Leech's paintings followed an
altogether more personal vision. He approached his painting in a more gentle
fashion, culminating in a style combining the Barbizon inspired work of Walter
Osborne with more colourful work of his Fauve contemporaries.

4 THE ROYAL ARCADE, OLD BOND STREET, LONDON W1X 3HD

TELEPHONE 071 493 4111  FAX 071 499 3260

*Hours Monday to Friday 10am – 5pm or by special appointment*

*Illustrated catalogue available*

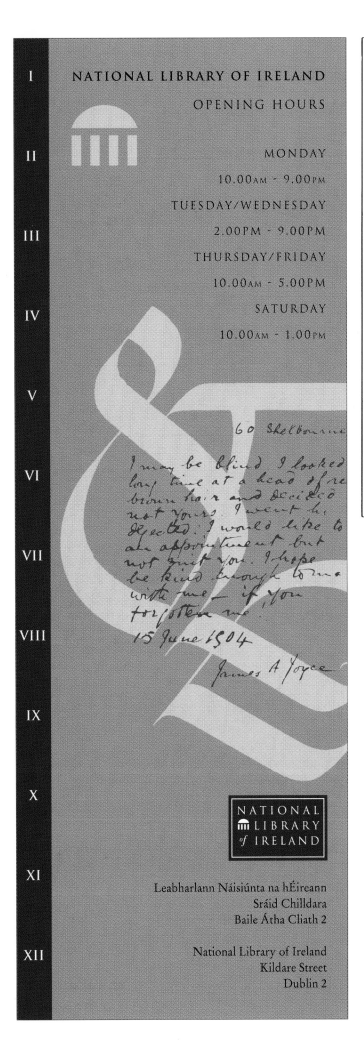

# NATIONAL LIBRARY OF IRELAND

## OPENING HOURS

MONDAY

10.00AM - 9.00PM

TUESDAY/WEDNESDAY

2.00PM - 9.00PM

THURSDAY/FRIDAY

10.00AM - 5.00PM

SATURDAY

10.00AM - 1.00PM

NATIONAL
LIBRARY
of IRELAND

Leabharlann Náisiúnta na hÉireann
Sráid Chilldara
Baile Átha Cliath 2

National Library of Ireland
Kildare Street
Dublin 2

Jack Butler Yeats, R.H.A. (1871-1957), *The 'Haute Ecole' Act*, signed, oil on canvas, 61 by 91.5cm.
Painted *circa* 1920, this work has by family tradition been known by different titles including
the present one (under which it was exhibited) as well as *Market Day, Mayo* and *The Long Car*.
From Sotheby's sale of Modern British *&* Irish Paintings in May 1992.

# The world's leading fine art auction house, at your service in Ireland

Your local Sotheby's representative is able to advise you on all aspects of buying and
selling at auction. Our experts travel to Ireland regularly and if you would like to discuss
the saleroom value of your pictures, furniture, silver, jewellery and other works of art,
our representatives would be pleased to make the necessary arrangements.

To arrange an appointment or for further information and for a free copy of
Sotheby's *Auction News*, please contact:

*Anne Dillon*
51b Dawson Street, Dublin 2. (01) 711786 *&* 711431

*William Montgomery*
The Estate Office, Grey Abbey, Newtownards, Co. Down. (024 774) 668

FOUNDED 1744

# MICHAEL ASHUR

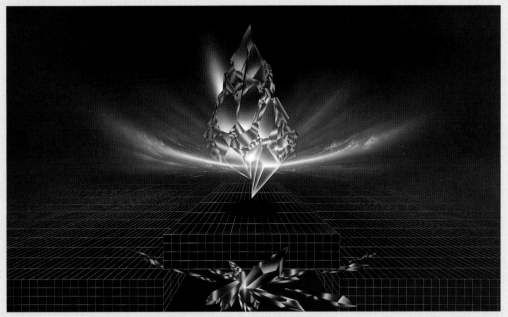

*Infinite illusion on canvas,* 188cm x 305cm

TELEPHONE DUBLIN 01–371580   FAX 01–360127

---

## PETER LINDEN

IRELAND'S MAIN DEALER
IN ANTIQUE & MODERN RUGS
CARPETS, RUNNERS, KILIMS
& TRIBAL WEAVINGS

Open Monday to Saturday 10am – 5.30pm
or by appointment

10 ROCKHILL (MAIN ST.)
BLACKROCK, CO DUBLIN
TELEPHONE (01) 2885875

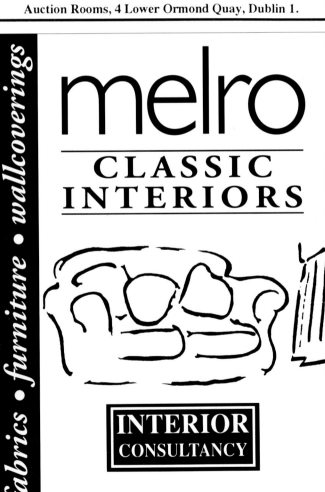
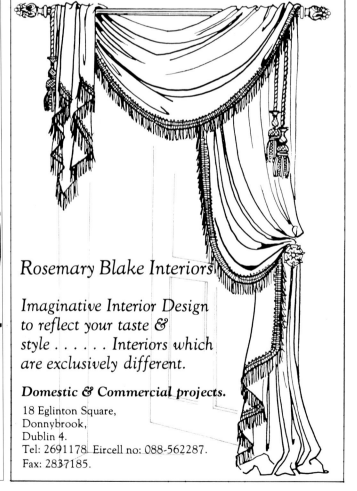

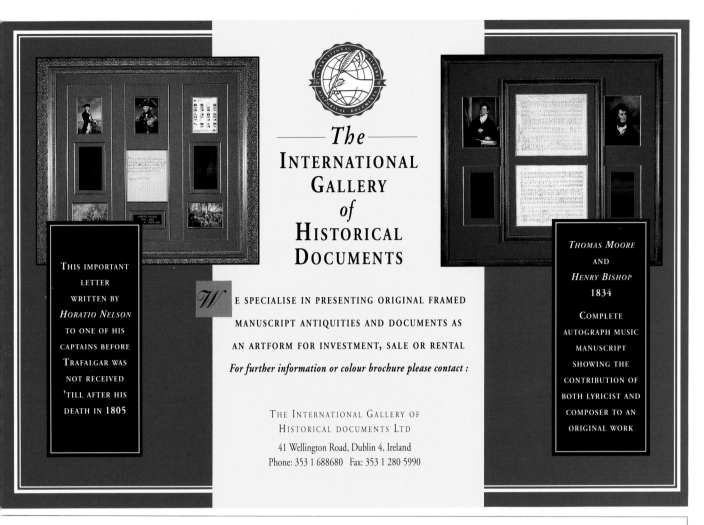

# MEALY'S

We conduct more Irish country house clearance sales than any other fine art firm.
We also conduct regular fine art, antique and specialised sales at our modern spacious auction galleries, Castlecomer, Co. Kilkenny, Ireland.

A 20th century Chinese Chipendale style gilt Wall Mirror by James Hicks, Pembroke Street, Dublin realised £15,900 including fees at one of our recent sales.

A satinwood and marquetry Grand Piano by Steinway & Son of New York & Hamburg realised £20,700 inlcuding fees at one of our recent sales at Castlecomer.

Catalogue subscription forms available on request.

## FINE ART AND RARE BOOK AUCTIONEERS
### MEALY'S LTD.

CHATWORTH STREET • CASTLECOMER
CO. KILKENNY • IRELAND.
TELEPHONE (056) 41229/41413 FAX: 05641627

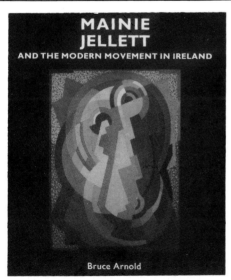

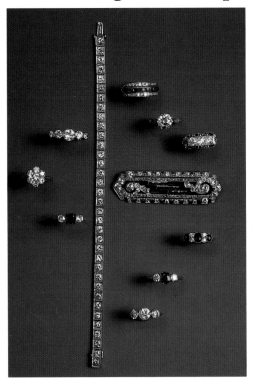

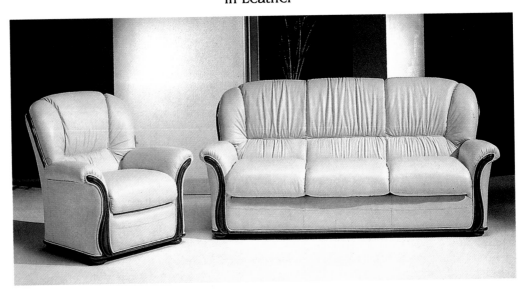

# THE CRAWFORD MUNICIPAL ART GALLERY CORK

Located at Emmet Place, beside the Opera House, in the heart of the city

The Crawford Art Gallery, the city art museum, is housed in one of the most historic buildings in Cork. The collection is particularly strong in late 19th and early 20th century Irish and British art and includes works by Daniel Maclise, James Barry, Harry Clarke and other Irish artists, as well as works by painters of the Newlyn School, such as Frank Bramley, Alfred Munnings and 'Lamorna' Birch. a collection of classical casts is housed in the magnificent Sculpture Galleries, along with works by nineteenth-century Irish neo-classical sculptor John Hogan, and more recent works by Cork sculptor Seamus Murphy. The collection also features recent and contemporary Irish art, with works by Louis Le Brocquy, Barrie Cooke, Mary Fitzgerald and Michael Mulcahy.

The Crawford Gallery is open from 10.00 to 5.00 Mon-Fri and 10.00 to 4.30 Saturdays. The Gallery restaurant is a favourite meeting place for lunch and is also open at night, from Wednesday to Friday.

The friends of the Crawford Gallery, an independent support organisation, organises coffee mornings, lectures and visits to museums and houses both in Ireland and overseas. For details, call Rosaline O'Brien at the Crawford Gallery, 021-273377 (mornings) City of Cork Vocational Education Committee.

*Tony O'Malley Hawk and Quarry in Winter: In Memory of Peter Lanyon 1964 (Acquired 1990)*

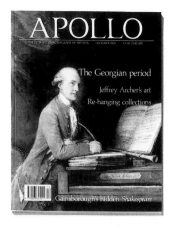
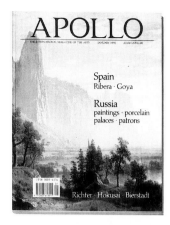

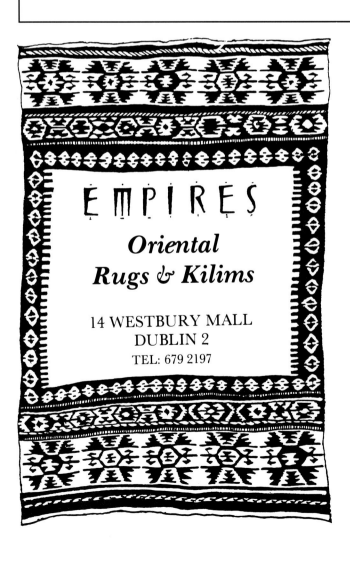

# Visit Ireland
# six times a year...

By reading "Ireland of the Welcomes" you will
be transported to another island – Ireland.
Discover its poetry, prose, artists and humour.
You will be our fireside guests on our travels
through the country, viewing our cities and
towns, enjoying our festivals and folklore.
All this by simply subscribing to
"Ireland of the Welcomes".

*Ireland's Premier Goodwill Ambassador.*

# 300
# And still climbing.

## Dash8
### *Far ahead.*

There have been many celebrations over the years marking the deliveries of Dash 8s to more than 50 operators all around the world. But there are two special circumstances which make a certain delivery in January, 1992 an especially significant event.

This delivery is important because it marks the entry into service of the 300th Dash 8 produced. And because this particular Dash 8 is being delivered to the USAir Group.

The USAir Group consists of 4 owned and 8 franchised USAir Express operators. These companies make up one of the world's largest regional networks, and one of our longest-standing customers.

The new aircraft will join the 43 other Dash 8s of the USAir Group fleet in servicing the airline's very busy Eastern U.S. routes - a job well-suited to the unique qualities of the Dash 8.

Many of the US Air Express operators have chosen to trust their success to the Dash 8's capabilities, relying on strengths tested through more than 2 million flights to deliver 99.2% dispatch reliability.

Our 300th delivery is tangible proof of our customers' belief that the Dash 8 is, clearly, far ahead. And still climbing.

## *de*HAVILLAND

# CALENDAR OF THE ART YEAR

## May

EVENTS

7   **Newman House**, 85-86 St Stephen's
    Green, Dublin. Restored Georgian houses.
    Opened to public.

7   *Until 9 May*
    *Berlin Soundworks*, concerts to coincide with
    *Berlin! The Berlinische Galerie Art Collection
    Visits Dublin 1991* (16 March-16 June) in the
    reopened **Hugh Lane Municipal Gallery.**
    Funded by Dublin 1991, the Goethe Institut,
    Dublin Corporation, The Berlin Senate and
    Lufthansa German Airlines. Catalogue,
    lectures.

11  Ceremonial floodlighting of restored
    **Custom House, Dublin**, by Office of
    Public Works. Eighteenth century pageantry
    and celebrations, including Handel's Water
    Music on the Liffey.

14  Belfast artist **Sharon Kelly** wins the annual
    Alice Berger Hammerschlag Trust award for
    visual arts.

16  *Until 19*
    Opening of **Fifth European Colloquium
    on Culture and Disability** by President
    Mary Robinson. Mansion House, Dublin.

25  Opening of the new **Irish Museum of
    Modern Art** in the Royal Hospital
    Kilmainham, Dublin by former Taoiseach,
    Charles J Haughey. Opening exhibition,
    'Inheritance and Transformation'. Also the
    Gordon Lambert Collection. (see IAR
    Yearbook 1991-92 pp. 61-73)

*Naum Gabo,* The Constructivist Torso, *1985.
Berlinische Galerie.*

*Richard Deacon,* Kiss and Tell *1989 'Inheritance
and Transformation', IMMA.*

26  Opening of newly restored medieval
    **Drimnagh Castle**, Dublin by President Mary
    Robinson.

30  British academic Mr Sandy Heslop BA
    nominated by board of assessors for vacant
    post of Professor of History of Art at
    University College, Dublin

31  University of Limerick announces new
    acquisitions for the *National Self-Portrait
    Collection.*

EXHIBITIONS

1   *Until 25 May*
    **161st RHA Annual Exhibition**,
    RHA Gallagher Gallery, Dublin.

1   *Until 25 May*
    **William Kelly - Recent Paintings**.
    Limerick City Gallery of Art, also
    Architecture Association of Ireland awards,
    1990.

4   *Until 22 May*
    **Barrie Cooke**, Kerlin Gallery, Dublin.

5   *Until 28 May*
    **Valerie Joyce and Paki Smith -
    Paintings**, Berkeley Gallery, Thomastown,
    Co. Kilkenny.

7   *Until 8 June*
    **Nick Miller - The Shadow Line**, City Arts
    Centre, Dublin. Opened by Michael
    Harding.

8   *Until 1 June*
    **BT New Contemporaries**; Arts Council
    Gallery, Belfast. Young artists' exhibition,
    tour, community programme.

---

### May 1991

If Dublin's year as European City of
Culture had any real resonance, it was
during May 1991. From start to finish, the
whole month was crammed with memorable festivities, climaxing with a splendid opening of the city's new **Irish
Museum of Modern Art**. The resonance
— or perhaps dissonance to some ill-
tuned ears — was first heard in early May
when, as part of the *Berlin!* exhibition at
the refurbished Hugh Lane Municipal
Gallery, three concerts of twentieth century German music were provided amidst
the work on show. Anyone already
suspicious of the tenets of Dadaism was
likely to have every prejudice confirmed
by these performances. which included
opportunities for Martin Miches' wonderful flute-playing machine.

An altogether more harmonious occasion came with the reopening of 85-86
St Stephens Green, better known as

*Newman House,* after extensive, although
still incomplete, restoration work over-
seen by architects Sheehan & Barry.
Owned by University College Dublin,
the two eighteenth-century houses
managed to generate modest controversy
amongst conservationists, not all of
whom approved of the windows' new glazing bars or the internal colour schemes.
Complete approbation, however, greeted
the ravishingly refurbished *Apollo Room*
and the new basement restaurant, *The
Commons,* which with extraordinary
rapidity, established itself as Dublin's
most fashionable meeting place.

Four days later, another of Dublin's landmarks, the Gandon-designed **Custom
House,** was unveiled after several years
of work on the heavily-damaged exterior.
Although the eighteenth-century fair in
front of the quayside facade was rather
more muted, not to mention cleaner,
than its original must have been, the
parade from St Stephens Green across the
city had an ample number of belles,

beaux, eccentrics and entertaining od-
dities.

As darkness fell, an orchestra moored
on a floating stage played Handel's Water
Music — no matter that this was composed more than half a century before the
Custom House was built — followed by a
truly spectacular fireworks display.

But most spectacular of all was the official opening of the *Irish Museum of
Modern Art at the Royal Hospital Kilmainham* which, for one afternoon, acted
as an open-air drawing-room for over
2,000 guests. Champagne, stout and
oysters were served in seemingly limitless
quantities; the only other element of the
day which appeared endless was Taoiseach
Charles Haughey's speech, presented on a
rather unsteady podium erected before
the building. Many of those present worried about the permanence of the timber
and corrugated iron pavilion erected in
the museum courtyard and designed by
architects O'Donnell and Tuomey to
accommodate *Brian Maguires's* prison

CALENDAR OF THE ART YEAR

9    *Until 31 May*
     **Damaris Lysaght**. Tom Caldwell Gallery,
     Dublin.

10   *Until 1 June*
     **Bernadette Madden, Batiks,** Gordon
     Gallery, Londonderry.

10   *Until 25 June*
     **Rosaleen Davey - New Works 1989-91**.
     Also **Mary Lohan - Donegal,**
     Taylor Galleries, Dublin.

13   *Until 7 June*
     **Tina O'Connell - Jelly Installation.**
     Temple Bar Gallery, Dublin.

14   *Until 31 June*
     **William Orpen - Hamlet Series**, European
     Modern Art, Dublin.

16   *Until 8 June*
     **Tighe O'Donoghue - New Atlantis**.
     Graphic Studio Dublin Gallery. Drypoints
     and etchings. Grant-aided by the Arts
     Council.

16   *Until 22 September*
     **In a State**, Kilmainham Gaol, Dublin.
     Painters and sculptors explore the question
     of national identity.

17   *Until 8 June*
     **Mary Fitzgerald - Counter act**. Oliver
     Dowling Gallery, Dublin.

24   **Watercolours by Joan Webb**, Kenny's
     Bookshop, Galway.

26   *Until 29 September*
     **Derek Hill Collection** at the Glebe
     Gallery, Churchill, Co. Donegal.

*Nick Miller, Chasm Gaps.*

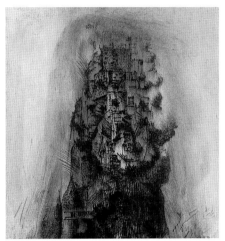

*Tighe O'Donoghue The Pillar.*

27   *Until 16 June*
     **NCAD 1991 Graduate Painters,**
     RHA Gallagher Gallery, Dublin.

27   *Until 19 June*
     **Ciaran Lennon**, Kerlin Gallery, Dublin.

30   *Until 15 June*
     **Patrick Scott - Paintings and Tables for
     Meditation**, Taylor Galleries, Dublin.

SALE RESULTS

PAINTINGS

28   William J Leech, **Sunlight on a Snow-
     Covered Landscape** £17,000; Laetitia
     Hamilton, **Currachs at Kilkee**, £4,000;
     Taylor de Veres, Dublin

29   Mary Swanzy, **Irish pastoral landscape**
     (lot 3, estimate £2,000/3,000) £4,500; Sir
     John Lavery, **Sok el Lechina, 1891.** (lot
     78; estimate £12,000/15,000) £19,000; W J
     Leech, **Fishing Boats, Concarneau** (lot 63;
     estimate £10,000/15,000) £21,000. James
     Adam, Dublin.

LITERATURE

Anne Crookshank and The Knight of Glin,
**The Painters of Ireland** (London 1979)
(lot 97; estimate £50/100) £170; Flora
Mitchell, **Vanishing Dublin** (Dublin 1966)
lot 102, £260; Walter Strickland,
**A Dictionary of Irish Artists**. 2 vols.
(Dublin 1913) £100. James Adam, Dublin

---

paintings. In fact, it stayed in place barely two months, later winning premier prize for 1991 from the Architectural Association of Ireland. Debate continues over the merits of this and, indeed, the £1 million transformation of a seventeenth century former hospital to the design of architect Shay Cleary. The glass and metal foyer and the gravel which supplanted grass in the courtyard generated a healthy public debate on the changing function of historic buildings. Of more immediate concern, many women also felt that only a man could put transparent glass steps on the museum's main staircase (not realising that a woman architect, Eva Jiricna, had already done so). On the opening day, few present seemed interested in climbing them to see the exhibitions upstairs, collectively called *Inheritance and Transformation*. This title was eloquently reflected in the upper landing where a small Paul Henry landscape hung above one of Richard Long's stone circles. The former was part of a loan from the

O'Malley collection; other loans, either temporary or long-term to the new museum, came from Gordon Lambert, Klaus Lafrenz and the Van Abbemuseum, Eindhoven, which for the first few months provided work by early twentieth-century masters such as Braque, Miro, Leger and Mondrian.

Festivities continued that evening with the opening of *Ciaran Lennon's* exhibition of new work at the Kerlin Gallery. Lennon was one of the first contemporary Irish artists to have work bought for the new museum's permanent collection.

Inevitably, the launch of this venture tended to overshadow all other events during May, including the following day's official opening of the restored *Drimnagh Castle* by the President, Mary Robinson. The only mediaeval castle in Ireland with its moat still intact, it had been saved from ruin largely through voluntary aid and the involvement of FÁS training schemes, responsible not just for the refurbishment of the building, but also for

the recreation of a formal seventeenth-century garden in the grounds.

Yet another of Dublin's most important buildings, *Kilmainham Gaol*, played host to an exhibition examining aspects of Ireland's national identity seventy-five years after the Easter Rising. Curated by the Project Arts Centre's Visual Arts Officer, Jobst Graeve, the show invited twenty-one artists to create site-specific pieces as a response to Irish history since 1796, the year this gaol received its first inmate. Naturally, the results were mixed, with some painters, such as Patrick Hall and Paddy Graham, treating the premises as no more than an extended gallery. More interesting were the installations by Dorothy Cross, Pauline Cummins and Alice Maher, all of whom used the space as a starting point for their work. John Kindness provided an Irish harp, the body of which was made up of ninja turtles in mosaic — a fitting and witty comment on the changing nature of Irish culture.

# CALENDAR OF THE ART YEAR

## June

EVENTS

*11*    Jack B Yeats, **Shelling Peas in Moore Street**, (stolen from Cothu exhibition in *Guinness Hop Store*, Dublin on 10 May 1991) recovered by Gardai in Dublin.

*19*    **Castletown Cox**, Co. Kilkenny, home of the late Brian de Breffny, sold for 'well over £1 million'. Sotheby's International Realty, London.

*25*    **The Great Book of Ireland** (see IAR Yearbook 1991-92 pp. 149-52) unveiled by former Taoiseach, Charles Haughey, Irish Museum of Modern Art, Dublin.

EXHIBITIONS

*4*    *Until 20 July*
**Ronan Halpin - Sculpture** and **Paki Smith -Paintings**, Limerick City Gallery of Art.

*5*    *Until 29 June*
**Basil Rakoczi**, European Modern Art, Dublin.

*19*    *Until 4 August*
**Nathaniel Hone the Younger (1831 - 1917).** Major retrospective. National Gallery of Ireland, Dublin. Sponsored by IBM. Catalogue by Julian Campbell (see IAR Yearbook 1991-92 pp 80-87)

*21*    **Sean Fingleton - Spirit and Matter**. Taylor Galleries, Dublin.

*27*    **Rietveld Furniture and the Schroder House**. Irish Museum of Modern Art. Seminar and exhibitions guide.

*Anne Madden, Sea-Box 1990.*

*Michael Mulcahy, Entrance IV, 1987.*
*The Art of the State.*

## July

EVENTS

*5*    *Until 7 August*
**Second National Small Works of Art Competition and Exhibition.** Opened by Patrick Murphy, Chairman of ROSC. *Sligo Art Gallery.* The winners were Annabel Langrish (painting), Mary O'Neill (sculpture), Mary McIntyre (open), Kathy Herbert (drawing), Aidan Linehan (print), Elke Thomas (student work).

*11*    **Jeffers Gallery, Main Street, Kinsale**, Co. Cork, opened by Conor Doyle. Group exhibition including Tim Goulding, Patrick Pye.

*15*    Irish Times interviews 'Women of the arts': **Barbara Dawson**, new Director, Hugh Lane Municipal Gallery, Dublin; **Christine Casey**, Curator, Newman House, Dublin; **Mairead Dunlevy** (of National Museum of Ireland) curator of new ESB Georgian House Museum, 29 Fitzwilliam Street, Dublin; **Pat Seager**, new Director. Irish Writers' Museum , Parnell Square, Dublin.

EXHIBITIONS

*1*    *Until 20 July*
**Thomas Ryan RHA, Retrospective,** Limerick City Gallery of Art.

*2*    *Until 28 July*
**Anne Madden Retrospective. Paintings 1950-90**. RHA Gallagher Gallery, Dublin.

*12*    *Until 31 July*
**Selma McCormack**. Tom Caldwell Gallery, Dublin.

---

### June 1991

After the previous month's crammed calendar, June seemed somewhat subdued, but was marked by a number of strong exhibitions at commercial venues, not least Samuel Walsh's *Fourteen Points of Entry* at the Oliver Dowling Gallery. Moving away from his customary monochromatic approach, Walsh's fourteen abstract meditations on the Stations of the Cross were bought by IMMA to add to its burgeoning collection. The museum offered a temporary home at the end of June to the heavily-publicised *Great Book of Ireland*. A secular version of the Book of Kells for our century, the volume contains three hundred contributions from almost every notable Irish writer and painter and was designed to raise funds for the Clashganna Mills Trust, which helps the disabled and their families. With a reputed price tag of £1 million, this book has so far remained unsold in a nation of avid readers. But then, any reader would

have trouble turning the pages in bed at night.

The National Gallery continued its long-running series of major retrospectives with a show devoted to *Nathaniel Hone the Younger*. Hone's widow left the contents of his studio to the Gallery and this source provided much of the work exhibited. In an effort at rehabilitation, preopening publicity suggested Hone was unfairly considered as a 'painter of cows' and pastoral scenes. The show was something of a disappointment, emphasising that the artist never really escaped from the influence of the Barbizon School and was certainly quite untouched by Impressionism or subsequent movements. Attendances at the show were modest by comparison with previous exhibitions; as usual with the National Gallery, the accompanying catalogue, written by Julian Campbell, was first-rate.

Another exhibition of historical interest was seen at Juliet O'Reilly's European Modern Art Gallery, showing work

by *Basil Rakoczi*, one of the driving forces behind the little-known White Stag Group of Dublin in the early 1940s. A month earlier, the same gallery had exhibited William Orpen's preliminary drawings and studies for *The Play Scene from Hamlet*, which now hang in Houghton Hall, Norfolk. Still more interesting studies were shown in *A Vision of the City: Dublin and the Wide Streets Commissioners*, a temporary exhibition organised by architect Niall McCullough in Newman House. The show served as a timely reminder that our predecessors needed no European edict to create their own city of culture; moreover, as the exquisite draughtmanship proved, urban planning over the past two centuries has become less rather than more cultivated.

### July 1991

July began with retrospectives by two of Ireland's most established (or should that be establishment?) painters. In Limerick, the President of the Royal Hibernian

12    *Until 25 August*
      **Maurice McGonigal RHA 1900-1979.**
      Opened by President Mary Robinson, Hugh
      Lane Municipal Gallery, Dublin. Catalogue
      by Katherine Crouan. Sponsored by
      Ericsson.

16    *Until 14 September*
      **Prints, watercolours, oils by Gerhard
      Richter**, Douglas Hyde Gallery, Trinity
      College, Dublin.

24    *Until 24 August*
      **Exhibition of Visual Art (E V + A)** from
      Limerick. Open submission selected by
      Germano Celant of the Guggenheim
      Museum, New York. Catalogue, talks. The
      City Centre, Dublin.

29    *Until-mid August*
      **The Art of the State. Twentieth century
      Irish Art from the State Collection,**
      Glebe Gallery, Donegal. Catalogue by
      William Gallagher. Also Glebe Gallery
      Collection. Office of Public Works.

## August

EVENTS

1     **John Baraldi** took up appointment as
      Artistic Director of *Garter Lane Arts Centre,
      Waterford.*

5     *Until 10 August*
      **Irish Antique Dealers Fair** and Exhibition,
      Mansion House, Dublin.

5     **Ha'penny Bridge** over the River Liffey,
      Dublin clothed in a giant garment by Belgian
      artist Lily van Oost, now living in Killarney.

*Gene Lambert,* Homage to Jonathan Wade.
*The Art of the State.*

*Tony O'Malley,* Atlantic Studio Inscape 1987.
*The Art of the State.*

EXHIBITIONS

2     *Until 6 September*
      **EspaCe - Irish and European Sculpture of
      the 90s.** RHA Gallagher Gallery, Dublin.

20    *Until 29 September*
      **Irish Watercolours and Drawings.**
      National Gallery of Ireland, Dublin.
      Catalogue; lectures.

24    **Ór - Ireland's Gold**. Opening of permanent
      exhibition of prehistoric gold, National
      Museum of Ireland, Dublin. (see IAR
      Yearbook 1993 pp. 149-52)

17    *Until 25 August*
      **Hughie O'Donoghue - Paintings and
      Drawings**. Kilkenny People Gallery,
      Kilkenny. (see IAR Yearbook 1990-91,
      pp. 144-53)

17    *Until 25 August*
      **Gillian Ayres - Paintings**. Butler Gallery,
      Kilkenny.

## September

EVENTS

10    **Artworks Gallery** opened in Cork.
      Contemporary painting, sculpture, print and
      photography.

15    **Pantheon Gallery** opened, 6 Dawson
      Street, Dublin. Irish and international
      paintings and sculpture.

23    **Irish Professional Conservators and
      Restorers Association** (IPCRA) series of
      conservation exhibitions in nine major
      institutions. (see IAR Yearbook 1993
      pp. 139-43)

---

Academy, *Tom Ryan*, showed work going back to the start of his career. Meanwhile, at the RHA's own gallery in Dublin, *Anne Madden* revealed forty years of assiduous labour. Curated by Siuban Barry and opened by the Taoiseach, Charles Haughey, the exhibition demonstrated just how fine a painter Madden had been, particularly during the 1960s. Later that month, the *Maurice McGonigal retrospective* at the Hugh Lane Municipal Gallery proved equally revelatory; the earliest pictures in the show indicated an enormous debt to the painter's uncle, stained glass artist *Harry Clarke*.

### August 1991

As saleroom prices indicate, McGonigal has never really fallen from favour, and work by other similarly well-loved Irish artists was on shown in the National Gallery's August exhibition of watercolours and drawings from its own holdings. All the best-known pieces were present, including Frederick William

Burton's *The Meeting on the Turret Stairs*, Sean O'Sullivan's sketch portraits and stained glass designs by Evie Hone. A lush repackaging of the National Museum's prehistoric gold collection — called Ór — opened in the same month while at the RHA Gallery, the Sculptors' Society of Ireland organised *EspaCe*, heralded as an exhibition of contemporary European sculptors. In fact, the show carried work by over fifty Irish sculptors and just twelve from the EC, one for each member state. Reversing these figures might have served a better purpose, because the Irish public already get ample opportunity to see work by the sculptors of this country and not enough chance to examine pieces by some of the contributors to this show such as Davis Nash.

Opportunities to see work by distinguished overseas artists are always provided by *Kilkenny Arts Week,* and 1991 proved no exception to that rule, with a fine show by *Gillian Ayres* at the Butler Gallery. The paintings' tropical richness offered a

striking contrast to the more low-key expressionist work of *Hughie O'Donoghue,* English-born but of Irish extraction, at the *Kilkenny People* offices.

As ever in this City during Arts Week, every available space was hijacked to house an exhibition, with mixed results. Outside the official show, the work often becomes shamelessly commercial with no motive other than financial profit to justify its display.

### September 1991

Speaking of commercialism, *two new private galleries* opened in September, both beginning with group exhibitions. In Cork, the Artworks Gallery arrived on an already-crowded contemporary scene, showing sculpture and prints by well-respected names such as Cathy Carmen and John Behan. And in Dublin, collectors Kevin and Gillian O'Brien reopened the Taylor Gallery's former premises at 6 Dawson Street under the name of the Pantheon Gallery. The debut show carried a

# CALENDAR OF THE ART YEAR

## EXHIBITIONS

3    Until 14
**Jane O'Malley. Recent Paintings and Works on Paper.** Taylor Galleries, Dublin

5    Until 27
**Sculpture by Aileen Mac Keogh**. Project Gallery, Dublin.

5    Until 28
**Sheila Maclean - recent paintings**, Gordon Gallery, Londonderry.

11   Until 4 October
**Irish Postage Stamp design.**
RHA Gallagher Gallery Dublin.
(see IAR Yearbook 1990-91 pp. 188-97)

14   Until 4 October
**Ignition. MA Show 1991. University of Ulster Faculty of Art and Design.** Irish Museum of Modern Art, Dublin.

15   Until 28 October
**Anita Groener - Paintings.** Taylor Galleries, Dublin.

17   Until 19
**European Large Format Printmaking Competition by Black Church Print Studio.** Guinness Hop Store, Dublin.

18   Until 17 November
**Kremlin Gold.** Irish Museum of Modern Art. Catalogue, lecture series.
(see IAR Yearbook 1993 pp. 208-16)

18   Until 11 October
**White Stag Group.** European Modern Art, Dublin.

Sean Keating, PRHA, Playboy of the Western World.

19   Until 10 November
**Irish Art and Modernism**, Hugh Lane Municipal Gallery, Dublin. Opened by Councillor Mary Freehill. Catalogue by S Brian Kennedy.

224  **Closed Circuits Opened.** Mixed media installation by Brian Connolly. The City Centre, Dublin.

25   Until 12 October
**Graham Gingles**, Fenderesky Gallery at Queen's, Belfast.

26   Until 19 October
**New Etchings by Patrick Hickey**, Graphic Studio Dublin Gallery.

## October

### EVENTS

1    Until 20 October
**Beckett Festival,** presented by The Gate Theatre in association with Radio Telefis Eireann and Trinity College, Dublin. Sponsored by Aer Lingus. All Beckett's nineteen plays performed at the Gate; his radio and television plays broadcast by RTE; seminars, lectures, discussions and exhibitions in Trinity College, Dublin.

7    Until 8 October
Sale of contents of **Castletown House**, Co. Kilkenny. Christies, Scotland, and Hamilton Osborne King, Dublin.

21   Sale of contents of **Streamhill House**, Doneraile, Co. Cork. Eighteenth and nineteenth century furniture, paintings etc. C Sheppard and Sons, Durrow, Co. Laois.

24   Until 10 November
Wexford Festival Opera

26   Until 8 November
Opening exhibition, **House of James Gallery**,Castle Street, Galway. Showing works by *Sean Keating*, PRHA.

26   Dr David James, former curator of **The Chester Beatty Library**, Dublin, charged with alleged theft of £400,000 worth of Islamic bibles and manuscripts from the Library, and remanded on bail.

30   Michael Diskin moved from Galway Arts Festival to replace Elizabeth McAvoy as Director of **Galway Arts Centre.**

---

pantheon of twentieth-century Irish art, including Evie Hone, Norah McGuinness, Louis le Brocquy and Tony O'Malley. At the Taylor Gallery's elegant new home, *Jane O'Malley* also had an exhibition of new work, in which luridly-coloured carnival-masked figures predominated, looking suspiciously like a sequence of holiday mementoes.

At the Rubicon Gallery, *Gene Lambert*, one of the driving forces behind *The Great Book of Ireland*, held his first one-man show since 1988. *Still Lives* consisted of nineteen paintings showing shanks of meat, not a subject to everyone's taste, most particularly the *Irish Times'* Desmond MacAvock, although the same newspaper's Chief Critic Brian Fallon later included the exhibition amongst the most notable of the year. The largest piece in the show was subsequently bought by Belfast's Ulster Museum.

Still more disturbing for some viewers were *Michael Coleman's* ripped black canvases at Oliver Dowling's Gallery. Their raw aggression contrasted with the tasteful harmony reigning nearby at the RHA Gallery, where An Post had organised a display of *Irish Postage Stamp design*. As David Scott noted in the *Irish Arts Review 1990—91*, an overwhelmingly bland modernism predominates in this area, where anxiety to appear contemporary runs into conflict with the commercial necessities of selling to a conservative market.

The largest exhibition of fine art printmaking ever held in Ireland was organised by the *Black Church Print Studio* at the Guinness Hop Store, since the Studio's own premises had been gutted by fire the previous autumn. Like the earlier *EspaCe* sculpture show, this one incorporated work by artists from all EC member states. And again, like *EspaCe*, twenty-five European artists shared the space with the same number of Irish printmakers, so that this country's contribution overwhelmed that of any other EC nation, providing an uneasy sense of imbalance to the whole show.

Imbalance of another kind was experienced at the *Irish Museum of Modern Art's display of gold from Moscow's Kremlin*. Quite what a show of this kind was doing in the museum was never adequately explained; certainly, the work seemed completely out of keeping with the new venue's professed philosophy of challenging attitudes with contemporary work. Hugely popular, with attendance figures of some 110,000 in two months, the bulk of the pieces on show were notable for their ostentatious vulgarity, culminating in a 1904 Fabergé egg depicting a miniature model of the Kremlin. This exhibition opened on the same evening as a group show at the European Modern Art gallery of work from the *White Stag Group*. Having already hosted exhibitions by *Kenneth Hall* and *Basil Rakoczi* earlier in the year, the Gallery now placed their work in the context of other White Stag members, including *Patrick Scott* and *Brian Boydell,* who today is much better-known as a composer. Ex-

## EXHIBITIONS

2    *Until 19 October*
     **Alice Maher.** Originated by Project
     Gallery, Dublin, and Triskel Arts Centre,
     Cork

3    *Until 19 October*
     **Word and Image** in *The Beckett Festival*,
     Douglas Hyde Gallery, Trinity College,
     Dublin.

3    *Until 26 October*
     **Cherith McKinstry – Recent Paintings,**
     Gordon Gallery, Derry.

3    *Until 2 November*
     **Carole Kay, Sonia Whitefield**, work by
     two young Northern Ireland photographers,
     Arts Council Gallery, Belfast.

5    *Until 30 October*
     **William Scott – Paintings**, Kerlin Gallery,
     Dublin.

9    *Until 15 November*
     **Una Sealy– Paintings**. The City Centre,
     Dublin.

11   *Until 26 October*
     **Cecil King 1921-86**, Oliver Dowling
     Gallery, Dublin.

14   *Until 28 October*
     **Paintings by Shaun Ferguson.** Solomon
     Gallery, Dublin.

15   *Until 20 December*
     Opening of **Crazy about Women** by Lady
     Marina Vaizey, art critic of *The Sunday
     Times*, National Gallery of Ireland, Dublin.

*William Scott, Dream III, 1969.*

16   *Until 20 May*
     **Indian Paintings** also **Western Prints and
     Drawings.** Chester Beatty Library, Dublin.

18   *Until 9 November*
     **Attitude**, group show. Orchard Gallery,
     Derry.

22   *Until 17 November*
     **Making a Modern Street**, proposals for
     inner city housing design by eight architects.
     Irish Museum of Modern Art. Opened by
     Senator Eoin Ryan.

23   *Until 23 November*
     **A Todo Color: in Full Colour.** Forty-two
     Spanish illustrators of Books for Children
     and Young People. Spanish Cultural
     Institute, for Dublin 1991. Library of the
     Royal Dublin Society. Opened by former
     Minister for Education, Mrs Mary O'Rourke.

24   *Until 9 November*
     **Tony O'Malley**, Taylor Galleries, Dublin.
     Catalogue, (see IAR yearbook 1993
     pp. 238-43).

30   *Until 17 November*
     **Edward Maguire RHA Retrospective.**
     RHA Gallagher Gallery. Catalogue by Brian
     Fallon.

## SALE RESULTS

### PAINTINGS

1    J H Craig, **Hornhead**, £3,600; W J Leech,
     **Sunlight on Sails, Concarneau**; £17,500,
     Colin Middleton, **Moneycaragh**; £5,200.
     Taylor de Veres, Dublin.

2    James Dixon, **Figures with Flags**, 1966. (lot
     29) Oil on board, est £800-1,200. Sold £950;
     Roderic O'Conor (1860-1940), **Rocky
     Coastal Landscape** (lot 79). Oil on board,
     est. £3,000-5,000. Sold £10,000; J H Craig
     RHA (1878-1968). **Cows at Sessiagh
     Lake**, (lot 73), Oil on board, est £7,000-
     9,000. Sold £5,500. James Adam, Dublin.

## PUBLICATIONS

15   Paul Durcan, **Crazy about Women**,
     National Gallery of Ireland, £9.95. Forty
     seven poems to accompany the exhibition of
     National Gallery paintings selected by the
     poet.

30   Brian Fallon, **Edward McGuire** (Dublin
     1991) £19.50. Illustrated biography
     published in association with retrospective
     exhibition in RHA Gallagher Gallery,
     Dublin.

---

amples of his painting also turned up at the exhibition *Irish Art and Modernism* mounted at the Hugh Lane Municipal Gallery. Examining the development of Irish art from 1880 to the early 1950s, the show looked cramped and confusing in four small upper rooms of the building. Only when viewed in conjunction with Dr S B Kennedy's substantial catalogue — which could not quite conceal its thesis origins — did the collection of pictures on show begin to make sense. For anyone unwilling to spend some £30 on a book, this important show must have been deemed a disappointment.

## October 1991

Irritation, rather than disappointment was the most frequent negative response to the National Gallery's winter exhibition *Crazy about Women*. Selected from the Gallery's collection by Paul Durcan and accompanied by a volume of forty-seven poems, the show was rather too self-consciously provocative to have any en-

during quality. Mr Durcan's book, on the other hand, sold over 23,000 copies and became the season's favourite Christmas present. Artistically more invigorating, the Kerlin Gallery showed a selection of work by the recently-deceased *William Scott* in early October. Cool, disciplined and quite uncompromising, these pictures from the mid-1960s to 1971 had an intellectual rigour equal to the work of *Samuel Beckett*, which was celebrated in a festival during the month's first three weeks. Aside from readings, discussions and performances there was a fine exhibition in the Douglas Hyde Gallery of images from Beckett's work, with contributions from artists such as Louis le Brocquy, Jaspar Johns and Robert Ryman. Still, the most powerful image of all remains Richard Avedon's quite remarkable photographs of Beckett, which were reprinted on the cover of the official festival programme. Portraiture was in favour during October, with a well-received show by *Una Sealy* at Dublin's

City Centre Gallery, and a retrospective of the late *Edward Maguire's* work at the RHA Gallery, in which portraits again predominated. Birds were Maguire's other abiding intrest, and these also featured strongly in the exhibition, which was drearily hung, so that one wall of portraits was followed by another holding ornithological subjects; the outcome was an unfortunate sense of monotony which did a disservice to this fine painter.

Attempting to escape from the monotonous tyranny of late twentieth-century design, a group of eight architects showed plans for *Making A Modern Street* at the Museum of Modern Art. In a more modest form, this exhibition had been seen earlier last year at the Riverrun Gallery, but on neither occasion did it sufficiently arouse the interest of any property developer willing to translate ideal into reality. Translating the written word into images, forty-two Spanish illustrators of children's literature showed their work as part of the Spanish Cultural

## November

E V E N T S

5   *(throughout November)*
Belfast- born John Kindness completes final construction of **The Waterfall of Souvenirs,** 14 foot high sculpture for new *Europa Buscentre*, Glengall Street, Belfast, incorporating ceramic souvenirs donated by the public. Arts Council of Northern Ireland.

18   **Dublin Writers' Museum** opened in nos.18 and 19 Parnell Square. Mid-18th century houses restored by Bord Failte, assisted by EC funds. Director, Pat Seager; Curator, Robert Nicholson.

27   **A Woman Reading a Letter** by Gabriel Metsu, part of the Beit Collection stolen from Russborough, Co. Wicklow, returned by Turkish authorities to the *National Gallery of Ireland*, Dublin.

E X H I B I T I O N S

1   *Until 27 November*
**Ivon Hitchens** and **Jack B Yeats**, Kerlin Gallery, Dublin.

1   *Until 23 November*
**John Behan - New Sculpture**, Gordon Gallery, Londonderry.

5   *Until 27 November*
**Irish Watercolour Society**, RHA Gallagher Gallery, Dublin.

6   *Until 19 December*
**Cecily Brennan**, Douglas Hyde Gallery, Trinity College, Dublin. Opened by playwright Frank McGuinness. Catalogue; talks.

*Cecily Brennan*, Line Fissure, Sulphur and Rope Lava.

*Jack B Yeats*, A New Town, 1947.

7   *Until 30 November*
**Gerhard Richter**, Arts Council Gallery, Belfast. Sponsored by Deutsche Bank.

14   *Until 30 November*
**Charles Tyrrell - New Work**, Taylor Galleries, Dublin.

14   *Until 30 November*
**Patrick Collins**, Tom Caldwell Gallery, Dublin.

18   *Until 19 December*
**Budapest!** A celebration of contemporary Hungarian art and culture for Dublin 1991. RHA Gallagher Gallery, Dublin and other venues.

21   *Until 14 December*
**New Work by Andrew Kearney**, Belltable Arts Centre, Limerick.

22   *Until 26 January 1992*
**Irish Art and Modernism, 1880-1950**. Ulster Museum, Belfast. (from HLMG) Catalogue by S B Kennedy. Sponsored by Northern Bank.

26   *Until 21 December*
**A Woman's Place**, City Centre, Dublin. Installations created by women's art groups, and 14 women artists in Tallaght, Crumlin, Finglas, Blanchardstown, Swords. Opened by President Mary Robinson.

26   *Until 31 December*
**The Paintings of Paul and Grace Henry - A Retrospective Exhibition**, Hugh Lane Municipal Gallery, Dublin. Catalogue; talks. Opened by President Mary Robinson. (see IAR Yearbook 1989-90 pp. 43-55, and IAR Yearbook 1993 pp. 174-78)

---

Institute's contribution to Dublin's 1991 celebrations. *A Todo Color: In Full Colour* was as variable as any other group show, but ought to have provided some inspiration for Ireland's own band of illustrators, the total number of which would certainly not add up to forty-two.

### November 1991

Illustration, along with almost every other aspect of the visual arts, was covered in a new annual produced by John O'Regan's Gandon Editions in early November. Already responsible for publishing a series of slim monographs on contemporary Irish artists, with *Portfolio*, O'Regan now expanded his field to include architecture, and what was described as 'time-based media' which proved to incorporate theatre, film and video work. An enormous number of full-colour pages alternated with dense — and even occasionally impenetrable — text, to make up a welcome addition to art publishing in Ire-

land. One of the artists given prominence in *Portfolio*, painter *Cecily Brennan*, had her own solo show in the Douglas Hyde Gallery during the same month. Ever since her exhibition of Howth rhododendrons at the Taylor Gallery in the mid-1980s, Brennan has enjoyed a reputation for producing lush, semi-abstract pictures. The latest work, often of surprisingly massive dimensions, possessed an altogether more severe tone than her earlier work, being based on the artist's visit to Iceland.

Landscapes also predominated in an arresting exhibition at the Kerlin Gallery which juxtaposed *Ivon Hitchens* with the somewhat older *Jack B Yeats*. Hitchens' barely-covered canvases came out better from the comparison, Yeats' paintings frequently looking too fussy and even, in several instances, rather coarsely finished. At the Taylor Gallery, *Charles Tyrrell* presented new work which was, as usual, quickly bought up by a Dublin audience

who all too rarely get a chance to see this Cork-based artist's paintings. Galway-based sculptor *John Behan* showed new work in Derry, while across the province, Belfast's Ulster Museum welcomed the *Irish Art and Modernism* show seen at the Hugh Lane Municipal Gallery earlier that year.

In turn, that space now accommodated a retrospective devoted to *Paul and Grace Henry*. His West of Ireland paintings have always attracted admiration, but Grace Henry's art has only recently begun to win favour in the salesrooms. She will probably never acquire the popularity in Ireland of her estranged husband, since, as this show once again demonstrated, the subject matter is both on a smaller, more intimate scale and also more French than Irish in inspiration. The exhibition was opened by the President, Mary Robinson who, that evening had performed the same honours at the City Centre, Dublin where *women's art groups* from the suburbs

# CALENDAR OF THE ART YEAR

## PUBLICATIONS

*1* **Squarings** - a hand made book of twelve poems by Seamus Heaney and four lithographs by Felim Egan. 100 copies only. Graphic Studio Dublin Gallery. (to be launched in Harvard University, Boston, May 1993).

*5* **Portfolio**, Ireland's new contemporary art annual (Gandon Editions, Dublin). Launched Temple Bar Gallery, Dublin.

*6* **Irish Arts Review - 1991-92** Launched in No. 90 Merrion Square, Dublin.

*22* S B Kennedy, **Irish Art and Modernism 1880-1950**. Published by The Institute of Irish Studies, Queen's University, Belfast, for the Hugh Lane Municipal Gallery of Modern Art, Dublin, to coincide with the exhibition. (See IAR Yearbook 1993, pp. 167-73).

## December

### EVENTS

*10* Mary Coll, formerly project director for Treaty 300, took up position as Artistic and Financial Director of the **Belltable Arts Centre, Limerick**, replacing Mairead Byrne, who has decided to write full-time.

*17* Total Government grant to the **Arts Council** cut by £244,000, a reduction of two per cent. (see IAR Yearbook 1991-92 pp. 99-106).

*19* Patrons' Evening. **Temple Bar Gallery Studios**. Opening speech by Dermot Egan, Chairman of Cothu.

*Mainie Jellett*, Composition, 1922. *IMMA exhibition.*

*Brian Ballard*, Daisies in a Glass Bowl, 1989.

## EXHIBITIONS

*1* *Until 29 February 1992* **Stephen Balkenhol**, innovative German wood sculptor. Irish Museum of Modern Art.

*3* *Until 20 December* **Let There Be Light**, O'Reilly Institute, Trinity College, Dublin. Science Faculty Quatercentenary Exhibition; travelled subsequently to the Ulster Science Centre, Derry; Birr Castle, Co. Offaly and The Linenhall Arts Centre, Castlebar, Co. Mayo. (see IAR Yearbook 1993 pp. 84-85)

*3* *Until 21 December* **Mainie Jellett and Abstract Cubism,** European Modern Art, Dublin. Opened by Bruce Arnold.

*6* *Until 22 March 1992* **Mainie Jellett: A Retrospective Exhibition**, Irish Museum of Modern Art. Catalogue by Daire O'Connell. Opened by President Mary Robinson. (see IAR Yearbook 1993 pp. 167-73)

*6* *Until 24* **Brian Ballard**, Kerlin Gallery, Dublin.

## PUBLICATIONS

*6* Bruce Arnold, **Mainie Jellett and the Modern Movement in Ireland**. Yale University Press. (see IAR Yearbook 1993 pp. 167-73).

*12* Daniel Grose (c. 1766-1838), **The Antiquities of Ireland. A Supplement to Francis Grose**. Edited by Roger Stalley. Irish Architectural Archive, Dublin. (See IAR Yearbook 1991-92, Book Review Section. )

were showing their work. Like all such exhibitions, this one was as interesting for what it said about the lives of the participants as for their art. Insight into the cultural life of post-communist Eastern Europe was provided by a mini-festival, *Budapest!*, at the RHA Gallery, sponsored by the recently-opened Hungarian Embassy. The centrepiece was an exhibition featuring work by twelve contemporary Hungarian painters and sculptors, some of whom had created pieces specially for the show at the National Sculpture Factory in Cork. A film series included features by the country's best-known director, *Istvan Szabo* — responsible for *Mefisto* and *Colonel Redl* amongst others— and there were also performances by the *Bartok Quartet* and ethnic music groups. Anyone looking for a slightly different taste of Hungarian culture could participate in the gourmet week run at the Westbury Hotel.

November witnessed both restoration

and destruction on successive days; the former when the *Dublin Writer's Museum* opened in Parnell Square after £2.3 million had been spent on two neighbouring houses which had suffered years of neglect from their owners, the City of Dublin VEC. But the damage done to these buildings — including the theft of several fine marble fireplaces — was surpassed by the fire which overnight struck *Slane Castle*, Co Meath on 19 November, the worst such disaster since the destruction of Powerscourt House in 1974. Fortunately, the superb gothic revival ceiling of the ballroom, dating from 1812, was saved and work began immediately on securing a roof over the entire property, restoration of which was expected to cost several million pounds. Leaking roofs were amongst the many problems which also faced the *Project Arts Centre*, which celebrated its *25th anniversary* towards the end of the month with an all-night party and the promise of refurbished premises

as part of the Temple Bar rejuvenation programme.

### December 1991

In the same district, *Amelia Stein* held a solo exhibition at the Gallery of Photography in early December. Called *Solomon's Children*, the show consisted of large black and white portraits of Ethiopian Jews newly-arrived in Israel; a change of subject matter from the rockstars more usually scrutinised by Ms Stein's lens. During the same month, another woman, Mainie Jellett, was the subject of a major retrospective exhibition at the IMMA. This exhibition had been heralded by a small showing of Jellett's drawings at the Wexford Opera Festival in October. IMMA's celebration, with full catalogue, coincided with the publication of Bruce Arnold's eagerly-awaited book *Mainie Jellett and Modern Movement in Ireland*. A little extra weight was added to the band-wagon by an exhi-

# CALENDAR OF THE ART YEAR

## January

### EVENTS

5     **Arts Council Gallery** badly damaged by large-scale bomb in Bedford Street, Belfast.

6     Dr Michael Ryan, Keeper of Antiquities at the National Museum of Ireland, appointed Director of **Chester Beatty Library**, Dublin.

13    **Bank of Ireland Show Awards** to Jobst Graeve and Pat Cooke, for **In a State**, at Kilmainham Gaol; Gene Lambert and Theo Dorgan for **The Great Book of Ireland**; the Samuel Beckett Festival at the Gate Theatre, Radio Telefis Eireann and Trinity College Dublin.

15    *Until 6 March*
**Japan at the Crawford** arts festival, opened by M. Yuzio Hatano, Ambassador of Japan. Exhibitions, demonstrations, lectures, music, tea ceremonies etc. Crawford Art Gallery, Cork. City of Cork Vocational Education Committee.

19    **Style, Centre, Identity**, Hugh Lane Lecture at the Municipal Gallery of Modern Art, Dublin, by Dr Rudi Fuchs, Director, Gemeente Museum, The Hague.

### EXHIBITIONS

1     *Until 31 January*
**Turner Watercolours**, also **Liber Studiorum** and **McNeill Bequest** of Miniatures. National Gallery of Ireland, Dublin.

*Toshikatsu Endo,* Untitled, 1983.

*Fergal Fitzpatrick,* Novice, 1991

4     *Until 31 January*
**Janet Mullarney 'The Straight and Narrow'.** Orchard Gallery, Derry.

7     *Until 8 February*
**Earth Air Fire Water**. The Sculpture of Toshikatsu Endo. Douglas Hyde Gallery, Dublin.

10    *Until 31 January*
**Sharon O'Malley, Ancient Presence.** Paintings. Project Arts Centre, Dublin.

11    *Until 29 January*
**Clement McAleer**. Kerlin Gallery, Dublin. (see IAR Yearbook 1993 pp. 233-37)

14    *Until 22 February*
**Fergal Fitzpatrick, Taken as Given**. City Centre Gallery, Dublin.

23    *Until 16 February*
**Joseph Hanly Retrospective.** RHA Gallagher Gallery, Dublin.

30    *Until 1 March*
**Edward Maguire RHA. A Retrospective Exhibition**. Originally scheduled for early January at the Arts Council Gallery, Bedford Street, Belfast, but postponed because of bomb damage. Ulster Museum, Belfast.

31    *Until 19 February*
**Elizabeth Magill. Belongings**, Kerlin Gallery, Dublin.

## February

### EVENTS

5     *Until 16*
**The Tower of Babel**. Dance theatre show. Irish Museum of Modern Art.

---

bition at European Modern Art, Dublin, setting Jellett's work in the context of 'abstract cubism'.

For several decades, Jellett has been regarded as a painter awaiting the popular appreciation which went to her less talented male contemporaries. Strangely, the concerted attention she received at the close of 1991 did not somehow lead to the emergence of that appreciation. Overall, the response to what was clearly meant as an act of restitution was muted; the subtlety of stylistic change during Jellett's last twenty years gave IMMA's retrospective a rather monotonous quality and certainly contributed to the low-key reaction.

### January 1992

No need to worry about the posthumous reputation of *Joseph Mallord William Turner*, whose watercolours were on display, as usual, for the month of January at the National Gallery. Equally small

pieces could be seen at the Rubicon Gallery's second annual exhibition of drawings by artists such as *Charlie Cullen* and *Lorcan Walshe*. And at the Kerlin Gallery, diminutive details appeared to obsess *Elizabeth Magill*, whose x-ray paintings examined the minutiae of handbags and briefcases. Up at the RHA Gallery, the relatively-youthful *Joseph Hanly* held a substantial retrospective, the impact of which was somewhat diminished by the force of repetition. This same problem had already affected the *Edward Maguire* exhibition, now installed at the Ulster Museum after a bomb had seriously damaged its intended Northern Ireland venue, the Arts Council's Gallery on Bedford Street.

*Japonisme* appeared to be back in vogue once again, evidenced by a number of exhibitions around the country, beginning with *Toshikatsu Endo's* carbonised installations at the Douglas Hyde Gallery. Like giant sticks of charcoal, they were

a world, not just a few counties, away from the daintier aspects of the *Japan Festival in Cork's Crawford Gallery*. Nineteenth century woodblocks, including examples by two masters of the form *Kunisada* and *Kuniyoshi*, vied for attention with Japanese dolls, art by four contemporary artists, prints by the staff and students of Tama College and a newly-installed 'Japanese-Irish Meditation Garden'. And the unmeditative could content themselves with cookery classes, flower arrangement and tea ceremonies.

### February 1992

More Japanese pottery and woodblocks, by *Takeshi Yasuda* and *Shiko Munakata* respectively, went on show at the Ulster Museum in early February, while at Dublin's Kerlin Gallery, the Spanish artist *Carlos Roig* showed a series of abstract canvases inspired by Zen contemplation. Still more stark, former performance artist *Nigel Rolfe* had a one-man installation

## CALENDAR OF THE ART YEAR

8    **New Irish Architecture 7**. Architectural Association of Ireland awards 1992 attracted 75 entries. Medal-winner: **The Irish Pavilion** - O'Donnell and Tuomey Architects. Exhibition at Irish Museum of Modern Art until 1 March, 1992 then touring. Book, **New Irish Architecture** (AAI, 1992)

12   President Mary Robinson announced sponsorship of **National Gallery of Ireland** by IBM to finance the tour to galleries in Chicago, San Francisco, Boston and New York of **Master European Paintings from the National Gallery of Ireland: Mantegna to Goya.**

18   Mr Nicholas Robinson, Chairman, **Irish Architectural Archive**, opened exhibition celebrating the quantity surveying work of Patterson, Kempster and Shortall over the past 130 years. Irish Architectural Archive, 73 Merrion Square, Dublin.

26   *Until 5 March*
     **Dublin Film Festival**

EXHIBITIONS

1    *Until 22 January*
     **Atlantic Skies.** Paintings on both sides of the Atlantic by Denise Ferran. (see IAR Yearbook 1993 pp. 224-32) The Gordon Gallery, Derry.

3    *Until 29 January*
     **With Respect To Mr Joyce.** Exhibition of oil paintings and prints by Gerald Davis for anniversary of birth of James Joyce. Davis Gallery, Capel Street, Dublin.

*Baron Gérard*, Julie Bonaparte as Queen of Spain (1808/9) NGI tour to USA.

*Denise Ferran*, The Bar Mouth, Malin.

4    *Until 8 March*
     **Contemporary Irish Art Society Exhibition**. Works purchased 1989/90/91 opened by James White. Lecture series. Also **Louis le Brocquy Room** (open until 29 March 1992) showing the artist's work for first 30 years of his career. Hugh Lane Municipal Gallery, Dublin.

5    *Until 16 June*
     **Imagining an Irish Past: The Celtic Revival 1840–1940.** 300 works of art, including some from National Museum of Ireland and Ulster Museum, exploring the rediscovery of medieval Celtic ornament. Catalogue; related events. The David and Alfred Smart Museum of Art, University of Chicago, USA.

6    *Until 29 June*
     **Paintings by William Kelly**. Project Arts Centre, Dublin.

11   *Until 7 March*
     **Nature Morte.** Exhibition of photographs by Michael Boran. Temple Bar Gallery and Studios, Dublin.

19   *Until 24 March*
     **Caravaggio and His Followers.** National Gallery of Ireland, Dublin. Catalogue by Sergio Benedetti.

21   *Until 12 March*
     **Nigel Rolfe – Hands**. Black and white photographs. Oliver Dowling Gallery, Dublin. To complement the installation **Resonator**, Douglas Hyde Gallery, Dublin.

22   *Until 11 March*
     Abstract paintings by young Spanish artist, **Carlos Roig**. Kerlin Gallery Dublin.

---

in the Douglas Hyde Gallery, called *Resonator*, which consisted predominantly of elegantly-spaced upturned terracotta flowerpots and enlarged black and white photographs of hands. Smaller hands were also in evidence at the simultaneous Rolfe show in Oliver Dowling's Gallery. And photography was again the medium for *Michael Boran's* Temple Bar Gallery exhibition, *Nature Morte*. The twenty-one hand-tinted pictures showed an assortment of toys set against different backgrounds, one often amusingly at variance with the other.

The National Gallery mounted a charming exhibition called *Caravaggio and his Followers*, in which the followers overwhelmed their leader. Based around its own collection of seventeenth century caravaggesque paintings, the only work by the master himself *The Supper at Emmaus* came on loan from London's National Gallery. Meanwhile, it was announced that forty-four European master-

pieces from our own institution would be taking an extensive tour around the United States of America, beginning in June. As if to make up for this deprivation, the *Contemporary Irish Art Society* held an exhibition at the Hugh Lane Municipal Gallery, showing its gifts to that venue over the past thirty years, as well as a selection of work purchased since 1989. Amongst the former, almost every expected name could be found; Cooke, Dillon, Souter, Scott, Ballagh and Le Brocquy, who also got his own room for two months containing work from 1939—67, much of which would have come as a revelation to anyone who only knew the later literary portraits. The CIAS's more recent acquisitions showed a refreshing diversity, ranging from Nancy Wynne Jones' *Shannon at Sunset* to Clifford Collie's *Memory*; two acts of remembrance that were far apart in appearance.

Form rather than appearance have long

been the concern of quantity surveyors Patterson, Kempster and Shortall, which celebrated 130 years of business with a fascinating exhibition of photographs and drawings at the *Irish Architectural Archive* opened by that organisation's chairman, Nicholas Robinson. One of the company's oldest clients is Trinity College, Dublin; PKS worked on the university's Graduate Memorial Building in 1892 and a century later is involved in the Beckett Theatre and Hamilton Library, both now nearing completion.

### March 1992

As part of its Quatercentenary programme, *Trinity College* also revamped the groundfloor of the Old Library in Front Square in a manner which was, quite frankly, unsympathetic to the architecture and motivated by a commercial concern to increase the number of visitors through the premises' gift shop. Both the Book of Kells and the Book of Durrow

## CALENDAR OF THE ART YEAR

## March

### EVENTS

2  **Ciaran MacGonigal** took up appointment as Director of the RHA Gallagher Gallery, Dublin.

10 Opening of exhibition of work of architect and designer, **Eileen Gray**, born Co. Wexford, 1878. Design Museum, London.

13 GPA with support of Henry Moore Foundation sponsor exhibition of work of **Alexander Calder**, one of America's best-loved sculptors of the 20th century. Exhibition (until 7 June 1992) at **Royal Academy of Arts**, London. Catalogue.

21 **Arts Council of Northern Ireland** announced opening of its temporary Gallery space, 56-60 Dublin Road, Belfast. Inaugural exhibition (until 4 April) **Contemporary Norwegian Ceramics** and some recent acquisitions from the Arts Council collection.

### EXHIBITIONS

5  *Until 27 March*
   **Boxes and Drawings by Graham Gingles.** Project Arts Centre, Dublin in conjunction with Fenderesky Gallery, Belfast. Catalogue.

7  *Until 31*
   **Alfonso Lopez Monreal.** New paintings and prints, Orchard Gallery, Derry. Catalogue.

11 *Until 11 April*
   **Father Jack P Hanlon 1913-1968. Paintings and Watercolours.** Pantheon Gallery, Dublin.

Gerard Dillon, Bathers Malaga.

Cecil Salkeld, Couple in a Bar.

13 *Until 25 April*
   **E V + A 1992.** Open submission show, selection by Lars Nittve (Director of Centre for Contemporary Arts, Malmo, Sweden). Limerick City Gallery of Art, the City Hall and Slattery's pub.

15 *Until 1 April*
   **Felim Egan**, Kerlin Gallery, Dublin.

16 *Until 28 March*
   **Power and Movement.** New age paintings by Georgina Heskin, Central Libary ILAC Centre, Dublin.

18 *Until 11 April*
   **An Installation by Andrew Kearney**, winner of Barclays Young Artist Award 1992, Temple Bar Gallery, Dublin.

20 *Until 27 March*
   Spring Show of Gallery Artists, including *Tim Goulding, Maurice Henderson.* Iverni Gallery, Kenmare, Co. Kerry.

24 *Until 16 April*
   **Robert Dawson Retrospective 1940–91.** European Modern Art, Dublin.

26 *Until 11 April*
   **T P Flanagan RHA, A European Journey.** Taylor Galleries, Dublin. (see IAR Yearbook 1993 pp. 144-48)

27 *Until 15 April*
   **Willie Doherty. New Colour Works**. Oliver Dowling Gallery, Dublin.

31 *Until May*
   **Beyond Description.** Recent loans and acquisitions from Irish Museum of Modern Art's collection, including works by *Sean Scully, Tony O'Malley* and *Marie Foley.* Irish Museum of Modern Art, Dublin.

were moved to a sterile shell called the Treasury and their former resting place, the first-floor library, has had its academic atmosphere destroyed by the intrusion of cash-tills ringing up sales in the shop downstairs. This extraordinarily crass refurbishment on the part of the college met with little public comment. A greater stir was caused by *Andrew Kearney's* installation at the Temple Bar Gallery, the interior of which was taken over by what can only be described as a corrugated-iron castle. Cramped for space, this towering edifice was best seen through the gallery's outside windows and even though it was meant to have been designed specifically for Temple Bar, probably looked better in Limerick's Belltable Arts Centre, where it had already been shown the previous winter. That venue was once again pressed into service for *Young EV+A*, part of Limerick's annual visual art extravaganza based in the City Gallery, Pery Square.

Long-established as an open-submission show of high calibre, *EV+A* each year invited a different non-Irish adjudicator to make a personal selection from the pieces offered. 1992's adjudicator, Lars Nittve of Malmo's Mooseum, made a choice which seemed to have no apparent theme, though award-winner Kate Malone's installation, *Lead Lady*, did share some similarities with the work of Dorothy Cross, another one of this year's award winners, as she had been in 1990.

Former EV+A prize-winner *Felim Egan* had a new show of his paintings at the Kerlin Gallery, spare in style though thankfully not in number. Up in Derry, a friend of Egan's, the Mexican artist *Alfonso Lopez Monreal* also presented new work at the Orchard Gallery, later transferring to the Arts Council of Northern Ireland's new exhibition space on Belfast's Dublin Road. Monreal's paintings, owing an obvious debt to the folkloric

traditions of his native country, had been seen the previous year at Dublin's Taylor Gallery, which in March held an exhibition of work by *T P Flanagan* called *A European Journey*, although the pictures on show differed little from those produced in the artist's home county of Fermanagh. At the Pantheon Gallery, a modest retrospective of *Jack Hanlon's* work was presented, mostly comprising watercolours found in his studio after the artist's death. Yet another retrospective — this time of the still-living *Robert Dawson* — was held at the European Modern Art Gallery; the opening brought together a galaxy of former models who had worked with Dawson when he was a photographer. And at Oliver Dowling's Gallery, *Willie Doherty* presented five of his large-scale photographic prints, as usual superimposed with cryptic captions, but this time in colour rather than the customary black and white.

# CALENDAR OF THE ART YEAR

SALE RESULTS

4    Cecil Ffrench Salkeld R H A (1908-68), **Couple in a Bar**, (lot 33). Oil on board, (est £2,500-3,500). Sold for £4,200; Gerard Dillon (1916-71), **Bathers, Malaga**, (lot 41). Oil on board, est. £2,500-3,500. Sold for £3,000. Taylor de Veres, Dublin.

PUBLICATIONS

4    Dermot Mc Guinne, **Irish Type Design**. Illustrated history of printing types for use in the Irish language. (Irish Academic Press). (See IAR Yearbook 1993 Book Review Section)

6.   **Organising an Exhibition** by Siobhan Barry; **Handle with Care!** by John Hunt; **Taxation Guide for Artists** by Martin Mulchrone; **Directory of Arts Managers in Ireland**, ed. Patricia Quinn. An Chomhairle Ealaíon, The Arts Council, Paperbacks, £3 each.

## April

EXHIBITIONS

1    Until 10 May
     **Sounding the Depths**. A Collaborative Installation by *Pauline Cummins* and *Louise Walsh*, artists in residence at Irish Museum of Modern Art for previous six months, and winners of Arts Council Bursary for 1991 to complete this work. Talks; discussions; workshops. Irish Museum of Modern Art, Dublin.

3    Until 1 May
     **Rainy Mondays Flicker By**. Film and mixed-media work by Orlagh Mulcahy. Opened by Paul O'Reilly, Director, Limerick City Gallery and Administrator of E V + A. Project Arts Centre, Dublin.

Carey Clarke RHA, Mr Tom Murphy, Playwright
RHA Exhibition.

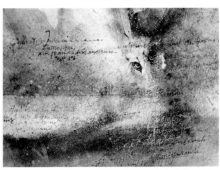

David McGrail, A Shadow exiled, fades
RHA Exhibition.

4    Until 22 April
     **Anne Madden – Drawings from Masks.** Kerlin Gallery, Dublin.

7    Until 30 April
     **New Paintings** by Derry artist, *William Kelly*. Flowerfield Arts Centre, Portstewart, Co. Derry.

8    Until 7 June
     Installation by Swedish artists **Jan Hafstrom** and **Cecilia Edefalk**, officially opened by H M The Queen of Sweden. Irish Museum of Modern Art, Dublin.

9    Until 2 May
     **Sitework: Architecture in photography since Early Modernism**. Orchard Gallery, Derry, with *Impact 92*, Derry City Council.

14   Until 6 May
     **Sean McSweeney.** Narrow Water Gallery, Warrenpoint, Co. Down.

17   Until 15 May
     **Pollen installation** by German artist *Wolfgang Laib*. Douglas Hyde Gallery, Trinity College, Dublin.

24   Until 30 May
     **Cut Here**. Recent paintings by Corinna MacNeice. Tom Caldwell Gallery, Dublin.

28   Until 5 July
     **Alberto Giacometti – The Artist's Studio**. Sculptures and paintings from the collection of the Tate Gallery, London. Opened by Mr Tom Kitt, Minister of State for Arts and Culture. Irish Museum of Modern Art, Dublin

29   Until 23 May
     **162nd Annual Exhibition**, RHA Gallagher Gallery, Dublin.

---

### April 1992

Substantial colour photographs were one element in an installation called *Sounding the Depths* at the Museum of Modern Art in early April. The two artists responsible, Pauline Cummins and Louise Walsh, also incorporated audio and video material into their work, a remarkable, if at times disturbing, examination of their own bodies. By comparison, *David Godbold's* cheeky juxtaposition of classical art with comic-strip characters at the Kerlin Gallery looked like childish provocation. Earlier in the month, again at the Kerlin, *Anne Madden* had shown a series of drawings from the old masters (amongst whom she included photographer Helmut Newton) which would not have disgraced an art student but seemed rather belated in so well-established an artist. Just as well-known, Sligo-based painter *Sean McSweeney* had

a one-man show at the Narrow Water Gallery in Warrenpoint, Co. Down, which has established a reputation for championing the work of Romanian as well as Irish art painters. From Germany, *Wolfgang Laib* installed a square of pine pollen on the floor of the Douglas Hyde Gallery. This could only be viewed from the venue's balcony, which ought to have eased the worries of any hay-fever sufferers — although since Laib trained as a doctor, presumably he could have prescribed the necessary remedy.

The sunshine of Spain predominated in *Martin Mooney's* elegant landscapes at the Solomon Gallery, where the skies of Cordoba looked inter-changeable with those of Dublin; if only it were so off-canvas also. And Cordoba provided the source of inspiration for *Brian Kennedy's* monoprints at Oliver Dowling's Gallery, bold abstracts in rich Moorish colours. More monoprints could be seen at

Dublin's Graphic Studio, which presented an exhibition called *Edition 1* and included work by Tony O'Malley, Mary Fitzgerald, Cecily Brennan and Charles Brady. This show had been selected by art collector Marie Donnelly and architect John Meagher, one of the board members of the Museum of Modern Art. So it seems fitting to conclude where this feature began, at the IMMA. Almost a year after it first opened this venue hosted a show based on *Alberto Giacometti's studio*, which had originated at Liverpool's Tate Gallery. Previously, such an exhibition would almost certainly not have come to Ireland and for this reason alone, the advent of IMMA looks set to have a profound influence on the development of art in Ireland long after happy memories of its opening have faded.

*Robert O'Byrne*

# THE THEATRE OF THE CITY: DUBLIN 1991

The fragmentation and destruction of our urban heritage by the twentieth century has been met by a counter-offensive launched by conservationists. With their campaign for the retention of existing fabric and the public's growing awareness of conservation issues, the pressures of nostalgia are also brought to bear on the new. In Dublin, planning and public opinion has preferred the new to ape the images of the eighteenth century. This is a lie without any attempt to replicate or develop the qualities the tradition of Georgian building exhibited. The result is a travesty, for the spirit of the past is not conjured up by quoting its forms. And for all this conservation and the getting up of contemporary building in eighteenth century drag, the fragmentation of the city has gone on unchecked. The magnificent endowment of a unique urban fabric, woven and fashioned over centuries, is still being torn and unravelled.

Dante's supreme work of poetic art, *The Divine Comedy*, can be viewed in such a way that it becomes a simile for the city of Dublin as it stood on the threshold of the twentieth century. Dante's masterpiece has been compared '. . . to a crystallographic growth which the unceasing drive towards the creation of interlocking

*With reference to Dublin's year as Cultural Capital of Europe, **John Olley** assesses some recent developments and aspirations in urban design.*

forms, penetrates and unites'. It is a 'live compaction, whose validation depends throughout on the quality of our reading, on our capacity, itself triggered and disciplined by the poem'. There is an overall design and there is local intensity so that the 14,223 verses form one single unified and indivisible stanza.[1] One might even be forgiven for believing that every word is related to each and every other word.[2] Dublin's 'crystallographic growth' took a millenium. Each age re-read the text and made its own distinctive contribution to the complexity and richness of the interlocking and united 'compaction'. Alas, the twentieth century has neither confirmed nor recognised the masterpiece which the centuries have compiled, perhaps this is because of the paucity of our reading.

On a clear day, as we come over the brow of the hill along the Swords Road by Whitehall, this route from the north leads our gaze to what was the location of the medieval city of Dublin. A spired

tower can be seen on axis against the backdrop of the Dublin Mountains. To its left and right is a veritable entourage of towers, spires and the green of copper clad roofs and domes. The road continues its easy descent to the Liffey, curving gently before aligning itself with a different spire in the straight stretch of Drumcondra Road. The road then drops down to the Tolka River and loses sight of the south side of the city. When we emerge from the dip, the new landmark returns to demand our attention. The classical spired tower of Francis Johnston's St George's Church is focused by two nineteenth century terraces to make it the axial marker along another straight length of road. Under the railway bridge and over the canal the spire edges to the left but never loses its authority as it towers over the terraces that line our route. Finally it vanishes — but only momentarily. As we cross Eccles Street, it reappears in all its glory, dominating and containing a short vista with its imposing classical portico boldly supporting the magnificent spire. Indeed the church is the focus of a set-piece design. Sited on the bend, it terminates the view in both directions along the road as well as presiding over Hardwicke Street which drops down the hill along a more axial line from its facade. St George's as

*The Custom House, Dublin*

# THE THEATRE OF THE CITY: DUBLIN 1991

the centre-piece of this urban tableau established a landmark in the extension of the Gardiner Estate, and as such it could be seen from Sackville Street (later to be extended to create the present O'Connell Street). The spire of St George's thus functioned to draw the gaze across from the northern route to meet the eastward drift of the city's centre of gravity as it forsook the medieval core in the late eighteenth century.

Distracted by this virtuoso piece of neo-classical planning, we have missed the arrival, as our axial marker, of the distant and dominating spire of St Augustine and St John (the late nineteenth-century church on Thomas Street). It asserts the presence of the Liberties on the other side of the Liffey. This landmark, growing larger every moment, leads us down Dorset Street as the visual connections into the inner city quicken in pace. Past Frederick Street, a glimpse of the Parnell Monument marks the north end of O'Connell Street. At the next junction, our path is crossed as St Mary's answers the cupola of the Rotunda Hospital down Granby Row and across Parnell Square. Then into Bolton Street and, to our right, we can look away from the city up Henrietta Street, a noble place for all its despicable neglect as the remains of

Dublin's most important and grandest ensemble of Georgian houses provides an architectural setting for the curved gateway of the entrance to the the later King's Inns.

The road bends sharply towards the south to confront us with the long perspective down Capel Street and the final approach to the Liffey. The vista is brought to a conclusion and climax beyond the river as the short rise of Parliament Street is blocked by the portico of City Hall and capped by the green copper dome.

Over Essex Bridge we straggle the wide watery boulevard of the Liffey and its Quays as they lay a powerful central east-west axis on the city to join land to sea. Along this line are located two of Dublin's grandest eighteenth-century public buildings: to the right the Four Courts and to the east, beyond Ha'penny Bridge as it braces itself between the Quay walls, the Custom House, which once mediated between sea and land both physically and fiscally.

Arrival at the City Hall has brought us before the present seat of civic government. Here we can discover another axis which ran from church to learning where architecture and urban design have precipitated this relationship in the real

space of the city. To the west the bulk of Christchurch Cathedral, anchored in the city by its robust tower, bars a distant view up Lord Edward Street. And to the east the wide facade of Trinity College encloses College Green as it broadens out from Dame Street.

Advancing towards Trinity we pass South Great Georges Street, whose straight stretch is visually contained at the first curve by the facade of the South City Markets (the most ambitious Gothic Revival building to infiltrate Georgian dominated Dublin). Just before the west face of Trinity College, Chapel Lane reveals the overbearing tower and spire of St Andrew's. This massive architectural block was strategically positioned in the plan of the church and its site when it was rebuilt after the disastrous fire of 1860. Now the spire exerts an influence on College Green, and as it rises clear of Suffolk Street, its foreground, it becomes an axial marker for the eastern approach to the city along Leinster and Nassau Streets. This is one of many examples where a public building has taken the opportunity to enter into a dialogue with the city, asserting its presence and becoming a figure in the urban landscape. It embroidered itself onto, and wove itself into, the fabric of the city — it discovered and

*Looking up Parliament Street towards City Hall.*

*The Custom House Dock Development — "tyranny of incoherence".*

# THE THEATRE OF THE CITY: DUBLIN 1991

created new patterns and relationships.

If, at the City Hall, we had turned right and journied west on that ancient route, we would have been accompanied by a series of orchestrated vistas that have been liberated by this reciprocal accommodation of building and city. Relationships have been contrived or discovered within the locality or across the city.

First we climb Lord Edward Street, which was cut in the nineteenth century in order to extend the line of Dame Street towards the Cathedral and give the church greater authority in the new burgeoning city to the east. Around Christchurch Place, flanking the great ecclesiastical vessel, we enter High Street, whose short straight length reveals our axial alignment with the Wellington Monument in Phoenix Park where it once signalled the boundary between city and country.

As the road snakes beyond High Street into Cornmarket, Thomas Street and on-to James Street, the churches of Sts Augustine and John, St Catherine and then St James take turns to allow their towers or spires to align our route. Like St Andrew's, both St James and St Catherine's strategically located their towers on difficult and concealed sites to assert their presence and to guide us west.[3] As Thomas Street gives into James Street, the truncated spire of St James moves to the side, allowing a distant spired tower to shift on and off axis before we can just distinguish, through the haze of the winter form of mature trees, the bulk of the Royal Hospital Kilmainham to which it belongs. We can imagine the importance the Royal Hospital once held on its prominent site above the Cammock River. It completed and closed the vistas presented on the journey from the city.

Over the centuries the fabric of Dublin was 'compacted', as new additions or redevelopments, large or modest in scale, contributed to the 'crystallographic growth'. A building of distinction would encourage the readjustment of its surroundings to make an architectural and urban virtue out of its specialness, or it might be picked up by some distant part of the city and incorporated into the composition of another locality. Alternatively, unpretentious insertions would be involved in the subtle fusing of one small development with another, transforming the ordinary to the extraordinary as each fragment worked to reveal and contrive echoes across the city and reflections across the street. Modest buildings played their part in two ways, either they acknowledged their immediate surroundings, submitting themselves to a setting from which a public building could emerge with importance, or they adjusted their posture to combine with humble neighbours to transform the commonplace to something exceptional, as the whole became much more than the sum of the parts.

In the eighteenth century, civic design came to the fore as both a priority and an active process, with the projects of 'improvement' being pursued by the Wide Streets Commissioners[4]. Charged with improving the infrastructure of transport routes within Dublin, their action was directed from a position of pride in the three-dimensional qualities of the city. The widening and straightening of routes served to provide the capital's public buildings with appropriate architectural perspectives to enhance rather than erode their appearance. Thus a dignified setting and approach was given to the Royal Exchange (now the City Hall), Trinity College and the Custom House. They extended Sackville Street to, and across, the river to feed into a pair of diverging streets in a gesture to link the north to the south of the city.

Such a corporate imperative to regulate and aggrandise the public realm was far from new in the history of cities. In 1299 the poetic genius, Dante, was a member of a communal commission which received authority to widen and straighten the streets of Florence.[5] Optimistic and positive interventions in cities have been and *are* possible. Additions and alterations can be both complementary to, and inclusive of, the existing fabric. While enhancing and reinterpreting the old, they can establish the integrity and modernity of the new. The past can be absorbed by the present to create a contemporary city.

Contrariwise 'My mind is ahistorical, I would welcome the clean sweep. I could build something better, I am sure of that, than has been left by our fathers.'[6] So wrote Wyndham Lewis with ruthless arrogance. He was painter, writer, critic and relentless irritant. Such an outburst became a *modus operandi* for the twentieth century. To illustrate it, Le Corbusier, one of the giants of twentieth century architecture, proposed his solution to the insalubrity and outmoded condition of Paris by formulating the *Voisin Plan* . 'Instead of a flattened-out and jumbled city such as *the airplane reveals to us for the first time*, terrifying in its confusion, our city rises vertical to the sky, open to light and air, clear and radiant and sparkling . . . The persistence of the present state of crisis must otherwise lead rapidly to the destruction of that past.' And for this, ironically, 'The districts of the *Marais*, the *Archives*, the *Temple*, etc., would be demolished.'[7]

In order to emphasise its modernity, the plan and its details depended on an act of radical disjunction from its spatial context. It uncompromisingly cut a segment from Paris and replaced it with a plan that simply refused any dialogue with the past or its three-dimensional surroundings. It entailed an inversion of the figure-ground relationship of the city. It terminated a tradition which favoured the creation of urban spaces, streets and squares carved out from the background of the built fabric, and, in its stead, planted a *Landscape* with autarchic objects. Its modernity was achieved by an inversion, isolation and exclusion. Although this particular heroic and aggressive act of planning and architecture was never carried out, Le Corbusier's scheme for Paris bequeathed a planning sensibility to the twentieth century for the use of both architects and civic officials. It could be applied to a quarter of a city or an individual site where each new intervention, whether large or small, would concern *itself* primarily with *itself*. This approach to design ignores any responsibility to the fabric of the city, but, more than this, it unravels and negates the cumulative and syncretic achievements of the past. This can be seen in Dublin today, whether as a result of new building, a scheme for conservation, the introduction of planting, or remarkably simplistic approaches to the solution of traffic problems. Each action is monocular and self-referential.

From the late seventeenth century onwards, the Liffey was treated as a positive element within the city. The previous practice of turning away from the water's edge was reversed. A generous quay was now addressed by the front facades of buildings. The discovery of the water's edge was completed by the Wide Streets Commissioners. The river became a grand watery boulevard, lined with quays and terraced with architecture. Its impor-

# THE THEATRE OF THE CITY: DUBLIN 1991

tance was celebrated in the late eighteenth century by positioning the Custom House and the Four Courts to address this artery which then united the south and the north of the city. The twentieth century again reversed the process, as planning blight, wilful neglect and gratuitous demolitions have turned the river and quays into a no-man's land separating north from south as a social and economic divide.

In 1991 the careful restoration of the Custom House endowed it with an almost luminous quality. However, surrounding developments have done much to dim its splendour, in particular, the Custom House Dock Development, which occupies a site of immense importance, where it could have contributed to the architectural backdrop of its distinguished neo-classical neighbour and at the same time risen to terminate the view from the heart of the city along the quays. Instead, it abdicated its responsibilities in favour of bullying the Custom House and coarsening the capital as it blesses the skyline with its tyranny of incoherence.

To mark Dublin's Year of Culture, the newly restored Custom House celebrated 200 years by becoming the focus and backcloth for a spectacle of fireworks, music and carnival, made all the more dramatic by its quayside location. The potential of the public building in the city was rediscovered for this special occasion, but, alas, its everyday life is circumscribed by a tight cordon of heavy traffic.

The motor car has played its own distinctive role in the restructuring of the layout and texture of many European cities. By construction and blight, swathes were torn through the fabric and communities of Dublin in the dash to establish new road systems. Little more was achieved than the destruction of the organism they claimed to serve. These new routes immediately filled up with traffic to harass pedestrians and residents alike with the evils of noise and atmospheric pollution. Cars were supplied by endlessly sprawling suburbs whose rapid expansion was stimulated by fiscal policy and incentives which recognised no responsibility for feeding profits back into an essential and efficient public transport system. A vicious circle was established whereby traffic converged on the inner city from the suburbs, and roads were built to service the perceived need. Such a vortex has enormous economic consequences, as more time is lost in the journey to work and more energy is burnt by stationary and slow-moving vehicles. Now, a return to living in the inner city has become an imperative to neutralise the centrifugal forces of expansion and the consequent disembowelling of the inner city.

In medieval Dublin the twilight zone was the rim, a tide mark of society's flotsam and jetsam. Viewed from the centre, a life of immorality, crime, poverty and disease was seen to inhabit and colonise the edges. The squalor of the margins has not been resolved by the twentieth century. Instead it has been squeezed to the centre by the halo of suburbia, or ejected and exiled to the wastes of the satellite new towns. The city was centripetal, drawing affluence and grandeur to its heart. Now Dublin is centrifugal as it disperses and dissipates material wealth and life to the periphery where they lose their intensity and energy, the concentric ripples spreading out to wash and erode an ever expanding shoreline. The inner city has become a kind of black hole into which the margins of society and life have collapsed.

As with some of today's squatter settlements and the shanty towns of Third World cities, the fringes of medieval towns, despite their privations and poverty, had a vibrancy and vitality all of their own. They might be compared with the margins of medieval manuscripts, where seedy and garrulous images run riot, and form a kind of critique on the prohibitions and prescriptions of the texts that occupied the centre stage of the sheet – a subversive life viewed from the centre, a carnival lived at the fringes. Where these communities have matured and acquired wealth for their own disposal, the physical fabric presents a compelling and fitting relationship between life and its architectural setting without recourse to pompous splendour. Here was demonstrated an inventiveness and ingenuity within the confines of limited means. Many surviving borghi of Italy, faubourgs of France and liberties of Ireland and Britain endorse the creative potential of a degree of self-determination.

The little inner-city residence which persisted in Dublin occupied two contrasting configurations. Firstly, fragments of the faded shadows of Le Corbusier's vision for the new city were erected on the urban steppes of the inner city clearances.

These slab-blocks have become physical fortresses rather than protected communities. Each unit is trapped in a hostile environment with no gradation between public and private, and little contact with its surroundings which lack social and spatial definition. Disjunction between inside and outside, public and private is absolute, the apartment a space capsule essential for survival in this hostile architectural environment. These are the scraps of a utopia stripped of its necessary elaborations and qualifications. By design, living was reduced to ergonomics, and architecture to Hannes Meyer's simplistic formula – function multiplied by economics. Dwellings were not even machines for living in, only cages for automata. This represented the final extinction of a tradition of designing for living in a city, a process at which Dublin once excelled.

A second location of the survival of inner city living lies in the interstice between the voids of planning blight or redevelopment. A particularly vibrant community occupies the remnants of the Liberties (whose name is descriptive of its origins as an area that was outside the early medieval wall of Dublin). Like the margins of the manuscripts, it enjoyed a certain freedom from the city's codes of financial and moral practice. This community has offered stiff resistance to road programmes and executive interventions that threaten to fragment its identity and degrade environmental conditions. It supports an active group preoccupied with upgrading the physical and social environment through the development of derelict sites for housing and social facilities. It possesses, in addition, a keen eye for the historical narrative of the area and its people. It is regrettable that the community's proposals and commitment to self-help have been met with indifference.

It seems that, with the passing of the grand Georgian town house, we have all been consigned to the servants' quarters instead of migrating to the piano nobile. There, one might find a paradigm for a quality of plan and proportion, an articulation of public and private, and the orchestrated interrelationship between community and intimacy, inside and outside, aspect and prospect – variety and richness in an unassuming and eloquent plan. From the grand houses of Merrion and Mountjoy Squares, to the modest

# THE THEATRE OF THE CITY: DUBLIN 1991

*From the exhibition,* Making a Modern Street, *showing a street of buildings, each designed by one of seven different architectural practices.*

*From* Making a Modern Street, *corner site.*

# THE THEATRE OF THE CITY: DUBLIN 1991

developments that ring the inner city, there was no process of miniaturisation terminating in meanness, but rather a paraphrase, more economic, yet maintaining generosity and dignity. Behind single storey facades of dimensions which would not shame a *piano nobile* in the city centre, an entrance and saloon of noble proportions precedes a split section with kitchen and service below and bedrooms above. Yet with this example available for re-interpretation to suit the conditions of the late twentieth century, recent building near the city centre has brought suburbia practically on to O'Connell Street. More sinister and depriving, along the Grand Canal, Georgian is travestied, for, behind a facade cluttered with anachronistic and misread eighteenth-century decoration, lurks a miniature back-to-back slab-block. A dwelling has become a commodity, not a setting to promote dignity in everyday life.

## MAKING A MODERN STREET
### A new design for city living

As a contribution to the Year of Culture, Group '91, a collective of young Dublin-based architectural practices came together to realise a project, *Making a Modern Street*. This was an expression of their continuing commitment to urban design and their belief in the need to re-establish the tradition of living in the city. Over the last decade, through exhibitions, proposals, research and publications they have done much to create an awareness of Dublin's distinguished urban heritage, and to help foster public perception of the potential of streets and squares to become the theatre for everyday life.[8]

On a derelict site in the Liberties, eight designs were combined to remake the identity of the public realm by completing the street. Each individual site was of equal area on a tapering parcel of land, and this allowed a variety of plot conditions from narrow and deep to broad and shallow. This ensured that the separate designs might have a value as a prototype, exploring the possibilities and potential of each condition. Furthermore, from plot to plot a great diversity of types was investigated; one, two, three-bedroomed or studio apartments, maisonettes and individual houses all sited above some form of commercial use. The formidable collective talent used great ingenuity in the pursuit of quality in each

interior, turning to advantage aspect and prospect, the relationship with the street, the community of site and plot as well as the possibility of wider views over the city and beyond to the Dublin Mountains. Access to communal and sometimes private outdoor space has established a rich interaction between inside and outside. For Group '91, the final project presented an architecture which '. . . *illustrates a wish to overlay on our tradition a delight and an excitement about modern architecture, maximising space, light, transparency and movement within the density of urban building.'*[9] Alas, this is more rhetoric than reality, a proposition and aspiration which, at the moment, eludes them. The project resides in an illusionary world. The built reality would not have confirmed the aspirations of the verbal prologue. Deep light wells pose as usable and delightful outdoor spaces. And the proclaimed interest in the luminous environment fails to investigate the subtleties required to compensate for the low levels of available light which result from such a demanding density of occupancy of the individual plots.

Through their past campaigns they have won a battle for the importance of the urban environment and they have composed an agenda which they must now address. The project is more than a polemical gesture, it is an attempt to relearn and to teach the interrupted tradition of urban design in which Dublin once excelled and with which it created its own distinctive character. It is an essential stage in the evolution of a simple, elegant plan as the mould for rich possibilities. This was the very hallmark of the Georgian house type. The process of refinement requires built examples to provide models — built examples to be investigated for their inner logic and qualities, not their circumstantial visual imagery.

As a proposition for a street, the total project looks like architectural anarchy. The combined facades present an undigested Babel of borrowed and concocted images, creating a cacophony rather than an exciting and stimulating visual tension. The hand of the editor is required. At times over-wrought, individual designs are in need of control by the removal of the superfluous and self-conscious architectural inventions that impede the eloquence of the proposition. It is here that a danger resides. Design

threatens to vanish into an image-laden conceit which will never intersect with social and physical realities.

However, within the collective design there are some intriguing fragments. The corner site tackled by McGarry, NiÉanaigh and Tynan, although it lacks some of the spatial verve aspired to in other schemes, has produced a remarkable design. It engages both streets in a complexity of relationships achieved by a very restrained plan and facade, and begins to reintroduce that lost urban design skill which once used the ordinary to create the extraordinary.

The problem tackled was monumental with a wide range of aspirations and accommodation packed onto a single site. The resultant complexity of the physical construction seems inevitable. However, a problem of strategy has arisen in this project, perhaps the consequence of a number of converging and inappropriate pressures. The Corporation donated one of its many derelict sites in the Liberties. The team worked to make the proposal a viable proposition for a developer by crowding in a large number of units. The result is a rather simplistic interpretation of the urban condition. A glimpse at Roque's 1756 map of Dublin would reveal an intensity of building on the street's edge to contain and define the public domain. But behind the dense layer of building that defines and contains the public realm, the plots allowed alternative methods of escape from the noise and social pressures of the street and city. Seen in this context, it is not necessary to build from boundary to boundary to simulate urban living, and neither does it make sense when the alloted site is surrounded by so many derelict voids. In the social context of the Liberties such a development seems alien. In the proposals of the community group active in the Liberties, this site, a couple of hundred yards from the bustle of Thomas Street was designated for social housing.

## STANHOPE GREEN
### Achievement in urban design

Across the city in Stoneybatter, there is an alternative approach to raising the dignity of inner city residence. The Sisters of Charity have donated part of their conventual site to establish sheltered housing. The vision was made reality by the tenacity of the Focus Housing

# THE THEATRE OF THE CITY: DUBLIN 1991

Association and their architect, Gerry Cahill. The short cul-de-sac of Stanhope Street leads through the gateway of the original convent to arrive in a new order and assurance for the socially vulnerable. This point of arrival is the most public place within a collective of buildings and spaces which together achieve a subtle grading from community to privacy, from enclosure to openness. Its dimensions are contained on the right by a surviving convent building, and, to the left, by a terrace of two-bedroom houses which withdraw slightly behind an area marked out by grass and cherry trees. While these houses engage with the public realm across the verdure, to the rear they open towards the sun and onto private individual terraces before joining the communal garden devoted to this group of ten homes for young families. The well-announced central entrance of the surviving convent building leads to the heart of the community. It is here that the caring administration welcomes and oversees the residents and their visitors. Above, and in the wings of this edifice, are ranged self-contained bed-sitting-rooms. These look south over the entrance 'piazza' and, from the upper floors, a panoramic view of the city can be enjoyed. Behind, the units open into corridors which, in turn, embrace a courtyard around which are ranged the 'public' activities and amenities

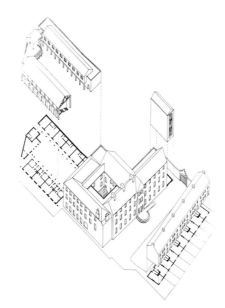

*Axonometric projection of Stanhope Green Housing, 1991. Drawn by Gerry Cahill Architects, Dublin.*

of the community. Below, a restaurant pushes a south-facing conservatory into this sheltered atrium whose bright yellow walls simulate the sun's cheerfulness even in its absence. The restaurant links through to the rest of the community to address another square. A colonnade marks out the rhythm of the units which flank the sides and lead to the closure of

the space by a workshop for training or recreation.

Stanhope Green is like a miniature city with a hierarchy and diversity of accommodation and spaces linked by its own public amenities. It is a good model for urban design and planning, since individuality and community are facilitated by a quiet and unpretentious architecture whose achievement is effortlessly to make a virtue out of the difficult parcel of land that is its site. In this, the project sets a paradigm for the making of a city where communities develop and coalesce, each having their own local facilities yet combining and complementing one another to promote a larger framework of public buildings and spaces.

It is interesting to compare Stanhope Green with Group '91's scheme for the Liberties. In Stoneybatter, the design produces an architecture and arrangement that cooperate to create cohesion in its resolution of a difficult site. In the Liberties the plots compete among themselves for architectural supremacy, outshouting one another with a jamboree of tricks and contortions. Whereas Stoneybatter used the site as a whole to provide for a generosity of space and outlook and a comfortable relation between privacy and community, the Liberties design attempted to put this complexity on each individual plot.

*Stanhope Green, the amenities surrounding the bright yellow atrium.*

*Stanhope Green, the Dublin skyline from an upper bed-sit.*

*Stanhope Green, the original convent building just inside the entrance gateway.*

# THE THEATRE OF THE CITY: DUBLIN 1991

*Stanhope Green, the colonnaded courtyard towards the restaurant.*

*Stanhope Green, the terrace bordering the entrance square.*

## TEMPLE BAR
### Creative evolution

If *Making a Modern Street* presented an unresolved collage, Group '91's winning entry for the Temple Bar Architectural Framework competition shows a pooling of their formidable collective skills to confirm their talent. It clearly demonstrated the rich possibilities of the use of a consortium of architects for dealing with urban planning. A single practice lacks the kaleidoscopic thought and invention which can be harnessed to produce richness and complexity, instead of the inevitable blandness of a single vision. Because of its uncertain future for over a decade, Temple Bar, at one time designated for total redevelopment as a transport centre, had neglected the maintenance of its physical fabric. Into this twilight zone of decay was drawn a creative spirit to reuse the derelict shell and produce an enclave of vitality with its own distinctive identity. A rich mixture of uses exploited the cheap rents in the area. It might be considered a kind of commercial equivalent of the fringes of medieval towns and the Liberties. The challenge is not to extinguish the vitality through real estate speculation and redevelopment, but to provide a framework for encouraging creative evolution on a path to prosperity.

Group '91 had picked through the fragments to discover routes through the area, punctuated by spaces that produce local focus. Seizing the opportunities of the circumstantial distribution of dereliction, the Group created a variety of places which become punctuations, points of arrival and settings for the various amenities existing or projected.

They have made a proposition to resolve the existing fabric into new and contemporary structures unearthed from the rich seams that history has laid down. They have referred to the city outside the bounds of the area, borrowing Christchurch Cathedral to compose a view or to lead Temple Bar across the Liffey with a new dynamic footbridge. At the level of strategy, it is a sensitive and ingenious proposal. They have re-established the tradition of urban design, and have begun to demonstrate how the past can be absorbed by the present to create a contemporary city. Within the overall plan they have speculated on the form of new building. Their designs for city-centre

# THE THEATRE OF THE CITY: DUBLIN 1991

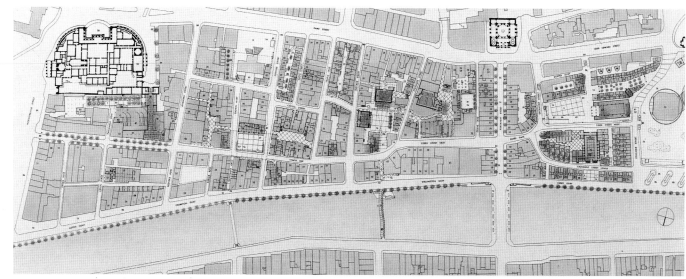

*Plan of the Temple Bar area, from* Temple Bar Lives *(Group '91, 1991). Winner of the Temple Bar Architectural Framework competition.*

living become convincing in this location, the very heart of Dublin. With rooftop gardens, they green the skyline but in the street their drawings present trees as graphic devices. Sprinkled liberally, they weaken the urban character in which Group '91 so much delight.

Over the past few decades trees have appeared in Dublin's inner-city, perhaps in emulation of the ubiquitous plane trees of the streets of London or the boulevards of Paris. However, they are not planted with an eye sensitive to Dublin's distinguished urban legacy so that they might enhance and reinterpret its qualities — instead they obscure and confuse. On a practical level, their heavy summer foliage helps to conceal street lighting thereby invading the pavements with a nefarious gloom, and the drains await the autumnal hazards. Have the prodigious dimensions of O'Connell Street become an embarrass-

ment which must be limited by planting? The Quays, as if in shame, are concealing themselves behind trees. Summer greenery blots out the Four Courts to all but the most oblique and fragmentary of views. But the greatest crime has been committed in front of Trinity College. The planting which forces the statue of Grattan to lurk in the bushes will, in time, totally obscure the central pavilion of the grand west facade of one of Dublin's finest collection of buildings as we approach College Green along Dame Street. Were the labours of the Wide Streets Commissioners in vain?

Dublin's year as the European City of Culture saw a number of projects realised and proposed which give cause for optimism. The fragmentation of a unique urban heritage has been arrested. Architecture is the very substance of the

theatre of the city and the stage for the local community. It has to allow the citizen, the resident and the visitor to inhabit its forms and spaces creatively in the same way that Bachalard suggests for the poem:

> *The image offered us by reading the poem now becomes really our own. It takes root in us. It has been given us by another, but we begin to have the impression that we could have created it, that we should have created it . . . the joy of reading appears to be the reflection of the joy of writing, as though the reader were the writer's ghost. At least the reader participates in the joy of creation . . .*[10]

It is only then that the city will become a work of art.

*John Olley*

*Dr John Olley is Lecturer in the School of Architecture, University College, Dublin.*

## NOTES

1. From 'Dante Now: The Gossip of Eternity in *On Difficulty and Other Essays*, George Steiner, 1978, Oxford.
2. George Steiner, 1991. Lecture at University College Dublin.
3. The tower of St. Catherine's was never completed and the spire of St. James's has been truncated since its de-consecration.
4. The works of the Wide Streets Commissioners was the subject of an exhibition at Newman House, Dublin, 1991, *A Vision for the City*, ed. Niall McCullough. They have also been studied by Edward McParland,: 'The Wide Streets Commissioners: their importance for Dublin

architecture in the late 18th and early 19th century', *Irish Georgian Society Bulletin*, XV, Jan–Mar 1972, pp. 1–32. Also 'Strategy in the Planning of Dublin, 1750–1800' in *Cities and Merchants*, ed. P. Butel and L. Cullen, Dublin 1986, pp.97–107.
5. Gene Brucker, *Renaissance Florence*, New York 1969, p. 27.
6. Wyndham Lewis, *The Caliph's Design*, 1919, republished in *The Essential Wyndham Lewis*, ed. Julian Symonds, London 1989.
7. Le Corbusier, *The City of Tomorrow*, 1924, trans. F. Etchells, London 1992, pp. 280, 287.
8. *Making a Modern Street* was first exhibited at the Riverrun Gallery, Dublin in May 1991.

Subsequently it was included in a more extensive exhibition of the individual members of Group '91, in Zurich in June and then it returned to the Irish Museum of Modern Art in the autumn of 1991. One member of Group '91, Niall McCullough published *Dublin: an urban history* in 1989 and in 1991 he organised an exhibition held in Newman House of the work of the Wide Streets Commissioners.
9. *Making a Modern Street*, the catalogue of the exhibition, 1991, p.12.
10. *The Poetics of Space*, Gaston Bachalard, 1964, trans. by Maria Jolas, pp. xix and xxii.

# 'TREASURES OF THE MIND'

In developing a policy for a treasures-type exhibition, it was felt that the greatest treasures of a university are the minds of its scholars and teachers, past and present. It was then decided that this might best be demonstrated in a portrayal of the achievements of the college's great alumni and the traditions they have nurtured. This would involve bringing out in two- and three-dimensional terms such abstract qualities as intellectual honesty and imaginative enquiry, willingness to experiment, to think creatively and a determination to question and to analyse; a concern to discover new solutions to problems while not disguising the existence of problems that stubbornly persist despite all efforts to dispel them. But the greatness of a university can also be measured in more tangible terms by focusing its teaching and learning resources, its library, museums and scientific equipment, its works of art and on the architectural environment it has developed and the way this promotes social interaction. Trinity College is as exceptionally rich in these latter 'treasures' as it is in the achievements of its graduates. The *Treasures of the Mind* exhibition set out therefore to present the rich resources of Trinity College in both areas in a manner that would be mutually illuminating.

But there is also, of course, a historical dimension. Trinity College is celebrating its *quatercentenary*, that is, 400 years during which it has striven to uphold the traditions and to create the environment that make it what it is. Different periods of its long history have brought out different facets of its character and that of the people who have created it. One of the challenges of this exhibition was trying, in a confined space, to do justice to the complexities of the College's past and

Trinity College Dublin was founded in 1592. The Quatercentenary Exhibition *Treasures of the Mind*, celebrating and illuminating its history and achievements, is described by the Exhibition Organiser, **David Scott**.

*The Charter of the University of Dublin (1591–92). Parchment, 57 x 73 cm.*

to the many changes that have taken place over 400 years. From its narrow and precarious beginnings in the late Elizabethan and early Jacobean eras, Trinity College had become, by the eighteenth century, a renowned institution, welcoming and nurturing some of the greatest minds of the period – Molyneux, Berkeley, Swift, Burke and others who were to create some of the most important works of literature and philosophy of the Georgian era. But Trinity also saw pass

through its gates other Irishmen such as Robert Emmet, Wolfe Tone and Thomas Davis who contributed in a different way to the nation's development, especially in the field of politics. Tensions between differing traditions were, of course, to intensify in Irish history throughout the nineteenth and well into the twentieth century, and these were reflected in the College's life in various ways. This exhibition set out to give a sense of these important developments and to confirm that, as the twentieth century draws to a close, Trinity College proudly embraces the diverse strands of Irish culture as they have developed over the centuries.

In celebrating the origins of Trinity College, at its quatercentenary, the exhibition naturally focused first on the origins of the university, backing up this with a lavish display of treasures associated with the college's founding and early development – the college Charter, drawn up in 1591–92, the fine portrait of Elizabeth I who granted it, the earliest plan of the college (shown for the first time in Dublin by kind permission of its owner, the Marquess of Salisbury). The College Mace, dating from the eighteenth century, as its magnificent Georgian silver attests, is shown as it symbolises the College's status as a corporate institution founded by Royal Charter; it thus bears Queen Elizabeth's motto, *semper eadem*. But later periods of vital historical importance were also explored, especially where Trinity men have had an important impact on ideas or events, as we saw, for example, in sections focusing on Revolution (Robert Emmet and Wolfe Tone) and on the Intellectual Revival (Thomas Davis and others). The contribution to science in Trinity College has been as important as its contribution to

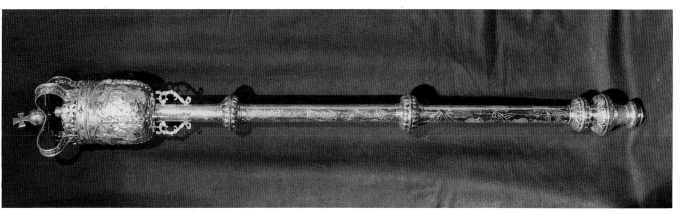

*The College Mace. Thomas Bolton: 1708–1709. Silver: 155 cm long.*

# 'TREASURES OF THE MIND'

literature and philosophy and this provided an opportunity to show in three-dimensional terms the environment, both physical and intellectual, conducive to successful experiment and research. The exhibition therefore reconstructed a fragment of Sir William Rowan Hamilton's observatory at Dunsink, and John Joly's office in Trinity College, where the latter was shown in dialogue with his life-long collaborator and colleague, Henry Horatio Dixon. The sections devoted to some of Trinity's great literary writers — Swift, Burke and Beckett, and also to those devoted to maintaining and renewing the impact of Irish language (Douglas Hyde, Mairtin O Cadhain) aimed by means of original photographs, diagrams and back-lit perspectives, as well as through a fine display of original manuscripts, paintings and sculpture, to bring to life and contextualise the great achievements of the college in literature.

The *Treasures of the Mind* exhibition was conceived, then, as a celebration of the university's long and valuable contribution to Irish life and to European culture and learning. It focused therefore both on the moments of significant change in the country and the college's history — the late Elizabethan period, the 1790s, the late nineteenth and early twentieth centuries — and on the periods of relative stability — the Georgian period, the early nineteenth and the later twentieth centuries — when some of the college's greatest achievements — in philosophy, science and literature — have been made. It also showed the value of university scholarship and research in the sciences and the arts and Trinity College's remarkable contribution in these areas, and to education in general. The function of universities as centres of teaching and research has never been more vital than it is today. This exhibition set out to show the continuing relevance of the objects and achievements of the past as well as the future potential of Trinity College.

In the context of Europe, 1992 was also a very significant year. The concept of an international Republic of Letters is especially relevant today and a display of the achievements of Trinity College's great scientists, philosophers and writers within the context of the Library shows how strong the links between Irish, British and continental learning have been. The receptiveness and contribution of Trinity scholars to European thinking was mani-

Wolfe Tone (1763–1798),
*contemporary engraving.*

fested in nearly every aspect of the exhibition: James Ussher was a scholar of international standing while Molyneux and Berkeley's confrontation of the epistemological problems raised in the seventeenth century by Descartes and Locke was to influence philosophical debate in Europe, and especially in France, for a century. Conversely, the political revolution in France was to have a profound impact on Tone and Emmet's thinking and, in the twentieth century, the Nobel prizewinner, Beckett, drawing on French and Irish elements, was to create a literature and a drama that both countries are happy to claim as their own. In the nineteenth century, William Rowan Hamilton was in touch with leading mathematicians and astronomers throughout Europe and it was, of course, with British colleagues in Cambridge that the Trinity Nobel prizewinning graduate, Ernest Walton, split the atom.

The exhibition was conceived to recreate a sense of how the university works as a space — both physical and mental. Michael Pickwoad's feeling not only for the beauty of the college buildings but also for their functional interrelationships, was reflected in the way he designed the display area. Trinity College is a series of harmoniously interrelated spaces — enclosed (common rooms, reading rooms, etc) and open (squares and gardens or parks) — which create opportunities for students and staff and the public to meet. It is a place of dialogue, discussion, exchange of ideas, built in such a way as to promote a meeting of minds. The opportunity to explore this potential is of course enhanced by the splendid new Colonnades gallery in which the exhibition itself is housed. Its series of lateral bays allowed the self-contained display of related items and yet opened them up to cross-reference in the broad open space of the main gallery. The central area also recreated a sense of the larger college campus. It did this in two ways. First, in its use of the eighteenth-century doorway motif which functions like the Campanile — poised between Front and Library Squares — as a meeting point of the various itineraries opened up around it. Second, in its focus on the library — for the central display of the essential contents of the early college library bore the same relationship to the exhibition as the Old Library with its historic Long Room (until quite recently the primary source of

Bay 3 of the Treasures of the Mind exhibition. Marble bust of Jonathan Swift (1667–1745) by Louis François Roubiliac, 1745 (Trinity College, Dublin).

View of the exhibition in The Colonnades of the Old Library, featuring a replica of an eighteenth-century College doorway.

# 'TREASURES OF THE MIND'

William Molyneux,
*engraving by P Simms. c. 1725.*

*Frontispiece design by F W Burton for*
The Spirit of the Nation, 1844.

Thomas Davis (1814–1845)
*Drawing by FW Burton.*
*National Gallery of Ireland.*

*James Malton (c. 1760–1803).* The Long Room of the Old Library,
Trinity College Dublin.

# 'TREASURES OF THE MIND'

knowledge) to the college as a whole. Movement around the exhibition space was encouraged by a broadly chronological lay-out, but this was not the only order in which it could be explored. And, above all, the exhibition was designed to appeal to the broadest possible public. In respect of this latter aim, we are grateful to the writer of the exhibition texts, Patrick Maguire.

The exhibition design attempted to elucidate scientific and academic thinking in its use of the window motif which, as a model of the mind, showed how thought projects itself either outwards onto the phenomena of the universe, whether it be the world of the natural sciences, the cosmos or the social and political world, or inward into the recesses of the imagination. These bifocal perspectives were reflected in the way each display area opened up different vistas. In the science areas, these were onto distant galaxies or future discoveries (as is the case with Hamilton, Dixon and Joly) while in history of literature the focus was rather on past or contemporary social or political situations. In the case of Swift, it is onto an imaginary world where the recognisable laws of human proportion have been disrupted. But it is a quality of Swift's eccentric vision that it has inspired countless artists since to re-invent ways of picturing the worlds encountered in *Gulliver's Travels*.

But the window metaphor also applies to the world of philosophical enquiry — especially to the field of perception to which Irish thinking has contributed so much. The vista in the 'New Learning' display opened out onto the Long Room in the eighteenth century as recorded in a print by Malton. It was precisely in questioning the status of sense data in relation to knowledge that thinkers such as Berkeley and Molyneux opened up a whole new field of philosophical enquiry. Conversely, the mathematical world of

*Unknown Artist*, Elizabeth I (1533–1603). Oil on canvas, 118 x 93 (based on engraving by Willian Rogers).

Plan of Trinity College (c. 1592) Parchment 30 x 32.5. Kindly loaned by The Marquess of Salisbury, Hatfield House.

pure relationships — more difficult to demonstrate in three-dimensional form — was mapped out in the catalogue essay on Hamilton's mathematics. Science and

the arts, maths and literature then had both inward and outward-looking modes. One display showed that Samuel Beckett sometimes worked out the plot sequences or choreography of his texts or plays with a mathematical elegance and exactitude that might have pleased a genius of mechanical optics or theoretical physics as great as Hamilton. Another showed that Hamilton was himself the friend of the great poet William Wordsworth.

Where space and viewers' patience made it impossible for all cross-references to be made or connections followed up, the exhibition catalogue provided supplementary perspectives. It incorporated contributions from a score of writers and specialists in the different disciplines, including essays on all the important developments on which the exhibition focused, a check-list of all the important objects on display, and a detailed bibliography. Lavishly illustrated in colour and black and white, the catalogue was beautifully produced by Sotheby's. In addition, the exhibition designer created a scale model of the central archway motif of the exhibition, based on an eighteenth-century doorway in the college. This item could be kept as a poster or cut out and assembled to form a scale model, forming in either case a special souvenir of the exhibition. There was also a short video programme on architecture, book conservation in the Library, and the *Book of Kells*.

*David Scott*

*Dr David Scott is Associate Professor of French and Fellow of Trinity College Dublin. He is also curator of the University of Dublin's modern art collection. His published work focuses on literature, contemporary art and textual and visual studies.*

*Treasures of the Mind* opened in the Colonnades, Trinity College, Dublin, on Charter Day 13 March 1992, and runs until December 1992.

# 'LET THERE BE LIGHT'

*And the Spirit of God moved upon the face of the waters. And God said let there be light...*

**Denis Weaire** describes how Art and Science are linked through the theme of Light in the Science Faculty Quatercentenary Exhibition in Trinity College.

*Mainie Jellett, Let There Be Light, 1942. Oil on canvas.*

As a universal theme for its Quater-centenary Exhibition the Science Faculty of Trinity College decided upon *light*, the source of life, the central puzzle of much of the history of science, the medium of vision and hence of the visual arts.

The history of the College is inter-twined with key events in man's search for an understanding of light. William Molyneux published the first book on optics in the English language in 1692. Berkeley's theory of vision followed not long after. MacCullagh, Hamilton, Lloyd, and FitzGerald all played crucial roles in the debate between wave and particle interpretations of light, which has continued for centuries and was resolved only by the uneasy compromise of quantum mechanics in this century.

These and more minor figures formed the central spine of the exhibition in a sequence of large portraits by Helen McMahon, a recent graduate of the National College of Art and Design. Included among these was Provost John Hewitt Jellett (1817–88), whose versatile accomplishments extended to the design of an instrument for measuring the polarisation of light. This handsome 'saccharometer', proudly exhibited by its Dublin maker more than a century ago, was on view once more, as were many other nineteenth-century optical instruments.

As it happened, the work of Jellett's grand-daughter, Mainie, was to provide the central symbol of this exhibition. *Let there be light* (1942) was one of the last of her paintings to be completed. It was cherished by her devoted sister Rosalind, who wishes it to rest in the College to which her family has given so much.

A striking background of wall panels improvised on the theme of light was provided by the work of Power Artz, an enterprising partnership of young spray-can artists, whose work can be seen on shopfronts in Temple Bar.

The unity of the arts and the sciences was further underlined by an exhibit of the colour photographic work of John Joly, mounted by the College of Technology. In the 1890s Joly hit upon the first practical one-shot system of colour photography. It was no accident; he had played with black-and-white photography, had studied colour perception and was aware of the possibilities offered by the latest scientific developments, such as chemical dyes and the ruling of diffraction gratings. Understandably fascinated by the process itself, he did not use it very imaginatively, copying book illustrations and portraits, together with uninspiring still life arrangements. There are rare exceptions nevertheless, in portraits and outdoor scenes. His series of pictures of a stuffed parrot is elevated to immortality by the remarkable survival of the parrot itself, recently rescued from obscurity in a cleaner's closet. Some might mischiev-ously suggest that the reawakening of the sleeping parrot is a fine metaphor for Trinity's resurgence in our national life.

The most important artistic exhibits were three new works by Alexandra Wejchert. Well known for her many striking sculptures and murals in major collections and public places, such as *Freedom* outside the AIB Bankcentre, Alexandra remains restless in pursuit of new media for her work. With the assistance of David Grouse, Senior Technician in the Physics Department, she produced her first two pieces in neon. Both looked very much at home in the central garden of Ronnie Tallon's O'Reilly Institute, where the exhibition was mounted. *Rising Blue*, a cluster of blue spirals, rose from the tropical plants like a symbol of growth and progress. It echoed the structure of the DNA molecule, the object of genetic research on blindness as featured in the exhibition. My own suggested title of *Blue Genes* for this piece did not, alas, gain favour. In another corner of the garden a bright yellow neon piece, *Arythmicmaze*, suggestive of a denser, horizontal mode of growth, nestl-ed comfortably. Over all towered the College's proud banana tree, auspiciously laden with fruit.

Alexandra Wejchert was startled to find such ready and enthusiastic collaborators within a science department. The stainless steel fabrication techniques which form the basis for much modern art are the stock-in-trade of physics tech-nicians, some of whose apparatus would, like the brass work of their Victorian predecessors, look well in any gallery. On a more experimental level, advanced semiconductor lasers were suggested as light sources for another work, in which the red laser light was guided through plastic rods, reminiscent of the infrared optical fibres which are used in today's telecommunication systems.

Some have said that Trinity's continu-ing development of new science buildings at the rear of the College, such as the William Rowan Hamilton Building, opened in 1992, represents a polarisation of the arts and the sciences. If so, the exhibition was a timely reminder of the universality of the creative process and the duality of man's enlightenment, reinforced three months later by the main Quatercentenary exhibition *Treasures of the Mind*.

*Denis Weaire*

*Dr Denis Weaire is Erasmus Smith Professor of Natural and Experimental Philosophy at Trinity College, Dublin.*

The Exhibition, *Let There Be Light*, took place in the O'Reilly Institute, Trinity College Dublin, 3–20 December 1991.

*Alexandra Wejchert, Rising Blue, 1991. Polished stainless steel and blue neon.*
*Arythmicmaze 1991, yellow neon.*

# JACK B YEATS – 'A COMPLETE INDIVIDUALIST'

After the death of Jack B Yeats in 1957, fellow members of the Royal Hibernian Academy summarised his achievement in their Annual Report:

> It has been said that he was influenced in his early days by the work of Goya, Watteau, Daumier and the Impressionists; this is possibly so, but, whatever the influences, Jack B Yeats was a complete individualist with a deeply sensitive personal vision and an equally personal means of expressing it. His subject matter was Ireland and her people, her towns, mountains and bogs; the Ireland of the landlord and the peasant, Parnell, the Land War, the Gaelic League, the Abbey Theatre, the rebellion, and finally the Republic. His paintings have that vitality which can only come from true artistry; they convince and vibrate with colour and movement showing an instinctively natural and unerring selectivity: Yeats was the true painter poet. His style of painting changed as every painter's does but the essence of the vision remained essentially the same. In his last years he used the palette knife and his forms played a subordinate role in brilliant and imaginative colour compositions.

The Academicians' eulogy, with its slightly meditative stutter, was appropriate to a painter who all his life was so completely unacademic that he was proud of being an academician. It sums up current attitudes at home and abroad to the originality and mystery of the mature Yeats. After his death in 1957, the debate began, centering on how important Jack B Yeats was to modern European art. Critics and art historians have been at pains to relate him to contemporary movements and to trace the direct influences of other greats on his work. While generally his individuality and Irishness have been acknowledged, it is now being recognised that his position in international art of the twentieth century is as valid as that of his brother in the literature of modern times.

The 1960s was a logical time for the debate to start because Yeats's agents, Victor Waddington in London and Leo Smith in Dublin, released to public view watercolours and ink drawings that had not been seen for over fifty years; and very soon a more rounded view of Yeats began to emerge. It had not been previously known that watercolour had been Yeats's main medium for a decade before he turned to oil. Waddington was uncertain of the dating of these works on paper, and imagined that some of the oils of the

**Hilary Pyle,** biographer of Jack B Yeats, and author of the new and definitive *catalogues raisonnés* of his work, assesses the status of Ireland's greatest twentieth-century artist.

*Jack B Yeats, Self Portrait, c. 1920. Pencil, 35.5 x 25.3 cm. National Gallery of Ireland.*

1920s had been painted much earlier than they had, even though stylistically they did not agree with such a view. One example was *The Circus Proprietor* of 1923, which was said to date from 1906 when it was shown in London in 1963.[1]

Part of the mystery of the magnificent Yeats that caused so much uncertainty was – what had he been doing until nearly the age of forty without a respectable oil painting to his name? But Waddington's interest was invaluable; and his monopolisation of Yeats – (with Smith he bought up all available canvases at current auctions so as to be able to continue his role as his dealer) – meant that Yeats's work was handled sympathetically, by connoisseurs who had known him personally, if only during his last years. Waddington offered six watercolours to the National Gallery of Ireland, to be purchased for the national collection, and reaffirmed his conviction of the importance of Yeats by presenting to the Gallery a pencil self-portrait, and later the only

known oil portrait of Jack Yeats as a young man by his father, John Butler Yeats.

In 1971, the centenary of Jack B Yeats's birth, a retrospective exhibition of his paintings and watercolours opened in Dublin, travelled in part to Belfast, and then afterwards *in toto* to New York. This year also saw the publication of his dramatic works in an edition edited by Robin Skelton, the first modern critic of his writings. To many people it came as a surprise that Yeats had written so much after the early arts and crafts miniature plays. I myself, though I had grown up with Yeats's Cuala prints, and his illustrations to Patricia Lynch's *The Turfcutter's Donkey*, had only discovered *Sligo* (published in 1930) in 1962 in the admirable Rosamund Stephen Library, in which most good literature up to the 1930s was to be found;[2] and I was captivated by the performance of *In Sand*, with its prologue *The Green Wave*, at the Lantern Theatre in 1964,[3] published for the first time by Liam Miller the same year. But in the 1970s, besides commissioning his biography from me, Routledge and Kegan Paul republished three of Yeats's forgotten prose works, *Ah Well*, *And to You Also* and *The Charmed Life*. The revived Cuala Press opened up the past further by publishing individual Yeats characters from the *Broadsides*. Yeats research became serious with the miscellany of Jack Yeats criticism edited for the artist's centenary by Roger McHugh; with Marilyn Gaddis Rose's *Jack B Yeats: Painter and Poet* issued as one of the European University Papers in Berne in 1972; and with the constant trickle of articles by various authors appearing in *Eire-Ireland*, *Studies*, *The Irish University Review*, and other publications from then on.

As an artist, however, the most important event for Yeats after his death was the *Post-Impressionism* exhibition in the Royal Academy, London, in 1979/80. Other Irish artists were there – Roderic O'Conor, Leech, Orpen, Osborne and Lavery. But, despite the very widely held opinion that Yeats's major work was done from 1925 onwards, the Royal Academy of Arts[4] had the wisdom to see that his work before that date was of importance. Within the limits which the exhibition set itself, 1880–1912, Yeats seemed to fit by a hair's breadth. He had only been painting seriously in oil for three years by 1912, which was when his *Circus Dwarf*,

# JACK B YEATS – 'A COMPLETE INDIVIDUALIST'

chosen for the Royal Academy exhibition, was first exhibited – though he had exhibited watercolours for a decade before that, some of these works showing post-impressionist tendencies. But from the beginning he had seen his oil painting in the context of the avant-garde. He showed some of the first examples in this medium at the second exhibition of the London-based Allied Artists' Association, with whom he continued to exhibit for years, and from 1910 he contributed to the *Salon des Independents* in Paris. He showed his work in the company of Degas, Monet, Bonnard, Van Gogh, Gauguin, Brancusi, Toulouse Lautrec and others at the International Society in London in 1911, and at the famous New York Armory Show of 1913. No wonder that when Sir Kenneth Clark arranged a joint exhibition for Yeats with Sir William Nicholson at the National Gallery in 1942, and in his article accompanying the exhibition in *Horizon* seemed less enthusiastic than he might (gossips said that he expressed regret that the pictures had looked better in Dublin), Yeats told a friend sadly that there was 'always a pull-back.[5] His complete individualism evidently baffled the English viewers of that later period.

The remainder of the 1980s, which saw exhibitions devoted to Yeats at the National Gallery of Ireland, the Hugh Lane Municipal Gallery, Dublin, and Sligo Art Society (as a major celebration of the centenary of his brother, W B Yeats), as well as two exhibitions of paintings mounted by Leslie Waddington in London, aroused an intense interest in Yeats's potential in the marketplace. A new scholarly interest in Irish art, resulting in first-class monographic catalogues and books on Irish art in general, increased the value of Irish works a hundred and thousand fold; and, when *The Harvest Moon* reached a record price of £280,000 at a sale in 1989,[6] not only was Yeats on a common footing with international post-impressionist painters, but dealers and connoisseurs outside Ireland began to ask why this was so. The results of such serious interest were seen in two historic exhibitions in places where Yeats had never been shown before, though during his lifetime and afterwards he had exhibited in Paris, Rome, all over Britain and the States, in Canada and in Scandinavia.

The exhibition in Monte Carlo, sponsored by the Jefferson Smurfit Foundation, was held at the request of the Irish Consul to Monaco within the context of the 12th International James Joyce Symposium, in June 1990. This selection of paintings and drawings from the collections of an Irish patron and his circle, presented in a high-powered setting of literary intelligentsia, and opened by Her Serene Highness Princess Caroline of Monaco, established Yeats successfully as a prestige symbol. From being a national artist collected throughout his lifetime and for a long time after it by artlovers from every level, who bought paintings, watercolours, drawings or prints according to their means because they liked them, or because a work struck some chord of significance for them, his importance for collectors was now demonstrably gauged by his desirability on the international market. Works doubtless selected for their aesthetic quality were cherished also for their financial value. Yeats, with the dramatic inflation of his works in the auction houses, had already drawn near to being an artist whom even galleries could not afford to buy. The exhibition exalted the artist even further by being shown subsequently in the National Gallery of Ireland – with a political benison – the addition of the

*Jack B Yeats,* Memory Harbour, *1900. Watercolour on card, 31 x 47 cm. Private Collection.*

*Jack B Yeats, That Grand Conversation was under the Rose, 1943. Oil on canvas, 35.5 x 53.5.*
*National Gallery of Ireland.*

*Jack B Yeats, My Beautiful, My Beautiful, 1953. Oil on canvas, 102 x 153 cm. Private collection.*

# JACK B YEATS – 'A COMPLETE INDIVIDUALIST'

Gallery's own holding of watercolours and drawings focusing attention on the national collection, and drawing Yeats back within the museum context.

The exhibition, both in Monaco and in Dublin, owed its success to the excellence of the collections from which it was drawn (which included the National Gallery of Ireland and the Hugh Lane Gallery in addition to private collections). The difficulty was what to select from these collections. What had originally been intended to be an exhibition of about sixty works, was narrowed down to forty-one for reasons of space, without diminishing the quality of the whole. It was possible to include examples from the earliest to the latest periods, in order to give a genuine account of the artist's career in its various manifestations. It would have been possible to do the same with a different selection of works, so numerous are the works of significance from the artist's hand. But

what was particularly interesting about the exhibition was that this selection came mainly from a small group of privileged private collectors, a princely offering in the modern sense. The presence of *Memory Harbour*, Yeats's watercolour of 1900, was a reminder of his early work as the source of his more famous mature pigmentedly-elated oils. After remarking with astonishment his colour and emotion in the intervening pictures, spectators focused on the large and unforgettable depiction of human love and inspiration, My *Beautiful, My Beautiful.* Barely sketched on to the canvas, in two striking images Yeats tells the whole story of a poor Arab's dilemma, forced to sell his steed, and then, moved by the loyalty of the special bond between them, refusing to part with the beast, accepting poverty and exile rather than betray the animal's dumb devotion. The climax of the tale is depicted in the huge figure of the horse

that surrounds the penitent suppliant, looking down at him with the light of forgiveness in its eye.

The second of the two recent and important exhibitions opened in Bristol in February 1991 – a collaboration between the Arnolfini in Bristol, Whitechapel Art Gallery in London and the Gemeentemuseum in the Hague. This exhibition was undertaken from a different angle than the Monaco one, under the happy misapprenehsion that Yeats was something new, an artist neglected since his demise. In England, leaving aside London, this was true; and the neglect was regrettable in that Yeats had learned his craft in England, working in London and Manchester, and exhibiting his watercolours from Devon until he was nigh on forty. It was appropriate that he should receive such a noble airing in Bristol, should be seen in London away from the Waddington ethos, and then go to the

*Jack B Yeats, The Clown Among the People, 1932. Oil on canvas, 46 x 61 cm. Private Collection.*

# JACK B YEATS – 'A COMPLETE INDIVIDUALIST'

Netherlands, where, like Bristol, the contiguity to the sea would have made Yeats's heart roll with pleasure. The Hague was a totally new venue for the artist, and interesting for obvious comparisons with Van Gogh. In some ways the method of compiling the exhibition was naive, though the organisers and authors of the catalogue had a refreshing outlook, and were fully conscious of the integrity of the artist. But the assumption that only his late works were of importance in the international field, and confining the exhibition to that period,[7] led to problems in the matter of selection, not only because of security, since these are regarded as his most valuable paintings, but also because of the risk in transporting such highly impastoed canvases.

The exhibition, like many non-commercial exhibitions before it, donned a different costume than planned for the occasion, yet was none the worse for this. Nearly half of the forty-five works were from public or private galleries (such as the Ulster Museum, the Tate, City of Bristol, Pyms and Waddington Galleries), themselves not without anxiety about the delicacy of the late canvases; and indeed some pictures were included whose condition was critical, and which should not have been exhibited without initial restoration. Many of the pictures on show were well known; yet they acquired renewed significance in this presentation from the context in which they were seen. The publicity that the exhibition in Monaco had enjoyed was nothing to that which haloed the show in the Arnolfini as its opening approached, and the limelight did not wane until well after the close of the three showings. As well as this, the dedication with which the directors of three such eminent galleries had addressed the exhibition undoubtedly increased scholarly interest in Yeats in a wide and constructive fashion. They were adventurous. It was the first time that Yeats's pictures had been seen in a public exhibition without their glass. Even the stark presentation in the Hague did not detract from the personality of the paintings, which in some ways benefited from being isolated like laboratory specimens. The pictures are strong enough to be seen in isolation. They invite and reward the closest scrutiny. Only the overall effect of the exhibition lacked the elegant and the earthy for a background to set off such remarkable works.

*Jack B Yeats*, Race Card Seller, 1909. *Oil on canvas, 35.5 x 25 cm. Commissioners of Public Works, Dublin.*

The show itself was full of what any show of Yeats should be full of, living moments preserved by the artist in immediate brushstrokes. It moved from a note of music in an Irish train through ecstatic, romantic, sweaty, poignant, tragic, revelatory snatches of life to the singular peace of the final canvas, *A Rose Among Many Waters*. A solitary figure, the artist perhaps, stands on the bank of a stream beside a waterfall (Glencar), his back turned to the sunlight. He fingers and smells a rose (the symbol which was so particularly his brother's and after that his own) as he faces the inner light of the shaded water. The water tumbles down, lit with gold and spattered with the ominous blood-red of sacrifice.

Visitors to the exhibition when it visited the Hague, many of whom came to his work for the first time, called it 'marvellous', and exclaimed – 'what colour!', 'what intense emotion!' They felt (as Yeats would have wanted them to) that each picture told some particular story that they did not always understand, but to which they responded. There was enormous enthusiasm for him as a pure painter, from a people who acknowledged that the visual came naturally to them, for whom the visual was paramount and the literary a very secondary affair.

Writing in *Trouw*,[8] Cees Straus was struck by the fact that here was an artist who did not base his style on some artistic programme or manifesto, but who painted instinctively, 'in such a pure form that one is inclined to characterise his work as "naive", however without the negative connotation that could go with the word "naive". ' Straus found Yeats more sedate and contemplative than the impressionists, and saw an obvious affinity between Yeats, Munch and Kokoschka. But 'there were too few events in his life that upset him. Munch and Kokoschka were more the therapists of their own souls and showed this in their works. Yeats does not seem to have been a very vexed person. He is above all a good observer who watches the world around him sharply. What he shares with Munch and Kokoschka is his technique of painting: broad, rapidly laid down, as if it has to respond directly to what he feels and thinks. It is his directness that makes his work so attractive.' Straus was also struck by Yeats's ability to end up in a fairytale world 'which puts a different face upon the original real situation. This could be called, literally "light", for Yeats uses light to give his realities a symbolic meaning'. He pointed out how light in Yeats's painting marks out the image, and models the story. 'You know that the situation in which the light manifests itself can be over immediately, but nevertheless you are allowed to see a glimpse of eternity.'

What Cees Straus suggests in his review, without actually stating it,[9] is the wholeness of Yeats's vision. Rather than analysing his own being, he wished to present life from personal experience in his creations, to reconstruct convincingly its multiple complexities, to reproduce the dichotomy of great moments and trivia, and in the momentariness of his images to recapture the incidental quality of life, its fragmented episodic nature, as well as its peaks of grief, joy, sensuality and communion. *Something Happening in the Street*, a picture of 1944 showing a maid servant peeping out through the panes of an upstairs bedroom to see what is going on below, is typical of his emphasis on the intrinsic importance of the everyday incident, learned perhaps from the impressionists.

His own life was marked by a series of dichotomies. He was born in London in 1871, of Irish parents. From the age of eight, he spent most of his schooldays in

Jack B Yeats, Death for Only One, 1937. Oil on canvas, 61 x 91.5 cm.
Private collection, on loan to the National Gallery of Ireland.

*Jack B Yeats, The Sea and the Lighthouse, 1947. Oil on canvas, 35.5 x 53.5.
Sligo County Museum and Art Gallery.*

# JACK B YEATS – 'A COMPLETE INDIVIDUALIST'

Ireland in Sligo, in the company of a grandfather who came from Devon, and whose vessels plied between Sligo and Liverpool, and had little to do with the rest of Ireland. Back in London in 1887 with his Irish family, he worked as a journalist illustrator while having sporadic formal training at art schools. In 1892, he took on his toughest job, as a poster artist commuting to David Allen in Manchester, while continuing to publish popular cartoons in *Paddock Life, Ariel, Judy* and other papers in London. This practice of combining the serious with the frivolous became a pattern of his creativity, notably when he was painting his most original and freely painted oils in the 1920s and 1930s, at the same time as contributing comic drawings with humorous captions to *Punch*.[10]

Other paradoxes may be seen in his living habits. At the moment he discovered the inspiration of Irish nationalism in 1898, he had just moved to Devon (drawn there probably by his West Country blood), and he continued to live there while painting only Irish subjects. He moved back to Ireland to live still by the

*Jack B Yeats,* Cartoon *in* Punch, *July 31, 1912.*

*Jack B Yeats,* "'Naturally I work better to a shanty'". Punch, *September 29, 1937.*

sea, at Greystones in County Wicklow, but, a solitary man,[11] he came close to a breakdown in such isolation, and moved up to the city in 1917 to live in Donnybrook. Evidently, though painting totally on his own, he depended on people, and on the company of people, in order to be able to create. In *A Morning in a City* (see illustration to Brian P Kennedy's article, 'The Oil Painting Technique of Jack Butler Yeats', in this issue), a scene just after dawn, when officeworkers, street sweepers, a flower girl and a barrow man (the subjects of his art) are hurrying to their daily activity, the artist is framed between the tall terraces of Dublin houses, wandering on his own, an idea which took root in two pen and ink self-portraits made over ten years before he painted the picture.

To pursue the paradox, though solitary as an artist, he took an active and interested part in current cultural affairs, firstly as a newly elected member of the Royal Hibernian Academy in 1916, and subsequently as a founder member of the Society of Dublin Painters in August 1920, which was when he agreed to give

*Jack B Yeats,* Dublin Newsboys, *1923. Oil on panel, 23 x 35.5 cm. Private Collection.*

# JACK B YEATS – 'A COMPLETE INDIVIDUALIST'

Jack B Yeats, The Barrel Man in Life in the West of Ireland, 1912.

Jack B Yeats, 'Will he catch them? c. 1912. Pen, ink and watercolour, 20 x 12.5 cm. Private Collection.

Jack B Yeats, The Scene of a Tragedy in A Broadside, February 1915.

his first public lecture on art. He was active in the Dublin Arts Club, and, towards the end of his life, on the Board of the National Gallery of Ireland. While convinced of the primacy of the visual image as a means for artistic expression,[12] he wrote one important prose work, six novels, and even more plays. Another anomaly was created by his settling permanently in Dublin half way through life, stating at the same time that every picture he painted (and every book he wrote) had a thought of Sligo in it!

Dichotomy was a natural product of his creative psyche and of his way of working. It underlies the paradox of the claim that he be regarded as a European genius at the same time as acknowledging that he played no part in any European movement. Yeats had been criticised at various stages of his career for failing to perfect a style which fits into the European pattern. 'Individualist', as the Academy called him, is an honest comment, translated by the modern pen of Rudi Fuchs into 'Irish loner'. Fuchs hails him as 'one of the great European painters', and applauds his aloofness, his refusal to take part in 'the explosive stylistic debate of the twentieth century'.[13] However the very ambivalence of Yeats's individualistic twentieth century approach is due to his sole aim to recreate life in his painting. 'A picture which is true is the memory of a moment which once was as it appears to the artist',

he said in Modern Aspects of Irish Art. 'The artist . . . feels he is part of everything that surrounds him. He knows what is happening every hour: the corn is springing, or a storm is coming and the floating archipelago of clouds are banking together. He may find himself in the very centre loop of a whirlwind. After a time the sun comes shouldering his way thro' the storm clouds and they scatter away, and under the sun the country lies like a new land; of all this the artist has been part'. It was for this reason that he could not yoke himself to any artistic rule. Such a move would preclude fidelity to life itself, to 'his pursuit of all that through its unpredictable, unarrangeable reality least resembles knowledge', as his brother put it.[14]

Yeats' theme of Life in the West of Ireland has been regarded for too long as simply an expression of nationalist emotion at a period when Ireland at last expected to be independent. The artist undoubtedly had nationalist ideals in mind. Twenty years after he had undertaken the theme in his exhibitions, Yeats reaffirmed that 'those painters who have the greatest affection for their country and their own people will paint them best . . . We must look to ourselves for the springs of our art. We must not look to Paris or London for a pace maker. Paris is the home of the very science of fashion and true painting has nothing to do with fashion', he said.

But the realisation that contemporary life was fundamental to 'true painting' was deeply imprinted in the artist long before he inadvertently happened on his exhibition title and theme.[15] When he worked as an artist reporter during the 1890s, picturing boxing matches and sporting events, he realised that Life was in the making around him, and that it was this phenomenon which was his subject matter. A journalist's training was an advantage when he began the practice of carrying tiny sketchbooks with him wherever he went, recording life as it happened, noting down amusing incidents, jargon and dialect, facts, useful addresses, as well as visual images – taking an interest also in the sprites who sold the journalists' ware. Irish life as he saw it, with a nationalist bias, was summed up in his book of drawings and reproduced paintings, Life in the West of Ireland, in 1912. The Scene of a Tragedy (a drawing referring to the shooting of innocent bystanders by the military during pre-war tensions, published in A Broadside, February 1915) was reportage on the spot, of an incident of national significance, which he recast a short time later, in similarly apolitical terms, in his painting Bachelor's Walk, In Memory. But in the mid-1920s he was increasingly aware of the limitations in a purely national view of life, when he found his individualistic style emerging of itself after years of preparation, and

*Jack B Yeats, The Man from Aranmore, 1905. Watercolour on board, 38 x 27.3 cm.*

# JACK B YEATS – 'A COMPLETE INDIVIDUALIST'

knew that what he must paint now was life in all its measure, mystification and manners, regardless of geographical or political boundaries.

From *Paintings of Irish Life* he turned to exploring *Lives* anywhere during the 1930s, in a superb series of drawings in seven volumes describing the many-layered and multi-faceted aspects of human existence. Alongside it, he wrote and published his version of Don Quixote's travels, *The Charmed Life*, which his brother called his 'Faust'. Jack Yeats's ultimate desire was, not to know all knowledge like Faust, but to reach a state where the knowledge of good and evil had been forgotten[16] (he painted *A Race in Hy Brazil*, a fantasy of the Land of Youth based on an Irish country race meeting, and *South Pacific*, where white clown and sooty Christy Minstrel sit down together in a paradisaical setting, about this time). Human life has of course to be learned, and Yeats had wisely studied, from his earliest years, every aspect he had experienced, from details of inn signs, or states of the tide, to different shades of emotion, and degrees of human relationships. When he was 'learning' landscape he wrote to John Quinn about the landscape that meant most ot him, Rosses Point in Sligo, pointing out that it was the internal rather than the external aspect of it that was important to him – 'the "nature" of it. Do you know that word "nature"? It means the heart, the marrow, the through and throughness'; and ten years later he was still in pursuit of the

*Jack B Yeats*, Illustration to 'John Francois' *in* A Broadside, *April 1913.*

'through and throughness' of nature and life when he told Quinn that the 'gay' moderns could not deter him from painting what he wanted, only 'what I have seen happen'.[17]

Yeats's 'learning' of life was not confined to studying nature and human nature, though he put these first. He was well aware of what was going on in contemporary art – enough to be able to give an honest opinion. From the time he first worked for illustrated magazines in London, or as a poster artist in Manchester, passing, rather than overt, references to

what he saw are evident in his work.[18] He probably visited exhibitions at the Fitzroy Club or commercial galleries as a young man in London, as well as noticing current reviews in the newspapers which he read. He attended exhibitions regularly in Dublin, and presumably did so on his few excursions abroad, though his sketchbooks show him always to have been far more interested in the people around him. His influences have been discussed elsewhere, and will go on being discussed by those who are anxious to fit him into some secure artistic pigeon hole. He claimed no direct influences, however, and obviously valued his individuality: indeed was individual (and workmanlike) in all aspects of his profession, organising his own exhibitions, transport of pictures, design of posters and so on until the age of seventy.[19] At the same time, his art cannot be described accurately as 'instinctive'. As Cees Straus has stated, he did not paint to a programme. His only manifesto was *Life*. But his very close observation of what he saw, and his rigorous training of his memory, were a result of personal deliberation in the matter of technique. Even in his earliest period, he could adapt the broad Morris-coloured idiom of *A Broadsheet* to the more restrained heroic lines, consciously deriving from traditional balladsheets, of *A Broadside*. His *Punch* style likewise developed from the strong definition of the first drawings, with their straight comedy, to a late, dancing, elvish hand, to match his more oblique mature wit. His

*Jack B Yeats*, The Fair of Ballinasloe *in* A Broadsheet, *March 1903. (Photograph courtesy of The Library, Trinity College, Dublin.)*
Two Traditional Broadsides *from the collection of Jack B Yeats.*

# JACK B YEATS – 'A COMPLETE INDIVIDUALIST'

*Jack B Yeats*, Something Happening in the Street, *1944. Oil on panel, 23 x 35.5 cm. Private collection.*

*Jack B Yeats*, Bachelor's Walk, In Memory, *1915. Oil on canvas, 46 x 41 cm. Private collection.*

# JACK B YEATS – 'A COMPLETE INDIVIDUALIST'

illustrations of all periods suit image to word and setting with a subtle understanding of the 'through and throughness' of his subject; and he wielded the brush in the same thoughtful way.

His father's view was, 'He has the habits of a man who knows his own mind';[20] and it is not surprising, therefore, that in the early 1930s – after he had attained the style he had strived for, but was painting comparatively little – that Jack Yeats should analyse colour in a way that has some bearing on his painting method. The date of the diagrams made in one of his late workbooks, which contains a conglomeration of notes of various kinds, is obscure. Pages torn from a lined notebook have been pasted in over a date which is probably 1933, and the colour wheel diagram opposite is dated either 1933 or 1937. The original pencilled triangle and graph, adjusted later in ink by Yeats, was probably jotted down first during a conversation with Dr Felix Hackett (whose name appears on the note), who was Professor of Physics in University College, Dublin, and who had bought a small landscape of Clonskea from Yeats at his exhibition in 1931. The CIE (Commission International de l'Eclairage) system of colourimetry, deriving all colours from three primaries, red, green and blue/violet, had only recently been adopted, and, in the diagrams (which do not appear elsewhere), Yeats records briefly how complementary colours are obtained from fundamental colours, using the additive method of combination. Hitherto his painting method may have been emotional and instinctive, influenced by what formal training he had, and by his own observation, but here he indicates a positive attempt to rationalise what he was doing in his new style; and the principles of the CIE colour wheel must be seen to have an effect on his subsequent approach to painting.

Yeats's oil painting technique is a matter of increasing interest. In his earliest paintings he experimented a great deal, basing his efforts on his knowledge of watercolour, and using linseed and poppy oil for a while. By about 1909, he had mastered a representational style that suited him and was partly influenced by his admiration for Sickert, in which forms are described in thin layers of restrained colour, brushed on freely within strong outlines. His preferred support for painting in these first oils, and later, was wood panel (he also used coarse canvas in the first period); and originally his panels were prepared by a local builder, who coated both sides of the panel with paint, over which Yeats put his own priming.[21] During the war he sometimes made up timber supports himself. Afterwards he was obliged to purchase commercially prepared board for his small paintings (the larger works were always on canvas).

His first representational style in oil gradually grew looser and more expressive, developing from a manner which was totally objective in its approach to one which was subjective and emotional. His essential technique in the late 1920s differed little from that of the earlier period, other than in the elated freedom of brushwork and artistic expression he had reached by breaking out of his original outline, allied to a new and brimming confidence in himself and in the lyrical heights a richer application of pigment could achieve with the aid of the palette knife. The 1930s saw a leaner period of painting, where images were conceived thoughtfully and individually (alongside a productive decade as a writer), often as poetic metaphors: but the use of colour during these years is often fantastic rather than lyrical, and pigment is generally used less lusciously, and more provocatively, than in the height of the 1920s. During the 1940s, when he abandoned writing, and became more prolific than ever as an oil painter, Yeats's style varied itself, going through a stage of contained personal expression with sparkling colour, through dryer opaque painting to a manner of ultimate freedom, his characteristic final period. Now he tended to wash and sketch over a primed surface with a wet loaded brush, and to build up his picture lightly, adding detail and figures with a palette knife as final flamboyant gestures.

As I have suggested elsewhere, his mature style cannot be regarded as wholly 'free', or 'automatic'. He always 'located' his subject in space, by working consciously with the centre of the canvas or board as a pivot. He drew with his brush, and consulted photographs, illustrations in periodicals and his own early sketchbooks, as well as continuing to work from life around him, thus preserving accuracy as well as the immediate living quality of his subjects. At this late period his technique involved the direct application of the pigment from the paint tube, adding a twist which sometimes resulted in a curl of colour, and frequently using the fingers instead of a brush. He always eschewed the use of varnish.

Technically, these late paintings (and mainly those from the late 1930s on) have

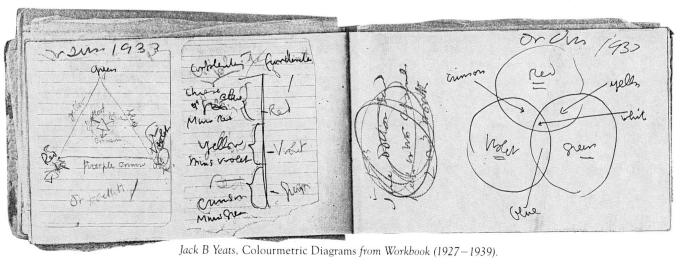

*Jack B Yeats, Colourmetric Diagrams from Workbook (1927–1939).*

# JACK B YEATS – 'A COMPLETE INDIVIDUALIST'

recently been presenting problems. One familiar devil is central heating. Cracking can sometimes be explained by the artist having used some too quick drying medium, or from his scumbling too thickly: but low humidity has been a hazard for the very fine toothed canvases Yeats employed from the middle 1940s, which have tightened, loosening the pigment which itself shrinks as a result of low humidity. The conservation department of the Victoria and Albert Museum was the first body to undertake the restoration of Yeats's work, the Keeper, Mr Norman Bromelle, coming to Ireland to wax rather than varnish the late works; and Kenneth Malcolm, his assistant, making a special study of Yeats's technique in the 1960s, using the same approach to Yeats as he adopted for paintings by Constable. He advised collectors to observe Yeats's instruction to keep the picture glazed in order to maintain the pigmented surface in good condition (and it is noticeable that pictures which have been preserved under glass in the temperate humid conditions in which Yeats and his first collectors lived, without central heating, have tended to survive without impairment). Andrew O'Connor of the National Gallery of Ireland, who has recently been restoring the national collection, is of the same opinion, pointing out that the grime which can dull a picture adheres to the glass rather than the pigment. Small areas of flaking pigment, due to drying out, have been his main concern.[22] He has made the decision to varnish pictures, despite Yeats's practice of non-varnishing, and uses a modern synthetic resin varnish which does not yellow. He feels that, besides providing a protection, the varnish assists fugitive colours, restoring the picture to its original brilliant state.

Yeats did not regard glass merely as a protection for his pictures, but, it seems, glazing for him was a substitute for varnishings, a means of adding a transparent lustre to his paintings without interfering with, or 'trapping', the living immediate quality of his pigment. From an early period he instructed that his pictures be framed under glass in 'antique' style frames (a matter about which he had to compromise during the War and afterwards, though he always kept to a similar style of frame, gilded where possible. When commenting on a method for painting in his lecture, *Modern Aspects of Irish Art* (1922), he recommended looking

*Jack B Yeats*, The Barrel Man, *1912.*
*Oil on panel, 35.5 x 23 cm. Private Collection.*

'through the frame' of the window to examine the view, and then drawing the window frame before committing the scene to paper. He was describing how the memory could be trained; but the indication is that he saw the picture as a framed object. To replace his traditional frames therefore, or to remove the glass, as has been a widening practice recently, whatever the interesting results, disregards the intentions of the artist, and ignores the manner in which he wished his pictures to be seen (rather like removing the frame of a Renaissance painting, and glazing it with clips).

Jack B Yeats studies, which have previously eluded the hungry academic adventurer, are now becoming more common, in the form of theses, articles and books. One – and possibly the most fruitful – form of research will be in the area of individual paintings, which, as in the case of *That Grand Conversation was under the Rose*, often grow out of some initially different theme to create a metaphor of metaphysical proportion. *The Grand Conversation under the Rose* is an Irish patriotic ballad of the Napoleonic era, which Yeats delighted in and illustrated in *A Broadsheet* in August 1903. In his play, *Harlequin's Positions*, he describes the

ballad as 'a song of great warriors', and its refrain is a channel for symbolism, both public and personal, in his oil of 1943, where he shows the artist (the clown) and his inspiration (the *haute école* rider), performers from opposite poles of the circus meeting privately, '*sub rosa*' – under the artificial rose which is fastened to the rider's whip. In effect the extrovert nationalism of the early period has been converted into deep poetic introversion, and the militant political song is now an anthem for private meditation. The horse alone is the common factor in both images!

Much can be deduced from this and other themes, carried silently by Yeats from his earliest drawings and sketches, to re-emerge after half a lifetime of gestation in some of his most enigmatic paintings. The clown himself, in various chronological manifestations, bears comparison with Rouault's clown. The ballad singer is another provocative figure who appears in the earliest period, with his ballad taking varous guises on his journey into the latest phase. The early drawings of barrel and maggie men side-shows at an Irish race meeting or country fair give rise to some of the most profound statements about mankind. Both in words – 'I'll show you Man upright defying the slings and arrows and getting away with it' (*The Old Sea Road*) – and images (*Defiance*) he translates harshly ironical entertainments into deeply intuitive visions of his fellow man.

A continual subject for investigation will be the ways in which Yeats blends reality and imagination together in his work.[23] It accounts for much of what appears to be inconsequentiality in both writings and paintings, the artist's instinctive reflection of Life itself; and it can reach heights of mystery, where land and water fuse with sky, and heaven leans down to illuminate earth (*The Sea and the Lighthouse*). The sea for Yeats was life with its mysterious sensuality. The beam of the lighthouse through the darkness represented spirituality, rooted in the concrete. Yeats was rare among artists in that the innocence and idealism that typified him as a young man stayed with him into old age. He did not ignore the tougher side of life, largely through is buoyant but canny sense of humour. Even moments of sensuality or cruelty observed in his late work are irradiated with a spirit of transcendence.

# JACK B YEATS – 'A COMPLETE INDIVIDUALIST'

How does one consider him in the context of post-modern art? No one imitates him any more – though there is no doubt of his influence on modern Irish painters like Le Brocquy, Collins, Davis, Souter, Reid and other contemporaries. But is he of importance in this new era of politically motivated, classless, psychoanalytical painting, with all its eclectic resources? The National Gallery treasures him among the masters of the centuries. For the Assistant Director, Brian P Kennedy, he is important to Irish painting for the original way in which he has captured the Irish spirit; and he regards Yeats's use of paint, promoting the luminous physical quality of the pigment, as something wholly individual. Dublin's Hugh Lane Municipal Gallery has always presented him as the leading Irish artist of the first half of the twentieth century. At the same time the Director of the Irish Museum of

Modern Art, Declan McGonagle, believes that Yeats is crucially important in an overall view of the contemporary Irish/international scene, and is to incorporate him in IMMA's programme during the next few years. All three museums welcome the current enthusiasm for his work, which has always been manifest in Ireland and now comes from outside the country.

Unexpectedly, the contemporary artist, both inside and outside of Ireland, tends to honour Yeats, and to admire and learn from his handling of colour and form. Frank Auerbach explained this to Mark Haworth Booth, while looking at some of Yeats's late paintings last year.[24] 'These are not stock figures – these are people he really saw. Even the people in Tiepolo have a sort of family likeness. These are all different, real . . . He's not obsessive – he's too interested in real

things. That's why he can make every mark of paint on the canvas count.'

*Hilary Pyle*

*Hilary Pyle, writer and art critic, was born in Dublin and is now living in Cork. She has worked in the Ulster Museum, Belfast, as Assistant Art Keeper, and in the National Gallery of Ireland as Librarian and Keeper of Prints and Drawings. More recently writing and lecturing, mainly in University College, Cork, and the National Gallery, she is also art critic of* The Irish Times, *the* Cork Examiner, *and RTE Cork and Dublin, and contributes to* Irish Arts Review, Hibernia, Circa, The Arts Review *(London),* The Woman's Art Journal *(Tennessee), etc. Biographies of the writer, James Stephens, and of Estella Solomons are among her published work. She is the author of the biography,* Jack B Yeats *(London, 1970) and of* Jack B Yeats in the National Gallery of Ireland *(Dublin 1986) as well as the major catalogues,* Jack B Yeats: His Watercolours, Drawings and Pastels *(Dublin 1992) and* Jack B Yeats: A Catalogue Raisonné of the Oil Paintings. 3 vols. *(London 1992).*

## NOTES

1. Waddington Galleries, *Jack B Yeats: Paintings*, 28 March – 27 April 1963, no. 1 (repro).
2. Incorporated with the Representative Church Body Library, originally in 52 St Stephen's Green, Dublin, and now in Braemor Park, Dublin.
3. *In Sand* was first produced by the Abbey Experimental Theatre at the Peacock Theatre, Dublin in 1949. It was revived by the Lantern Theatre, at 38 Merrion Square, Dublin, opening on Tuesday, 29 September, 1964. Liam Miller, one of the directors of the theatre, published *In Sand* with *The Green Wave* from the Dolmen Press in June 1964.
4. Anna Gruetzner was the author of the catalogue note on Yeats, no. 357.
5. Terence de Vere White, *Sunday Telegraph*, 15 October, 1989.
6. James Adam (Dublin) sale, 28 September, 1989.
7. The Whitechapel Gallery redressed the balance in a small way by showing examples of sketchbooks in London during the exhibition, which took place 16 February – 24 March, 1991, Arnolfini, Bristol; 5 April – 26 May, 1991, Whitechapel Art Gallery, London; 21 June – 15 September, 1991, Haags Gemeentemuseum, the Hague.
8. 'Haags museum ontdekt in Jack Yeats schilder van formaat', 23 Juli 1991, 12. I am indebted to Jan van Putten for the translation.
9. Apart from Pierre Schneider's rather rarefied comments in *Les Lettres Nouvelles*, April 1954, and Rudi Fuchs's succinct and commendably brief *Eulogy* in the Arnolfini catalogue, this is one of the few critiques of substance from the continent.
10. He contributed to *Punch* under the pseudonym 'W. Bird' from 1910–1941.

11. Painting 'high solitary art'. Samuel Beckett, *Les Lettres Nouvelles*, April 1954. Beckett told Thomas MacGreevy (TCD Mss. 131) 'what I feel he gets so well, dispassionately, not tragically like Watteau, is the heterogeneity of nature & the human denizens, the unalterable alienness of the 2 phenomena, the 2 solitudes, or the solitude & the loneliness, the loneliness in solitude, the impassable immensity between the solitude that cannot quicken to loneliness & the loneliness that cannot lapse into solitude . . . perhaps that is the final quale of Jack Yeats's painting, a sense of the ultimate inorganism of everything . . . A painting of pure inorganic juxtapositions, where nothing can be taken or given & there is no possibility of change or exchange.'
12. In his lecture on art, composed in August 1920, he described painting as the greatest medium of all for the communication of the thoughts and feelings of mankind, 'even greater I believe than literature' (Ms. 10, 478, National Library of Ireland).
13. *Jack B Yeats: the Late Paintings* (1991) p. 11.
14. W B Yeats, *On the Boiler* (1939) p. 36.
15. Like the impressionists, who adopted a name summarily invented for them, Yeats took his title from a critic's dubbing his first exhibition of Devon watercolours as *Life in the West Country* and converted it for his exhibition of Irish subjects to become *Life in the West of Ireland*, later *Paintings of Irish Life*.
16. J W Purser, *The Literary Works of Jack B Yeats*, pp. 164–66.
17. 26 June 1903, 15 December 1913. New York Public Library Manuscript Collection. Yeats's methodological approach to landscape painting is described at length in the

introduction to my catalogue of his oil paintings *Jack B Yeats: A Catalogue Raisonné of the Oil Paintings*, 3 vols, (André Deutsch, London, 1992), and the Life theme is discussed in my catalogue of the watercolours, *Jack B Yeats: His Watercolours, Drawings and Pastels*, (Irish Academic Press, Dublin, 1992). See also 'Memory Harbour: Jack Yeats's painting process' by James White, in *Theatre and the Visual Arts: A Centenary Celebration of Jack Yeats and John Synge*, edited by R O'Driscoll and L Reynolds, 1972, 9–17.
18. In his late workbooks, jotted references to Joyce and Lawrence indicate that he approached modern writing in the same relaxed but observant way.
19. Note also his correspondence with Elkin Mathews about *A Broadsheet* and his book, *A Little Fleet*, Ms. 4558, National Library of Ireland.
20. *Christian Science Monitor*, 2 November, 1920.
21. Kenneth Malcolm, Victoria and Albert Museum to author, 24 May 1967. I am also indebted to Matthew Moss, Restorer at the National Gallery of Ireland at that time, with whom I consulted about Yeats's technique.
22. Andrew O'Connor in conversaton with the author, December 1991. It may be noted that the paintings of AE (George Russell, 1966–1935), who had a similar palette, have tended to flake in the same way as those of Jack Yeats.
23. See Hilary Pyle, ' "My unshatterable friend of clay": fantasy in the paintings of Jack B Yeats' in *More Real than Reality: the fantastic in Irish Literature and the Arts*, ed. by D E Morse and C Bertha, 1991, pp. 97–110.
24. *Jack B Yeats: the Late Paintings*, 1991, 32.

# JACK B YEATS AND JOHN QUINN

Hilary Pyle, in her biography of Jack B Yeats[1], has described the role which the American collector, John Quinn — better known as the patron of Jack's father, John Butler Yeats — played in Jack's career. The two first came into contact in the autumn of 1901 when Jack, then aged thirty, was still relatively unknown as a painter. He had done some book illustration, had exhibited at the RHA (in 1895), and, from 1897, had staged one-man exhibitions in London and Dublin of his watercolour drawings of life in the west of Ireland. To that date, he had not, however, seriously attempted oil painting.

John Quinn (1870–1924)[2], who was born of Irish immigrant parents in Ohio, was a brilliant financial lawyer who had established his reputation in New York by the age of twenty-five. He was a singular man with a keen appetite for reading and self-education. Developing an early interest in contemporary literature, he proceeded to collect first editions and autograph manuscripts with a particular focus on the works of Yeats, Lady Gregory, Douglas Hyde, and other writers of the Irish Literary Renaissance. His first personal contact with this world took place in November 1901 when he wrote to Jack Yeats as a result of reading an exhibition review from *The Dublin Express* which described the paintings of both Jack and his father, J B Yeats.[3] Thereafter, Quinn was to become an inordinately generous friend of Ireland.

He advised and helped W B Yeats in securing American copyright for his writings and organised Yeats's first lecture tour of the States in 1903–04; he arranged a similar tour for Douglas Hyde and worked for the advancement of the Gaelic League; he sponsored the Abbey Theatre's American tour in 1911–12; he financially supported John Butler Yeats — more or less — over the fifteen years of the latter's stay in New York; and he acted as friend and patron to a host of other Irish artists and *literati*: Joyce, AE, Synge, Padraic Colum, James Stephens, Nathaniel Hone,[4] Sarah Purser (who, on first meeting Quinn, 'looked at him hungrily to paint him'[5]), and others.

His greatest friend, among all his Irish friends, was perhaps Lady Gregory whom he first met on her home territory in 1902[6] and his most intimate contact with the 'Celtic Twilight' came twelve years later when, on the conclusion of the

One of the earliest collections of the work of Jack B Yeats was assembled in New York by his friend, the collector John Quinn (1870–1924). In their spirited correspondence over twenty years, **Homan Potterton** finds new light is shed on the character and development of the great Irish artist.

*John Butler Yeats*, John Quinn, 1912.
Pencil on paper, 7¾ x 5 in.
*Hirshhorn Museum and Sculpture Garden,*
*Smithsonian Institution, Gift of Joseph*
*H Hirshhorn, 1966.*

Abbey's American tour, Lady Gregory stayed with him in New York: for a brief few days the couple became lovers.[7]

In time, Quinn's interests were to develop away from Irish literature and painting to the art of the avant-garde in Europe and, by the time of his early death in 1924, he had assembled 'the most important modern art collection in the United States before the Depression'.[8] It numbered more than fifty works by Picasso and as many by Matisse, Derain, and Rouault as well as outstanding examples by Cézanne, Van Gogh, Gauguin, and Seurat.

Quinn was passionate about collecting but had no interest in consigning his art collection to posterity: he left directions for it to be sold after his death. But the

record of his activities as a collector, in the form of more than twenty years of carefully preserved correspondence with artists, he bequeathed to New York Public Library[9] Amidst this archive are the letters he and Jack Yeats exchanged over almost twenty-three years, letters which document Jack's career and development, his ideas and enthusiasms, and, above all, his character.

\* \* \*

In the autumn of 1901 Jack Yeats held an exhibition of his work in Dublin[10] at the same time as the exhibition, (organised by Sarah Purser), of the paintings of his father, John Butler Yeats and the landscape painter, Nathaniel Hone.[11] T W Rolleston wrote a review of Jack's exhibition in *The Dublin Express* and this review was sent to John Quinn in New York.

Quinn's first letter to Yeats is not preserved in the New York Public Library archive but letters from both Jack (J–Q: 18.11.01) and JB (JB–Q: 19.11.01) in reply answer the enquiries that he made. Quinn had obviously asked if he might purchase a painting from Jack called *Midsummer Eve;* he asked about the size of Jack's paintings, and he asked about prices. Confused in some way as to the identities of Jack and J B, he also enquired about several of JB's pictures including *King Goll* and the *Portrait of John O'Leary* as well as the possibility of there being a portrait of W B Yeats.[12]

Writing from his home in Devon[13], Jack remarked how flattering Rolleston's notice had been and, at the same time, he sent Quinn a copy of AE's notice of the exhibition from *The Freeman's Journal* (23 Oct 1901); he regretted that *Midsummer Eve* had already been sold but sent a list (with prices) of the pictures that were still available, adding a description of them as an afterthought. Remarking that the largest of his paintings were about 30 by 22 inches ('most about half that size') he suggested that they could 'travel all right rolled or flat'.

From the list which Jack supplied, it is clear that Quinn expressed interest in some of the pictures which remained unsold[14] — *The Unicorn* (no. 2 below), *After the Harvest's Saved* (no. 1) and *The Banner* (possibly no. 14) — and Jack offered to show them to him on his visit to London the following summer (J–Q: 21.7.02). Jack proposed noon on Saturday 26 July at Blenheim Road, Bedford Park[15]

# JACK B YEATS AND JOHN QUINN

– 'I hope you will not mind going so far into the suburbs' – and the visit, Quinn's first meeting with the Yeats family, was obviously a success. He and Jack's sister Lily, found much to talk about – Lollie (his other sister) thought they were greatly attracted to one another'[16] – and Quinn also took to Jack. He bought some of Jack's pictures (he sent a cheque a day or so later)[17], invited him and his wife[18] to spend the evening with him – 'Thank you very much for last night's pleasant time which my wife enjoyed greatly as did I', Jack wrote afterwards (J–Q: 27.7.02) – and when they parted it was with a promise to meet again the following Tuesday.

JB, who was in Dublin, heard of the encounter and wrote excitedly to WB (JB–WB: 31.7.02): 'John Quinn is the nearest approach to an angel in my experience. He has bought ten of Jack's (paintings) . . . He and Jack have been going about London together. Jack is just the man to guide a newly arrived American among the mysteries of London'.[19]

As it happened, Jack and Quinn lunched the following Thursday when they discussed Quinn's plans for his first visit to Ireland. Jack was about to set off for Coole[20], and Quinn also intended visiting Galway but since he had not appeared there by 12 August, when Jack was on the point of returning to Dublin, Jack wrote to him giving his Dublin address. He told Quinn of the Feis that was to take place in Galway later in the month (with a play in Gaelic by Douglas Hyde) and he offered to accompany Quinn there, should he so wish. (J–Q: 12.8.02)

In the meantime Quinn, who was still in London, firmed up on his purchases and ordered from Jack *After the Harvest's Saved* and *The Unicorn* – both of which had been praised by AE in his *Freeman's Journal* notice – as well as the set of five small sketches (*The Bay Pilot, The River Pilot, The Stevedore, The Ganger,* and *The Gang*) now in Sligo Museum (no. 4). He changed his mind about one picture, *The Kindly Donkey*, which he had already reserved, and asked instead for *The Emigrant Girl* (no. 6) and *The Man of the*

West (no. 5). (J–Q: 16.8.02).

By the time of the opening of Jack's exhibition (at the Central Hall, Westmoreland Street) on Monday 18 August, Quinn had still not arrived in Ireland. He was enjoying himself in London where he met, among others, Sir Charles Dilke to whom he recommended the poetry of Jack's brother, WB (J–Q: 16.8.02). Jack now wrote encouraging him to come for the Dublin Horse Show the following week – 'Wednesday would be a good day' – and he suggested The Shelbourne Hotel with The Gresham or The Metropole as second choices. (J–Q: 23.8.02).

When Quinn eventually did arrive, Jack took him round. They saw 'little plays being rehearsed' which were to be performed in Dublin the following October (J–Q: 29.10.02) [21]; Quinn bought some pictures from Jack's exhibition (nos. 7, 8, 9, 10, 11, 12, 13); and then, as Quinn later described it, 'on a Sunday (August 31st) [he] travelled with Jack . . . from Dublin, through Mullingar to Athenry, and thence by side-car to Killeeneen, in

*Jack B Yeats,* Fortune and her Wheel, *1902. Watercolour, 10¾ x 17 in. Sligo County Museum and Art Gallery. (See Checklist No. 9).*

# JACK B YEATS AND JOHN QUINN

*Jack B Yeats, The Bay Pilot; The River Pilot; The Stevedore; The Ganger; The Gang. 1902.*
*Five watercolours each 4¼ x 3¼ in. Sligo County Museum and Art Gallery. (See Checklist No. 4).*

county Galway . . . to a 'Feis' that was to be held that afternoon where the blind Connacht poet Raftery was buried. The Feis was held on rising ground in a field beside the road. There were perhaps a hundred side-cars and other vehicles and five or six hundred men and women at the meeting. On a raised platform sat Dr Douglas Hyde, the President of the Gaelic League; Edward Martyn from Tillyra Castle (sic); Lady Gregory from Coole; and others in charge of the Feis. W B Yeats, the poet, and his brother, Jack B Yeats, the artist, and myself stood in the crowd and watched the spectacle.[22]' Jack promised Quinn 'a little drawing as a memento of the Feis' and sent it to him in October, 'I

. . . now send it hoping it will give you a memory of the scene' (J−Q: 29.10.02).[23] When Quinn offered to reimburse Jack for the fares and expenses of the trip to Galway, the painter refused. Quoting a story of 'the old horse trainer who was drinking Green Chartreuse by the tumbler when the noble owner said to him, "that cost 15/= a bottle", Jack wrote Quinn about the cost of the jaunt to Galway, 'I can say as the old trainer did, "and worth it too sir"' (J−Q: 11.9.02).

Quinn enjoyed himself with his new Irish friends and was pleased when, for example, Lady Gregory mentioned him in a letter to Jack; he asked Jack for the letter only to be told 'I may have torn

it up . . . (but) I may find some other in which she speaks of you'! (J−Q: 11.9.02). Quinn also asked Jack for the press notices of his exhibition and these were sent off to New York[24] together with 'three little Irish primers for which I have done the sketches'[25].

After some time at Rosses Point, Co. Sligo in September − 'this place is the finest in the world, I am renewing the blood of my youth' (J−Q. 11.9.02) − Jack and Cottie had returned to 'a long mild but wet autumn' in Devon by October; their 'Irish terrier, *Hooligan* by name, was mighty glad to see us when we arrived' and Jack sketched the dog's greeting on his letter to Quinn (J−Q: 29.10.02).

# JACK B YEATS AND JOHN QUINN

Back in his office, Quinn set about generating interest in Jack's work. 'I will paint away at the best Irish stuff I can, with the idea of an exhibition in New York', Jack replied to his encouragement (J−Q: 15.12.02) while at the same time acknowledging an order for the *Broadsheet* from Quinn's Harvard friend, the actor-stage manager Townsend Walshe. He sent Jack some books − one about the painter RMA Stevenson − and he suggested that space might be found in some future *Broadsheet* for Fanny Parnell's poem, *After Death*, all seven verses of which he copied out for the painter (Q−J: 5.12.02). The poem, as Quinn pointed out, was called *Post Mortem* in Brooke's *Treasury of Irish Poetry* but *After Death* in Sparling's *Irish Minstrelsy*. When Jack published it in the *Broadsheet* (April 1903) he 'did not think either of the titles quite right so gave it none as we do not know what she called it' (J−Q: 28.4.03). Nor did Jack illustrate the poem: 'it struck on too fine a note for ordinary illustrating, so I just put a sunburst at the top, as an emblem of the Ireland that will rise up one of these days fit and well.'

Jack sent Quinn a copy of his miniature play, *The Treasure of the Garden* (J−Q: 5.12.02)[26]. Quinn subsequently had it performed: he wrote to Jack in May 1903, 'I have received in a box from (Elkin) Mathews the stagings . . . Walshe and I together are going to rig the things up . . . and give the show' and with a later letter Jack included a review of the play from the *Sligo Champion*: 'they don't know I'm grown up (and) think I must still be the little fat boy who used to leg it round the town picking up the gossip of the shops and the buttermarket, attending fires, circusses, and the arrival of steamboats' (J−Q: 16.1.03).

In early January 1903, Jack and Cottie visited London and made arrangements for an exhibition at Walker's from 5th February to 6th March: 'I will have the remains of the Dublin show − a dozen pictures which I have not shown before and also a few painted during the last few months' (J−Q: 16.1.03). When the exhibition, which consisted entirely of watercolours ('I only very occasionally do any oil work') opened in London, Jack sent Quinn some of the notices − 'you will see how stupid the London journalists are about Irish subjects' (J−Q: 14.2.03) − and he promised to let Snyders, the *New York Herald* critic, have

a ticket for the show. Quinn requested him to select 'three or four' pictures for him (J−Q: 12.3.03) from the exhibition and Lady Gregory too was pressed for her views. She agreed with Jack's choice of *The Big Peddler* (no. 15), *Dancing for a Cake* (no. 16), and *The Squireen* (no.17) and when Quinn insisted on a fourth painting, *Catching the Donkey* (no. 18) was reserved for him. (J−Q: 23.3.03).

In the meantime, *The Unicorn* (which Quinn had purchased the previous summer) had only now arrived from exhibition in Cork[27] but Jack promised to have it despatched forthwith: 'it would be a pity to wait for the Governor's (J B Yeats's) picture of Russell (which Quinn had commissioned) as the Dublin Academy, where it goes, does not close till the end of June' (J−Q: 14.2.03). The news from London was that Strang was etching a portrait of WB but as far as 'the story of Miss Maud Gonne's engagement to John McBride' was concerned, nobody 'knows whether it is true or not' (J−Q: 14.2.03). The Strang etching interested Quinn more than the possible marriage and he replied to Jack asking for more information about it.

Back in Devon, Jack continued to work on the *Broadsheets*[28] which he 'hoped to make more Irish in 1903'. The February number had verses by AE and a Lady Gregory translation of Douglas Hyde; Fanny Parnell's poem − 'with its fine idea' − was scheduled for the April issue; and the 'fine rattling verses, *The Last Prayers* and *Port of Holy Peter*', in a recent issue were by 'a young man called John Masefield . . . a Welshman but very keen on Irish things' (J−Q: 12.3.03)[29]. When Jack told Quinn that Masefield 'has some wild notion of going through Ireland with a pack this year; he thought of going as a tinker but I put him off that idea, because in Ireland the country people don't like tinkers they think there's something not right about them' (J−Q: 28.4.03), Quinn was very much attracted by the idea and proposed joining them. Even when it later transpired that, on account of his marriage that summer, Masefield could not contemplate such a trip (J−Q: 28.4.03), Quinn still pressed Jack to organise it: 'a tramp together down in the West, say from Galway to Sligo or anywhere around in the country where we could walk and ride as we pleased and where you could sketch to your heart's content while I loafed and read' was how

he described his ideal (Q−J: 1.5.03).

Writing to Quinn at the end of April, Jack told of sending three pictures 'to a big free pictures exhibition in Canningtown (a desperately poor part of the east of London) . . . I think the poor like pictures best: they look at them like a child looks at a picture book and that's the right way'. He reported on work in progress, 'I have done one pretty big (picture) with a lot of figures it is a little Irish race meeting on the sea-shore − and will I think give the visitors to my show something to look at for a good long time. It will appeal I think to "the people" over in Dublin − where I'll be having a show some time in the summer . . .' He feared, however, that he would not be 'flush enough for the adventure in New York in November', by which he meant the exhibition of his work which Quinn had been proposing; but if Quinn came to Ireland they could go into everything 'and see what the whole thing would cost' (J−Q: 28.4.03).

Jack was by now (May 1903) at work together with Cottie, designing banners of saints for Loughrea Cathedral[30] which were 'to be embroidered at Dun Emer[31] by my sister and her work girls'. He had completed St Patrick and St Asicus, Cottie had worked St Ita and St Patrick's sister (J−Q: 21.5.03). He was also preparing for a Dublin exhibition (at the Central Hall, Westmoreland Street) in late August (J−Q: 23.6.03), and at the back of his mind was always a New York show: 'a month on your side and a successful show would be a delightful experience!!!' (J−Q: 23.6.03).

Quinn came to Ireland again that summer. He was at The Shelbourne by 13 August; later went to Coole − 'your visit did us all good, that friendly voice from the new world cheers us inhabitants of the old' Lady Gregory wrote to him afterwards (Lady G−Q: 10.9.03). On his return to Dublin he visited JB, Lily and Lollie at their home, Gurteen Dhas, near Dundrum and proposed to WB that he should embark on an extended lecture tour of the States. He bought five pictures (J−Q: 10.9.03) from Jack − *Telling the Cards* (no. 19), *A Boreen* (no. 21), *To Catch the Liverpool Boat* (no. 20), *The Pirate* (no. 22) and *The Crucifixion* (no. 23) − and commissioned of JB a portrait of his own mother, to be painted from photographs. A record of his expenses from the trip, jotted on the back of an envelope dated 24 August 1903, is among Quinn's letters to

# JACK B YEATS AND JOHN QUINN

AE and shows that he paid JBY £100, Jack, £200, and Russell £110. Quinn also made definite plans for Jack's visit to New York, arranging too that Cottie would accompany him (J–Q: 16.10.03).

After his show ended in Dublin, Jack and Cottie went down to Coole. WB was also there and so was JB, and Jack wrote his sister Lily 'an amusing letter about a trout. Willie caught his first. Lady Gregory had it solemnly cooked for his breakfast but Papa got down first and ate it all up, when Willie appeared Papa drew his attention to the beautiful pink colour of the little bits of fish remaining'. (Lily–Q: 22.9.03). At Coole, JB was engaged in painting Lady Gregory's son, Robert and also Douglas Hyde: 'the head is splendid', Jack wrote to Quinn, 'but the knees will have to be worked at a bit. But that can be done from anybody' (J–Q: 10.9.03). Then JB was to paint Lady Gregory's sister-in-law, Mrs Persse but, complained Lady Gregory to Quinn (12.9.03), when she 'arrived by arrangement, on Monday for her portrait, (JB) had no canvas! And then we telegraphed to Jack who was coming next day to bring one, and he arrived without taking any notice of the telegram, and three days were wasted and both artists are so very artistic, one feels they have done quite the right thing!' The house party attended a Feis and Sports at Ardrahan, Jack and Cottie went out on the lake boating, he 'looked around for ideas down the little town of Gort, and about generally' (J–Q: 10.9.03), and then they moved on to stay with Uncle George Pollexfen (Lily–Q: 22.9.03), at Rosses Point: 'to me the most beautiful place in the world', as Jack described it to Quinn, 'but that is not alone from its outward beautifulness (which might not strike all people as much) but because of the "nature" of it. Do you know that word "nature"? It means the heart, the marrow, the through and throughness' (J–Q: 26.6.03).

After a week staying with John Masefield in London, the Yeatses were back in Devon by early October. Jack had completed a new children's play, *The Scourge of the Gulph*, which Elkin Mathews published in book form[32] and he was able to send it to Quinn in November (J–Q: 25.11.03). He also designed a bookplate for Quinn to be printed by his sisters at Dun Emer (Q–J: 13.2.04) but this project was beset by difficulties. 'We have not been able to put

*Jack B Yeats*, The Crest of the Hill, *1904. Watercolour 28½ x 21 in. Sligo County Museum and Art Gallery. (See Checklist No. 26).*

the name of the press on them' wrote Lily to Quinn (25.11.03), 'because Jack did not put it in the drawing, and as he had the block made, I did not know until too late. Then I tried printing Dun Emer Press at the bottom in our type but it looked horrid, did not go at all well with the drawing, and looked like a cheap advertisement. As this plan failed I had a little block made of the words Dun Emer Press and tried it but we all decided against it. I wrote and pitched into Jack for not putting it on the original drawing where it would have looked alright.' Eventually, when the fifteen hundred plates were printed, the sisters mailed them to Quinn but 'in their innocence of our customs laws . . . declared the value at six pounds six and lo! and behold you I had to pay $7.75 duty on them besides fifty cents expressage' (Q–J: 13.2.04).

By early in 1904, Jack was seriously planning his New York debut. The St Louis World's Fair was to take place that year, and Jack thought of sending some of his pictures – 'about half a dozen only' – for inclusion in the Irish section (J–Q: 10.1.04)[33]. If he did so, it would lessen the number of works in any one-man show (unless he sent them on to St Louis afterwards) and he really needed Quinn's reaction as to whether a Spring exhibition in New York was a possibility.

Although Quinn was at this stage busy 'engineering' (to use Jack's word) WB's triumphant lecture tour of the States and sending newspaper clippings and magazine articles back to Ireland that recorded its progress (Q–J: 13.2.04), he found time to discuss Jack's proposed exhibition with the art critic of *The Evening Sun*, Fitzgerald. Between them they decided that Clausen's Gallery was 'the best and in fact the only place to have the exhibition in. The larger galleries like Macbeth's and Durand–Ruel's . . . only exhibit French pictures or large groups of pictures that are sure of commercial success . . . '. Furthermore, Jack should plan to come soon and not 'under any circumstances' later than the middle of April. The St Louis Fair was to open on 1 May and Quinn advised Jack that he should by all means exhibit there, which he would be able to do after a show at Clausen's: Sarah Purser was to show stained glass and Quinn presumed that Lily and Lollie would be sending work from Dun Emer[34]. Jack should get in touch with T P Gill at once about the Fair and, assuming that other Irish artists were to exhibit in the Irish section, should arrange to have his paintings hung with them.

In regard to the New York exhibition, Quinn agreed to arrange terms with Clausen and suggested that Jack should 'bring as many of his good pictures as he can . . . and at least forty or fifty' of them (Q–J: 13.2.04). When the time came, he would also take care of the customs arrangements. Referring to a current economic recession – 'even rich people feel poor and people of moderate wealth have been much reduced . . . this winter has been one of the poorest for the buying of pictures that there has been for many years', Quinn warned Jack that he need not expect commercial success but 'your brother's lectures here and all the talk there has been about the name Yeats ought to help along your show'. He invited Jack and Cottie to stay with him – 'there is a quiet room in my apartment which your brother has used' (Q–J: 13.2.04) – and promised 'I am sure you and Mrs Yeats will have a good time' (Q–J: 15.2.04).

With WB away for six weeks on the West Coast (Q–J: 15.2.04) where he gave about twenty-five lectures, Quinn had time to plan Jack's exhibition. As promised, he met with Clausen and engaged the Gallery from 28 March for a three-week

# JACK B YEATS AND JOHN QUINN

period as well as agreeing the financial arrangements. Having had to pay $7.75 duty on the bookplates which Lily and Lollie had sent him, Quinn was conscious of the bills Jack might have to pay at Customs if he imported his pictures in a regular way: 'I am going to rob Uncle Sam of seven times that much if I can for your benefit' he declared. After consultation with Clausen, he proposed that Jack should send him about twelve or fifteen pictures to his home address, without insurance and and without any declared value, and that a week or so later he should send another batch to his business address; he should bring about another twenty or so with him. Quinn would declare a low value on the pictures he received and pay a small amount of duty and Jack should do the same when he arrived. With regard to the catalogue, Jack should send copies of previous catalogues as well as some reviews and articles including a recent one by D S McColl.

Quinn's concerns extended beyond the safe (and economical) import of Jack's pictures to the passage of Jack and Cottie themselves and in a very long letter (Q−J: 15.2.04) he set out instructions. A first class passage was recommended; the Atlantic Transportation Line would be about $25 to $30 cheaper than the American Line but the latter would be better. If WB did not intend sailing as early as 9 March, they would be able to get his steamer rug when he arrived − as it was, they would miss him, 'we will pass him on the high seas I suppose' (J−Q: 1.3.04) − so they should provide themselves with at least one rug as well as a heavy ulster. Jack would have to declare his profession and his intentions (strictly a visit and no mention of the exhibition, Quinn recommended) as well as the fact that he was not a polygamist and on no account should he declare any Russian sympathies; the deck-steward should be tipped two to three shillings, the bath-room steward − three to five, the boots − two and six, and the cabin steward ten − but only after they had landed, otherwise he would desert them and not disembark their belongings.

Jack acted quickly and immediately sent off twenty pictures to Quinn (J−Q: 1.3.04) declaring their value at twenty-two pounds; another parcel, this time with nineteen, would go by the next steamer; and, as Quinn had instructed, he would bring the balance of the sixty or so

*Jack B Yeats, The Car is at the Door, 1904. Watercolour, 21 x 15 in. Sligo County Museum and Art Gallery. (See Checklist No. 28).*

he hoped to exhibit with him. The fourteen pictures he intended for St Louis were to go separately. He and Cottie were booked to sail on 12 March and would travel on the *Mesaba* arriving in New York on the 21st. (J−Q: 9.3.04). They were looking forward to the adventure: 'we have both longed for a great many years to see the shores of America' (J−Q:1.3.04). He would wait to see Clausen before deciding on prices for his work but thought of charging the same as in Dublin.

Hilary Pyle[35], by reference to Jack's *Sligo*[36] and other material, has pieced together beautifully Jack and Cottie's peregrinations during their seven-week stay in New York. Jack later referred to the metropolis as 'that little one-night stand they call New York as the music hall song went' (J−Q: 4.12.07), and wrote that 'from a pleasure point of view (they) both had a fine time' (J−Q: 6.6.04) and 'did not regret going a bit'. Quinn enjoyed their company and wrote to WB as well as to the Yeats sisters to tell them as much. 'He is one of the most simple and unaffected kind-hearted genuine and sincere men I have ever met, and I like him more than I can tell and have been delighted to have him with me' was how he described Jack to WB (Q−WB: 14.5.04)[37] and, when Lily received a similar encomium, she replied, 'I am very glad you had Jack long

enough with you to get to know him and find out how lovable he is. People don't know and he gets put rather in the shade by "Big" brother.' (Lily−Q: 12.6.04). The studio photograph of Jack which accompanied a short notice of the exhibition in *The Lamp*[38] showed the artist, cigar in hand, and the sisters thought it 'very good indeed, the best photograph we have seen' (Lily−Q: 17.5.04). When the couple returned − they sailed from New York on 15 May aboard *The Celtic* −their letters were 'full of tales of their travels which they have enjoyed greatly' but Lily wished that 'we had Jack himself for an hour or two, that would be better than twenty letters' (Lily−Q: 12.6.04).

\* \* \*

Initially, Quinn reported favourably on the collection: 'Jack Yeats has sold a fair number of pictures', he wrote to AE, 'and has had some good notices from the critics and has had troups of people in to see his show. He and Mrs Yeats are delighted with New York and I believe that he has seen more of the City than I ever have' (Q−AE: 2.5.04). Apart from the exhibition, Quinn also arranged that Jack was commissioned by *McClure's Magazine* to provide illustrations for the two stories by WB − *Hanrahan's Vision* and *Hanrahan's Curse* − that (again through Quinn) the magazine had just purchased: 'This will put a little additional money in his purse and will also be his first introduction to the American magazines', Quinn wrote to WB (Q−WB: 14.5.04). But the commission was not a success and Jack later wrote to Quinn (J−Q: 20.8.04): 'You will be sorry but McClures don't care about my pictures to Willy's stories. They were as good illustrations as ever I did . . . of course they were quite nice about it − But you know publishers don't care a rap whether illustrations are right or wrong in character and detail − as long as they can give their readers what'll satisfy them'.

After all his endeavours, Quinn must have been disappointed at this news and nor can he have been impressed by Jack's somewhat arrogant tone particularly as his initial enthusiasm for the exhibition was by now considerably modified: 'He is too careless' he reported to AE (Q−AE: 2.5.04), 'his drawing is very bad in some of his pictures, and out of the sixty-three he exhibited, some eight or ten were too badly drawn and badly coloured to be

# JACK B YEATS AND JOHN QUINN

shown out of a school of painting. He hurt his good ones by showing his bad ones . . . He has undoubted gifts, but somehow his pictures seem only superficially attractive'. Quinn took up the same theme with WB: 'Jack . . . doesn't take himself as an artist seriously enough, I wanted to tell him that while a large part of his work was very fine, more of it was very crude both in drawing (and) coloring but after just hinting at it once I stopped and did not mention it further. No artist can paint fifty or sixty fine pictures every year any more than a poet can produce seven or eight volumes of good poetry a year. If Jack would perfect his technique and improve his drawing and his coloring, he might have a chance to make himself a very great name as an artist. But if he keeps on as he is, by the time he is forty he will be, I fear, a young man with a brilliant future behind him. This is a part of the matter that I am afraid his wife does not appreciate' (Q−WB: 14.5.04).[39]

Apparently, Quinn addressed the same topic with JB and Lady Gregory, but when Lily heard about it she was furious. She wrote to her father, '(Jack) is all right and knows what he is doing. He never drifts. Willy and Lady Gregory are both too ready to criticise and direct. They forget Jack is at the beginning and is seven years younger than Willy. What of Willy's technique seven years ago? . . . Don't worry Jack. He wants encouragement, and his work is beautiful and his own. When we are all dead and gone great prices will be given for them. I know they will' (Lily−JB: 27.7.04)[40].

Quinn's long-standing enthusiasm for Yeats's work may have been tempered after discussion with some of the New York artists and critics, and he must have been influenced in some way by reviews of the exhibition such as those which appeared in the *New York Times* (5 April 1904): '(The Exhibition) has the personal charm of sketches made by a tourist during a stay in the West of Ireland . . . they might be those of an amateur who is not without all knowlege of the poster art of France. (The artist) manages to give the impression of movement to his little figures, though his drawing is often queer, and in some instances childish . . . rough notes for illustrations rather than well-considered pictures, yet the very hit-or-miss way in which they are knocked off is not without its attraction . . . the impression one gets is of the amateur rather than

the professional . . . while his inexperience often leads him into compositions that only a novice would attempt. Mr Yeats has keen appreciation of the humorous and a decided talent for catching a character. He has the stuff in him, perhaps, for a caricaturist. In any case, there is much work ahead of him before he can be taken seriously for an artist.'

When anyone later asked him how he got on in America, Jack replied that he 'cleared expenses − which is a sort of half truth as of course it paid all *my own* expenses well, not counting Mrs Yeats'. (J−Q: 21.6.04). The Macbeth Gallery retained fourteen of his pictures[41] : he 'may do something with them as I fancy he has a clientele who would believe what he said' (J−Q: 6.6.04). Otherwise, only two pictures sold and it was left to Quinn to help with the expenses by purchasing ten drawings at the conclusion of the exhibition.[42] In contrast to the tremendous success of his brother's tour of America, Jack's visit was a very muted affair and, even though his father, JB, lived in New York from 1907 until his death in 1922, Jack never again crossed the Atlantic.

In the years that followed, Quinn was to buy a further six paintings from Jack; he continued to subscribe to the *Broadsheet* − 'Your new *Broadside* comes along regularly . . . although I don't think I like it as much as I did the old and bigger broadside' (Q−J: 20.12.08); and he lent all his pictures by the artist to the Irish Industrial Exposition at Madison Square Gardens in 1905. On a placard that he placed in that exhibition, he referred to Jack as 'Jack B. Yeats, G.I.P.'. When 'several people wanted to know what "G.I.P." stood for . . . I told them that it was a new decoration of the Royal Hibernian Academy and that it meant "Great Irish Painter"' (Q−J: 13.10.05).

Although Quinn and Jack were only ever to meet twice again after Jack returned from America − on Quinn's visits to London and Dublin in October 1904 and August 1909 − the two men corresponded on a regular basis until Quinn's death in 1924. Initially, Jack wrote fairly frequently and reported all his doings. That summer, on their return from America, he and Cottie attended the opening of Hugh Lane's exhibition of Irish Art at the Guildhall, London[43] where JB's portraits 'looked well' and his own pictures were 'very well-placed' (J−Q: 21.6.04). Later in the year, when Quinn was planning his

trip to Europe, Jack wrote from Devon: 'I am sorry you don't think you will be able to look us up − I wish I could go to Ireland and have a day or two's walking − but I will be going over later in the year and must stay at my work till then' (J−Q: 20.8.04). When Quinn was in London in October, however, Jack went up to see him.[44] At home that Christmas, when he entertained the Valley children − 'as (Mrs Jack) does always at Christmas' (J−Q: 13.1.05) − he performed a shadow show for them[45] , but afterwards wrote wistfully to Quinn, 'I would like to be giving entertainments to Irish children, they would be such a much brighter, quicker audience'.

His exhibition in 1905 at Baillie's Gallery in London − 'a very out-of-the-way place' − was not a success (J−Q: 11.8.05). In June that year, he and Synge travelled in the West of Ireland − in 'the congested districts of Connemara and up as fas ar Belmullet' − with Synge writing articles and Jack making drawings for the *Manchester Guardian* (J−Q: 11.8.05).[46] His exhibition in Dublin in September 'was quite successful clearing a nice little lump' − and after it was over he spent about ten days in Manchester making drawings of the city for the *Manchester Guardian* (J−Q: 10.12.05).[47] Quinn had intended visiting Dublin at the time of the Dublin show but because he was 'up to my neck in preparations for the Douglas Hyde lectures . . . in November' (Q−J: 30.8.05) he cancelled his visit.[48] Nevertheless, he ordered two pictures to be selected for him and Jack subsequently informed him (J−Q: 27.9.05) that 'they' had picked out 'good ones' for him: *There was an Old Prophecy found in a Bog* (no. 35) and *Political Meeting* (no. 34). It was, however, only after many difficulties that Quinn received the pictures. Initially he asked Jack to hold them − 'Russell has some pictures of mine . . . and I may decide to have yours sent with them' − (Q−J: 13.10.05); then, in July the following year, he asked Jack, 'How could your two pictures be sent? Could they be rolled up?' (Q−J: 12.7.06). When Jack replied 'they are on stiff card so they could not be rolled and sent in a cylinder' (J−Q: 28.7.06), the matter again fell into abeyance. When in 1907, Quinn bought further paintings by AE, he proposed that Jack's watercolours would be despatched with them (Q−J: 21.8.07) but he warned Jack, 'Egan is a very bad packer', and for

# JACK B YEATS AND JOHN QUINN

*Jack B Yeats, The Race-Course, Town of Galway, 1907—10.*
*Watercolour, pastel and pencil on paper, 12½ x 19½ in.*
*Hirshhorn Museum and Sculpture Garden, Smithsonian Institution,*
*Gift of Joseph H Hirshhorn, 1966. (See Checklist No. 30).*

*Jack B Yeats, The Political Meeting, 1905.*
*Crayon and watercolour on card, 21 x 28½ in.*
*Sligo County Museum and Art Gallery. (See Checklist No. 34).*

some reason the pictures remained in Dublin until one of Quinn's employees collected them there in June 1908 (Q–J: 4.6.08 and Q–J: 20.12.08). By this stage Quinn was cross: 'hereafter I am going to limit my buying of pictures on the other side to my being there personally present, and save troubling those that I buy them from, and save myself trouble (Q–J: 4.6.08). Jack defused the situation by writing to Quinn (Q–J: 27.7.08) in an amusing way, 'It is a great shame that Noble Buyers like yourself should have any bother about getting your pictures across the Atlantic. If I had a long low black-hulled schooner of my own I'd go into the picture delivery business myself' and to these words he appended a sketch which Quinn 'enjoyed' (Q–J: 20.12.08). It showed Jack smuggling pictures by passing them from a schooner to a small row-boat in New York harbour with the Statue of Liberty and 'the very guns of the frowning forts' in the distance.

The reprint of *The Fancy* (a book of verse by Keats's friend, John Hamilton Reynolds, that was originally published in 1820) with an introduction by Masefield and illustrations by Jack — 'there are some delightful sonnets to pugilists in it' (J–Q: 11.8.05) — came out at the end of 1905[49], and he sent Quinn a copy: 'It isn't great poetry, but some of the short verses are very cheerful kind of reading — and I think Masefield's introduction is the very best thing of that sort of "*make shape and perfection*" as they used to say under the

old prints of race horses' (J–Q: 28.7.06). That summer he and Cottie spent time at Clifden. Writing from The Quay House Hotel in early September (J–Q: 7.9.06) where they had been 'for the last fortnight', Jack described for Quinn 'doing some landscapes, bathing and rowing about the little bays'. They were there again the following year 'painting landscapes in oils': 'this painting landscape is very useful to me, and exciting work and a rest from picture making where, beyond the ordinary difficulties of painting, you have all the composition of your figures and the "idea" of your picture to keep a grip on' (J–Q: 16.9.07). It was not just landscape painting that Jack was developing at this time, but painting in oils as well. 'I have been painting away doing a little more in oils than usual' he wrote to Quinn in 1908 (J–Q: 7.7.08). Returning to the West the following summer when they stayed with Arnold Harvey (Robert Gregory's former tutor and one of Jack's lifelong friends) 'who has now a living with a nice vicarage' (J–Q: 18.12.08) on a peninsula between Sligo and Galway Bays, he reported 'we have come early this year as last year we were late and it was divilish cold for painting out of doors. It is no pleasure to sit on a desolate coast, perched on a damp rock with the cold showers sweeping over you and your paint and a drop on the end of your nose' (J–Q: 21.5.09).

That same year, on Synge's death, Quinn suggested to Jack that he 'ought to

sit down and write something about him' (Q–J: 15.5.09) for possible publication in the New York papers, and Jack did 'throw together some little things about him' (J–Q: 21.5.09) although he later apologised, 'I am sorry to have bothered you to get those little notes I scrawled about Synge typewritten' (J–Q: 19.6.09)[50]. Writing from Ballycastle, Co Mayo (May's Hotel), when Quinn's visit to Ireland seemed imminent, he suggested 'perhaps you could come away to some quiet place like this for a couple of days. Where . . . you could lie on your back in the heather or on the rocks by the sea or tramp along the coast . . .' Quinn himself expected to be 'in Dublin a day or two and then a day or two at Lady Gregory's, and then I expect to go over to Hyde's place' (Q–J: 24.6.09); but, in the event, he spent only a few days in Dublin and most of his time in London. There he met Hugh Lane: 'I think that (he) is a very good sort. I never could understand why almost everyone in Dublin who mentioned Lane's name seemed to smile. After all the man has done something fine and big, yet everyone seems to laugh or smile when his name is mentioned. I suppose if they could do worse than laugh or smile they would do so.

They did worse before he succeeded. Now that he has succeeded, all they can do is to laugh and smile' (Q–J: 29.11.09).

By 16 August 1909, Quinn was in Dublin where he stayed for a few days and took the opportunity to add to his col-

# JACK B YEATS AND JOHN QUINN

lection eight pictures by AE, six by Nathaniel Hone, and two by Jack (nos. 37 & 38). It was on this occasion too that he quarrelled with WB — a rift that was to last five years — but he consolidated his other Irish friendships and he was to remain a faithful correspondent of AE, Hyde, Lady Gregory, TW Rolleston, and, not least Jack Yeats, until the end of his days.

After spending some time in London, Quinn returned to Dublin for a day, Saturday 28 August, when he went out to see Lily and Lolly; 'saw about one act of *Bunco Podsnap*[51]; 'met Sir Walter Armstrong, Director of the National Gallery . . . and we talked pictures for two or three hours with Sarah Purser, the artist and the cleverest woman in Ireland, as sort of official referee . . .' (Q to Walshe, 3:9:09); and left Dublin 'at some ungodly hour Sunday morning . . . (for) . . . a cold, hard dreary ride . . . from Dublin to Queenstown' (Q–J, 29:11:09). There, leaving Ireland for the last time ever, he embarked the *Lusitania* for New York.

The two pictures which Quinn bought from Jack on his 1909 visit were *The Sea Fog* and *Washing the Circus Horses* (nos. 38 & 37); and although over the years that followed he often attempted to buy more — 'I want to buy two or three more of your important things' (Q–J: 30.1.14)[52] — these pictures, together with *The Old Road to Cahirciveen* (no. 39) which he bought from the Independents' exhibition in New York in 1923,[53] completed his collection of Jack Yeats. By the time of the International Exhibition of Modern Art in New York ('The Armory Show')[54] in 1913, he was still intent on promoting Jack's work and he selflessly suggested that the painter should send over new work rather than be represented by earlier pictures from his own collection. He wrote to Jack (Q–J: 21.12.12), 'They said something a little while ago about making a selection from your water colors that I have, but perhaps it would suit you better to have some of your later work exhibited. I am told that you have been doing a lot of interesting things, and in oil . . . if you would care to send a number of oils . . . cable me. Personally I shouldn't send any watercolours.' Jack agreed with him: 'it is better to exhibit oils in a public exhibition than watercolours. Watercolours get slaughtered . . . by high keyed neighbours' (J–Q: 7.1.13). He cabled that he would send five oils[55] and, in the event,

Quinn lent one watercolour, *The Political Meeting* (no. 34), so that Jack's earlier style was also represented.

By the time of the Armory Show, Quinn was well on his way to being the foremost collector of modern art in America and his Irish collection naturally paled in comparision to the works by Picasso, Matisse, Rouault, Cézanne, Seurat, Gauguin, and others which he was now pursuing. Initially it was Augustus John — 'a most interesting man . . . a great painter' (Q–J: 29.11.09) — whom he first met in London in 1909, who educated his taste towards modern French art.[56] Quinn had first heard of the artist through his Irish friends. John had made a drawing of WB at Coole in 1907, and when Quinn heard about it he asked Jack what he thought of John's work (Q–J: 10.12.07). Jack replied (J–Q: 6.1.08) that he had not seen WB's portrait but that he had 'seen some of John's painting which I liked very much but I have not cared very much for the drawings of his which I saw except two or three etchings'.

In 1910, Jack and Cottie left Devon, where they had lived for thirteen years — 'it was too rediculously (*sic*) out of the way' (J–Q: 20.12.10) and moved to Red Ford House — 'an amusing house' — in Greystones.[56] They had always longed for Ireland, a yearning Jack had expressed in a letter to Quinn in 1906: 'You say I miss a lot not being in Ireland. I don't think I miss much from a financial point of view but I know I miss lots of the joy of life, its a queer thing to live in an alien country — But I wouldn't give a thrawneen to live in Dublin. I would want to be somewhere in the west by the sea . . .' (J–Q, 7.9.06). When they eventually made the move, he reported 'I am very glad to be in my own country. I lived for years in England but the Anglo-Celtic brotherhood never even sprouted in my case . . .' (J–Q: 20.12.10).

Jack's move to Ireland came at about the same time that Quinn's interest in the art of the moderns was developing and as a result, Paris rather than Dublin, became his main focus of attention. Thereafter, he and Jack corresponded less regularly, perhaps just exchanging letters at Christmas, but between them they touched on a variety of subjects. In 1913, Jack reported on the general strike in Dublin — 'my sympathies are all with the workers, who have never had quite enough to eat. But I object to any help from England' (J–Q:

22.11.13); later, he wrote of the 'public meeting here in Dublin about getting back the Lane Pictures from London' (J–Q: 24.12.17). Quinn, in turn, gave such news as the great success of the Armory Show in New York. Jack — who was never enthusiastic about contemporary art — also had views about that Show: 'the great good these wild Post-Impressionists and Futurist painters will do, will be that they will knock the handcuffs off all the painters. There must be no more you-must-not-do-this or that. We can now do anything we like and no old lady of either sex will be able to say "Oh my! you mustn't paint sunlight shadows without some pretty mauve in them" . . . Art critics stop using a new eye at the age of about forty-five. I walked through the Lane Gallery here with Bernard Shaw one time. He only liked one picture really. That belonged to the time when he was between forty and fifty'. (J–Q: 14.6.13). Jack returned to this theme in a later letter: '. . . the moderns . . . these gay souls will do good in unshackling painting. But so far they do not shake me in my plans, which are only to paint what I have seen happen'. (J–Q: 15.12.13).

It was not the first time that Jack had aired his views on art to Quinn. On his visit to New York in 1904 he had, as Quinn reported to AE, expounded 'his theory that the chief aim of a picture should be to tell a story, and that an Irish peasant is a better judge of art than a Whistler or Corot'. At the time, Quinn thought that this 'theory is all wrong; it enables him to please himself and wife with easy results but never will produce great art. Millet and Corot and Rodin didn't go on the "peasant theory"; they had their own ideas but never for a moment undervalued technique. Jack B Y undervalues technique. But of course these are only the views of an outsider who doesn't know art and I shouldn't care to be quoted'. (Q–AE: 2.5.04). A year or so later, Quinn was more confident in rejecting Jack's ideas. Writing again to AE, he reiterated, 'I do not believe in Jack Yeats' theory of painting at all, that the peasant — even the unspoiled peasant — even the unspoiled Irish peasant — is a better judge of a painting than an art critic. These are Tolstoi's views in his book "What is Art?" I believe that the best judge of a painting is a painter. I would rather take your judgement, for example, if I wanted to select five Whistlers

# JACK B YEATS AND JOHN QUINN

out of a group of twenty of his best works than I would that of the most unspoiled Irish peasant there ever breathed'. (Q–AE: 4.8.05).

Also at the time of his New York exhibition, Quinn felt that Jack 'really ought to take more pains with his work; to exhibit fewer pictures; to associate more with artists and critics; to live either in London or Paris, where he will see other men's work' (Q–AE: 1.7.04); but this too was a concept which Jack rejected. 'These silly young modern writers on art, don't know a bit more, than the nice old lady, who thinks a broken down windmill is *Artistic*, but a windmill in working order is most inartistic. I do not keep on meeting young artists and learning what the fashion is with them, and I think this is a very good thing for me – they are such a lot of sheep. They use one common mind' (J–Q: 13.1.05). In a later letter he returned to this theme: '. . . a little while ago the fashion with the critics was to say that there was nothing in a picture but light and shade and colour, nothing else meant anything, and Velasquez[58] was the man that they swore never cared tuppence about the man or the scene he painted. He was all for the light shade and colour, and perhaps the way he slung the paint. Now they are beginning to discover that, even if he *thought* he wasn't interested in anything else, he was all the time *selecting* and *selecting* and painting the *idea* just as much as anyone else' (J–Q: 10.12.05). '. . . I believe that all fine pictures and fine literature too to be fine, must have some of the living ginger of life in them' he wrote later. 'I know there have been fine painters who said there was nothing in their pictures but *light and shade and colour* but such men may paint better than they know . . . I should not be surprised if one asked one of the great old painters what he thought of his own Venus if he would reply, that the handling of the paint was the only thing that made the picture worth anything and that was why he painted it. Now this would not be true he would be deceiving himself. If he spoke the truth he would say "I painted it because she was such a dam fine gall"' (J–Q: 7.9.06).

Jack's 'peasant theory' extended also to the theatre. 'The Abbey Theatre . . . is getting good houses this winter, the best they have had yet' he wrote of the 1905 Dublin season. '. . . by reducing the price of the cheapest seats they get if not a cultivated artistic crowd an honest one that is not afraid to have feelings and show them and of course they still get the polite people in the stalls. I do not believe in polite people anywhere and especially do I doubt them when they come from Merrion Square, Dublin' (J–Q: 21.12.05).

At the end of 1915 Jack became ill for the first time – 'I escaped anything like a regular breakdown' he wrote to Quinn (J–Q: 21.1.16) referring to his bout of depression – and then in 1917 he and Cottie moved from Greystones to Marlborough Road in Dublin[59]: 'I think we will like being nearer to our human friends', he informed Quinn (J–Q: 1.11.17). 'I have a good studio in this house with a good light and a spacey outlook over a little light square to the west and over a field to some wooded grounds on the east. But it is a little odd after looking over just a few fields to the Irish sea as we did from the Greystones house. I send you some five reproductions and photographs of my later pictures. They are all in oil. I have not painted in watercolour for a long time now'.

In his letters from these years, Quinn's principal concern is the failing health of JB Yeats who was still in New York and for whom Quinn felt responsible – 'he is thinner . . . and a little whiter . . . he has been working vigorously on the portrait of himself . . .' (Q–J: 26.6.19); '(he) has done about 30,000 words of his memoirs which I rescued from destruction' (Q–J: 10.1.20); '. . . his being here the last two years has worried me dreadfully . . .' (Q–J: 12.6.21); and finally, after JB's death at the age of eighty-two in 1922, 'although I feared (he) might not go through the winter, when the last attack seized him, it was a shock . . .' (Q–J: 4.5.22).

More shocking was the death from cancer of Quinn himself just two years later at the early age of fifty-four. Jack had written to him for the last time the previous Christmas: 'Willy is very pleased with his Nobel Prize . . . my sister Lily has been ill . . . there has been a little pumping up of excitement here over the appointment of a new Director for the National Gallery in the place of Langton Douglas. The piercing cry of "Job" was raised. But I don't think there was anything in most of the letters to the papers more than the flake white that those bad painters put on the crests of their dead waves to give them an appearance of friskiness. But I am not thrilled by the business of collecting the dismal old masters' he continued and then his last words to his friend and patron of more than twenty years were surprisingly tactless: 'Collecting for its own sake has reached the very young. Children of five or six now picket the tobacconists for cigarette pictures. The wise ones play pitch and toss with them, head or harp, plain or picture.' (J–Q: 18.12.23). It was a curious dismissal from Jack of what had, after all, been Quinn's lifelong passion.

After his death, Quinn's art collection was, in accordance with his wishes, dispersed mainly at auction[60]. In directions which he had given his executors six years earlier they had permission to dispose of his 'advanced art work' privately, but Quinn had felt that most of his earlier purchases '. . . the Russell things, the Jack B Yeats things, the Nathaniel Hone things, the Mr Yeats things . . . are quite sane'[61] and that they would do well in the saleroom. A selection from his collection, including some works by Jack[62], were exhibited at a Memorial Exhibition in New York in January 1926, and the principal auction took place in February the following year[63]. It included thirty-two pictures by Jack, several of which were bought by old friends of Quinn. These included the Irish writer (and British Vice-Consul at Baltimore), Ernest Boyd; his old Harvard classmate, Cornelius J Sullivan; and the Abbey actor, J M Kerrigan.

Thus was dispersed one of the earliest collections of the work of Jack B Yeats. By the standards of his later paintings in oil, John Quinn's group of watercolours by Jack, mainly dating from his early years, was modest enough but it was witness to an artist who by the age of forty, in Quinn's words, 'had a brilliant future behind him'. That 'future' is documented in the spirited correspondence between Jack and Quinn, a correspondence which, in its way, is almost as important for our understanding of Jack as the pictures he painted at the same time.

*Homan Potterton*

*Homan Potterton was Director of the National Gallery of Ireland from 1980 to 1988.*

NOTES OVERLEAF

CHECKLIST OF PAINTINGS BY JACK B YEATS IN THE QUINN COLLECTION ON PAGES 113 AND 114.

# JACK B YEATS AND JOHN QUINN

## NOTES

1. Hilary Pyle, *Jack B Yeats* (London, 1970) referred to hereafter as Pyle 1970. See also Hilary Pyle, *Jack B Yeats: His Watercolours, Drawings and Pastels* (Dublin, Irish Academic press, 1992) and *Jack B Yeats: A Catalogue Raisonné of the Oil Paintings*. 3 vols. (London, André Deutsch 1992).

2. For Quinn see, B L Reid, *The Man from New York: John Quinn and his Friends* (New York, 1968) referred to hereafter as Reid.

3. For J B Yeats see, William M Murphy, *Prodigal Father: the Life of John Butler Yeats (1839–1922)* (Ithaca & London, 1978) referred to hereafter as Murphy 1978.

4. For Nathaniel Hone and Quinn see Homan Potterton, 'Nathaniel Hone and John Quinn: a Correspondence' in Brian P Kennedy (ed.), *Art is my Life: a Tribute to James White* (Dublin, 1991), pp. 133–53.

5. Quoted in Joseph Hone (ed) *W B Yeats* (London, 1962) p. 183.

6. Quinn himself described his first meeting with Lady Gregory in John Quinn, 'Lady Gregory and the Abbey Theatre', *The Outlook*, 16 December 1911, pp. 916ff.

7. See Daniel J Murphy, 'Dear John Quinn' in Ann Saddlemeyer & Colin Smythe (eds.), *Lady Gregory, Fifty Years After* (Gerrards Cross, 1987) pp. 123–30 and 410–11.

8. For Quinn the collector, see J Zilczer, 'The Noble Buyer': *John Quinn, Patron of the Avant-Garde*. Exh.Cat. Hirshhorn Museum (Washington, 1978).

9. John Quinn Memorial Collection, Rare Books and Manuscripts Division of New York Public Library (Astor, Lenox and Tilden Foundations). Additional letters are among the Jeanne R Roster–William M Murphy Collection in the same location.

10. 'Sketches of Life in the West of Ireland' shown at 9 Merrion Row, Dublin, 23 October – 2 November 1901.

11. 'A Loan Collection of Pictures by Nathaniel Hone, RHA and John Butler Yeats, RHA' and shown at 6 St Stephen's Green, Dublin, 21 October – 3 November 1901. Catalogue by Sarah Purser, George Moore, and F York Powell.

12. Writing from 52 Morehampton Road, Dublin on 19 November 1901, JB replied: 'King Goll has been sold & John O'Leary's portrait was painted for subscribers who presented the picture to Mr O'Leary. I believe the final home of the picture will be the Dublin National Gallery – If you cared for a copy of the picture I could easily get permission to make one & would do it for £30 – My son W B Yeats possesses a portrait of himself done by me two years ago. It remains however my property & I could dispose of it to you for £20 – It is a life size head & considered very like by my son & his friends –.' This letter is reproduced by Murphy 1978, pp.234–45.

13. 'Caislean na Seilmide, (later, Cashlauna Shelmiddy) Strete, nr. Dartmouth, S. Devon' where Jack lived from 1897. For the house, see Pyle 1970, pp. 41, 48–50.

14. Quinn's earliest letters are not among the papers in NYPL (his first letter to Jack in the Collection is dated 5.12.02) but it is possible to deduce the substance of the corre-spondence from Jack's replies.

15. 3 Blenheim Road, Bedford Park where JB and his family lived from 1888 until 1902. For this house see Murphy 1978, p. 154.

16. Quoted by Murphy 1978, p. 238.

17. 'Thank you for your cheque for the pictures for which I enclose a receipt'. (J–Q. 29.7.02).

18. Mary Cottenham White, always referred to as Cottie. She and Jack met at art school and married in 1894. She was a native of Devon which probably accounts for the couple making their home there from 1897 onwards although the Yeats family also had connections in Devon. (Pyle 1970, p. 39).

19. Joseph Hone, *J B Yeats: Letters to His Son W B Yeats and Others, 1869–1922* (New York, 1946), p. 73. It is not possible to be certain which pictures Quinn bought in London and which he bought later in the month at Jack's exhibition in Dublin: *The Emigrant Girl*, for example, was bought in London but was nevertheless exhibited later in Dublin. Pyle 1970, p. 81 says that Quinn bought eight pictures at the Exhibition.

20. Coole Park, Gort, the home of Lady Gregory. For a description of Coole by Quinn, see John Quinn, op. cit. 1911, pp 916ff.

21. In seeing these rehearsals, Quinn was actually witnessing the birth of the Irish National Theatre the first performances of which were in October 1902. The programme as planned in August, however, was subsequently changed (see Murphy 1978, p.246) so it is not certain exactly which plays Quinn saw but Lady Gregory wrote to him the following November (Lady G–Q: 8.11.02): 'We have had a busy fortnight here in Dublin. The little dramatic company has made a good start. A play by one of the young men (Fred Ryan) *The Laying of the Foundations*, has been very successful and *Cathleen ni Houlihan* and *Pot of Broth* (both by W B Yeats). These are the three favourites, and the acting was wonderfully good, especially the acting of W Fay in *The Pot of Broth*. They are throwing off the conventions of English acting, and may develop an art of their own. Except on Saturday when the hall was crowded, the audience was small. The "respectable" classes being afraid of dangerous novelties, but a small profit, about £10 was made so it doesn't matter. The "respectable" classes are very funny here. A clergyman living in Merrion Square said to old Mr Yeats "I shall be able to go and see the plays in the Antient-concert Rooms, of course one could not go to St Theresa's Hall". Mr Yeats answered "After all Christianity did not begin in Merrion Square".

22. Quinn, op. cit. 1911, p. 916.

23. The drawing may simply be the Feis programme annotated with sketches of WB, Hyde, Quinn, Jack and Lady Gregory now in the Berg Collection, NYPL (reproduced in Reid, p. 9). More possibly it is *At the Feis* for which Jack invoiced Quinn 7 guineas on 10 September 1903 (no. 14 below).

24. Notices from *The Leader* (30 August), *Daily Independent* (19 August) and *United Irishman* (23 August) by AE are amongthe Foster-Murphy papers in NYPL.

25. Probably the books in Irish for the Irish Book Company which Jack illustrated, N

Borthwick, *Ceachta Beaga Gaeilge* (Dublin, Irish Book Company, 1902–06).

26. *The Treasure of the Garden*, written and illustrated by Jack B Yeats (London, Elkin Mathews, 1903). See Pyle 1970, p.p. 64–5 for a description of the play.

27. International Exhibition, Cork, 1902.

28. *A Broadsheet*, edited by Jack B Yeats. Illustrated by Pamela Colman Smith; Jack B Yeats; and others. (London, Elkin Mathews, 1902, 1903). The Broadsheet was later published in a revised format as *A Broadside*, edited and illustrated by Jack B Yeats and published by Dun Emer and Cuala Presses, 1908–15. See Pyle 1970, pp. 67–68 and Murphy 1978, pp. 244, 334.

29. For Jack's friendship with the poet John Masefield, see Pyle 1970, pp. 73–80 and *passim*.

30. See Pyle 1970, p. 69. For this and the other important Arts and Crafts commissions for Loughrea, see J. Sheehy, *The Rediscovery of Ireland's Past : the Celtic Revival 1830–1930* (London, 1980) p. 157.

31. For Dun Emer see Sheehy, op. cit., pp. 158 ff. and N Gordon Bowe, 'Two Early Twentieth Century Irish Arts and Crafts Workshops in Context: An Túr Gloine and the Dun Emer Guild and Industries', *Journal of Design History*, Vol. 2, Nos. 2 & 3 (1989). Also see Murphy 1978, pp. 240–1, 258–60.

32. *The Scourge of the Gulph*, written and illustrated by Jack B Yeats (London, Elkin Mathews, 1903). See Pyle 1970, pp. 64–65 for a description of the play.

33. The Louisiana Purchase Exposition, St Louis, Missouri, 1904. For the Irish exhibit see Sheehy, op. cit. pp. 133–34; also, N Gordon Bowe, 'The Irish Arts and Crafts Movement (1886–1925)', *Irish Arts Review Yearbook 1990–1991*, p. 180. Although there was an 'Irish Village' at the Exposition with a 'brave show' of Irish arts and industries the collection of Irish paintings which Hugh Lane planned to send did not travel on account of insurance problems. See Sheehy, op. cit., pp. 107–08 and Murphy 1978, p. 271. As late as 1 March 1904, Jack nevertheless informed Quinn: 'I sent on Saturday to the gent in London who is collecting the pictures for St Louis 14 pictures, these go straight to St Louis – I think they are good pictures and ought to do me good'. Pyle 1970, p. 209 also indicates that Jack's pictures were exhibited at St Louis.

34. Quinn was correct in his presumption. Lily wrote him later (Lily–Q: 11.10.04): 'I have a lot of work at St Louis, have heard nothing at all of it since it left here in March last.'

35. Pyle 1970, pp. 83 ff.

36. Jack B. Yeats, *Sligo* (London, Wishart, 1930).

37. The letter is given in full in A. Himber (ed.), *The Letters of John Quinn to William Butler Yeats* (Ann Arbor, 1983), pp.59–60.

38. *The Lamp* (May 1904). For a description of Jack and Cottie as they appeared at this time, see Pyle 1970, pp. 82–83.

39. See n. 37.

40. Quoted in Murphy 1978, p. 267.

41. The pictures retained by Macbeth were as follows:- Exh. cat. no. 1: *Outside the Hurley Match*; no. 2: *Harnessing the Long Team*; no. 7:

A Cross-Champion; no. 8: *Political cartoons*; no. 27: *The Regatta*; no. 29: *The Whirley Horses in the Rain*; no. 34: *The Duck Hunt*; no. 37: *Robert Emmett in 1898*; no. 40: *Let me See the Wan fight*; no. 45; *Looking at a Horse*; no. 46: *A Bottle of Florida Water*; no. 55: *The Island King*; no. 61: *Hop, Step and Leap*; no. 62: *The Hibbidy Hibbidy*.

42. Jack sold twelve pictures. Of these I bought ten, amounting to $430; Mrs (Helen MacGregor) Byrne bought one small one, and one small one was sold to another person' (Q–WB: 14.5.04). Subsequently Quinn gave one of the pictures he bought, *Bonfire Night* to a friend, Tom Kelly (J–Q: 20.8.04). The other pictures he bought are nos. 24–31 and no. 14 below.

43. Exhibition of Irish Art, Guildhall, London, 1904.

44. Jack was not in Ireland at the time of Quinn's visit as the detailed diary of the trip kept by Quinn makes clear. The diary – 26 pages of typescript – is in the Foster-Murphy collection (NYPL). Quinn arrived in Ireland on 25 October 1904. Jack later wrote to Quinn, 'we have been home ever since we saw you in London' (J–Q: 13.12.04).

45. For Jack's entertainments, see Pyle 1970, pp. 61ff.;

46. The articles, which were published in June and July 1905, were suggested to Synge by Masefield who wrote for the *Manchester Guardian*; Synge asked Jack to accompany him. See Pyle 1970, pp.87–90.

47. These were published in the paper, March–May 1906.

48. At Quinn's suggestion, Douglas Hyde as President of the Gaelic League lectured throughout the States between mid-November 1905 and mid-June 1906. The tour, which Quinn organised in its entirety, was a triumphant success and raised £55,000 for the Gaelic League.

49. J H Reynolds, *The Fancy* (London, Elkin Mathews, 1905). See Pyle 1970, pp. 78ff.

50. The notes were published as 'A letter about J M Synge' in the *Evening Sun*, 20 July 1909 and 'Memories of Synge' in the *Irish Nation*, 14 August 1909.

51. *The Shewing up of Blanco Posnet* by George Bernard Shaw. The play had been banned in London by the Lord Chamberlain and only performed in Dublin after Lady Gregory had intervened with the Castle and the Viceroy. Quinn wrote to Jack (Q–J: 29.11.09): 'The play was a ghastly joke . . . Shaw had better stick to what he knows, or thinks he knows; or if he goes into a region unknown to him, let him stick to the Superman region where nobody can successfully contradict him'.

52. Lily, in her letters to Quinn, often attempted to interest him in particular paintings by Jack. 'My sister tells me you were asking about . . . *Memory Harbour* (J–Q: 6.7.16) – it belonged already to WB; and 'Lily said that you had a beautiful painting of Rosses Point . . .' (Q–J: 12.6.21). In response to this enquiry Jack sent off a photograph of *Approaching Rosses Early Morning* (J–Q: 15.7.21).

53. Society of Independent Artists, (New York, The Waldorf Astoria) 1923. *The Old Road to Cahirciveen* was no. 676 while *The Lift in the Long Car*, Jack's other picture in the Exhibition was no. 675. Jack sent pictures to the New York Independents every year between 1921 and 1926.

54. 'International Exhibition of Modern Art, Association of American Painters and Sculptors, Inc.' held at the 69th Regiment Armory, New York, 17 February – 15 March 1913. See M Brown, *The Story of the Armory Show* (New York, 1963).

55. He sent *A Stevedore* (no. 352), *The Barrel Man* (no. 353) *Strand Races* (no. 354), *The Last Corinthian* (no. 355), and *The Circus Dwarf* (no. 356).

56. See Zilczer, op. cit., p. 21; and Reid, pp. 72 ff, 104ff, and *passim*. Quinn was bowled over by John and paid him an annual stipend in

return for an unspecified number of paintings. In 1911 he went to Paris and the South of France with John, a trip that was to influence his collecting enormously. Quinn was also impressed by John's sister, Gwen: he corresponded with her and collected her work.

57. For a description of this house, see Pyle 1970, p. 110.

58. Jack's reference to Velàsquez was occasioned by the London National Gallery's public appeal to save *The Rokeby Venus* for the Nation. 'They are trying to raise £40,000 in London to buy a Velasquez – *Venus with Cupid and a Mirror* – so there is a lot about Velasquez in the papers.' (J–Q: 10.12.05).

59. The house, no. 61, was previously the home of the de Vere White family and is described by Pyle 1970, pp. 120–1.

60. For the dispersal of the Collection see Reid, pp. 637–62. The exhibition, "The Noble Buyer": John Quinn, *Patron of the Avant-Garde* (Hirshhorn Museum, 1978) re-assembled part of the Collection and the catalogue documented further, though not all, art works that had once belonged to Quinn.

61. Quoted by Reid, p. 640 from a document drawn up by Quinn in 1918.

62. The catalogue of the Memorial Exhibition listed eleven works by title (nos. 4, 7, 8, 9, 14, 30, 31, 34, 39, 41 and 43 below) as well as '33 watercolours of Irish subjects'. 'Memorial Exhibition of Representative Works Selected from the John Quinn Collection', Art Center, New York, 7–30 January 1926. The catalogue of the Exhibition is *John Quinn, 1870–1925* (sic). *Collection of Paintings, Watercolours, Drawings and Sculpture*. Foreword by Forbes Watson. (Huntington, New York, 1926).

63. *Paintings and Sculptures. The Renowned Collection of Modern and Ultra-Modern Art formed by John Quinn and including many examples purchased by him directly from the Artists.* American Art Association, Inc., New York, 9–12 February 1927.

---

## CHECKLIST OF PAINTINGS BY JACK B YEATS IN THE JOHN QUINN COLLECTION

Jack Yeats recorded selling 41 pictures to Quinn (information from Hilary Pyle). Thirty-five of these were in the Quinn Sale in 1927 and it is documented that Quinn gave one picture (no. 32 below) to his friend Tom Kelly. Eleven pictures are listed by title in the catalogue of the Quinn Memorial Exhibition in 1926 as well as 33 watercolours of Irish subjects. (*John Quinn, 1870–1925* (sic). *Collection of Paintings, Watercolors, Drawings and Sculpture*. Foreword by Forbes Watson. (Huntington, New York 1926)). This would imply that Quinn may have owned as many as 44 paintings by Jack except that the Memorial Catalogue cannot be regarded as reliable. Of the five pictures known to have been owned by Quinn that were *not* included in his Sale, three (Nos. 4, 26 & 28 below) were later owned by James A. Healy who presented them to Sligo Museum. Healy also owned a further two pictures (Nos. 9 & 34 below) which he also gave

to Sligo. In the data given below 'Purchased' refers to the date Quinn acquired a painting from Jack; 'Quinn Sale' refers to the auction of Quinn's collection of Paintings and Sculptures at the American Art Association Inc., New York, 9–11 February 1927; and the following abbreviations are used: Pyle 1992 W – *Jack B. Yeats: His Watercolours, Drawings and Pastels* (Irish Academic Press, Dublin 1992); Pyle 1992 O – Hilary Pyle, *Jack B. Yeats: A Catalogue Raisonné of the Oil Paintings*. 3 vols. (André Deutsch, London 1992).

(Measurements are given in inches).

1. *After the Harvest's Saved*
W/c. 16 x 11½; signed, l.l.
Prov: purchased August 1902 (7 gns); Quinn Sale lot 295(b), bt. William A. Brady, Jr. ($30, together with no. 3 below). Ref: Pyle 1992 W, no. 323.

2. *The Unicorn*
Crayon and w/c, 22 x 30; signed, l.l.
Prov: purchased August 1902; Quinn Sale lot 191, bt C J Liebman ($40).
Ref: Pyle 1992 W, no. 351.

3. *The Shadow on the Road*
W/c, 10 x 14; signed, l.r.
Prov: Quinn Sale lot 295(a), bt. William A Brady, Jr. ($30 together with no. 1 above).
Ref: Pyle 1992 W, no. 348.

4. *The Bay Pilot; The River Pilot; The Stevedore; The Ganger; The Gang.* (Five watercolours mounted together)
Each w/c, 4¼ x 3¼.
Prov (for the set): purchased August 1902 (7 gns): James A Healy, by whom presented to Sligo County Library & Museum, 1965. Ref: Pyle 1992 W, nos. 276–80.

5. *The Man of the West*
W/c, possibly 10 x 7.

# JACK B YEATS AND JOHN QUINN

Prov: purchased August 1902 (7 gns); possibly Quinn Sale lot 276 (b), – as 'Interior with figure' – bt. J M Kerrigan ($15 together with no 25 below).
Ref: Pyle 1992 W, no. 400.

6. *An Emigrant (The Emigrant Girl)*
W/c, 20 x 15; signed, l.l.
Prov: purchased August 1902 (7 gns.); Quinn Sale lot 313, bt. Marie Sterner ($20).
Ref: Pyle 1992 W, no. 399.

7. *Simon, The Cyrenian*
Oil on millboard, 18½ x 24½; signed, l.r.
Prov: purchased August 1902; Quinn Sale lot 91, bt. Mrs Ernest Boyd ($45).
Ref: Pyle 1992 O, no. 2.

8. *The Actor (Willie Reilly)*
Oil on millboard, 24 x 18½; signed, l.r.
Prov: purchased August 1902; Quinn Sale bt. Ernest Boyd ($30).
Ref: Pyle 1992 O, no. 3.

9. *Fortune and her Wheel*
W/c 10¾ x 17; signed, l.r.
Prov: purchased August 1902; Quinn Sale lot 40, bt. F J Deordan ($20); James A Healy, by whom presented to Sligo County Library & Museum, 1965.
Ref: Pyle 1992 W, no. 417.

10. *The Ballad Singer's Children*
W/c, 10 x 14; signed, l.r.
Prov: purchased August 1902; Quinn Sale lot 39(a), bt. Samuel Lustgarten ($40 together with no. 21 below).
Ref: Pyle 1992 W, no. 403.

11. *Dog watching a Seagull*
W/c, 19 x 14¼ signed, l.r.
Prov: purchased August 1902; Quinn Sale lot 53, bt. Samuel Lustgarten ($40).
Ref: Pyle 1992 W, no. 390.

12. *A Tale of Piracy*
W/c, 10 x 13¾; signed, l. r.
Prov: purchased August 1902; Quinn Sale lot 416(a), bt. Cornelius J Sullivan ($45 together with no. 18 above).
Ref: Pyle 1992 W, no. 425.

13. *Beside the Western Ocean*
W/c, 16½ x 20½; signed, l. l.
Prov: purchased August 1902; Quinn Sale lot 436, bt. Ernest Boyd ($35).
Ref: Pyle 1992 W, no. 404.

14. *At the Feis*
W/c 14½ x 10.
Prov: purchased October 1902 (7 gns.); Quinn Sale lot 430 (a) – as 'The Orator' ('The Politician' in the Memorial Catalogue) – bt. Ernest Boyd ($30 together with no. 19 below).
Ref: Pyle 1992 W, no. 491.

15. *The Big Peddler*
W/c 21½ x 15¼; signed, l. l.
Prov: purchased February 1903; Quinn Sale lot 444 (illus. in Catalogue), bt. Scott & Fowles, New York ($40).
Ref: Pyle 1992 W, no. 272.

16. *Dancing for a Cake*
W/c (measurements unknown).
Prov: purchased March 1903.
Ref: Pyle 1992 W, no. 477.

17. *The Squireen*
W/c, 12 x 15.
Prov: purchased March 1903; Quinn Sale lot

298 – as 'The Thruster' – bt. Ernest Boyd ($25).
Ref: Pyle 1992 W, no. 330.

18. *Catching the Donkey*
W/c, 10½ x 14½; signed, l. r.
Prov: purchased February 1903 (5 gns); Quinn Sale lot 416(b). bt. Cornelius J Sullivan ($45 together with no. 12 above).
Ref: Pyle 1992 W, no. 442.

19. *Telling the Cards*
W/c, 10½ x 14½; signed l. l.
Prov: purchased August 1903 (7 gns.); Quinn Sale lot 430 (b) – as *Two female figures seated by placid green water, conversing* – bt. Ernest Boyd ($30 together with no. 14 above).
Ref: Pyle 1992 W, no. 490.

20. *To Catch the Liverpool Boat*
W/c, 28½ x 21; signed, l. r.
Prov: purchased August 1903 (12 gns.); Quinn Sale lot 192, bt. Samuel Lustgarten ($55).
Ref: Pyle 1992 W, no. 480.

21. *A Boreen*
W/c, 10 x 14; signed, l. l.
Prov: purchased August 1903 (7 gns.); Quinn Sale lot 39(b), bt. Samuel Lustgarten ($40 together with no. 10 above).
Ref: Pyle 1992 W, no. 441.

22. *The Pirate*
W/c, 28½ x 21; signed, l. r.
Prov: purchased August 1903 (10 gns.); Quinn Sale lot 57, bt. Cornelius J Sullivan ($50).
Ref: Pyle 1992 W, no. 495.

23. *The Crucifixion*
W/c, 13¼ x 28¾; signed, l. r.
Prov: purchased August 1903 (10 gns.); Quinn Sale lot 46, bt. Max J Sulzberger ($15).
Ref: Pyle 1992 W, no. 327.

24. *A Young Man's Troubles*
Crayon, 5½ x 18½; signed, l. r.
Prov: purchased April 1904; Quinn Sale lot 268, bt. W C Murphy ($25).
Ref: Pyle 1992 W, no. 267.

25. *It Must Have Been an Allegory*
Tinted drawing 3½ x 6; signed, l. r.
Prov: purchased April 1904; Quinn Sale lot 276(a), bt. J M Kerrigan ($15 together with no. 5 above).
Ref: Pyle 1992 W, no. 180.

26. *The Crest of the Hill*
W/c, 28½ x 21; signed, l. l.
Prov: purchased April 1904; James A. Healy by whom presented to Sligo County Library & Museum, 1965.
Ref: Pyle 1992 W, no. 503.

27. *The American Tablecloth*
W/c, 11½ x 17; signed, l. r.
Prov: purchased April 1904; Quinn Sale lot 43, bt. Samuel Lustgarten ($15).
Ref: Pyle 1992 W, no. 186.

28. *The Car is at the Door*
W/c, 21 x 15; signed, l. r.
Prov: purchased April 1904; James A. Healy by whom presented to Sligo County Library & Museum, 1965.
Ref: Pyle 1992 W, no. 504.

29. *The Day of the Sports*
Crayon and w/c, 13 x 18½; signed, l. r.
Prov: purchased April 1904; Quinn Sale lot 303, bt. J.M. Kerrigan ($15).
Ref: Pyle 1992 W, no. 321.

30. *The Melodeon Player*
W/c, 12½ x 19½; signed, l. l.
Prov: purchased April 1904; Quinn Sale lot 301 – as 'The Race-Course Town, Galway' – bt. Edward W. McMahon ($30).
Ref: Pyle 1992 W, no. 373.

31. *Donkey Races*
W/c, 11 x 17; signed, l. r.
Prov: purchased April 1904; Quinn Sale lot 421, bt. F. J. Deordan ($15).
Ref: Pyle 1992 W, no. 105.

32. *Bonfire Night (Midsummer Eve)*
W/c, size unknown.
Prov: purchased April 1904; given by Quinn to his friend, Tom Kelly (see note 42), although also listed in 1924 inventory. (Information from Hilary Pyle).
Ref: Pyle 1992 W, no. 168.

33. *The Man who Told the Tales*
W/c, size unknown
Prov: purchased April 1904.
Ref: Pyle 1992 W, no. 282.

34. *The Political Meeting*
Crayon and w/c on card, 21 x 28½; signed, l. r.
Prov: purchased September 1905 (12 gns.); Quinn Sale lot 415 (illus. in Catalogue), bt. Cornelius J. Sullivan ($90); his widow's sale (Parke Bernet, New York), 6–7 December 1939, lot 150, bt. James A. Healy by whom presented to Sligo County Library & Museum, 1965.
Ref: Pyle 1992 W, no. 517.

35. *There was an Old Prophecy Found in a Bog*
W/c on card, 14¼ x 10½; signed, l. l.
Prov: purchased September 1905 (7 gns.); Quinn Sale lot 54, bt. J. M. Tobin ($65).
Ref: Pyle 1992 W, no. 550.

36. *A Warning Against Book-Borrowers*
W/c, 10¼ x 7; signed, l. r.
Prov: commissioned by John Quinn, March 1907 (5 gns.); Quinn Sale lot 417, bt. F J Deordan ($80).
Ref: Pyle 1992 W, no. 624.

37. *Washing the Circus Horses*
Crayon and w/c, 10 x 14; signed, l. r.
Prov: purchased August 1909 (7 gns.); Quinn Sale lot 170, bt. Mrs D.J. O'Brian ($40).
Ref: Pyle 1992 W, no. 679.

38. *The Sea Fog*
W/c, 14 x 10½; signed, l. r.
Prov: purchased August 1909 (7 gns.); Quinn Sale lot 305, bt. J. Toner ($50).
Ref: Pyle 1992 W, no. 666.

39. *The Old Road to Cahirciveen*
Oil on panel, 9 x 14; signed, l. l.
Prov: purchased 1923; Quinn Sale lot 445, bt. Cornelius J. Sullivan ($55).
Ref: Pyle 1992 O, no. 163.

40. *The Concert*
Crayon, 12 x 18¼; signed, l. r.
Prov: Quinn Sale lot 397, bt. Ernest Boyd ($15).
Ref: Pyle 1992 W, no. 298.

41. *The Rain! The Rain! (Return from Galway Races)*
Pencil and w/c, 11¼ x 14¼; signed, l. r.
Prov: Quinn Sale lot 422, bt. J.M. Kerrigan ($12.50).
Ref: Pyle 1992 W, no. 378.

# THE OIL PAINTING TECHNIQUE OF JACK B YEATS

In the already extensive and ever growing literature about the art of Jack Butler Yeats (1871–1957), there is nothing specifically about his highly personal oil painting technique. The National Gallery of Ireland has initiated a programme of conservation to address problems which have arisen in some of its Yeats collection, and the preliminary results of this investigation are presented here.[1]

In recent years, the National Gallery of Ireland has done much to enhance the reputation of Yeats as arguably the premier Irish painter of the twentieth century. The publication of a fine catalogue of the Gallery's extensive collection of his works[2], and the establishment of a Yeats Room at the Gallery following refurbishment in March 1990 have helped to stimulate interest in his art. In June 1990, an exhibition titled *Images in Yeats*[3] was shown at the Centre de Congrès in Monte Carlo and, the following month, it received critical acclaim when exhibited at the National Gallery of Ireland. The Gallery did not permit any late oil paintings to travel to Monte Carlo, and in 1991, the Gallery maintained this policy by refusing to lend to an exhibition, *Jack B Yeats: the Late Paintings*[4] which opened at the Arnolfini Gallery, Bristol, and travelled to the Whitechapel Gallery, London, and on to the Municipal Museum (Gemeentemuseum) in The Hague. The decision not to lend to this exhibition sparked off some adverse criticism, but the Gallery view is that the late paintings are, in most instances, too fragile to endure the movement involved in international touring exhibitions. This may be borne out by the fact that some of the paintings shown in the exhibition had flakes of paint gathered inside the glass at the bottom of the pictures. This is not to suggest that the works were carelessly handled but that they were perhaps not in fit condition to travel. One large, important late painting had bits of paint stuck to the glass where the canvas at some stage had come in contact with it, irretrievably damaging some areas of *impasto*.

Close examination of the National Gallery of Ireland's Yeats paintings revealed that some of the late works required urgent attention. There was considerable flaking and cracking of the paint surface. In a dramatic and considered published statement designed to jolt owners of Yeats paintings into paying attention to the condition of their pictures, it was suggest-

The unique methods used by Jack B Yeats in his late oil paintings, recently conserved in the National Gallery of Ireland, are described, for the first time, by **Brian P Kennedy**.

*Jack Butler Yeats RHA. Photograph by Adolf Morath, (1948).*

ed that some of the late works were 'falling apart'.[5] This description worried one prominent art dealer, who perhaps feared that prospective buyers would be dissuaded from investing in Yeats. These fears are groundless because careful attention by trained restorers can arrest the deterioration of Yeats's paintings.

Yeats came to oil painting when he was about thirty years of age (his earliest known oil painting dates from 1902). The condition problems common in his late oil paintings have much to do with his limited academic training in the studio principles of the oil technique. While he was painting slowly and methodically, this deficiency did not manifest itself. His early oils in the National Gallery of Ireland like *Before the Start* (1915) and the middle period oils like *The Liffey Swim* (1923) are in excellent condition; it is the later oils which are problematical. Yeats realised that he could best express himself in paint by using his brushes sparingly, employing a palette knife instead, and by squeezing his oils directly on to the canvas from the tubes. On occasion it would appear that he used the pointed, wooden end of his brush to incise the canvas,

especially when adding his signature. In his late works, form becomes subservient to the tremendous power of pure colour. He delighted in the plasticity of oil paints and their capacity for surface variation. Yeats was proud of the startling colours and the tactile quality of his painting, so much so that he would not permit colour reproductions of his works in his dealer's exhibition catalogues. The passion with which Yeats employed his oil paints was quite at odds with his sober and reserved public image. But one feels instinctively that Yeats loved his paints, the smell of them, the consistency of the thick liquid and its capacity for varied means of application.

If Yeats used his paints passionately, it should be stated that there is nothing passionate about his subject matter. He idealised female beauty and loved romance but the theme of sensuality never features in his work. In this respect at least, Yeats was in sympathy with the atmosphere of the Irish Free State (1922–48) which cast a repressive legal blanket over the whole area of human sexuality. It is odd that Yeats made very few references in his pictures to religious practice, a dominant part of Irish cultural life. Perhaps it was because he lived in a self-consciously Catholic country, or because of his Protestant background, or his free-thinking father, but Yeats in both his writings and his paintings is a convinced humanist who never preaches. He is always on the side of the underprivileged, the marginalised, the outsider, those who lead an unsettled lifestyle: gypsies, circus artists, actors, sailors, tramps, jockeys, travellers.

By squeezing oils directly on to the canvas, Yeats abandoned the use of linseed oil and turpentine. His oils, therefore, may at times have had no binding medium to help them to adhere to the canvas and this has caused shrinkage. Yeats tended to use glazing pigments as body colours and this is another reason why his paint layer is often weak. (Glazing means the application of thin, transparent layers of paint over already laid colours. For example, to make a red more translucent, a glaze of alizarin crimson could be applied; similarly, aureolin on yellow.) Yeats disliked varnishing his pictures and relied on glass for protection. He insisted that purchasers of his pictures should retain the glass because it was better to have dirt attach itself to glass (which can be cleaned)

*Jack B Yeats, The Scene Painter's Rose, 1927. Oil on canvas, 46 x 61 cm. Private collection.*

# THE OIL PAINTING TECHNIQUE OF JACK B YEATS

than that it should stick to the paint layer itself.[6] The fact that Yeats glazed his paintings has been of value in a way he never imagined. Any paint which falls off his canvases is evident to the careful viewer who can then seek to prevent further losses. It is curious how few owners of Yeats paintings bother to clean the glass regularly. It is little wonder that some pictures look like new when a mere cleaning of the glass removes decades of dirt. It is also worth mentioning that Yeats specified grand swept-and-carved frames for his pictures. He felt them to be appropriate to his dramatic images and it is sad that some Yeats paintings now carry ugly frames which are wholly inconsistent with the artist's wishes.

Yeats said that he would have preferred to paint on wood instead of canvas but for the problem of warping[7]. He purchased pre-primed off-the-shelf shop canvases and was not rigorous in his use of further coats of primer. However, he regularly allowed the luminosity of the white priming coat to enhance effects of light and shade in his pictures. He also left areas of the priming coat untouched by oil colours to help to create a sense of depth and resonance. Some time in the 1940s he stopped adding further protective layers to his pre-primed canvases, a problem which was exaggerated by his use of pure oil paint. The reason for this casual approach to technique was due to Yeats's desire to proceed directly to the creative act of picture making. In one way, it was this very disregard for academic rules which enabled Yeats to develop such dexterity in his use of oil paints. In his anarchic technique lies his greatness as an artist. In 1947 Yeats explained in an interview with Eamonn Andrews:

> I would say you could not possibly understand all of any painting of mine anymore than you could understand all of the feelings of any living being. There's no book of words, no direction by which you or anyone else can understand all about painting. If there were such a book it would ring the knell of painting. I dislike the word art as painting. There is only one art and that is the art of living. Painting is an occupation within that art and that occupation is the freest of all the occupations of living. There is no alphabet, no grammar, no rules whatever. Many hopeful sportsmen have tried to invent rules and have always failed. Any person or group of persons who try to legalise such rules do a disservice to this occupation of

living. They forget that painting is tactics and not strategy. It is carried out in the face of the enemy.[8]

There is little evidence of under-drawing in Yeats's late pictures. His father, the distinguished portrait painter, John Butler Yeats, lamented that his son did not take more time to study the human figure and to practise the art of drawing as the basis for oil painting. Women, for example, are depicted frequently in the late paintings but Yeats's niece, the painter Anne Yeats, has remarked: 'I personally do not find his women very convincing: I feel there was a moment in his painting career when he stopped looking at women and that from then on they become formalised or idealised'.[9] But while Yeats's understanding of human anatomy may have been limited, his father's criticism should not be read as implying that Jack did not take time to draw, although it is true that he did not use drawing as underpinning for his oil painting and instead came to abandon it in favour of a form of free oil painting. Yeats's use of drawing had a different purpose, as his sketchbooks and notebooks prove beyond question. There are about two hundred of them (each measuring 9 x 13 cms.), begun in 1894, and continuing up to the 1950s. At first they were records of things he had seen, but later they became semi-abstract compositions of lines and squiggles, distilled memories. In 1943, Rupert Strong wrote perceptively: 'Mr Yeats has a Wordsworthian conception of art as emotion recollected in tranquillity. He paints all his pictures from memory, never using a model or working out of doors from life. He does not paint what he sees, but what his imagination does to what he sees'.[10] Yeats did not keep conventional diaries because he believed that a man's private life was his own business. His sketchbooks and notebooks are, in a real sense, his personal diaries. He told Sir John Rothenstein: 'I believe that the painter always begins by expressing himself with line — that is, by the most obvious means; then he becomes aware that line, once so necessary, is in fact hemming him in, and as soon as he feels strong enough, he breaks out of its confines'.[11]

Anne Yeats has provided us with a delightful description of her uncle's working method:

> For the whole of his career he succeeded — whatever his reason may have been in doing

so — in keeping his whole method of work secret. It was always a great mystery to people where and how he painted his pictures. There were never any visible traces of work in hand in his studio; there were no palettes or brushes lying around, no paint tubes, no paint rags or overalls, no smell of turpentine, no half-finished sketches or paintings. There was indeed an easel to be seen, but nothing else, and his hands were always clean and well-kept. He had a kind of painting cupboard with drawers at the top that opened out like an old-fashioned washstand with places for materials. Also in his studio was a large turf basket for the waste paper he used to clean his palette, which was cleared out each day, leaving no trace.[12]

Yeats required total peace and quiet in which to work and if he was interrupted, his work would be finished for the day. His wife, 'Cottie', would sometimes forget this, but he solved the problem of interruptions by tying a pipe cleaner around the door handle as a warning. James White has written about a visit to the painter's studio: 'He received me with his usual old-world courtesy and took me in to the private place where the painting was done — always in electrical light as I had heard previously and never in the presence of anyone else'.[13] He had a pink paper rose tied to the top of his easel and said that he painted sub rosa, that is he did not offer explanations about the meaning of his pictures. They were conversations 'under the rose' and it was for each viewer to decide on an interpretation. As Yeats put it: 'If ten people look at my painting and it works for them all in different ways, then it's a good painting'.[14]

The ritualistic aspect of Yeats's creative method is evident in Anne Yeats's comment that: 'He used to keep his paintings for six months in racks in his studio before letting them out or allowing anyone at all to see them. He kept meticulous work-books and opposite [the note regarding] each painting, when it was ready to leave his studio, he drew a picture of a seagull — his signal that it was ready to fly away'.[15]

When Hilary Pyle had Yeats's paints analysed, she found that he had used the relatively confined colour range of yellow, red, blue and green, in addition to black and white.[16] He used different shades of each colour and mixed them to create variations of hue and tone. Yeats allowed his paints to exert their power over him. He described the effect to his dealer, Victor Waddington: 'When I begin a paint-

# THE OIL PAINTING TECHNIQUE OF JACK B YEATS

*Jack B Yeats*, Men of Destiny, *1946. Oil on canvas, 51 x 69 cm. (NGI 1134).*

ing I think I'm in control, but after a while the paint controls me, and as I go on, we work together . . . the title comes later'.[17] This comment should not be read as implying that Yeats began a picture without a subject in mind but rather as his way of explaining the impulse which compelled him to paint. Yeats told the critic, John Berger: 'You can plan events, but if they go according to your plan they are not events'.[18] By the time he ceased painting in 1955, Yeats had completed 1,200 oil paintings and 700 drawings.[19]

Yeats refused to admit to admiration of any great painters of the past except Goya. He told Terence de Vere White that Velasquez was 'a good painter but a journalist', Rembrandt was 'a journalist, painting the same thing over and over again', and Tintoretto produced 'The best journalism, but journalism just the same'.[20] This may

have been bravado but Yeats shows little direct influence from other painters. He is a classic individualist. His late style recalls the work of Rouault, Ensor, Munch, Kokoschka, even Jackson Pollock, but such relationships are most likely coincidental. Yeats was never an abstract artist. His work always remained figurative in intent, even though, as in *Grief* (1951, National Gallery of Ireland), his lines blur, his forms become indistinct and his colours explode. He told Serge Philipson that *On the Hazard* (1911, Private Collection) owed some debt to Daumier.[21] Yeats was clearly influenced by his father but Hilary Pyle agrees with Terence de Vere White that he was most deeply influenced by Walter Sickert.[22] She points out that Yeats, in his early works, adopted Sickert's use of short, thick strokes of paint and his manner of

correlating colour. It was through Sickert, she argues, that Yeats received the impact of Degas. Yeats had a very good sense of how to organise a picture and this was probably due to his study of the works of the French master.

The first picture in the National Gallery of Ireland's collection to receive treatment in the restoration studio was *Men of Destiny* (1946) which was lined successfully by Sergio Benedetti in 1986. Lining is seen as a major intervention on any Yeats painting, because of the risk of flattening the heavy *impasto* during the lining process. In the case of *Men of Destiny*, lining was necessary because the canvas was bulging in two places and there was also a hole in it. The more recent conservation work on Yeats's paintings, begun in 1991 by Andrew O'Connor is primarily corrective rather than preventive in

*Jack B Yeats, A Morning in a City, (prior to conservation), 1937. Oil on canvas, 61 x 91 cm. (NGI 1050)*

*Jack B Yeats, A Morning in a City, (detail, centre top left, under raking light)*

*Jack B Yeats,* About to Write a Letter, *(prior to conservation), 1935. Oil on canvas, 91 x 61 cm. (NGI 1766).*

*Jack B Yeats,* About to Write a Letter,
*(centre detail revealing the dense application of paint strokes which Yeats employed to build up his picture surface).*

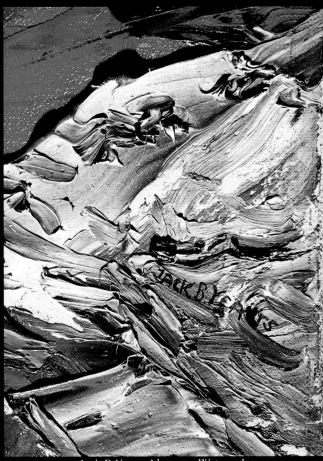

*Jack B Yeats,* About to Write a Letter,
*(detail, lower right corner).*

# THE OIL PAINTING TECHNIQUE OF JACK B YEATS

*Jack B Yeats*, The Cavalier's Farewell to his Steed, *(prior to conservation), 1949. Oil on board, 36 x 46 cm. (NGI 1374)*

nature.[23] The main feature of this work has been the injection of adhesives in localised areas to consolidate the paint layer. This is a safe, conservative solution to the problem of flaking paint and *craquelure*. All the conservation work has been documented by Michael Olohan, the Gallery's photographer, and the resulting pictures dramatically reveal Yeats's rapid, vigorous and exciting procedure.

When *About to Write a Letter (1935)*[24] was taken to the restoration studio, its surface was found to be very dry and dusty. It appeared that the picture had never been varnished. The strong, rich colours reinforce the drama of the scene in which a tall, gaunt figure hovers beside a table. There was some cracking of the paint sur-

face particularly in the red of the curtains to the top right of the picture. The paint surface was cleaned using slightly dampened cotton swabs. The canvas is of the commercially prepared pre-primed type typical of Yeats. It was in relatively stable condition although the stretcher wedges required tightening and three had to be replaced. Apart from two areas of lifting *impasto*, there was little sign of flaking. These areas were treated by injecting PolyVinyl Acetate (PVA) resin followed by gentle manual pressure and removal of excess adhesive. The picture was then varnished using ketone resin brushed on in two coats. Finally, the glass, which was very dirty, was cleaned. The effect of this treatment was to transform the appearance of the picture. The photo-

graphic details of the standing figure and of the area around the signature in the bottom right corner reveal the dense application of paint strokes which Yeats employed to build up his picture surface. The paint is applied like icing on a cake, whipped up, dabbed on and dragged along the canvas. In the area of the signature, the paint is applied in a highly articulated way. In contrast, in the area to the left of the man's head, the primed surface has only been casually brushed with green paint. The picture is a masterpiece of painterly expression.

The next painting to be treated was *A Morning in a City (1937)*.[25] It appeared to be in poor condition with extensive *craquelure* visible in most areas of the picture. Only the lower right hand corner of the

# THE OIL PAINTING TECHNIQUE OF JACK B YEATS

painting required treatment for flaking. Dilute PVA adhesive was injected under the affected area followed by gentle pressure. The painting was surface cleaned and it was decided to fill in the network of hairline cracks using a reversible water-based paint. This retouching was especially necessary in the red areas where the colour was separating. Finally the glass was cleaned. Photographic documentation included the use of raking light to focus in on the retouched areas. Detailed photographs of the paint surface reveal, once again, Yeats's extraordinary mastery of colour. The area at the centre, top left of the picture, which includes the sky and the tops of some Georgian buildings, is magnificent in photographic detail. The windows of the buildings are defined loosely with thick lines of paint like congealed blood. The morning sky is stained with yellow, white, red and blue. In the centre of the picture, the artist stands erect, staring intently at the viewer. He is surrounded by, yet aloof from, the flurry of activity, the people going to work, the newspaper boy, the postman, the man with the wheelbarrow. Yeats is stating that he is a man of the city but he is also the detached artistic observer.

The final painting to be treated was *The Cavalier's Farewell to his Steed* (1949).[26]

*Jack B Yeats*, The Cavalier's Farewell to his Steed, *(detail, to right corner, flaking paint).*

This small picture was painted on board and, as can be seen clearly in the photographic detail, there was a large piece of flaking paint in the top right-hand corner which required attention. It would appear that other areas of the painting had suffered paint loss over the years. This picture is an excellent example of Yeats's practice of leaving large areas of the barely primed board unpainted so that

it creates a resonating background. In an image which is fleeting and transitory, the cavalier doffs his hat to the spotted horse on the merry-go-round. The paint was applied in a hurried, almost slapdash manner. The effect is one of pure theatre, the cavalier's dramatic gesture as he heads off into the sunset. The flaking paint was affixed with PVA resin, the picture was cleaned using a moist cotton swab and then it was varnished with ketone resin. The glass was cleaned and the painting was replaced on exhibition.

The conservation programme will continue on other paintings by Yeats which require attention. It is already clear that Yeats's paintings respond well to treatment. There are inherent problems associated with his painting technique but his mastery is such that private owners should be prepared to invest in the future of their works by having them examined by experts and any necessary remedial work carried out by a qualified restorer. If nothing else, at least the glass can be kept clean.

*Brian P Kennedy*

*Dr Brian P Kennedy is Assistant Director of the National Gallery of Ireland. His monograph* Jack B Yeats, *was published in 1991 in the National Gallery of Ireland/Townhouse* Lives of Irish Artists *series of which he is the editor.*

---

## NOTES

1. The author wishes to acknowledge the kind assistance of the following people in the preparation of this article: Andrew O'Connor, Michael Olohan, Sergio Benedetti, Raymond Keaveney, Dr Michael Wynne, Ciaran Mac Gonigal and Dr Hilary Pyle.
2. Hilary Pyle, *Jack B Yeats in the National Gallery of Ireland*, Dublin, 1986.
3. Hilary Pyle, *Images in Yeats*, Dublin 1990. This splendid catalogue was printed by the exhibition sponsor, the Jefferson Smurfit Foundation.
4. Rudi Fuchs, Stephen Snoddy and Mark Haworth Booth, *Jack B Yeats: The Late Paintings*, Bristol, London and The Hague, 1991.
5. Brian P Kennedy, 'Jack B Yeats: An Irish Romantic Expressionist', *Apollo*, March 1991, pp. 193–5.
6. Anne Yeats, 'Jack Yeats', in Robert O'Driscoll and Lorna Reynolds (eds.), *Yeats Studies*, No. 2, 1972, p.3.
7. Hilary Pyle, *Jack B Yeats: A Biography*, revised ed., London, 1989, p.135. (Hereafter noted as Pyle, *Biog.*).
8. Radio Eireann interview with Jack Yeats by

Eamonn Andrews, 1947.
9. Anne Yeats, *op. cit.*, p.1.
10. Rupert Strong, *Irish Art Handbook*, Dublin, 1943, p.33.
11. Pyle, *Biog.*, p.127
12. Anne Yeats, *op. cit.*, p.2
13. James White, 'Memory Harbour: Jack Yeats's Painting Process', in Robert O'Driscoll and Lorna Reynolds (Eds.), *Yeats Studies*, No. 2, 1972, p. 16.
14. Jack Yeats in conversation with Victor Waddington, quoted in M G Rose, *Jack B Yeats: Painter and Poet*, European University Papers series XVIII, Vol. 3, Berne and Frankfurt, 1972, p.11.
15. Anne Yeats, *op. cit.*, p.2.
16. Pyle, *Biog.*, p. 135. Jack Yeats used the following paints, all manufactured by Winsor and Newton: white — Flake White but mainly Titanium (which has advantages over Flake White in that it is not poisonous, is less susceptible to discolouration, is opaque and mixes well with other pigments); black — Ivory Black; Green — Winsor and Cobalt Greens; yellow — Winsor Yellow, Cadmium and Aureolin; red — Scarlet Lake, Alizarin Crimson, Scarlet Vermilion and Rose Doré;

Blue — Chinese Blue, Cerulean Blue, New Blue and Winsor Blue, Manganese and Prussian Blue.
17. M G Rose, *op. cit.*, p.12.
18. John Berger, 'Jack Yeats', *New Statesman and Nation*, 8 December 1956.
19. Yeats returned to his studio in 1956 to have a look at his paintings. In his record book, he marked up the final paintings which were ready for release.
20. Terence de Vere White, *A Fretful Midge*, London, 1957, p.119.
21. *Jack B Yeats 1871–1957: A Centenary Exhibition*, London, 1971, No. 28, p.147.
22. De Vere White, *op. cit.*, p.120, and Pyle, *Biog.*, p.108.
23. The descriptions of conservation treatment which follow rely heavily on Andrew O'Connor's excellent notes.
24. See Hilary Pyle, 'About to Write a Letter", *Irish Arts Review*, Vol. 2, No. 1, Spring 1985, pp.43–7.
25. See Hilary Pyle, *Jack B Yeats in the National Gallery of Ireland*, Dublin, 1986, pp. 66–7.
26. *Ibid.*, pp. 80–1.

# 'SAGE' – EVELYN MONTAGUE'S FABRIC ART

The traditional art of patchwork has been revived in Ireland recently with astonishing and rapid success. Guilds have been formed in the North and South drawing in new members to be trained by existing practitioners, and through sewing bees achieving a continuous output of individual or group-made quilts. These may be seen regularly at exhibitions of the Irish Patchwork Society or at shows abroad. Quilt making is now regarded as an important element of the current art crafts movement. Not only does the modern quilt perpetuate itself in the traditional way as a vehicle for feminist self expression[1], but it has been prominent in this country in facing public issues, increasing public awareness of the Aids venom, for example, or approaching with suitable ambiguity the question of celebrating the French Revolution on its bicentenary.

For Evelyn Montague, whose recent exhibitions have marked a breakthrough from traditional quiltmaking to a more personal form of expression, the essence of quiltmaking as a form of statement or diary of experience from women who were otherwise inarticulate is still recognisable in her work, particularly in her theme *Reliquaries*. Speaking of the nineteenth century pioneer women who left the East Coast of America to go to the West, bringing quilts made for them by their friends, she comments, 'If they made it on such a tough trek, they taught communities out there to make quilts. It assuages the pain of exile.' Being an exile is an integral part of her work. 'It's very likely that none of this would have happened if I had stayed in Paris. And I find among colleagues that exile is a muse, it's a very important part of quiltmaking.'[2]

Patchwork for her in the early 1970s represented a means of finding a sense of identity in a new land. She came to quilting without any particular interest in sewing, and with no training other than a demonstration from a friend in the elementary techniques. Born in Paris in 1946, she had taken a degree in American Studies at the Sorbonne intending to continue with her research, and instead came to Cork in 1972 with her husband, the poet John Montague. 'I found myself out on a limb. Touching fabric prevented me from going crazy'.

For ten years she made templates, quilting traditional designs in hexagons and mosaic. She immediately related to the

Patchwork has become for the French artist Evelyn Montague, now living in Cork, a fluent medium in which she expresses the feminine psyche. **Hilary Pyle** outlines the development of her colourful and authentic art form.

*Evelyn Montague,* Homage to Bill Hayter, *1986, cottons, 84 x 133 cm. Private collection.*

*Evelyn Montague,* Third Eye, *1985, cottons, 169 x 169 cm. Private collection.*

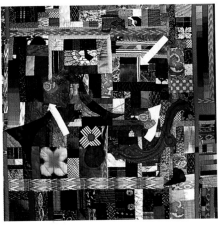

*Evelyn Montague,* Ikat 'n' Blues, *1991, mixed fabrics, including 18th century ikats from Japanese peasant kimonos, 122 x 122 cm. Private collection.*

technique, perfecting it until it became second nature to her. The necessity of spending so long at single pieces gave her the opportunity to reflect on how closely the medium related to the feminine psyche. The craft thus, as an act, became real and tangible, a flexible channel through which personal attitudes and philosophies had room to expand themselves.

Her first one person exhibition, at the Triskel Arts Centre in Cork in May 1983, was remarkable for the explorative way in which each quilt was approached. Evelyn Montague has always maintained that she does not spend time thinking about the image, but rather sees the image merging gradually as the idea on which she meditates comes to completion. Themes tend to come from her own life – as in the imaginative *To Rochestown and Back* – or they are excited by situations of topical and usually Irish interest. But her investigation of the origins of quiltmaking has affected the nature of her work strongly. *Hospitality Sign*, using the motif hung by native Indians over the lintel of the door, was deliberately fashioned by her from rustic materials in order to capture the palpable nature of the idea.

The exhibition was traditional but it was also experimental, respecting different kinds of fabric for their individual associations. At this stage, concern for the human implications inherent in such a medium sometimes warred with the quality of craftsmanship. But it was obvious that Evelyn Montague had reached a point of crisis where her understanding of the objectives of the traditional craft, with its possibilities for personal statement, were at odds with a deeper urge towards creative self-expression. Her titles, and her preoccupation with metaphor of some kind or other, were indicative of a wish to regard the medium more seriously, not merely as a craft. Tapestries created in recent decades by le Brocquy and Scott could possibly offer patterns for a new approach, but these were by artists who normally worked in paint, and Evelyn Montague wanted to use patchwork not as an alternative, but as her main and fluent art medium.

The breakthrough came with *Third Eye*, first exhibited at the annual exhibition of the Patchwork Society at the Crawford Gallery in Cork, in 1985. Initially an excitement of melting colours and shapes, it also conjures up a moment of deep revela-

*Evelyn Montague, Reliquaries II, 1991, mixed fabrics, 154 x 150 cm. Private collection.*

# 'SAGE' – EVELYN MONTAGUE'S FABRIC ART

tion. Regarded more closely, the square in circle motif emanates from a yellow cross form in the centre (for the artist implying the human figure with limbs outstretched rather than the traditional sacred symbol), outwards through red and orange, and thence to blue on the circumference, interchanged with purple, the movement revolving eventually back to the central core.

Evelyn Montague regards the sudden emergence of this first *mandala* (deriving much from the painted *mandalas* of Jung) as her 'Damascus'. Not unlike a St Brigid's Cross in its visual impact, it opened the way to a series of different *mandalas*, which as a group relate to the seven energy centres of the body, and were consciously worked by the artist as a form of spiritual exercise. None of the subsequent *mandalas* is as potent as the original *Third Eye* (which was later shown at a conference on spirituality in India); but they are an important theme and they mark a decisive point in the artist's development.

Evelyn Montague looks on the *mandala* objectively as a geometric formation, where the circumference has to relate to the centre, take the centre towards the edge and bring it back in again; but she is also aware of it as a mental game common to all cultures, from the time of the neolithic circle up to the medieval labyrinth or ecclesiastical rose window, and still preoccupying modern artists. The fact that the *mandala* is worked in stone or glass as well as paint has perhaps given her more confidence when interpreting it in fabric.

*It relates to the eternal riddle of the place of man inside the cosmos. I was interested in Jung's work in this area. It's because I made those mandalas that I was able to go into self-expression – I have no doubt that the other quilts could not have come otherwise. I needed to find myself in the cosmos – though I'm not saying I found it!*

Very critical of her own work, Evelyn Montague felt that the theme failed to sustain itself visually throughout the series. However, she had left traditional patchwork behind, and now launched into a series of exciting compositions, each, through some pressing theme, attempting to resolve a problem of technique, so that gradually her style became more fluid, and suited to self-expression. Already a moving force in the Irish Patchwork Artists Guild of Ireland, she now

exhibited abroad, with the French Association of Patchworkers and in the United States, Japan, Austria, Germany, Belgium and Scandinavia. While serving on the board of the American Irish Quilt Association as the first European member, some Japanese women presented her with scraps taken from the kimonos of eighteenth century workers. These were to form the basis of her *Ikat 'n' Blues*, and find their way into *Reliquaries II*, which she regards as her most important work.

*Ikat* came about partly through an effort to come to terms with the colour blue. The artist has seen a relationship between her medium and music when it comes to colour:

*Particularly when a quilt is over, I may hit a dry patch and not know what to do next. I make a colour scale, just as a composer may do scales – to limber up. It starts the body, it starts the blood. The colours are states of mind. Of course blue is calm: contemplation. It was a colour I had trouble with. I was more at ease with red and yellow in the three primaries, but I forced myself to use blues, because how can you not use blues? It's one third of the creation. My first attempt was the Mandala . . . My second attempt was the first Ikat. I had to use those blues because those Japanese women had given me those presents of pieces of kimonos, and I had to honour them. Then I did the first Ikat 'n' Blues. The solution to the boredom that comes out of blue – (because blue is so sedate!) – was to use the contrary on the colour scale, which is orange. Having done one, and knowing that you could make blue very lively so long as you used orange, I began using red and green, and a bit of orange because it's wilder. So I'm happy with blue now. You can make yourself be friendly with colours.*

So far has her appreciation of the expressive powers of colour developed that she realises that the way colours are assembled can be explosive, or subversive. Her own work, however, rather than being political, tends to grow increasingly introspective. *Homage to Bill Hayter* of 1986, which demonstrates how she can now use shape and colour in visual counterpoint so as to recreate the dynamism of a jazz melody with all its colour and rhythm, has an excitable revelatory mood amidst the lament. This was followed by *Décembre en Dordogne*, a more muted but equally rhythmical collage, composed of verticals and curves, with elusive autumnal references. Later still *Citizen* was a metaphor of the birth of her first child, with reference to the French

bicentenary celebrations of 1789; and the *Puer in Tenebris* series contemplated more personally the effects of childhood trauma.

Her second one person exhibition, held at the Riverrun Gallery in Limerick in 1989, showed how she has transformed patchwork into an authentic fine art form as expressive as oil painting. Her theme, '*Mandalas* and other Expressions', underlined her preoccupation with metaphysical concerns; yet she remained true to the essential purpose of patchwork as a means of working the scraps of material remaining from life's experiences into memorable patterns. While emphasising her break with tradition, she has never ceased to be aware that the quilt is first and foremost a body cover, and to be sensitive to this concept in her work. Her quilts are for hanging on the wall, their use symbolic rather than functional, but their content continues to examine the human inheritance of customs, emotions and beliefs at the same time as having broken down the divide between craft and contemporary art.

*Her cloths can be innocent of purpose,* writes Kathleen Raine[3] '*when, new off the bolt, they look fresh as gouache pressed out of its tube. Cut out from gowns of women of her family, they can appear knowing and familiar, yet manipulated with such intimacy, they suggest mystery, all the secrets taken to the grave. The mystery becomes total when she uses old ikat from kimonos worn by eighteenth century Japanese peasants. By juxtaposing them with contemporary blue fabrics she seeks to give them a new definition and future.*

Evelyn Montague's skill lies partly in her choice of materials – laid out according to individual colour tone in a glass fronted cupboard in her studio, like oils arranged on an artist's palette. She looks carefully for what she needs. In America the market is prepared for art quilters as well as traditional quilters. But in France she goes to interior designers' shops, to buy the best of fashion design in small quantities.

*You don't agonise. You know immediately the fabric is the portrait of an emotion or a situation or a thing that exists. You get a bit of snakeskin because you never know when you will want – not to do a snake – but to have the spirit of a snake enter into a quilt. Brick red is a state of mind for me, and I know every now and then that I have to have it, that state of mind.*

Otherwise she dyes cloth, adapting the

# 'SAGE' – EVELYN MONTAGUE'S FABRIC ART

technique of batik in her own way in order to achieve full expression. Her random manner, now developed in a totally different direction from her original orthodox use of templates, derives partly from the traditional crazy technique which gave late nineteenth century quilters a certain freedom. It arose also from a reluctance to discard the trimmings of materials, which still may have meaning. She has invented a technique of applying the pieces to backing in a wild way by using a vanishing plastic as a bond, and so she has created her distinctive style.

Her most recent exhibition, *Lineage of Cloth*, shown in Castletownshend in the summer of 1991, showed seven large and important hangings; but the greater number of the works were small and many were framed. The small colour studies owed much to Paul Klee whom she admires intensely. In some ways they recall the elemental gouache studies made by Hone and Jellett when they were attempting to master abstraction. But she herself sees them in relation to Klee's small works. More subtle were the *Steles*, inspired by ancient classical headstones. 'Things have happened, and have to be mourned, but not in a sad way. It is the same with reliquaries. Such and such a saint has died, but the saint has left substance. A box is made to contain a bit of bone, but it isn't just for the bone, it is for the substance.' The *Stele* works advanced the flexibility of her technique. Through them she learned to mix fabric as if it were paint, from a confusion of colour in the centre drawing light out fluidly to travel to the composition's edge.

Borders are as conventional in these works as in her more conventional tapestries, bringing order to the visual chaos of the centre. She regards the *Steles* as pioneer work, framed in order to make viewers look at textile art differently.

*I'm granting myself the arrogance of presenting the framed object to the viewer and saying, Well you like it or you don't, but don't come questioning me as to what's in it. Because that's what painters do. I'm tired of people coming close to examine the cloth and to touch the stitching. Nobody asks a painter how the brush relates to the paint.*

Her other recent theme on a small scale was the *Ego* series, introspective yet relieved by the humour of the pun in the title. 'The egg is perfection,' she says. 'It's male and female, and it's important for me. It's the future.' The egg shape enters into her large and striking *Lances*, with its suggestion of aggression and the consequent reaction presented in bright, heraldic, and slightly satirical imagery. The inspiration is taken from African warriors, as seen in books and magazines, but gradually the notion acquired the idea of 'reliquaries', and of civilised form being put on to the barbaric. 'Things that are precious relate enormously to a quilt.'

'Reliquaries', because of the nature of her medium, is a persistent theme, to which she continues to return, as has been indicated above, even as a secondary and underlying reference. Her first hanging entitled *Reliquaries*, closer to collage than patchwork, gathered together fabrics worn by three generations of the women of her family, with lace, pearls, buttons, and strips of tapestry spelling out the accumulation of traditions, sentiments, and deeper emotions. Her more recent *Reliquaries II*, described by Kathleen Raine as a 'Life Quilt', shows her to have identified herself fully with a post modernism which perceives all experience in aesthetic terms.[4] In it, Evelyn Montague, very conscious of her French Huguenot background, sees herself as a Renaissance person.

*All of the Renaissance came out of the Reformation, when they made man aware of being more angel than beast. Yet the Reformation artists were not allowed to worship and reproduce the Holy Face. I would see the Protestants of the Reformation as being just as spiritual as anybody else, only more intellectual; so they were, I would say, the ancestors of abstraction. I really feel it in my person, I am quite certain of that. The human has this need to express the spirituality, and if you can't do it through the face, you are going to do it through other shapes as for instance in the work of Klee – which is very spiritual.*

*Reliquaries II* is an image of her studio, where whatever may provide inspiration hangs on the wall – 'my studio being the

place where I'm really me. It's most fundamental'. The diverse objects represented – the head of an African woman, a Commedia dell'Arte stage, a Polynesian man, scraps from kimonos of the Noh Theatre – related to each other only in the sense that she put them there. But gradually the window, the wall and the table conjure up the physical and visible past, present and future, while the floating colourful emblems with their literary and artistic connotations suggest a past, present and future of the subconscious.

There's a tactile artistry about the tapestry, the image planes retiring into the cloth or pushing outwards imperiously, all with the fluidity of an interior by Andrea del Sarto, or by Giorgio de' Chirico. Regarded by Evelyn Montague as her masterpiece, it might be described in psychological terms as her 'apologia'. Embroidered at the heart of the patchwork are the words of her husband, John Montague – his poem, 'Sage', written in memory of Morris Graves (the American painter whose philosophy led him to pursue what he imaged by way of the inner eye):

*On the way towards a new art
she halts where the red earth
drinks warmth all day, to turn
towards evening, a flaring red.
The sparkle of this dry light
breeds a wisdom, where herb, moth
blend fragrances, and the cricket
rubs its metal legs against the night.*

Hilary Pyle

## NOTES

1. See Pat Ferrero, Elaine Hedges, Julie Silver, *Hearts and Hands: the influence of women and quilts on American society*, 1987, p. 11, etc.
2. In conversation with the author, 11 November, 1991.
3. Introduction to *Evelyn Montague – Lineage of Cloth: an exhibition of quilts and other textile objects* shown at Warren's Boathouse, Castletownshend, Co. Cork, August-September 1991.
4. Elizabeth Wilson, *The Sphinx in the City* (1991) pp. 135–6.

# MARINOT GLASS IN IRELAND

An important collection of glass by the renowned French artist Maurice Marinot is perhaps one of the most surprising and, to a certain extent, undiscovered pleasures of the National Gallery of Ireland's holdings. The glass was donated to the Gallery by the artist's daughter Florence Marinot in 1970. Her gift also included a number of her father's oils, watercolours and drawings.

Marinot, who is today chiefly remembered for his historic role in the development of twentieth century studio glass, was also a painter of considerable fame. He was born in Troyes in 1882 where his father was a manufacturer of millinery.

An important collection of studio glass by the French artist Maurice Marinot (1882–1960) is in the National Gallery of Ireland. The significance of the artist and his work is outlined by **Wanda Ryan-Smolin.**

Following an unspectacular school career at Troyes he went to Paris and entered the Ecole des Beaux-Arts in 1901, where he chose to study under the academic painter Fernand Cormon. Cormon, who was not as liberal as Marinot had hoped,

found his nonconformist attitudes hard to take and asked him to leave. Marinot, however, continued to attend the studio in the master's absence, availing himself of the models, and also studied on his own at the Louvre. Marinot's nonconformity was publicly confirmed when he exhibited two paintings at the Salon d'Automne in 1905 and was criticised along with his friends Matisse, Dérain, Vlaminck, Van Dongen and others as 'a Fauve'. The term Fauve was adopted by the group following the critic Louis Vauxcelles' now famous outburst 'Donatello au milieu des fauves' which he is said to have exclaimed when confronted with a bust in the Renaissance

*Etched Vase with internal bubbles in clear glass, 1927, height 14 cm (NGI, 12,024) and clear stoppered bottle in green glass with internal design in black, 1926, height 18.5 cm (NGI, 12,009). Both signed* Marinot.

*Bottle with internal crackled layer of black and red in clear glass, 1927, height 22 cm (NGI, 12,011). Signed* Marinot.

*Green and red tinted bowl with internal bubbles, 1927, height 10.5 cm (NGI, 12,015) Signed* Marinot.

*Stoppered bottle in tinted green glass with internal bubbles and rust coloured streaks, 1926, height 14 cm (NGI, 12,008); furnace modelled bottle in grey glass with internal bubbles, 1927, height 16.5 cm (NGI, 12,021), and stoppered bottle with internal marbled layer of brown red and white in clear glass, 1927, height 15 cm (NGI, 12, 023). All signed* Marinot.

*Stoppered bottle in clear glass with internal bubbles and surface applied trails, 1927, height 22 cm (NGI, 12.025). Signed* Marinot.

*Covered vase with internal black bubbles in clear glass, 1927, height 28.5 cm (NGI, 12,027). Signed* Marinot.

style amongst the violently coloured paintings of this group of young artists. Marinot continued to be associated with the Fauves for a number of years and exhibited regularly at the Salon des Indépendants and the Salon d'Automne.

In 1911 Marinot visited, at Bar-sur-Seine, a small glass works belonging to his friends Eugène and Gabriel Viard. This was to stimulate a passion for working in the glass medium which lasted almost twenty years. The Viard brothers accommodated him in every way and put all the facilities of the glassworks at his disposal. He began by decorating plain glass vessels with enamel paint. At first he chose suitable glass vessels from the factory's repertoire. Later he had pieces specially made to his own designs. His enthusiasm for this new medium was such that he ceased exhibiting his paintings altogether and began instead to show his glass to the public. In 1912 he exhibited his glass for the first time in the *Maison Cubiste* designed by André Mare for the Salon d'Automne. The facade was by Raymond Duchamp-Villon, the interior decoration by Mare and others, the paintings by Fernand Léger, Albert Gleizes and Jean Metzinger, and the glass (enamelled vases, bottles and a decanter) by Marinot. Once again Marinot found himself associated with the avant-garde when the *Maison Cubiste* was singled out by the press and the public for some praise and much criticism. In the following year Marinot had his first one man exhibition of glass at the Gallery of Adrien Hébrard.

Hébrard was well known as a bronze-founder (most notably of Degas' work) and as a dealer. Amongst the artists whom he promoted at his rue Royale gallery were the studio potter André Metthey (1871–1920) who was also associated with the Fauves, and Georges Manza-Pissarro (1871–1961), the son of Camille Pissarro who, like Marinot, was producing glass vessels decorated in enamels. At this early stage in his glass career Marinot used the enamels to create simple and consciously naive graphic designs with flower, bird and figure motifs. Although his motifs were figurative, there was a strongly geometric aspect to his early designs for glass that can be identified with the Art Nouveau of Mackintosh in Edinburgh and Hoffaman in Vienna. His range of colours was generally limited to the French national colours which he apparently chose especially for their

patriotic associations[2] as well as purple, yellow and gold.

The first World War interrupted Marinot's work at the Viard factory. He was called up in 1914 and in 1917 he was sent to Morocco where he found time to paint and did many watercolours and drawings of the local people and their customs. After the war he returned to Bar-sur-Seine and began his difficult apprenticeship as a glass maker. This was a turning point in a career which led him gradually away from being purely a decorator of glass to becominng a creator of glass. He continued to work for some years with enamel while acquainting himself with the processes of acid etching and wheel cutting as well as with the physical and chemical properties of the glass itself. By 1923 he had mastered the craft sufficiently to be able, not only to decorate the glass in a number of techniques, but also to blow his own glass.

The shapes of the glasses that he made were inspired by the traditional glass of various regions and periods. His preference was however for the solid simple forms of traditional French glass rather than the skilful creations of the Venetians:

> 'Je les préfere, aux tours de force orgueilleux et aux jongleries des Vénitiens, leurs matières plus robustes, leurs formes plus simples et plus ordonnées, sont plus belles de l'amour du verre que de l'orgueil du verrier'.[3]

At this stage Marinot was thirty years of age and faced an enormous challenge in trying to master a skill which normally required a long training period beginning virtually in childhood. He was aware of the difficulties that he faced but was determined to go ahead as he recognized the greater potential for artistic expression which glass blowing offered:

> 'Les deux qualités essentielles du verre sont la transparence et l'éclat. Le mode de travail qui n'appartient qu'à lui et fait le mieux valoir ses deux qualités significatives c'est le soufflage.'[4]

His experiments with acid etching, a technique in which selected areas of a piece of glass are treated with hydrofluoric acid which bites into its surface to create a pattern, were of particular significance to his developing style. In order to produce a strong contrast between the etched pattern and the main body of the glass, Marinot found it increasingly necessary

to work with very thick gathers of glass. From the start of his apprenticeship, Marinot had been fascinated by the decorative effects of bubbles within the body of the glass and he had begun by experimenting with *malfin* glass, which because of its impurities (including bubbles), was normally discarded. Eventually he was able to control the size, density and colour of the bubbles which he often dispersed throughout the glass. He also developed another method of internal decoration which involved trapping a layer of coloured glass between two layers of clear glass. This was achieved by applying metal oxides to the surface of a gather of molten glass which was then blown into a gather of clear glass. An important element in the procedure was the mixing of the metal oxides which determined the colours. Also crucial was the application of the oxides which ultimately dictated the pattern of the colour ground. The patterns of these colour 'sandwiches[5] were nearly always abstract although evocative of natural phenomena, and have been likened to ferns, moss, river beds, veined leaves, tree bark and other organic forms.

By this time Marinot was exhibiting his glass annually at Hébrard's, was receiving much acclaim for his work and was recognized as one of France's foremost 'decorative artists' (though he himself never accepted the title decorative artist or indeed even that of 'glass artist' but preferred instead to be called a glass-maker). In 1925 he was appointed Vice-President of the selection committee of the *Exposition International des Arts Decoratifs et Industriels Modernes*, the landmark exhibition from which the term Art Deco derives. Marinot's work was displayed in a number of the exhibition pavilions, and most notably in the Pavilion of an Ambassador and in the Museum of Contemporary Art designed by the firm of *Süe et Mare*. Marinot's friend Andre Mare together with Louis Süe founded a successful partnership with the name *Compagnie des Arts Français* for which several young designers and craftsmen produced simple but expensive household furnishings in a distinctly Art Deco style.

It has often been noted that Marinot's swift recognition as a glass-maker had much to do with his already privileged position as a successful painter. From the onset his work was viewed more as art than craft since he was, in effect, simply

# MARINOT GLASS IN IRELAND

adapting his painting style to suit the glass. It became increasingly obvious to his contemporaries that his glass could not be classified as decorative art in the nineteenth-century meaning of the term with its implied status lower than painting and sculpture. His own view on the matter was clear:

'Je m'élève contre le mot de décorateur ( . . . ), ma verrerie est un acte aussi gratuit que la peinture ou la sculpture.'[6]

That he felt obliged to explain his point of view, is indicative of the fact that the nineteenth-century classification of the arts which placed all craft lower than painting and sculpture was still very much alive when Marinot was working, despite the achievements of the artists who through their work in the Arts and Crafts movement had begun to change the public's perception of craft as an inferior art form.

Marinot's last ten year phase of glass making was for him the most significant:

'A partir de 1927, je commence cette nouvelle période, la plus passionnante: c'est le modelage à chaud et en force dans des pièces très épaisses et d'un seul bloc.'[7]

At this stage in his career Marinot concentrated on hot work, (modelage à chaud) where the pieces were worked on or modelled at the furnace by means of simple tools and occasionally by the application of heavy gathers of molten glass to the exterior.

It is to this exciting period of transition that the Marinot glass in the National Gallery of Ireland belongs. There are twenty pieces in the collection and they date to the years 1926 and 1927. They are broadly representative of all his most important techniques and forms and they illustrate both the diversity and uniqueness of his individual pieces and the unity of his work as a whole. The overwhelming feature of the entire collection is the sheer weight and massiveness of each piece. It is this feature of Marinot's work more than any other that led his glass to be universally regarded not as decorative art but rather as pure sculpture. The fact that every piece can clearly be identified with a functional object was according to him, purely accidental; none of them were intended to carry out the function that their name or shape suggests.[8] The repertoire of vessels in which Marinot chose to express himself was limited to a small range of bottles, vases, goblets,

Maurice Marinot, A study for David, 1905, signed M Marinot, oil on canvas, 27 x 22 cm (NGI, 4020).

chalices and paper weights (though these are very rare). Particularly characteristic of the bottles are the spherical stoppers which he nearly always made to go with them. They are made either in an identical or contrasting glass to that of the bottle, but what makes them noteworthy is that they are uniformly small in relation to the size of the bottle. Their function seems to be to highlight the bulk and weight of the accompanying bottle. Although certain basic bottle and vase shapes were continually repeated, it is extraordinary that no two pieces of glass are exactly the same; they are rather variations on a theme.

Marinot's method of working was extremely methodical. He started with numerous drawings of a particular shape, followed by a systematic study of alternative decorative schemes. In addition to using drawings he also let the weight and other physical characteristics of the glass direct him while he was working, and he drew inspiration from the making process which he then used as a point of departure for subsequent work. It had been estimated that throughout his entire career in glass he produced no more than about 2,500 pieces in all with an annual output never in excess of 200. This was due to his practice of destroying anything which did not satisfy him completely. The processes which he used were time consuming

(particularly acid-etching) and it was not uncommon for him to have a single piece of work in hand for several months.

The NGI collection has several examples of acid-etched vessels, where the thick body of the glass has been heavily eaten away. These include the chalice with diamond pattern (NGI, 12,018), the rounded bottle with square neck and base (NGI, 12,016), the vase with etched-out squares (NGI, 12,024) and the bottle with stylized mask motifs (NGI, 20,017). All are in clear glass, some displaying internal bubbles. The striking contrast in all these pieces between the clear smooth body of the glass and the rough sheen of the etched areas, coupled with the extraordinary depth of the etching, is typical of Marinot's work in this technique. Also notable is the strongly geometric quality of the abstract motifs which reflects the modernist aesthetic of the period, for despite the relative isolation in which Marinot worked and lived at Bar-sur-Seine, he remained in touch with the spirit of his most progressive contemporaries.

For Marinot the physical characteristics of glass, its translucency, clarity and brilliance were of primary interest. This is particularly reflected in his use of the ice-glass technique. A particularly handsome piece in this technique is the bowl in crackled blue-green glass with internal bubbles, (NGI, 12,019). The Venetians of the sixteenth century had frequently used this method whereby the glass, still hot from the furnace, is plunged into cold water and then reheated to produce an overall crackled effect. Marinot's work can be seen as a distillation of nature with effects of still or running water and cracking or melting ice. His own description of glass as ' . . . une sculpture d'eau, une architecture de glace'[9] is an apt one.

Marinot's smooth walled vessels are in complete contrast to the acid-etched pieces. These equally heavy pieces are original both in the classical simplicity of their shapes and in their internal colouring and bubbling effects. In some cases the internal colouration is dispersed like a mist, or spread by way of tinted bubbles within the body of the clear or tinted glass. This effect is seen in the bottle with dark green bubbles and brown-red streaks in clear glass (NGI, 20,008), and in the semi-spherical bowl with red and green bubbling (NGI, 12,015). In others the colour is applied to the interior of the vessel

# MARINOT GLASS IN IRELAND

in a definite pattern, as in the *bottle* with an internal black design in green glass (NGI, 12,009). But the most intriguing and beautifully coloured pieces are those done in his 'sandwich' technique where a layer of textured colour is trapped between an inner and outer layer of clear glass. Interesting examples are the large *bottle* with an internal crackled layer of black and red in clear glass (NGI, 12,001), the flat *bottle* with an internal marbled layer of brown, red and white in clear glass (NGI, 12,023), and the cubic *paper weight* in clear glass with an internal black sphere surrounded by gold bubbles (NGI, 12,013).

The colours in Marinot's work appear to change according to the intensity and angle of the light source under which it is viewed. The outer layer of clear glass has a distinctive magnifying quality which illuminates the trapped colours which appear to float in the depths of glass. There is a very sensuous quality to these sculptures in glass which have both visual and tactile appeal. To appreciate their beauty fully it is almost essential to touch the smooth and rough surfaces and to feel the immense weight of the pieces.

Marinot's growing interest in '*modelage à chaud*' is reflected in the NGI collection in a number of pieces. One small densely bubbled *bottle* in grey glass (NGI, 12,022) perfectly conveys the artist's working method. After blowing, the bottle was subjected to fairly intense modelling with a variety of both traditional and specially designed tools to produce a faceted body with a flattened profile. The walls of the *bottle* have been squeezed together at the centre to form a diamond-shaped depression. This type of work, which involved shaping the piece from within and without by blowing and modelling, was for Marinot a fundamental part of the creative process.

The natural development of Marinot's furnace work led him to use one of the most ancient techniques of glass-making, that of decorating the body of a piece with applications of molten glass. The large conical covered *vase* in clear glass with internal black bubbles (NGI, 12,027) has, for example, a line of heavily applied lugs around its circumference. The protruding lugs correspond with the rounded shape of the lid giving the piece an added dimension. Similarly, the flat square-necked *bottle* in clear glass (NGI, 12,025) has an organic looking pattern of applied

*Maurice Marinot, Florence in a Hat, 1924, oil on board, 41 x 33 cm (NGI, 4021).*

trails in thick glass on both sides. The design of both the *vase* and the *bottle* highlight a new departure in Marinot's work in which convex elements take precedence over concave ones. These purely sculptural concerns, visible in all his late work, placed Marinot in a position of major historical importance in the field of glass-making. Marinot's work was recognized as breaking new ground not in the technical sense but in a much more fundamental way through the expression of the natural beauty inherent in the glass itself. His originality lay in the individuality of his thick walled, heavy vessels decorated in a broadly minimalist manner.

Marinot's glass continued to attract much attention in the 1930s and was included in numerous exhibitions both in France and abroad, with a major individual exhibition taking place in New York at the Brummer Gallery in 1932. In the same year he was made a *Chevalier de la Légion d'Honneur* and, in 1937, he became an *Officier de la Légion d'Honneur*. A documentary film showing Marinot at work was made in 1933 by Jean Benoit-Lévy and René Chavance. His career in glass ended as abruptly as it had begun when the glassworks at Bar-sur-Seine closed down in 1937.

His characteristic style in glass proved inspirational to a number of his contem-

poraries with Henri Navarre (1885–1971), André Thuret (1898–1965) and Georges Dumoulin (1882–1959) being among his better known followers. All of these artists produce heavy-walled furnace-worked vessels with a variety of internal colour effects and surface applications. However it is the numerous factories (including Daum, Steuben, Kosta, Orrefors, and Baccaret) who developed stylized production-line versions of his glass that have truly popularised his ideas.

Marinot gave up exhibiting his paintings when he started his glass career and did not recommence until after 1937. During his many years at the glassworks he had nonetheless continued to paint in the evenings and while on holiday. His style from 1905 to 1911 was fiery in colour and similar to that of the other members of the Fauve group, but his imagery tended towards an intimate and calm view of the world reminiscent of the Nabis. In *A Study for David* (NGI, 4020), an oil of 1905, there is a strong sense of line and the scene, despite the decapitated figure at David's feet, is composed in a light-hearted series of decorative arabesques. A number of drawings and watercolours in the NGI also date to this Fauve period. In their lively treatment of Parisian café society (e.g. *Dancer*, NGI, 7345), they illustrate Marinot's affinity with the art of the Impressionists. This affinity surfaces again in a more significant way in Marinot's late glass where his preoccupation with questions of light, colour and transparency are similar to those which Monet had earlier explored.[10] The style of these early paintings and drawings compares closely with that of Marinot's first enamel designs for glass which were also generally of a decorative graphic nature. After 1911 his style changed radically and he entered what is known as his 'black period' characterised by tones of black and grey and roughness of contour. Victor Arwas[11] has noted that his style in these years was very close to that of his friends André Dérain, André Dunoyer de Segonzac and Othon Friesz. The move to Bar-sur-Seine at this time appears to have prompted a change in subject matter with landscape becoming increasingly important. *A Landscape in the Forest of Othe*, of 1929 (NGI, 4018), is an example of the rather heavy realism that pervaded his painting at this time.

Other landscapes by Marinot in the NGI are much later and indicate a return to a more graphic, linear style. Portraiture played a significant role in his oeuvre throughout his career. In the period 1911 to 1937 his portrait subjects were limited to his family and very close friends. The portrait of his daughter *Florence in a Hat*, of 1924 (NGI, 4021), is in sharp contrast to the portraits of his early years such as that of his wife *Marcelle* of 1904 (NGI, 4019). A composition of strong contrasts and angular shapes, it is in many ways compatible with Marinot's acid-etched glass of this period. The *Self-Portrait*, a pen and ink drawing of 1953 (NGI, 7248) reveals a man of strong resolve and considerable physical presence, both qualities which surely were decisive factors in his success as a glass-maker. Other themes which preoccupied Marinot as a painter were bathers, a type of intimate genre and still-life; all of these are represented in the National Gallery's collection which consists of eight oil paintings and twenty watercolours and drawings.

After the second world war the direction of Marinot's painting style changed and colour emerged again as a dominant feature in a series of sun-filled landscapes. A pastel *Evening Sun* of 1958 (NGI, 7343), painted just two years before the artist's death, is characteristic of this last phase of his work. The intense light which radiates from the sun and almost obliterates the landscape has a dazzling, even blinding quality which many have observed as Marinot's instinctive desire to return through the medium of painting to the scorching flames of the glass furnace.

Marinot's exit as a painter from the public arena in 1913 (his work was included in the famous Armory Show in New York in that year) had been so absolute that his painting was totally forgotten by critics and historians. It was not until after 1945 when he began again to exhibit (most notably at the Charpentier Gallery in Paris in 1948) that attention was again focused on his painting. From 1950 onwards he won wider acknowledgment for his achievements as a member of the Fauve movement and his early works were included in collective exhibitions of their works at the Musée National d'Art Modern in Paris in 1951 and 1966. However, much of Marinot's work of both his early and middle period was destroyed in 1944 when his studio was bombed during the Liberation of Troyes. It has been estimated that over 2,500 paintings and

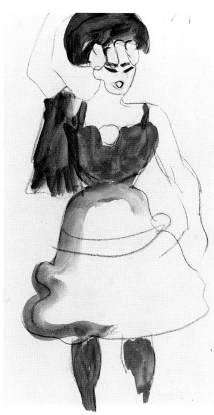

*Maurice Marinot, A Female Dancer, 1906, stamped: ATELIER marinot, black crayon, pencil and watercolour on paper, 31.5 x 25.5 cm (NGI, 7345)*

*Maurice Marinot, Marcelle, 1904, oil on canvas, 24 x 19 cm (NGI, 4019).*

drawings as well as a great deal of glass was lost at this time. Luckily some work which was stored elsewhere escaped destruction including those works now in the NGI. Towards the end of his life Marinot made a compilation of published material relating to his life as an artist to which he added his own personal notes and reflections on his work in glass. His task was greatly hampered by the loss of so much relevant documentation in the bombing of his studio. None the less these notes, which have remained unpublished[12] have served as the basis for many of the articles[13] written about Marinot in recent years.

Since his death at Troyes in 1966, Marinot has captured the interest of many. His work, particularly his glass, has been continually exhibited and major retrospectives were held in Lyon in 1965 and in Paris in 1990. As a man of independent means Marinot was not forced to sell his work and as a result very little of his glass and far fewer of his paintings ended up in private collections. He did, however, have a number of important patrons who avidly bought his glass, including Baron Robert de Rothschild, Jacques Zoubaloff, M. and Mme. Louis Barthou, and Baron and Baronesse Gourgaud. All of these patrons were great collectors and benefactors and between them they donated a considerable amount of the artist's glass to national institutions in Paris.[14] Today the majority of Marinot's glass is, in fact, in public collections due to the great generosity of Florence Marinot who inherited the artist's large personal collection. She began donating to institutions in France and abroad in the 1960s with the Victoria and Albert Museum in London being one of the first foreign museums to benefit when it received a donation of eleven pieces of glass in 1965.[15] She continued donating sizable collections of her father's work (normally including both glass and paintings in her gifts) during the 1970s so that now Marinot glass can be seen in well over thirty museums throughout France and in an equal number of museums abroad.[16] Dublin's collection is the only one in Ireland and compares very favourably with those of other European museums which on the whole tend to have much smaller selections of his glass. In the United States he is best represented in New York, the biggest collection being in the famous Corning Museum of Glass

# MARINOT GLASS IN IRELAND

which has twenty-nine pieces of glass. By far the largest collection, however, is in Brussels where Florence Marinot donated over a hundred pieces of glass as well as many paintings, watercolours, drawings and working studies for glass to the Musées Royaux d'Art et d'Histoire.[17] Also included in that magnificent bequest were all Marinot's glass-making tools which are now permanently displayed there together with his work.

In his glass Marinot was, in many respects, following the lead given by those pioneers of art glass, Emile Gallé (1844–1904) and to a lesser extent Louis Comfort Tiffany (1848–1933). Both of these artists had begun their activities in glass by experimenting with a variety of modern and ancient methods of both internal and external decorating, and through their creative work had highlighted the potential of glass as a medium of artistic expression. What sets Marinot apart from these famous predecessors and from his highly successful contemporary René Lalique (1860–1945)[18] is that he was not involved in industrial production. Instead he worked with only a boy to assist him and without the support of the traditional team of glass workers. Although he had his bench and tools supplied by the factory, none of his designs from 1923 onwards were produced by the factory. He did not manufacture any commercial lines of glass but instead created each piece as a separate one-off original work without the use of any moulds. It was essential for his own creative sensibilities to be in physical contact with his medium, it was the very making of the piece that gave him inspiration. It is in this context that Marinot can be seen as the most significant precursor of the contemporary studio glass movement.

*Wanda Ryan-Smolin*

*Wanda Ryan-Smolin M.A. (Jagillonian University, Cracow) was formerly on the staff of the National Gallery of Ireland (1981–89) and a lecturer in the National College of Art and Design (1988–91). She is the author of King's Inns Portraits (Dublin, 1992).*

## ACKNOWLEDGMENTS

I would like to thank the following people for their assistance in the preparation of this article, Dr Helmut Ricke (Kunstmuseum Düsseldorf), Jennifer Opie (Victoria & Albert Museum), Jane Adlin (Metropolitan Museum of Art), Susanne Frantz (Corning Museum of Glass) and particularly Paula Hicks, Adrian Le Harivel and Maighread McParland (National Gallery of Ireland).

## NOTES

1. See Jean-Luc Olivie, 'Maurice Marinot: l'oeuvre en verre' in *Maurice Marinot. Peintre et Verrier,* exhibition catalogue, Museé de l'Orangerie, Paris, 1990, p. 34.
2. See *Maurice Marinot, Peintre et Verrier,* op, cit., p. 98.
3. Maurice Marinot, *Le métier du verre soufflé',* L'Amour de l'Art, no. 5, September 1920.
4. Ibid.
5. Ada Polak, 'Maurice Marinot's Glass. The Extreme Rarity of his "Sandwiches" in *Connoisseur,* May, 1965, no. 637, pp. 21–23.
6. See *Donation Florence Marinot,* (exhibition catalogue, Musée des Beaux-Arts de Rouen with introduction by François Bergot), Rouen, 1985.
7. Maurice Marinot, 'Lettre', in *Les Beaux Métiers Artistes-Artisans,* Paris, 1943.
8. See M Vaizey, 'Collection of Mr and Mrs Robert Walker' in *Connoisseur,* no. 182, April, 1973, pp. 239–40.

9. Marinot, 'Lettre', op. cit.
10. See Michel Hoog, 'Marinot chez Claude Monet' in *Maurice Marinot, Peintre et Verrier,* op. cit. pp. 11–17.
11. Victor Arwas, *Glass, Art Nouveau to Art Deco,* London, 1987, p. 223.
12. Typed copies of Marinot's notes were distributed to a very small number of select museums by Florence Marinot.
13. Marinot has been the subject of numerous articles in journals and magazines but has only once been the subject of an independent monograph: G. Janneau, *Le verre et l'art de Marinot,* Paris, 1925. However his work has been treated extensively in many exhibition catalogues and is the subject of an unpublished thesis, *Maurice Marinot, Maitre verrier* written by Beatrice Thévenard under the direction of Pierre Vaisse at the Université de Paris-X Nanterre, 1988.
14. The largest collections of Marinot glass in

Paris are in the Petit Palais, the Musée des Arts Decoratifs and the Musée d'Art Modern de la Ville de Paris.
15. See R J Charleston, 'The Glass of Maurice Marinot', *Victoria and Albert Museum Bulletin,* July 1965, vol. 1, no. 3, pp. 1–8.
16. For a complete list of museums containing Marinot glass, see H Hilschenz-Mlynek and H Ricke, *Glas – Historismus Jugendstil Art Deco,* (glass catalogue of the Kunstmuseum Düsseldorf), Munich, 1985, vol. 1, pp. 313–14.
17. See H Fettweis, *Marinot, La donation Florence Marinot aux Musées Royaux d'Art et d'Histoire,* Brussels, 1972.
18. See Philippe Garnier, 'Glass Between the Wars' in D Klein and W Lloyd (eds.), *The History of Glass,* London, 1984, pp. 221–26 for an interesting comparative discussion of Lalique and Marinot.

# BELFAST HARBOUR OFFICE: A HAVEN OF ART

**Eileen Black** outlines the history of one of Belfast's splendid Victorian buildings and its art collection.

The headquarters of a port authority may seem an unlikely setting for an interesting and historic accumulation of paintings, sculpture and furniture. Nevertheless, Belfast Harbour Office contains just such a collection, built up since the mid-nineteenth century mainly as donations by numerous Harbour Commissioners. The art collection, catalogued by the author in 1983[1], includes a few seventeenth and eighteenth century portraits by unknown artists, nineteenth-century Italian and French sculpture and bronzes, nineteenth-century Irish paintings and sculpture, and an assortment of paintings by twentieth century northern Irish artists such as Joseph W Carey, Frank McKelvey and Maurice Wilks. The chief interest of the collection lies in its local historical relevance. Many of the landscapes are valuable as records of Belfast and its environs in former times. Probably the most interesting earlier views of the locality are a number of scenes by Hugh Frazer (fl. 1813–61), the first Ulster landscape painter of note and an important figure in Belfast's artistic community during the 1830s. There are also numerous portraits of commissioners, many of whom were leading figures in the development of the town over the years. These include Sir Edward Harland (1831–95), founder of the major shipbuilding firm of Harland and Wolff, Sir Daniel Dixon (1844–1907), Belfast's first Lord Mayor (in 1893), and Sir James Musgrave (1829–1904), a prominent merchant and local figure.

The origins of the Belfast Harbour Commissioners extend back to 1785, when The Corporation for Preserving and Improving the Port and Harbour of Belfast (commonly called the Ballast Board) was established by Act of Parliament. Of the fifteen Board members, three were honorary and never attended meetings: Arthur Chichester, 5th Earl and later 1st Marquis of Donegall, John Foster, Speaker of the Irish House of Commons and John Beresford, Chief Commissioner of Revenue in the Irish government.[2] The remaining twelve were all local merchants and shipowners. The Board held meetings in various buildings in town until it acquired its own premises,

*Unknown artist,* Belfast Harbour Office, *c. 1854, pencil and watercolour on white paper, heightened with white, 56.5 x 79 cm. Courtesy Belfast Harbour Commissioners.*

# BELFAST HARBOUR OFFICE: A HAVEN OF ART

the Ballast Office on Merchants' Quay. (The office had an observatory on its roof, to enable the Harbour Master to have a clear view of the port and channel seawards. This feature can be seen in the painting by James Glen Wilson). The Board remained in operation until 1847, when it was replaced by a new body with wide-ranging powers, the Belfast Harbour Commissioners. The Commissioners, however, continued to use the old Ballast Office until 1854, when they moved into a resplendent new building in Corporation Square, designed by their own engineer, George Smith. The Ballast Office was subsequently demolished to make way for the Custom House, designed by Charles Lanyon and completed in 1857.

As befitted the Commissioners' status as one of Belfast's most important bodies,

the new office was impressive and dignified. A drawing by an unknown artist (perhaps Smith himself?) shows the early building as a compact two-storied Renaissance *palazzo*, with a Doric portico and clock tower with a belfry.[3] (This latter feature was not merely ornamental but was of prime importance to the smooth running of the harbour, being the public clock 'by which the hour of sailing of Steam Vessels plying from or within the Harbour of Belfast shall be determined.'[4] Steamers were forbidden to leave until the stated time and masters of rival passenger steamers were regularly fined for trying to cast off early). The Clarendon dock, seen to the right of the painting, is no longer there, having been filled in between 1965 and 1967.

The inauguration of the office on 7

March 1854 was the occasion of much celebration and civic pride. Over one hundred guests were present, including the Commissioners, their friends and the official staff of the Harbour Office. Among the numerous speeches, that by Commissioner Thomas McClure struck a prophetic note: 'We have but attained a certain point from which we are about to start to a far higher and prouder position than we have hitherto acquired . . . we have before us the prospect of prosperity which will go on increasing in an accelerated ratio compared with our previous advancement.'[5] Within thirty-six years, in consequence of the expansion of the port and Belfast's rise as one of the leading industrial cities in the British Isles, Smith's building was found to be inadequate. In 1890, the Belfast architect

*Belfast Harbour Office, enlarged by WH Lynn and completed in 1895. The modern office block, opened in 1971, can be seen to the rear of the building. Courtesy Belfast Harbour Commissioners.*

# BELFAST HARBOUR OFFICE: A HAVEN OF ART

William Henry Lynn was commissioned to design an extension.[6] This later building retained the seaward face of Smith's office but absorbed two-thirds of the original entrance front into one of the two new wings which formed the main front.[7]

The enlarged office was officially opened by Earl Cadogan, the Lord Lieutenant of Ireland, on 18 January 1896. The inauguration, held in the large colonnaded Public Room, with its fine vaulted ceiling and heraldic stained glass in the clerestory lunettes,[8] was a splendid affair, with three hundred guests including the Duke and Duchess of Abercorn, the Marquis and Marchioness of Londonderry and Lord Castlereagh. James Musgrave, chairman of the Board, in his address to the Lord Lieutenant, quoted a set of interesting statistics illustrative of the growth of the port since the beginning of

the century. In 1800, the tonnage of ships trading to Belfast was 5,500; by 1896, it had grown to 2,150,000 tons. In 1800, the income of the port was a mere £2,748; by the time of the opening of the enlarged office, it had risen to £140,000. The splendid new building was indeed visible proof of Belfast's increased prosperity.

The Lord Lieutenant's observation, in his speech to the assembled worthies, that 'before long it will be necessary for you, if you continue to increase your operations on the same scale . . . to add at least two more wings to the building',[9] did not, however, become a reality until 1967, when the Commissioners found it necessary to add a new office block to the rear of the Harbour Office. The old and new buildings, connected by an overhead corridor on two floors, operate as one unit. The traditional Board Room, Committee Rooms and Public Room in the old

building retain their former use, while the modern office block, completed in 1971, functions as an administrative centre.

As far as is known, the first painting to be acquired was Thomas Robinson's *Review of the Belfast Yeomanry by the Lord Lieutenant, the Earl of Hardwicke, 27 August 1804*. Presented, in 1852, by the Rev Thomas Romney Robinson DD, the artist's son, it contained portraits of several important local figures including a number of Ballast Board members. The picture, the most prestigious in the Collection, has an interesting history. Robinson, an English portrait, landscape and history painter, who worked from 1801, in Belfast, began the painting (which has also been called *The Entry of Lord Hardwicke into Belfast as Lord Lieutenant, 27 August 1804*) in October 1804. According to a local newspaper, Robinson hoped to defray the cost by receiving 'subscriptions

*Thomas Robinson*, Review of the Belfast Yeomanry by the Lord Lieutenant, the Earl of Hardwicke, 27 August 1804, *oil on canvas, 162.5 x 244 cm (sight). Courtesy Belfast Harbour Commissioners.*

# BELFAST HARBOUR OFFICE: A HAVEN OF ART

from one guinea upwards . . . all persons so subscribing may have their portraits introduced without further expence.'[10] In what appears a shrewd move aimed at the vanity of Belfast's nobility and gentry, he continued: 'It will be curious to hand down to other generations, the likenesses of the principal inhabitants of the present day, assembled in one of the most beautiful parts of the town (Donegall Place). An additional increase to the undertaking (is) that the ladies will be introduced as gracing this interesting scene.' Provided he received one hundred and fifty guineas, the picture would become the property of the subscribers, who could place it wherever they wished in town.

Robinson, however, apparently failed to raise the amount he sought − there are only forty-four major figures in the picture. In a conversation with the well-known local figure Martha McTier in March 1807, he told her that he had approached the Marquis and Marchioness of Donegall in the hope that they would purchase the painting.[11] That idea had unfortunately come to nothing as the Donegalls' affairs in Belfast were in ruin by December 1806.[12] Disillusioned with the picture, he had decided to give it up but was persuaded by William Sinclaire, one of those included in the painting, to finish it, on the understanding that Sinclaire would either buy it or assist with costs. That too had fallen through as Sinclaire died on 11 February 1807. According to Mrs McTier, Robinson hoped that somehow the painting would be acquired for Belfast's Exchange Rooms.

Despite the setbacks, Robinson completed the picture by the summer of 1807 and included it in an exhibition of his paintings at the Exchange. However, his plan to raffle it on 1 September came to nothing, possibly because of lack of subscriptions. Obviously still anxious to sell, he altered the background, added a statue of Nelson and exhibited the work at the Society of Artists in Dublin in 1809, with a new title *A military procession in Belfast in honour of Lord Nelson*. (There was never such a statue in Belfast). Notwithstanding the popularity of the hero of Trafalgar, the painting still failed to sell and remained in the Robinson family's possession until presented to the Harbour Commissioners. The picture, which contains several members of Belfast's leading families including the 2nd Marquis of Donegall, is one of Robinson's few extant history pieces. A better-known example of his work in this genre is his *Battle of Ballynahinch*, completed some four and a half months after the battle on 13 June 1798 between Crown troops and the

*James Howard Burgess,* View of Queen's Bridge, Harbour and Timber Pond, Belfast, 1858, *oil on canvas, 68.5 x 95.2 cm.*
*Courtesy Belfast Harbour Commissioners.*

# BELFAST HARBOUR OFFICE: A HAVEN OF ART

United Irishmen (Aras an Uachtaráin, on loan to the National Gallery of Ireland).

As stated above, many of the landscapes in the collection are interesting records of nineteenth-century Belfast. Two such are *View of Queen's Bridge, Harbour and Timber Pond, 1858* by James Howard Burgess and *Belfast Harbour, Ferry Steps, 1851* by James Glen Wilson. Burgess (c. 1810–90), a landscape painter, ran a drawing academy in Belfast during the late 1840s and early 1850s and contributed a number of views to Mr and Mrs S C Hall's *Ireland, its Scenery, Character, etc*, published 1841–43. The painting, which is finely executed, depicts the Queen's Bridge, erected 1842–43, and the Custom House (the pedimented building to the left), completed in 1857 on the site of the old Ballast Office. The Cave Hill, one of Belfast's landmarks, dominates the background. Wilson's painting shows a Greek brig berthed at the Donegall Quay. Behind the vessel is one of the cross channel steamers which plied to Liverpool or Fleetwood. The Ballast Board observatory can be seen in the right background, rising above the goods shed on the quay. Wilson (1827–63), whose work was discussed in a previous yearbook, painted around Belfast during the early 1850s, before commencing a career as a ship's artist with the Royal Navy.[13]

Among the seventeenth-century portraits, that of Justin of Nassau (1559–1631), from the studio of Jan Anthonisz. van Ravesteyn, is of particular interest. The painting, purchased by the Harbour Commissioners in 1940, was traditionally thought to represent Hugh O'Neill, 2nd Earl of Tyrone (1540?–1616), until research indicated that the sitter was in fact Justin of Nassau, son of William I of Orange. This identification is based on comparison with a similar portrait in the Rijksmuseum, Amsterdam, ascribed to van Ravesteyn's studio.[14] The painting, the best of the early works in the collection, is delicately handled and has considerable merit.

Of the sculpture, one piece stands out as an example of virtuosity, the *Veiled Lady*, from the workshop of Pietro Bazzanti. Bazzanti founded his sculpture studio in Florence in 1822 and the business remained in the family's possession until about 1940. Although under different ownership, however, the firm still trades under the family name. Bazzanti employed numerous artists to work in his studio; the

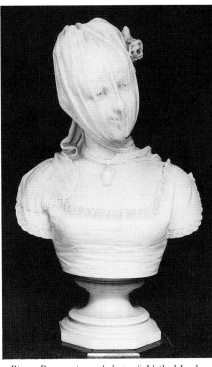

*Pietro Bazzanti, workshop of,* Veiled Lady, *marble, height 114 cm. Courtesy Belfast Harbour Commissioners.*

*Veiled Lady*, a mid-to-late nineteenth century piece, is by one of his anonymous employees. The carving of veiled figures first became popular in the eighteenth century, when the Venetian sculptor Antonio Corradini (1668–1752) made it his speciality. By the mid-nineteenth century many sculptors had popularized the theme for workshops like Bazzanti's. The *Veiled Lady*, smiling enigmatically through her diaphanous covering, appears almost to breathe with life. The piece is a striking and noteworthy example of the sculptor's art.

The Commissioners' collection comprises over one hundred paintings, fifteen sculptures and four bronzes and is added to on occasion by portraits of Chairmen and scenes of the harbour area. The former normally show sitters wearing the Commissioners' uniform, that is, a cream waistcoat with gilt buttons, blue tie and lapel ribbon with official insignia. The wearing of uniform dates back to Queen Victoria's visit to Belfast in August 1849 when, in honour of the occasion, the Commissioners decided upon a standard ensemble: blue dress coat with inscribed gilt buttons, white waistcoat, blue

trousers, black stock and a round hat. An example of an early coat is on display at the Harbour Office. That the coat has been kept and the wearing of uniform maintained, says much for the Commissioners' sense of history and their feeling for the importance of tradition.

The collection is not open to the public, but can be seen on request. In a city which has relatively few interesting and historic buildings, a visit to Belfast Harbour Office is well worth the effort.

*Eileen Black*

*Eileen Black is an Assistant Keeper in the Ulster Museum, with curatorial responsibility for the pre-twentieth century oil painting collection. Her publications include catalogues on James Glen Wilson (1980), Samuel McCloy (1981), the Harbour Commissioners' collection (1983) and on an area of the museum's holdings,* Irish Oil Paintings, 1572–c.1830 *(1991). She was also a contributor to, and the compiler and editor of, a major museum catalogue,* Kings in Conflict: Ireland in the 1690s *(1990). She has, in addition, contributed articles on art and on local history to numerous journals. Her particular interest is art in Belfast in the eighteenth and nineteenth centuries.*

## NOTES

1. Eileen Black, *Paintings, Sculptures and Bronzes in the Collection of The Belfast Harbour Commissioners*, Belfast, 1983. All references to the Commissioners' collection comes from this source.
2. Robin Sweetnam and Cecil Nimmons, *Port of Belfast 1785–1985: An Historical Review*, Belfast, 1985, p. 4.
3. Paul Larmour, *Belfast: An illustrated architectural guide*, Belfast, 1987, p. 55.
4. Black, p. 43.
5. *Belfast News-Letter*, 8 March 1854.
6. For a discussion of Lynn's career, see Martyn Anglesea, 'The Lynn brothers, architect and sculptor', *Irish Arts Review*, Yearbook 1989–90.
7. Larmour, p. 55.
8. Ibid.
9. *Northern Whig*, 20 January 1896.
10. *Belfast News-Letter*, 9 October 1804.
11. *Drennan Letters*, edited by D A Chart, Belfast, 1931, p. 375. Mrs McTier's letters to her brother, Dr William Drennan, provide a fascinating glimpse of Belfast social life of the late eighteenth and early nineteenth centuries.
12. W A Maguire, *Living like a Lord: The second Marquis of Donegall 1769–1844*, Belfast, 1984, p. 32.
13. Eileen Black, 'James Glen Wilson of Ireland and Australia: an enigmatic artist', *Irish Arts Review*, Yearbook 1990–91.
14. Reproduced in *All the paintings of the Rijksmuseum in Amsterdam*, Amsterdam, 1976, p. 700.

# CONSERVATION 1991

The Irish Professional Conservators' and Restorers' Association was founded in 1982 by a small group of concerned professionals anxious to promote here in Ireland the practice of conservation and restoration to internationally accepted standards, to provide a forum for discussion and to disseminate technical information. It is a broadly based Association with membership coming from all over Ireland, and representing many specialisations – archaeological artefacts, books, ceramics, furniture, gilding, manuscripts, oil painting, photography, plasterwork, textiles, works of art on paper, etc. While this is not an exhaustive list it does demonstrate the wide range of expertise existing here. Over the last ten years the Association has grown steadily and now represents almost one hundred practising conservators and restorers working in public institutions and from private studios.

Membership of IPCRA is not confined solely to conservators. There is an associate membership available to those with an interest in the subject but who are not practitioners. While there are relatively few such members this is an area where expansion is needed in order to draw more concerned people into the debate and so help support the aims of the Association. Two major meetings are held each year. There is also a series of lectures on conservation topics and seminars are organised on specialist subjects.

Since its foundation the Association

*The Irish Professional Conservators' and Restorers' Association is ten years old.* **Grellan Rourke** *describes its developments in the areas of exhibitions and training.*

has been very concerned with training. To date, most conservators have had to go abroad to train, often with great difficulty and at great personal cost. There is a far greater awareness of conservation now than at any other period and many young people are seeking careers in this field. In addition there have been many enquiries from abroad from those interested in coming to Ireland to seek training. Alas, there is very little on on offer. Since 1985, a sub-committee has been working to set up a Materials Conservation Course here but while a foundation course has been envisaged for aspiring conservators it has been impossible to secure funding to set it up. There is abundant recognition for the need to establish formal training but resources have not been forthcoming. Nevertheless, in the interim, the Association has been active in providing supplementary training for existing conservators and courses of short duration have been run in recent years which have proved to be both very successful and self-financing.

Collaboration with other professionals is essential; the conservator does not work in isolation. Often it will be necessary to seek the assistance of a scientist to help fully understand complex technical problems or there may be occasions when the services of an art historian may be required. There are many areas of joint interest and joint conferences are worthwhile. Recently IPCRA joined with the Association of Irish Art Historians to organise a colloquium entitled *Integrity and Interpretation – the Conservation/Art History Interface.* This was housed by the National Gallery of Ireland and took place last September. There were speakers from institutions like the National Gallery, London, the Tate Gallery and the Canadian Conservation Institute. The highlight of the three-day event was a superb lecture on the restoration of the Sistine Chapel ceiling by Dr Fabrizio Mancinelli, Technical Curator of the Vatican Museum. His visual presentation was a tour-de-force and captured the process of conservation in great detail. This event gave an opportunity for art historians and conservators to come together to discuss important international projects.

This is a need to promote greater awareness of conservation and make it more accessible to the general public. Mindful of this, the Association set about compiling the *Irish Conservation Directory* which was published in 1988. This publication set about introducing the public to the workings of conservation, explaining the issues involved, with particular emphasis on preventive conserva-

*Turn of the century tinted photographic portrait on gelatine coated paper. The portrait has been severely damaged by mould and very badly torn and scratched.*

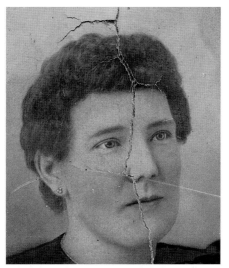

*The gelatine coating is very sensitive to moisture with a resultant loss of image, consequently conservation treatment of the paper is limited.*

*Restoration work only, carried out with a repair to the back of the picture using Japanese tissue and rice starch paste. The portrait is then finally retouched.*

*Majolica vase, blue, green, yellow on cream and black background, c. 1750, height 46 cm, broken in about 20 pieces and missing one snake handle.*

*Vase restored, handle and part of lip remodelled and hand painted.*

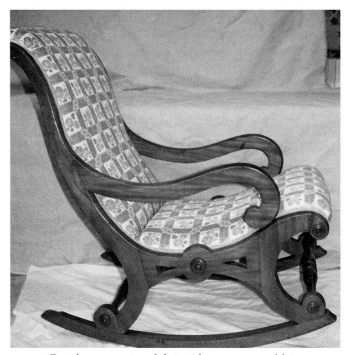

*Early Victorian mahogany rocking chair sadly neglected.*

*Complete restoration of chair with contemporary fabric.*

CONSERVATION 1991

tion, and guidance on how to choose a competent conservator. The Directory has been well received and hopefully will become a permanent reference work to help the public in matters of conservation. Work on a new edition is now under way and this will be published in 1993 once sponsorship has been secured.

With the publication of the *Irish Conservation Directory* the Association began to adopt a more public image. While the Directory was a step in the right direction it didn't make conservation available to people in a tangible way. If the public were to understand more about the subject they would need to experience it more visually. And so the idea of a series of conservation exhibitions took root, and events were planned to take place during 1991 to coincide with Dublin's period as European City of Culture. A two-pronged presentation was envisaged — the first, to show people what was being achieved in their national institutions; the second, to demonstrate the range of expertise available in Ireland, and to explain the problems the conservator encounters and how these are dealt with.

IPCRA approached institutions throughout Dublin with the idea, agreeing to act as co-ordinator, and the response was very encouraging. It was essential that all the exhibitions would run together for a core period. For varying reasons some institutions were unable to participate but, in the end, eight mounted conservation exhibitions. An important aspect of the exhibition concept was that people should see the conserved objects themselves as representing the range of conservation work undertaken in each institution. An exhibition trail was devised which included Archbishop Marsh's Library, Kilmainham Gaol, the National Gallery, the National Library, the National Museum including the Natural History Museum, the Royal Dublin Society, the Royal Irish Academy and Trinity College. The event was launched in the National Museum on the 23 September by Eamon de Buitleir who has done much over the years to promote conservation. To coincide with these exhibitions there was a series of complementary lectures and demonstrations on conservation and related topics; these were held at the different venues and ran over a period of six weeks.

In late October, IPCRA's own exhibition was launched by President Mary Robinson in the Bank of Ireland Exhi-

*Meissen figure, predominantly cerise, green, c. 1750, height c. 23 cm, after restoration. The figure was bonded with Hyxtall glue, left arm and missing pieces of glaze filled in with porcelain filler and hand painted.*

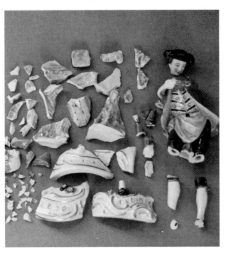

*The Meissen figure, broken in 73 pieces when a mirror fell on it.*

bition Centre in Baggot Street, Dublin. The President gave a splendid address to an enthusiastic crowd in which she said that our heritage could only be effectively preserved if there were programmes for training in conservation, good facilities and adequate funding. She expressed the hope that resources would be found to achieve these goals.

The primary function of the IPCRA exhibition was educational and, in order to get the message across to the lay person, a very visual format was devised, incorporating some three-dimensional objects. The photographic display showed procedures and techniques with relevant documentation to guide the viewer through the various stages in the preservation of artistic and historic works. In all, fifteen areas of specialisation were represented. The importance of keeping records and of actually recording the process of conservation was stressed. Emphasis was also put on preventive conservation, where a full treatment is not possible; this included advice on correct storage and display procedures, proper environmental control and the protection of objects from further damage.

The exhibition also included examples of restoration, and an explanation of the difference between restoration and conservation, which seeks to stabilise and preserve the object without its being materially altered. The approach will vary according to the function and purpose of the object — a painting has aesthetic value, whereas a chair or clock will have primarily functional demands made on it. The concept of the patina of age, and how this is an integral part of the object itself, was explained. As little intervention as possible was advised, the emphasis being on caution.

This exhibition has now assumed a new form to allow it to travel, as was envisaged from the outset. In this way it will reach a large population spread throughout the entire country. The Exhibition will move to local museums and similar institutions where each will add a local dimension to the display. This will help emphasis the importance of conservation in the preservation of local heritage and will broaden the public perception of the role of conservation in museum management. The exhibition has had a successful run in Monaghan County Museum and will shortly be opening in Derry. Future venues will include Armagh County

Museum, Donegal County Museum, Clonmel Museum and the Crawford Gallery, Cork. Negotiations are still underway regarding other venues throughout the country. This travelling exhibition will run well into 1993, and may well later travel to Scotland. At each venue an explanatory booklet about the exhibition and conservation is being distributed free of charge; in this way the exhibition will continue to have an impact after it has moved on. IPCRA is grateful to the National Heritage Council who provided the funding for this publication.

There is no point undertaking conservation work unless there are adequate conservation facilities, and here in Ireland these are very meagre indeed. There is an urgent need to set up a range of professional conservation laboratories and workshops, an enormous and varied amount of cultural material is in need of conservation, much of it in our national institutions. These bodies need to be given the resources to deal with the problem. It will be a long-term task but one which should begin without undue delay. Our heritage is our finest asset and what is lost can *never* be replaced. Most visitors from abroad come here to experience our heritage; it is a vital resource and if it is well taken care of it will continue to be of benefit to our economy. Investment in conservation is investment in our future.

There is need of an overall conservation policy in this country. At the conservation colloquium last autumn, a full day was devoted to presentations on current policy by directors of our national institutions. It provided a good opportunity to assess individual conservation policies insofar as they exist. Before the formation of a national conservation policy it will be necessary to assess future needs and, to do this, a national survey must first be undertaken to provide an accurate inventory of material with initial condition reports. Such a survey would paint a more complete picture of what needs to be done and, more importantly, what objects most urgently require conservation. This, in turn, will give an indication of future demands on conservators and give direction to where training in conservation will be most needed.

The issue of training is so important that IPCRA felt it necessary to set up a more formal body in order to pursue the matter with greater authority. A lot of ground work was necessary to achieve this

*Joseph Michael Wright the Elder*, George Villiers, 2nd Duke of Buckingham, 1669. *Cleaned, relined with wax resin, supplied with new stretchers and restored.*

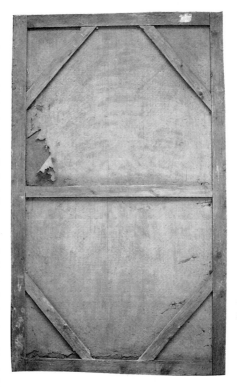

*Verso — Before restoration.*

*Verso — After restoration.*

# CONSERVATION 1991

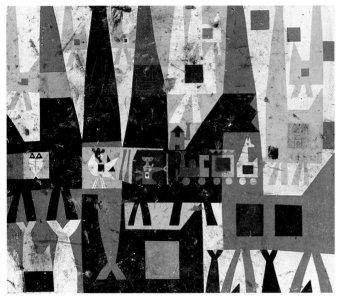

*Painting by the Irish artist, Colin Middleton, RUA, suffered bomb damage. Before and after restoration.*

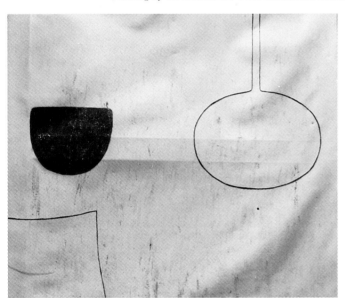
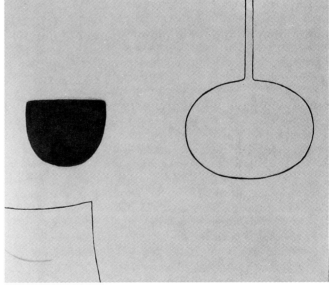

*Painting by William Scott, CBE, suffered blast damage. Before and after restoration.*

and after two years of intense preparation the Institute for the Conservation of Historic and Artistic Works in Ireland was formed. This Institute, incorporated last autumn, is charged with education matters in relation to conservation and has already been active in running short courses for both conservators and allied professionals. In the fullness of time, it will become the professional body dealing with conservation in Ireland, formulating conservation policy and being available for consultation by Government on matters relating to conservation.

It will be responsible for setting standards, devising a code of ethics, promoting training and research, publishing, organising conferences and establishing a conservation centre in Ireland to the highest international standards.

IPCRA is a small voluntary body; it has achieved a considerable amount in a short time thanks to the dedication of its members. It receives no funding and consequently its resources are very limited. Nonetheless the Association will readily make itself available to offer advice and direction whenever necessary. In the

future, as the Association becomes more firmly established, it will be able to provide a greater service to the community. Conservation is a very worthy and worthwhile pursuit and IPCRA is dedicated to excellence in this field.

*Grellan Rourke*

*Grellan Rourke is a conservation architect.*

For further information on the Association or to enquire about the itinerary of the Travelling Exhibition, please contact either the Chairman or the Honorary Secretary, IPCRA, 48 Woodleigh Park, Goatstown, Dublin 14.

# CLASSICAL WATERMARKS

T P Flanagan's recent tour
through Italy and Greece
inspired a series of watercolours
'redolent of place'.
**Christina Kennedy** discusses
them with the artist.

For over two centuries there has existed in Ireland a strong tradition of landscape painting. Today, when we come to consider this dialogue between the artist and his natural environment, nowhere is the tradition more sustained than in the paintings of T P Flanagan, PPRUA, RHA. For many, his vision is synonymous with the landscapes of the northwest of Ireland. He has also painted the demesnes of country houses like Lissadell, Castlecoole and Florence Court. His friend, the poet Seamus Heaney, once described him as 'a haunter of demesne and ditchback'. He returns again and again to the places that haunt his mind's eye; his distillations redolent of place, instant yet timeless, local yet universal. In fact, it is difficult today to visit certain stretches of Fermanagh, Sligo or Donegal without one's responses being informed in some way by Flanagan's vision. To quote Heaney again 'our senses have been tinctured by his sensibility'.

In the summer of 1988, T P Flanagan travelled through Italy and Greece. Although he was intent on keeping a pictorial diary, at the time he had no desire to take these sketches and notations any further. Over the last eighteen months, however, he has had recourse to them when 'in the light of what I had been doing here in Ireland, suddenly, they became of help'. The result of this is a series of watercolours inspired by the sketches and the impressions from his 'Grand Tour' of three and a half years ago.

While T P Flanagan's landscapes of the northwest have come to be regarded signatory, this series of watercolours, though different in location may be considered an 'affirmation'. True, he included overtly classical elements in his paintings before — particularly in his lyrical depictions of such eighteenth-century houses as Castlecoole. More important, however, is an instinctive truth to classical principles that underlies all his work. His is an emotional response with a classical translation informed by what Heaney describes as 'a sort of pining that stirs the unconscious'. If Flanagan's formal principles were 'affirmed' or 'validated' by his journeys through Italy and Greece, so too, in a cathartic way, were his range of palette and his personal 'envelope of light' (a phrase coined by Corot). His travels abroad had the effect of 'verifying' his sense of place with its attendant sureties and idiosyncrasies. He came back

'terribly keen to paint an Irish landscape'. That said, the travel sketchbooks and notes have since precipitated a specific body of work which, in location, are quite separate from the mainstream of T P Flanagan's work, although similar in technique and feeling.[1]

Since T P Flanagan rarely paints 'on site', his working method is well suited to travel. Usually, he will attempt to capture his immediate response to a place through a series of sketches in pencil and crayon: 'I try to record my inspiration in front of nature . . . but to get down the purity of the idea . . . it has to do with selecting, editing, emphasising'. At times he uses photography: 'to capture the details that I wouldn't have time to spend drawing from life — like the contour of a classical cornice, or whatever'. As with almost all of Flanagan's watercolours, each of the European works conforms to a standard format. He employs a rectangular sheet of paper, 22 by 30 inches; sometimes, he divides up the sheet. This standard size has become 'almost a type of view-finder' for him. Superimposed on his vision 'it proportions, coordinates, disposes'.

Quality and diffusion of light, and the colours it effects, has been a fundamental concern in all of Flanagan's paintings. He describes his reaction to the Mediterranean sunlight:

*What strikes you when you go abroad is the constancy of light, of an even light — brilliant, clean. There is no twilight such as we have in Ireland. Twilight is very important in order to come to terms with direct light. The gradual fading of light in Ireland, unlike the Continent, makes for a totally different approach to the way one paints light or is attracted to light. As against that too, in Italy and Greece you can get pure colour in the sky which has a very odd habit of creating, if you look straight into it, a particular type of darkness. If you were going to paint pure Tuscan sunlight in the middle of the day, although you know the sky is a splitting Cerulean blue, you would be far better to paint it somewhere between Davies Grey and Paynes Grey because on paper that would give you the intensity of light that is*

*almost like ashes . . . the light burns so heavy that it loses colour if you look up into it.*

Given that the moist, Irish countryside with its ever-fluctuating weather conditions and effects of light has consistently influenced T P Flanagan's palette in the past, what were his sentiments when faced with a Mediterranean scheme of colour?:

*It's only when you go to Italy that you realise the true meaning of earthcolours . . . you can take the ochres and siennas from your pencil-case, place them on the ground and there they already are! . . . it's incredible to stand beneath a complete raw sienna cliff. Somebody said to me recently that the Irish countryside would make you an expert on greys. Equally, Italy and Greece would make you an expert on ochres. . . . I was reminded of when I was a schoolboy reading the Homeric epics . . . I used to wonder how could a sea be 'wine-dark'? We now know, of course, that the Greek heroes moved about the navigable sea — close to the shores of the islands and the great height of the mountains with their intense sienna and ochre colouring reflected into the still, blue sea, and on hitting the sea it became purple and deep red — hence your 'wine-dark' sea. It was a marvellous colour . . . a marmalade and burnt geranium red which reflected down into the waters.*

T P Flanagan is particularly receptive to those factors, intangible as well as tangible, in a given environment which both inform and describe its sense of place:

*When the artist travels to a new environment he will obviously be concerned with the sort of space he finds himself in, the sort of physical volume around him, and that will also include the quality of stillness and silence. There is nothing more intriguing in a truly pastoral landscape than the quality of stillness and silence. I'm not so much talking about the incidental noises like running water or the sound of a bird or a passing breeze but there is a sort of great, enveloping, tonal dome that you find yourself under that is peculiar to each place. Donegal has its own stillness and silence and, interestingly, I found a very close equivalent to that in Greece. The colours are different but it's that funny relationship of space, stillness and silence in a different landscape that can have cross-cuts into other experiences.*

What struck Flanagan very forcibly on his travels through Italy and Greece was the scale he, at times, encountered, particularly when journeying through the Peloponnese. Here were sheer mountains

# CLASSICAL WATERMARKS

and deep gorges 'on a scale totally shocking' and incomparable with any in his Irish experience. His one regret is that he didn't get the opportunity (through lack of time) 'to face the total challenge of that enormous scale'. He hopes, some day, to return and embark upon a series of studies to resolve this. 'I was reminded of something somebody wrote about Turner (not that I'm comparing myself to Turner!), but when he first went to Switzerland and Italy his eye was so completely thrown (by the sense of scale), that when accommodating himself again to the British landscape, in attempting that same sense of scale he began to leave things out'.

T P Flanagan also mentions Poussin in relation to the evocation of scale in the classical landscape. He is a great admirer of Poussin and, indeed, of his disciple Cézanne. Kenneth Clark, quoting Hazlitt, wrote of Poussin: 'he applied nature to his own purposes, worked out her images according to standards of his own thoughts'.[2] Poussin dwelt on the notion of the landscape as a harmonious balance of the horizontal and the vertical. In a fundamental way this aesthetic informs all of Flanagan's work. While his paintings have variously been described as elegant, lyrical, civilised, Claudian even, it would be wrong to neglect their inherent Cartesian quality. The artist

testifies to this: 'no matter how rough around the edges you want it to be . . . there are basic structures, scaffolding. I would say that I use the same compositional discipline for a painting like one of the Boglands as I would in, for example, the *Villa Lante* . . . structurally I like to order things'.

However, it was less the existing sense of order which inspired T P Flanagan to sketch the *Villa Lante* than the 'lovely interplay of the man-made and the natural', where the artificial became naturalised 'by accident rather than contrivance'. The artist prefers it that way: 'when I was about eighteen I read a book entitled *On the Pleasure of Ruins*, which gave me a feeling for things not perfect, that once were'. Flanagan was fascinated, in particular, by the quality of the light at the *Villa Lante*, especially by the black shadows cast by the strong, Italian sunlight:

*It was the dramatic darkness to the right of the villa in the full middle of the day and the sun being trapped by the great, heavy, green growth there . . . and the absolute, almost nudity of the urns — I liked the way they formed a nice sort of balance . . . they seemed of stone or marble, above and reflected in the water . . . and then the cypress trees and hills behind and everything conspiring to, as it were, complement echoes — artificial forms echoed by natural forms and natural forms, one almost felt, growing in sympathy with architectural forms.*

Painted almost in *grisaille* but for the splashes of dappled green light, *Fountain of the Giants, Villa Lante* is a wonderful study of reflected and refracted light on stone and marble. Beneath a cascading fountain surmounted by playful *putti*, reclines a giant holding a cornucopia, his languorous form echoing, yet softening, the insistent horizontals and verticals of the composition. Their presence is further mollified by the impressionistic technique employed by the artist, with the result that the forms seem to emerge, almost by accident. In the case of the giant: 'I didn't begin by drawing in that figure . . . I painted in all the dappled light, and he seemed to want to be there and I coaxed him out of the paper'.

In the great tradition of classical landscape painting, *Road to Orvieto* exudes a calm, simple grandeur and captures the very essence of the *campagna* in the full heat of the Italian summer. Here the landscape rendered itself easily divided, visually, into its component parts, for direct translation by the artist to his paper in washes of pure colour. There was no danger of overworking: 'its own simplicity forced you to stop . . even the farmhouse, from that angle, was practically without windows . . . simply an architectural form'. The heat of the day transfixed all forms and: 'lent such dignity and quiet that you didn't want any cloud . . . just

*T P Flanagan, Road to Orvieto, 1991, watercolour 33 x 68.6 cm.*

*T P Flanagan,* Fountain of the Giants, Villa Lante, *1991, watercolour 56 x 76.2 cm.*

*T P Flanagan,* Villa Lante, *1991 watercolour 56 x 76.2 cm.*

*T P Flanagan*, Plains of Argos from Mycenae, 1991, *watercolour 56 x 76.2 cm.*

# CLASSICAL WATERMARKS

that burning feeling'. The sense of receding space in this composition is further heightened by the incursion of the road into the fields: 'every inward movement takes on specific creativity because one is pitting it against a series of horizontals and verticals . . . the tyre-tracks in the wet tar on the road are like a graphic statement − a piece of drawing . . . and those marvellous umbrella pines give a triumphal presence, a sense of procession, to the road . . . one can understand from where the Romans got their feeling for ceremony'.

All of the sketches made by Flanagan reflect aspects of places to which he personally responded, rather than depicting any 'typical', formal view. For instance, although the Baths of Caracalla hold much interest for him, he has yet: 'to get around to seeing what way to treat them':

*What particularly interests me is somewhere between the monumental arches, that is, the basic interior structures that have been robbed of the marble, and the fragments of the Baths themselves and what remains of them in the ground − fragments of mosaic, for instance. . . . part of a dolphin or an edge with a Greek Key or egg-and-dart pattern − and to relate these fragments in some way to the arch and to do so without doing a formal view, because it is so much a fragmented place . . . all bits of a bigger story.*

In the *Plains of Argos from Mycenae*, Flanagan testifies to his innate interest in the fragments of fallen civilisations and in the immutability of a landscape which man once controlled but has, sooner or later, had to surrender to the forces of wild nature.

*What interested me was the feeling of enormous permanence of the landscape . . . hills that have been there since prehistoric times, and that primal feeling − like a great*

*throb, almost, coming out of the ground. Everything is desolate, broken . . . man's taming influence on this landscape has been a temporary one. Nature keeps coming through − like those wonderful thistles with that sort of spinning movement like little burnt-out suns. All that exists of man's influence is a short flight of steps. In the context of this landscape they invite you to speculate on a type of drama, if you like. You could imagine players going up those steps onto a level platform, or celebrants with masks, to perform some rite. Individual boulders, like fire-bricks, storing heat . . . cast shadows of browns and greens which almost vibrate . . . the whole landscape has a very hallucinatory quality.*

T P Flanagan's senses were particularly heightened when visiting amphitheatres. In his depiction of *The Amphitheatre, Pompeii by Moonlight*, he has imbued his description of the place with an intense pathos. He cannot recall ever having experienced in Ireland such a sense of 'the residue of the past', especially poignant 'at night with the warm smell of the pines'. Bathed in moonlight, this great, tiered arc seems to act as a receptacle for the reflected light of the moon. Beyond the sentinel cypresses Mount Vesuvius rises in the background:

*It was one of those occasions of moonlight almost creating a snow-like effect together with a mist gathering on the hot land in the cool evening . . . Vesuvius became a type of Alp . . . I was interested, not in the silver of the moon on the olive trees but in that which was trapped in the cypresses . . . in the Pompeiian moonlight there was an enormous profusion of mauve, purple and blue colours and of rich darks without, necessarily, the intrusion of black.*

The amphitheatre inspired two very separate images in Flanagan's mind − on the one hand of 'a great piece of metal jewellery, like an adornment under the

mountain'; on the other 'a drum on which all sorts of things were enacted, and upon the surface of which were produced sounds that were, on the whole, very mournful'. The sketches and the finished painting they inspired have brought Flanagan back to thinking about 'the sort of generic significance of the circle, square and triangle . . . shapes that we take for granted today'. He is now thinking of working on a series of large oils 'based on the idea of the circle as an arena'. This in turn, he says will present him 'with the challenge of how much parochial detail to retain'.

For over eighteen months now T P Flanagan's recollections of his travels in Italy and Greece have variously begun to find their way from his mind's eye and onto paper. This series of paintings is not his only output during this time but is concurrent with his ongoing enquiries into the Irish countryside.

These paintings have, however, raised a number of issues, formal and intuitive, and have left the way open for the artist to explore. Wherever the location, there is a special symbiotic relationship between Flanagan's perception of the landscape and his manipulation of the medium of watercolour. In critical terms, he has made a major contribution to this medium in Ireland.

*Christina Kennedy*

*Christina Kennedy is a free-lance art lecturer and exhibitions organiser.*

NOTES

1. All quotes in this article are from the author's interview with T P Flanagan, 26 January 1992.
2. Kenneth Clark, *Landscape into Art*, (Pelican), 1956, p.80.

# BRONZE AGE GOLD AT THE NATIONAL MUSEUM

In August 1991 the National Museum opened a new permanent exhibition of its unrivalled collection of Bronze Age goldwork from Ireland. *ÓR – Ireland's Gold* occupies the main hall of the Kildare Street building which has been extensively restored in recent years. The exhibition at the National Museum has been generously supported by the Boyne Valley Honey Company.

The National Museum's collection of Bronze Age goldwork is one of the largest and most important in Western Europe. It owes its existence to the vision and efforts of the Royal Irish Academy which from its foundation in 1785 devoted much time and effort to collecting archaeological objects from Ireland. Shortly after its foundation, the Academy established an Antiquities Committee to look after all antiquarian pursuits including the formation of a collection of archaeological artefacts. Irish prehistoric gold ornaments found an important place in the collection from the beginning. Throughout the succeeding century many prominent antiquarians including General Vallencey, George Petrie and Sir William Wilde served on the Committee. The collection grew by donations and purchases and gradually developed into a museum of Irish antiquities. Important acquisitions included the gold torcs found at Tara, Co Meath, in 1810. A very significant addition was made in 1841 by the purchase, through public subscription, of the collection of the late Dean Dawson of St Patrick's Cathedral. It included the large gold dress-fastener from Castlekelly, Co Roscommon, the bulla from the Bog of Allen and the gold collars from Ardcrony and Borrisnow, Co Tipperary. Other important pieces of prehistoric goldwork were acquired by the purchase of the collection of Major Sirr, also in 1841. Throughout the nineteenth century the collection of Bronze Age goldwork continued to grow and many important papers were pubished in the Academy's *Transactions and Proceedings*. Following an agreement between the Academy and the Government the complete collections of antiquities were transferred to the new Museum of Science and Art (now National Museum of Ireland) in Kildare Street in 1890.

In 1862 the first corpus of the gold collection was published by Sir William Wilde. The catalogue was arranged in typological groups and was very well illustrated. Almost sixty years later, in ·

A spectacular collection of gold ornaments found in Ireland, dating from as early as 2200 BC, is now on permanent exhibition in the National Museum of Ireland. **Mary Cahill** describes some of these national treasures.

*Gold Foil-Covered Lead Bulla, Bog of Allen. Later Bronze Age c. 800–700 BC. National Museum of Ireland.*

1920, E C R Armstrong, then Keeper of Irish Antiquities, published his comprehensive *Catalogue of Irish Gold Ornaments*, which contained descriptions and illustrations of almost 500 gold objects.

The discovery in 1932 of a gold collar at Gleninsheen, Co Clare, added another important object to the collection and in each succeeding decade new discoveries were made throughout the country. Several important private collections were also acquired. The discovery of a hoard of boxes, discs and dress-fasteners at Ballinesker, Co Wexford, in September 1990 and the purchase of the Northumberland Collection in December 1990 have enriched the National Collections immeasurably.

The immense quantity of Bronze Age gold from Ireland suggests that rich sources of gold were known. Although gold has been found in Ireland at a number of locations, particularly in Co Wicklow and Co Tyrone, it has not been possible yet to identify where the prehistoric sources were but those most likely to have been recognised and exploited by prehistoric people are alluvial deposits from rivers and streams. This placer gold is weathered out from the parent rock and can be recovered using simple washing techniques such as panning.

In Europe the earliest evidence for goldworking dates to the 5th millennium BC. By the end of the 3rd millennium, gold working had become well established in Ireland and Britain, together with a highly productive copper- and bronzeworking industry. While we do not know precisely how the late Neolithic people of Ireland became familiar with metalworking, it is clear that it was introduced as a fully developed technique. Essential metal working skills must have been introduced by people already experienced at all levels of production, from identification and recovery of ores through all stages of the manufacturing process.

During the Earlier Bronze Age, between 2200–1700 BC, the goldsmiths produced a limited range of ornaments. Their principal products were sundiscs, usually found in pairs like those from Tedavnet, Co Monaghan, plain and decorated bands, and expecially the crescentic gold collars called *lunulae* (Latin for 'little moon'). These objects were all made from sheet gold – a technique which is particularly well demonstrated by the *lunulae*, many of which are beaten extremely thinly. The *lunula* from Rossmore Park, Co Monaghan exemplifies the high level of control and skill achieved by the earliest goldsmiths. During this early period decoration consists mainly of geometric motifs such as triangles, lozenges and groups of lines arranged in patterns. Incision using a sharp tool and *repoussé* (working from behind to produce a raised pattern) were the principal techniques employed.

At about 1200 BC there was a remarkable change in the types of ornaments made in the workshops. New gold-working techniques were developed and new styles began to appear. Twisting bars or strips of gold became the most commonly used technique and a great variety of twists can be seen. By varying the form of the bar or strip of gold used, and by controlling the degree of torsion, a great range of styles can be produced. Torcs, varying in size from earrings such as those from Castlerea, Co Roscommon, to waist torcs like the exceptional pair from Tara, Co Meath, are represented. Many of these ornaments required the use of very large amounts of gold, suggesting that a new source for gold had been discovered. Meanwhile the use of heavy sheet gold continued, as can be seen in the massive

*Gold Nugget, Co. Wicklow. National Museum of Ireland.*

*Pair of Gold Lock-Rings, Co. Limerick. Later Bronze Age c. 800–700 BC. National Museum of Ireland.*

*Gold Lunula, Rossmore Park, Co. Monaghan. Earlier Bronze Age c. 2000 BC. National Museum of Ireland.*

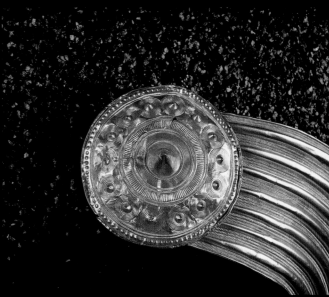

*Gold Collar, detail of terminal. Ardcrony, Co. Tipperary. Later Bronze Age c. 800–700 BC. National Museum of Ireland.*

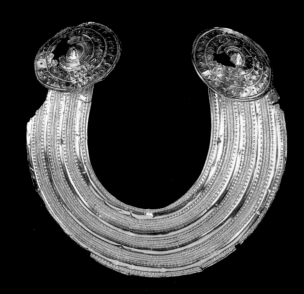

*Gold Collar, Borrisnoe, Co Tipperary. Later Bronze Age 800–700 BC. National Museum of Ireland.*

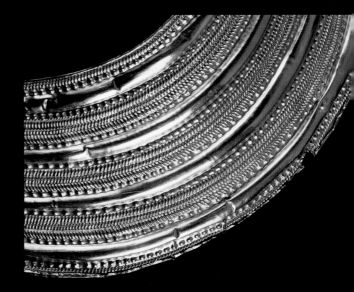

*Gold Collar, detail, Borrisnoe, Co. Tipperary. Later Bronze Age 800–700 BC. National Museum of Ireland.*

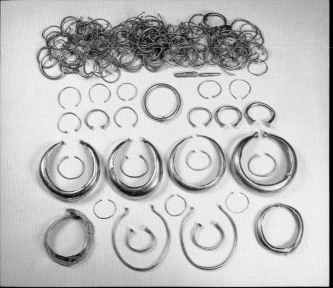

*Hoard of Gold Ornaments including collars and bracelets, Mooghaun, Co. Clare. Later Bronze Age c. 800–700 BC, National Museum of Ireland.*

*Two Gold Discs, Kilmuckeridge, Co. Wexford. Earlier Bronze Age c. 2200–1800 BC. National Museum of Ireland.*

*Gold Dress-Fastener, Clones, Co. Monaghan. Later Bronze Age c. 800–700 BC. National Museum of Ireland.*

*Hoard of Gold Balls, Tumna, Co. Roscommon. Later Bronze Age c. 800–700 BC. National Museum of Ireland.*

*Two Gold Armlets, Skreen, Co. Sligo and Dysert, Co. Westmeath. Later Bronze Age c. 1200–1000 BC. National Museum of Ireland.*

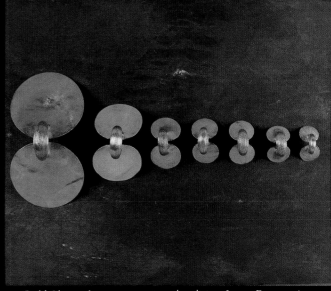

*Gold Sleeve fasteners, various localities. Later Bronze Age c. 800–700 BC. National Museum of Ireland*

# BRONZE AGE GOLD AT THE NATIONAL MUSEUM

armlets from Derrinboy, Co Offaly.

Between 1000–850 BC there seems to have been a lull in goldworking, as there are few gold objects which can be dated to that time. It may be that this apparent gap is caused by changes in hoarding practices which have made it difficult to identity objects of this period.

However, the succeeding phase was an extremely productive one and is noted for the great variety and quality of both gold- and bronzeworking. The goldsmiths developed to a very high degree all the skills necessary to make a range of ornaments of various forms and technique. The same care and attention to detail was applied to objects large and small, irrespective of whether they required the expenditure of vast quantities of gold or only a few grammes.

The goldwork of this period can be divided into two main types. Solid objects, cast or made from bars and ingots, such as the bracelets, dress-fasteners and neck-rings, contrast dramatically with the delicate collars, boxes and discs made of sheet gold. Gold wire was also used in a number of ways, expecially to produce the ornaments called lock-rings. Thin gold foil, sometimes highly decorated, was used to cover objects made of other metals such as copper, bronze or lead. This technique can be observed at its best in the *bulla* from the Bog of Allen — a heart-shaped lead core covered by a highly decorated fine gold foil. The purpose of this and other similar objects is not fully understood but they may have been used as amulets or charms.

Decoration is an important feature of Later Bronze Age goldwork. Many different motifs were used to achieve the complicated patterns which often cover the entire surface of the object. Among the most popular designs are arrangements of geometric patterns, concentric circles, raised bosses — domed or conical — and rope and herring-bone patterns. The goldsmiths used a variety of techniques to produce these motifs, including combinations of repoussé and chasing, stamping with specially made punches, as well as incising the surface of the gold.

Our knowledge of Bronze Age goldwork from Ireland is largely dependent on the discovery of groups of objects in hoards. At least 160 hoards of the Later Bronze Age have been recorded from Ireland. One of the earliest references known is to

a hoard — now lost — of gold ornaments found at Ballymorris, Co Laois, in 1670. Hoards have been found accidentally during the course of various activities including turf-cutting, ploughing and quarrying. They are almost never discovered during archaeological excavations because the places in which they were deposited are remote from settlements, workshops or burial sites.

Several different types of hoard have been identified. These include founders' hoards consisting of scrap metal; merchants' hoards containing objects for trade and ritual; and votive hoards deliberately deposited with no intention and, in many cases, no possibility of recovery. Hoards can contain a mixture of tools, weapons and personal ornaments, or they may consist of a single object type. Several hoards of gold ornaments are known, while others contain a mixture of gold and bronze objects and may sometimes contain also necklaces of amber beads. Where tools and weapons occur together with ornaments or jewellery, it has been suggested that these may represent the personal regalia of an individual.

In Ireland the number of spectacular discoveries from bogs suggests that they were regarded as special places by the people of the Bronze Age particularly during its later phases. In the eighteenth century a remarkable series of discoveries was made in the Bog of Cullen in Co Tipperary. A very large number of bronze and gold objects was found during turf-cutting over a period of about seventy years. Contemporary records describe a variety of gold ornaments including several large collars and vessels. Many finds of bronze weapons were also made. Today only one gold object can be positively identified from the Bog of Cullen. It is the decorated terminal — the only surviving fragment — of a once-magnificent dress-fastener. This object passed through generations of the Damer family (some of whom lived at Shronell, Co Tipperary, and in Dorset) until it was acquired by Birmingham City Museum. Many nineteenth century gold finds were probably melted down by jewellers for re-use. Indeed one documented case describes the use, as fillings for teeth, of part of a gold dress-fastener from near Bansha in Co Tipperary by a Clonmel jeweller, watchmaker and dentist.

A large hoard of gold ornaments found in 1854 in marshy ground close

to a lake at Mooghaun North, Co Clare, contained over 150 objects. It was discovered accidentally by workmen building a railway between Limerick and Ennis, near a lake about two miles from Newmarket-on-Fergus, Co Clare. Accounts of the discovery differ in detail but it seems that, in the immediate aftermath of the discovery, much of the hoard was sold to dealers and jewellers and ended up in the melting pot. Some reports say that the hoard was found in a small, rectangular structure made of stones in which the objects were arranged in layers.

The exact composition of the hoard will probably never be known but, in June 1854, a portion of it consisting of 146 objects weighing over 11lbs (5 kilos), was exhibited by Dr J H Todd at a meeting of the Royal Irish Academy. The hoard consisted mostly of bracelets but also included at least six gold collars and two neck-rings. These heavy sheet gold collars are deeply curved and have small solid terminals. They are known only from Mooghaun. Likewise, the gold neck-rings have not been found elsewhere. It is difficult to explain the reason for the deposition of such a huge wealth of gold. Its discovery close to a lake in what may have been once marshy ground suggests a ritual deposit but the reported use of a stone-lined box may suggest that the objects were hidden during a period of stress.

Today only twenty-nine original pieces can be identified from Mooghaun. It seems that the vast bulk of it was melted down and we can now gain no more than an impression of its original size and splendour.

During the Bronze Age, Irish goldsmiths did not function as an isolated group of specialist craftsmen on the western shores of Europe. While they maintained links with Britain and Europe, drawing some of their inspiration from trends current abroad, they always imparted a characteristically Irish style to each product. At the same time they constantly expressed their own individuality and creativity by producing at all periods gold ornaments which are unparalleled elsewhere. They have left us a great national inheritance which serves as an inspiration and an aspiration.

*Mary Cahill*

*Mary Cahill is an Assistant Keeper in the Irish Antiquities Division of the National Museum of Ireland.*

# SIR ALFRED CHESTER BEATTY AND HIS LIBRARY

In April 1964, thanks to the efforts of the Irish Government, Sir Alfred Chester Beatty was granted a private audience of Pope Paul VI. During this visit to Rome he was also introduced to the Vatican Library, an experience which gave him singular satisfaction. Afterwards, he wrote to Thomas McGreevy, 'After seeing the Vatican Library, I am afraid I was suffering from a swollen head.'

This was the understandable reaction of an owner whose holdings rivalled, and in many ways surpassed, the magnificence of one of the greatest libraries in the world. Chester Beatty had for many years sent a copy of each new catalogue of his collection as it was published to Cardinal Tisserant at the Vatican Library, an ordinary courtesy. He was first recognised as a major collector when he loaned some items to the Persian Exhibition in London in 1931.

The reasons for his gratification were many. In Dublin were held the oldest known versions of the Greek Bible, or Septuagint, and of the New Testament, written on papyrus. The Gospels of John and Luke were therefore older than any others then known, older than the Codex Vaticanus or the Codex Britannicus of the British Library, both dated to the fourth century, and until the discovery of the Beatty papyri in 1930 believed to be the oldest versions of the New Testament.

*The Chester Beatty Library in Dublin houses one of the world's most magnificent international collections.* **Kate Robinson** *describes some of its highlights.*

Further, in 170 AD a Syriac Priest, Tatian, had written a Diatessaron, or 'harmonization' of the four Gospels which was widely used throughout the Middle East as a Mass Book until a new edict ordered that each of the four Gospels must be read separately. It fell into disuse and the eventual suspicion was that it had never existed. Then, in 1956, a Commentary on this work, written in the fourth century A D by St Ephraem, one of the Fathers of the Church, and quoting extensively from the original, was discovered at the Chester Beatty Library. The implications from a textual point of view were profound.

Chester Beatty was born in New York in 1873 in a house on the site now occupied by the Rockefeller Centre. His paternal antecedents were Irish: his great-grandfather, David, is buried in the Churchyard of Armagh Cathedral with his wife and ten children, of whom Chester's father was one. His mother's family, original English colonists, had settled in Boston in 1635.

Chester attended Columbia Univer-

sity, whose School of Mining Engineering had a considerable reputation. He graduated in 1898 with marks that put him top of his class in every subject except one and total marks that were among the highest ever achieved in the School's history.

It was tragedy that really led Beatty to create this major collection. In 1911 his first wife died from typhoid fever, leaving him with two young children, a boy and a girl. By this time his great mining skills had made him a multi-millionaire. Shortly after his wife's death he himself was given only a short time to live, since he had contracted silicosis, the miners' dread occupational disease. He survived, but could never return to active mining which he had so thoroughly enjoyed. He lived until he was 93.

In 1913, Beatty remarried, Mrs Edith Duke of New York. He had bought the magnificent Baroda House in Kensington Palace Gardens the year before and the family now settled permanently in London. But he had not shot his bolt with the mining industry. In December 1914, he launched his new survey company, the Selection Trust, with a total capital of £20,000. It was to become at one stage the wealthiest firm in the world. Meanwhile he had discovered that London, though unrivalled as a business base had also the unkindest climate. Its notorious 'pea-souper' fogs could be fatal for anyone with

*Fragment of St Luke's Gospel. Third century papyrus. Chester Beatty Library, Dublin.*

Chinese Jade Book. Buddha Enthroned with Worshippers. *AD 1732.*
*Gold on jade. 24.1 x 9.0 cm. Chester Beatty Library, Dublin.*

*Gospel Book in Bosnian Cyrillic: Finest calligraphic example extant.*
*Beginning of the Gospel of St. John. Late 14th – early 15th century: post 1371.*
*Tempera on vellum, 16 x 10 cm. Chester Beatty Library, Dublin.*

*Qur'an: Naskh Script. Turkey. 14th century AD/8th century AH. Tempera on paper. 35.6 x 26.2 cm.*
*Chester Beatty Library, Dublin.*

# SIR ALFRED CHESTER BEATTY AND HIS LIBRARY

delicate lungs. In 1914 his doctors advised him to go away for the winter and the Beattys visited Cairo for the first time. So balmy was the climate that they bought a house there and eventually built one to their own design.

A story, perhaps apocryphal, illustrates Beatty's predilection. It is told in Arthur Wilson's entertaining biography. Sitting in the front row at one of the big auctions in New York were a man and his son, aged ten. What they had been waiting for was eventually presented with great ceremony to the assembled connoisseurs, 'a fragment of mineral calcite, in a delicate shade of pink overlaid with crystals of apatite . . . (which) perfectly formed, sparkled in what little light infiltrated the smoky atmosphere.' In response to the auctioneer's request for a bid, the boy offered 'ten cents.' Despite many pleas no other bid was tendered and Chester Beatty walked proudly home with his first treasure.[1]

By 1914 a catalogue of his snuff-bottles gave the number in his possession as 1,674. They attracted Beatty's interest because so many of them were made from semi-precious or precious stones. Jade held a particular attraction for him because of its rarity, and many of these exquisite miniatures were carved from it. The Collection now numbers less than a thousand but it represents the highest quality among collectable items and the greatest variety in design and materials including ivory, porcelain, chalcedony, glass, crystal and other stones.

Quality was always a pre-eminent requirement for this collector, who would replace an item he already possessed for a better example if it became available. 'Quality, quality, always the quality,' he wrote to his Librarian, AJH Wilkinson in 1955.[2]

Though he never claimed to be a scholar, and technically, of course, he was not, his eye could put many a scholar to shame. The collection was his, his design, his acquisition, his great love, and until the day of his death gave him the most intense pleasure that beauty can bestow on the refined soul.

Beatty's experience in Cairo was probably the turning-point in his life, notwithstanding his spectacular career in mining and its abrupt end. It was here that he came into contact with the dazzling, virtuoso magnificence of Islamic art, encapsulated in the pages of the Qur'an.

*From* Ise Monogatari, *Beginning of 16th Century. Painted Book. 29.8 x 22.3 cm. Chester Beatty Library, Dublin.*

Shah Abbas in Qazvin, Iran, Shah–Namah: "The Simurgh Carrying the Infant Zal to her Nest." 1587–1597. *Chester Beatty Library, Dublin.*

His fortune allowed him to acquire magnificent specimens of this unrivalled art-form. His wife, herself a connoisseur of standing, supported him in all his searches while simultaneously making impressive collections of her own, including French nineteenth century paintings and Western illuminated manuscripts of the medieval period.

After her death in 1952 her prestigious collection reverted to Beatty. He hoped to make a gift of a large number of the paintings to the National Gallery in Dublin, but death duties in England necessitated their sale. It was the finest among them, including many Impressionist and Post-Impressionist works, that had to go. Nevertheless, he did give a large number of paintings and drawings to the Gallery.

His collection of Qur'ans led Beatty's imagination to a new and perhaps impossible dream: 'To show in one place every material on which man has communicated with man in all parts of the world and through all periods of time.'[3]

As a result, his searches led him as far back as the Babylonian Empire to the first known examples of human script on the clay tablets of up to 2,700 years BC. Those in the collection are commercial records, accounts, transactions written with a stylus on the wet clay in a cuneiform script sealed with the cylinder seals of the scribes employed to write them. A number of these seals can also be seen beside the tablets.

Following this, chronologically, is an Egyptian papyrus written in early hieratic script in 1160 BC, during the reign of King Rameses V in Thebes. To quote Sir Alan Gardiner who edited the text when it was published for Chester Beatty in 1931: 'Here, for the first time, we have a long mytholigical narrative composed solely for literary and non-utilitarian purposes, and here too, on the *verso,* are the most complete, intelligible and poetic love-songs which Ancient Egypt has bequeathed to us'.[4]

A translation of the poem reads:

*Seven days from yesterday I have not seen*
*my beloved*
*And sickness hath crept over me,*
*And I am become heavy in my limbs,*
*And am unmindful of my own body.*
*If the master-physicians come to me,*
*My heart hath no comfort of their remedies,*
*And the magicians, no resource is in them,*
*My malady is not diagnosed.*
*Better for me is my beloved than any*
*remedies,*

# SIR ALFRED CHESTER BEATTY AND HIS LIBRARY

*More important is she for me than the entire*
*compendium of medicine,*
*My salvation is when she enters from*
*without,*
*When I see her, then am I well;*
*Opens she her eye, my limbs are young*
*again;*
*Speaks she, and I am strong.*
*And when I embrace her, she banishes evil,*
*And it passes from me for seven days.*[5].

Another papyrus, *The Book of the Dead of the Lady Neskhons*, written about 300 BC, is in perfect condition and the hieroglyphics can be easily interpreted by the expert. These 'books' were sheets covered with magical texts and images called vignettes which the Egyptians placed in the tomb with the bodies of their deceased to help them pass through the dangers of the Underworld and attain an afterlife of bliss in the Field of Reeds, the Egyptian Heaven.

Papyrus, the great plant that grows in the marshes of the Nile and other Middle Eastern sites, provided the first writing material, from which the name 'paper' is derived. It was the invention of the Egyptians who had been using it, as we have seen, for more than a thousand years BC. It was not to be challenged until the invention of parchment by the Greeks at Pergamum. But neither it, nor vellum, nor leather ever totally replaced papyrus in the Mediterranean region or the Middle East. It was really only replaced with the invention of paper and the printing-press in the fifteenth century. Other writing materials shown in the Library are slates and wax tablets used in Greece and Rome from very early times.

It seems that the codex form of the book was never used by the Greeks, Romans, or in the East, their literature being usually written on scrolls. Investigations indicate that the codex was first used by the Christians, and this fact is emphasised in the papryus codices of the Old and New Testaments in the Beatty Library. It is argued that passages needed for liturgical or other reference could be more quickly found in a codex than in a scroll.

By 300 AD the codex had achieved parity with the roll. Although it has never been proved, it is possible that the codex was first produced in Coptic Egypt. In the Beatty Library the oldest, on vellum, is a gospel book written in Egypt and bound with wooden covers and leather spine and dated to the sixth or seventh century, and there are a number of other wooden and

*Ethiopian: Miracles of Jesus. Christ with Simeon. Second half of 18th century. Tempera on parchment. 36 x 29.4 cms. Chester Beatty Library, Dublin.*

*Firdawsi of Bursa, Sulayman–Namah: The Queen of Sheba. 1453 AD/857 AH Tempera on paper. 44.3 x 31.0 cm. Chester Beatty Library, Dublin.*

leather bindings of approximately the same date, also of Egyptian origin. Vellum and parchment facilitated the development of the decorated or illuminated manuscripts which were brought to perfection during the first millenium AD. Many such books of Christian origin are contained in the Library, from Western and Eastern Europe, Russia, Armenia and Ethiopia.

Typical of the fine discrimination of Chester Beatty is the delightful 'Rosarium,' a little book containing miscellaneous prayers which once belonged to King Philip II of Spain, that strange recluse who spent so much of his time in prayer, a reluctant ruler. The thirty-three illuminations have been attributed to Simon Bening of Bruges, and the book is only one of three surviving manuscripts from the hand of this, the last and greatest of Flemish miniaturists who died in 1561. It was hardly known until it was reproduced in facsimile in 1986.

The 'Book of Hours' was a desirable possession and royalty and nobility often competed to own the most brilliant example. There are many in the Library, one of the most famous being the *Coetivy Hours*, made for Prigent de Coetivy, Admiral of France, who himself was the owner of a celebrated library. It dates from the first half of the fifteenth century and contains 148 miniatures attributed to the Bedford Master. The oldest vellum manuscript in the Collection is the Flemish *Stavelot Bible* which dates from the year 1000 AD.

One item in the collection is remarkable for its historiated initials. It is an eleventh or twelfth century version of St Augustine's *De Civitate Dei*. A most powerful, logical treatise, it encapsulated the Saint's philosophy of the world and mankind, and had an influence that extended throughout the Christian world and beyond its own time.

Not all the Western manuscripts are gospel or prayer-books. A splendid version of the *Thebaid* by the Roman poet, Statius, is lavishly illustrated with miniatures painted mainly in grisaille. It is the only book known to have been illuminated by Altichiero Altichieri, one of the great fresco painters of the Trecento in Verona.

To Chester Beatty, the most important part of his Collection was the Islamic section. Magisterial in its holdings of the sacred Qur'an, which are unmatched outside the Topkapi of the Sultans, it

*Hiroshige, Small Lane at Atago. From Series, 'One Hundred Views of Famous Places, in Edo.'*
*19th century. Woodblock print. Chester Beatty Library, Dublin.*

新玉の天氏々きるとあ○○きる
日とい○○きの諍の初春

弥生蕃雛丸

り○○○○あ○○○
○の○れ○○多れ
○○○○○○○
○○○○て

四方真顔

友や唯よ
まり○○は
や○りを
る○そ
○○ひ
初諍の
撑

三千舘挑實

北溪

*Hokkei, Rooster Threatening a Painted Cock. 1825. Surimono. 21.9 x 18.9 cms.*
*Chester Beatty Library, Dublin.*

represents every period and every locale in which Islamic spirituality was practised. The most precious of the Qur'ans is that written by Ibn-al-Bawwab in Baghdad in 1001, and which shows the earliest form of the Naskhi script surviving. One of the three greatest calligraphers in all Islam, he was, unusually, also the illuminator of his own work. Ibn-al-Bawwab's claim to fame was to have perfected the style of writing invented by Ibn-Muqla in the early tenth century and to have created from it an elegant and beautiful art-form. He was reputed to have copied the Qur'an sixty-four times.

Arabic calligraphy is the Queen of the Arts. The Qur'anic text, which is always written in Arabic, must aspire to absolute perfection and beauty. We are told that 'the Qur'an was transmitted to the Prophet Muhammad in the Arabic tongue, through the intermediary of the Archangel Gabriel, and it therefore has the status of Divine speech. The Prophet heard . . . a voice commanding him: 'Recite! for thy Lord is most Beneficent. He has taught the use of the pen. He has

*Turkish.* Two Lines of Persian Verse illustrated by a Banquet Scene. *16th–17th century. 41.5 x 27.2 cm. Chester Beatty Library. Dublin.*

taught man that which he knew not." (Qur'an, XCVI, 1–5.)[6]

It is a short distance from here to the marvels of penmanship that decorate the pages of the vast number of Arabic manuscripts that are preserved in the Library.

In 1985 the Chester Beatty Library welcomed two unusual visitors, the Crown Prince Akihito and his wife Princess Michiko, now Emperor and Empress of Japan, during their State Visit to Ireland. They came to view the Japanese artefacts which are many and varied, ranging from tsuba, or sword-guards, to *inro, netsuke,* painted scrolls, printed books, as well as the famous collection of woodblock prints.

The Crown Prince was impressed by the splendour of the section, the quality of the items. A special exhibition of Surimono showed him what he could no longer see at home in such profusion. These prints were published privately on refined paper with technical intricacies that were not possible on the more popular publications. That is not to say

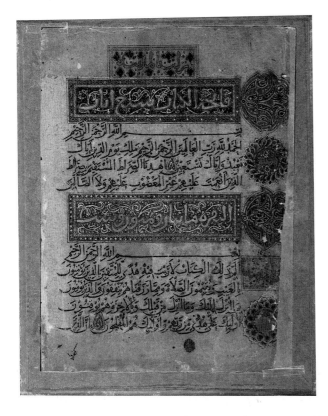

*Ibn-al-Bawwab, Qur'an: Naskh Script. Baghdad. 1001 AD/391 AH. Tempera and ink on paper. 17.7 x 13.7 cm. Chester Beatty Library Dublin.*

# SIR ALFRED CHESTER BEATTY AND HIS LIBRARY

that the ordinary prints were not spectacular — art history proclaims their influence. So highly reputed are these that some years ago Mr Tatsuo Endo, who represents the thirtieth generation of art restorers in his family, came to Dublin to restore them, staying for a month.

In March 1991, a great privilege was bestowed on the Chester Beatty Library when His Holiness the Dalai Lama came to open the Buddhist Exhibition, which presented artefacts from the sources of the religion throughout Eastern Asia, a unique collection which to his surprise lacked a bell, one of the most essential items in Buddhist ritual. He presented one, thus completing the range of exhibits illustrating this great religion.

The Parabaiks, large folding books from Burma, show the story of the Buddha's life in highly-coloured paintings lavishly decorated with gold. They may be all the more precious now, due to the on-going disturbances in that country.

The Chinese had a penchant for distinction — they made not snuff-boxes but snuff-bottles; they carved convoluted

*Bichitr, Portrait of the Emperor Jahangir, (1605 – 1668.) 17th century. Tempera on paper. 38.7 x 27.5 cm. Chester Beatty Library, Dublin.*

cups from rhinoceros-horn; they engraved precious documents on jade. The *Diamond Sutra (Prajnaparamita)* is still one of the most popular Buddhist scriptures in China or Japan and there are two versions in the Library, one complete, the other shortened, both texts engraved on jade. The older, dated 1723, was probably made for the Emperor Qien-Lung (1736 – 95). It is written in gold on fifty-three folios of pale green jade with a 'frontispiece' of three folios showing a continuous line-drawing of Buddha enthroned with guardians and worshippers.

The condensed version of the same text is written, also in gold, on eight extremely thin sheets of green jade. It belonged to the Dowager Empress Cigi who died in 1908. Another book, dated 1760, is presumed also to have been made for the Emperor Qien-Lung. Inscribed on blue jade, it purports to show the portraits of the original sixteen Lohans, or priests, of Buddhism in beautiful line-drawings engraved in gold.

A great curiosity is a printed document which is probably the oldest in the world.

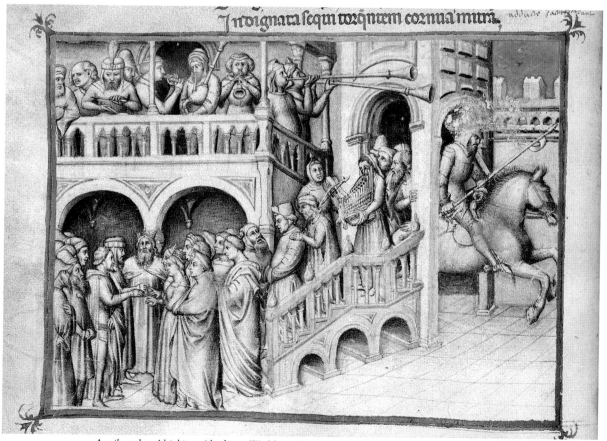

*Attributed to Altichiero Altichieri, Wedding Scene from Statius: Thebaid. Late 14th century. Grisaille on vellum. 17.3 x 22.0 cm. Chester Beatty Library, Dublin.*

# SIR ALFRED CHESTER BEATTY AND HIS LIBRARY

Made in Japan in 768 AD, on the order of the Empress Shotoku, it is a mystical Buddhist formula chanted for a specific spiritual purpose. A million copies were printed, each to be placed inside a miniature pagoda of cypress wood, these to be preserved in the ten largest Buddhist temples in Japan.

Apart from all these attractions, there are many splendid examples of the bookbinder's art, and over 20,000 Western European graphic works: engravings, both from metal and wood, etchings, lithographs, made by many of Europe's most famous artists.

The Dürer wood-engravings of *The Apocalypse* and *The Life of the Virgin* have been exhibited recently. But less well-known is the collection of Goya's *Disasters of War*, which is the complete issue of the second edition published by the Academy of San Fernando, Madrid, in 1892. Goya's *La Tauromaquia*, a collection of thirty-three plates, which had a strong influence on Picasso, is represented here by two editions, the second of 1855 and the third of 1876, plus seven additional plates.

Goya's graphic works reached the highest artistic expression of which etching was capable. Like Rembrandt, he created original works rather than, as was more usual, using the medium to reproduce other artists' paintings.

Rubens, Delacroix, Corot and Whistler are all represented in this collection, as well as the astute Giuseppe Castiglione, a Jesuit Missionary who arrived in China in 1715. He gained such confidence of the Emperor, Qien-Lung, and showed such skills as an artist, that he was appointed Court painter, a post he managed to retain through the reigns of three Emperors.

The *Loggie* of the Vatican Palace are a source of considerable artistic enjoyment to the traveller visiting Rome. They con-

*Nar-Singh, Akbar-Nama: Jesuits challenge Islamics to Ordeal by Fire. Mughal. c. 1602–5. Tempera on paper. 22.5 x 12.4 cm. Chester Beatty Library, Dublin.*

sist of thirteen vaulted bays forming a gallery sixty-five metres long and four metres wide. Each of the first twelve bays was frescoed with scenes from the Old Testament designed by Raphael; the thirteenth had scenes from the New Testament; and in between, the famous *grotteschi* decorations which influenced artists and stuccodores for generations. Popularly known as the 'Raphael Bible', it is one of the great achievements of the

High Renaissance. The frescoes were engraved and hand-coloured in gouache by Giovanni Ottaviana and Giovanni Volpato in the eighteenth century and a number of these can be seen in the Library.

This is merely a taste of a well that cannot be drained, so deep and rich is it. Every item is a new adventure, a new vision, an introduction to an unknown world, sometimes strange, sometimes quickening the mind with a quiver of intuition. It is a remarkable tribute to the passion of its creator, one which the Irish people must develop a passion to protect, because it holds so much of the grandeur that is in humanity.

*Kate Robinson*

*Kate Robinson is an art historian, critic and curator. She is a Guide at the Chester Beatty Library and Gallery of Oriental Art.*

## ACKNOWLEDGMENTS

*I am indebted to* The Life and Times of Sir Alfred Chester Beatty, *by Arthur Wilson, published by Cadogan Publications; to Brian P Kennedy's study,* Alfred Chester Beatty and Ireland, 1950-1968, *published by Glendale Press, Dun Laoghaire; and to the monograph,* The Chester Beatty Library, Dublin, MCMLVIII, *by R J Hayes, Hon Librarian.*

## NOTES

1. Arthur Wilson, *The Life and Times of Sir Alfred Chester Beatty*, London 1985.
2. Chester Beatty Papers, quoted in Brian P Kennedy, *Alfred Chester Beatty and Ireland 1950-1968*, Dublin 1988, p.89.
3. Jan Chapman, 'Chinese Jade Books in the Chester Beatty Collection,' *Arts of Asia*, May–June 1983.
4. Sir Alan Gardiner
5. Leonard Cottrell, *The Lost Pharaohs*, London, 1956. Translation by Sir Alan Gardiner, p.5.
6. Y H Safadi, *Islamic Calligraphy*, London 1978, p.9

# 'THE CITIZEN' AND 'THE SUBJECT': RICHARD HAMILTON AND IRELAND

Between 1949 and 1981 events both in Richard Hamilton's personal life and in Ireland itself had developed so as to give his interest in Irish themes a more disturbing emphasis. It is for this reason that a particular character in *Ulysses* whom Hamilton had represented in 1949 now takes on a special significance. The subject of Hamilton's *Finn MacCool — first study* (1949) is a semi-legendary figure, an Irish poet and Chieftain leader of the *Fianna*, the warrior force from which the Fenian Society (Irish Republican Brotherhood) took their name. Organised in 1858 by James Stephens, the IRB was committed to the achievement of Irish independence throughout terrorist tactics and violent revolution, rather than through parliamentary or constitutional reform.

Hamilton returned to the subject of Finn MacCool in 1982 and the source of *Finn MacCool — working drawing* (1983) 'became identified, in my renewed consideration of the mythic character, with a photograph of a nationalist detainee, Raymond Pius McCartney, on hunger strike in the Maze prison in Northern Ireland.[1]

Hamilton also spoke of the 'dirty' protest when in conversation with Richard Cork: '. . . it's a question of jumping in when a chance offers itself, when the image itself is so compelling. You can't go out and find it.'[2]

Yet, however detached Hamilton appears to be from the realities of Northern Ireland, he makes clear his position as a viewer of 'the troubles' in *A Cellular Maze*. 'Being with Rita Donagh keeps me close to the troubles. She was born of Irish parents in the Industrial Midlands of England. I was born in London. Our home is now in an ideal English country landscape. To be haunted by Ireland's problems may seem a little artificial. But our experience is not a rare condition: most British people feel Ireland's difficulties as a constant intrusion'.

Hamilton has stated his own abhorrence of the IRA's campaign of terror, but at the same time he acknowledges the human sacrifice of the hunger strikers in the extremity of suffering they inflicted upon themselves for their principles. This dichotomy of feeling — a respect for the dignity of the protest, counterbalanced by horror at the terrible crimes committed — is a potent element in the meaning of *The Citizen*. Hamilton and Donagh use the media, factually and emo-

**Stephen Snoddy** discusses two companion paintings by Richard Hamilton, whose work is on exhibition in the Irish Museum of Modern Art from October 1992 until January 1993.

tionally, to construct their work, yet the distinction between their work is one of mood; it could be compared to that between different pitches of sound. Donagh's is a quiet, measured, self-reflective approach, like the softness of an echo compared to Hamilton's big-bang, raw and direct style of *The Citizen* and *The Subject*. As Samuel Beckett once remarked, 'Alone together so much shared', Hamilton and Donagh strike a lyrical chord and a double sense of being at once intimately close to, and at a distance from, their powerfully-charged motifs. Hamilton's identification with Ireland can therefore be seen in terms of the broad subjects of his work — contemporary history; media, technology and communication; mass culture; the iconography of modern society — but along with these he refers us to his sense of an ancient and primitive self, whereby the contemporary is interwoven with the mythic past and the public 'secondary' media experience with the private human emotion.

In wall murals across Northern Ireland, William III still rides into battle at the Boyne. These are associated with the commemorative summer parades by Orangemen, while the Republican wall murals often centre on notions of Mother Ireland and of a new Ireland. It is easy to dismiss both as mindless sectarian graffiti, but perhaps it is much more accurate to describe the wall murals tradition in Northern Ireland as a folk art that is omnipresent. Just as the kerb stones are painted red, white and blue, or green, white and gold to mark out a territory, so the murals are part of the street iconography of Northern Ireland. Hamilton, again through the media, was to respond to the many indigenous street images he saw on television and in a letter to the author, 13 November 1991, he recalled the circumstances of his embarking on painting *The Subject*. 'Having completed the painting *The Citizen*, I remembered all the exposure given to the other faction. "Orangeman" seemed the natural complement to "Blanketman" so

I began to research material for a companion painting. The project was given some impetus when I was invited to make a contribution to the TV series of Paintbox programmes called *Painting with Light*.'

On behalf of the Republican prisoners at the Maze/Long Kesh[3] prison outside Belfast, Bobby Sands went on hunger strike on 1 March 1981,[4] the fifth anniversary of the date on which the government had started to phase out special status which had existed between 1971 (when internment without trial was introduced) and 1976. Special status meant that those prisoners who were interned (under the Special Powers Act) were treated as political prisoners and not as 'common criminals'. The hunger strike was to peak at Easter of 1981, the anniversary of the 1916 Uprising, a potent symbol of Republican resurrection. It was to be the climax in the prisoners' four year campaign for political status. This campaign had begun with the 'blanket' protest, in which prisoners convicted of what would, in other times, be described as politically motivated offences refused to wear prison uniform, the badge of a common criminal, and covered themselves with the only clothing at hand — their blankets. The 'blanket' protest became the 'no wash' protest, then the 'no slop out' protest, and finally the 'dirty' protest, in which Republican prisoners smeared their own excrement on the walls, floors and ceilings of their cells. Their vow to fast to death if necessary was made in order to attain their five demands: to refrain from prison work; to associate freely with one another; to organise recreational facilities, to have one letter, visit and parcel a week; and to have lost remission time restored.

Both the government and the hunger strikers rigidly maintained their respective positions. There were few real efforts to negotiate a solution. On the one side there was a simple refusal to consider concessions on any of the demands; on the other a simple refusal to consider anything other than concessions on all five. As a consequence, the hunger strikes polarised Northern Ireland to an extent that no single event since 1969 had, or has since. Within the Catholic community the ambiguous relationship between militant Republicanism and the Catholic Church was unveiled, between ancient mythologies of blood sacrifice and the statement of Pope John Paul II, on his visit to Ireland in 1981, 'murder is murder and must not be called by any other name.' Within the Orange community, responses to the hunger strikes exposed the depth and intensity of a hatred of Republicanism, a deep-rooted fear of Catholicism, and the extent to which these factors were thought to be fused. Both communities were caged inside traditional ideologies which would not and could not be unlocked overnight. A historical twist to the situation was that it was the siege of Derry, in 1689, which had provided Protestantism with its enduring slogan, 'no surrender', when their enemies had attempted to starve the Protestant people into submission.

The showing of *The Citizen* and *The Subject* side by side in London in summer 1991 evoked in me an immense feeling of personal sorrow. It is important to view them as *companion* paintings (this is the only the way I have viewed them, literally and symbolically) and thus more fully to understand the convictions, postures, fanaticisms and dualities which these images are about. It was noticeable that a British audience felt somewhat removed from the symbolism of the images and side-stepped the iconography of the paintings, thereby being able to discuss them only in relation to Hamilton's use of technology. It was as if the paintings called for a collective re-examination of a part of history which had become taboo. Such images correspond to a contemporary history and situation, and ask questions of the viewer's position towards the subject of these paintings. An Irish showing of the paintings should permit a more direct look, and place the work more closely in the context of political and social events. It is the reality of the paintings that can only be the subject of the debate.

The actions of the hunger strikers were beyond Protestant comprehension. They were seen by the world at large to be victims, but to Protestants, victimhood is not self-inflicted. For the ordinary Protestant takes refuge in the reason for the supreme sacrifice (as when, for example, thousands of young Northern Irish Protestants gave their lives in the trenches at the Somme during World War I), rather than in the process of the sacrifice itself. A Protestant would justify and find ways of contributing to, and living for, a country (the work ethic), while the hunger strikers chose ancient Gaelic laws of self-

*Richard Hamilton (b.1922) The Citizen (1982–83)*
*Oil on canvas 200 x 100 cm (x2).*

denial and sacrifice. It is what the historian A T Q Stewart calls a 'nightmarish juxtaposition of the folk memory of Jungian psychology'; not only were the hunger strikers asserting claims to Protestants' physical territory but they were invading the loyalist psyche.[5]

To keep the nationalist cause at the top of the political agenda and in touch with international consciousness, Republican prisoners carry on the fight by resisting the prison regime. Maintaining the struggle within the prison is part of the psychology of 'the long war'.[6] This claustrophobic tension exists alongside the celebratory triumphalism of the Orangeman stating his claim to march the route of his forefathers.[7] *The Citizen* and *The Subject* are opposing images of incarceration and freedom, yet their conjunction evokes the survival of the species syndrome. Each opposing side is a closed

world with an unchargeable internal code of its own, impervious to the passage of time. The inflexible, no-compromise stance is so deeply rooted in both communities that everything conforms to an action-response pattern that endlessly repeats itself.

*The Citizen* and *The Subject* correctly portray Northern Ireland's politics as a battle between two irreconcilable groups. Conforming to the two sides' intransigent stereotypes, they glare at each other. One evokes a screaming silence, the other a screaming defiance. Both attract a macabre fascination through their military associations and each signals a staunch/devout will, a stubborn intolerance and a fanaticism masquerading as nobility of cause.

In Hamilton's words, 'What we had heard of the blanket protest, mainly through the propaganda agencies of Sinn

# 'THE CITIZEN' AND 'THE SUBJECT': RICHARD HAMILTON AND IRELAND

*Richard Hamilton (b.1922) The Subject (1988–90)*
*Oil on canvas 200 x 100 cm (x2).*

strongly held convictions that one belongs to a certain human grouping. This segregation of human beings into distinct groups can be defined as a 'sense of national identity', when people find it necessary to identify themselves with a particular tribe. *The Citizen* and *The Subject* have this sense of national identity. They both use history as a weapon against each other. History is defenceless, it can be used and manipulated to maintain the polarisation between the tribes.

Religion in Northern Ireland is a powerful early learning tool in each side's perception of the other. Childhood upbringing and shared family experience make the religious aspect of 'the troubles' reach the deepest levels of the human psyche. *The Citizen* and *The Subject* convey this depth. They give a strong sense that while the individual is grounded in the world of his ancestry, his power is the collective power of the tribe.

The Orangeman is very much a fact of life in Northern Ireland. Nearly one third of adult male Protestants belong to an Orange Lodge. *The Subject* in his regalia of an assertive power strides out triumphantly emphasising his supremacy. A dignified gentleman in his Sunday best, he is a staunch defender of Ulster's glorious past. *The Subject* is also a 'citizen'; a citizen who loves his Queen and Country; a citizen who would die in its defence; a citizen who is obedient to the forces of law and order; a citizen who believes in the democracy of one man, one vote. *The Subject* is as much about nationalism as *The Citizen*; both identify with a strong sense of self and a fanatical devotion to the same cause of defence of 'the nation', *The Subject* proudly commemorating and proclaiming his 'victory' at The Boyne; *The Citizen* symbolising a sacrificial martyrdom recalling a mythological past. Their meeting brings a troubled history up to the present and into the future. History in Ireland replicates itself and, in a country where people pride themselves on their memory, the future is therefore weighed down with a sense of the inevitable, that is, there is no hope of compromise. They are mirror images reflecting the human tragedy of using force to settle arguments, as Odysseus, in Book Nine of *The Odyssey* describes his adventures among the one-eyed Cyclopes, who are 'giants, louts, without a law to bless them.'

*The Citizen* and *The Subject* are a reflection on the political conditions in which

Fein, could not prepare us for the startling photographic documentation on TV. The picture presented, first by Granada Television and later by the BBC, was shocking less for its scatological content than for its potency. An oft-declared British view of the IRA as thugs and hooligans did not match the materialisation of Christian martyrdom so profoundly contained on film. One became acutely aware of the religious conflict that had resulted in civil inequalities that gave a platform for IRA activity. The symbols of Christ's agony were there, not only the crucifix on the neck of the prisoners and the rosary which confirmed the monastic austerity but the self-inflicted suffering which has marked Christianity from the earliest times'. The prisoners claimed the high moral ground because their fast to death reinforced their identification as martyrs. By fusing the ancient myth of militant

nationalism and of heroic sacrifice with the central characteristics of Irish Catholicism, penitential fasting, atonement for wrong-doing and self-denial, we can understand the context of Father Matt Wallace's statement: '(They) were almost akin to Christ-like.'[8]

Nationalism has a power over people's minds and hearts. The defence or cause of 'a nation' is one of the few commitments for which people will kill others or voluntarily lay down their lives. The psychology of nationalism is powerfully connected to a sense of self. It is the need for people to belong to a group which is linked by culture, customs, religion and a common history. Only the collective group can give meaning and fulfilment to individuals within the group, and it is the pack instinct which is the driving force. The packs have leaders who perpetrate primitive tribal rituals by imposing

1½ million people are forced to live in Northern Ireland. It is a situation reflective of the impossibility of consensus. Through generations of political manipulation and intransigence, the communities have been 'misplaced' by history. The younger generations have turned to political violence as a means of escape from the sectarian dilemma in which they have been put by the intolerance of their ancestors. Any interpretation of these paintings cannot dismiss the moral questions they ask; to do so is to ignore the content in favour of the aesthetic considerations. Hamilton has insisted on his right to paint images of such directness that they demand a response, not an averted glance. Although everything in these works is dependent on the 'content', we have become sanitised or practised at resisting images of raw power. Yet, though we may turn a blind eye, these paintings are located in the *mind's* eye. We hover between not wanting to remember and not being able to forget.

Whatever judgement posterity may reach, these images grasp a painful and sorrowful reality, a sense of anger and frustration, sadness and grief. They cast shadows upon us; we cannot be oblivious to their presence. They touch a nerve, a trapped nerve, yet by their existence they confirm a future. Regretfully, a predictable future of the zero-sum game, a Beckettian game of waiting, 'The light glitters an instant and then it's night once more' (*Waiting for Godot*). An endgame, a game over which the spoils cannot be shared or negotiated, but only won or lost.

*Stephen Snoddy*

*Stephen Snoddy is Exhibitions Director, Cornerhouse, Manchester. Previously he organised the travelling exhibition* Jack B Yeats: the Late Paintings. *This essay is an abridged version of the essay* Yes and No *which appears in the* Richard Hamilton Retrospective Exhibition Catalogue, *available from Tate Gallery Publications, Millbank, London.*

## NOTES

1. Work in Progress, Richard Hamilton, Orchard Gallery, Derry, 1988, Terry Eagleton, p. 8.
2. 'Epiphanies', Richard Hamilton in conversation with Richard Cork, BBC Radio 3, 1 April 1985.
3. It is Long Kesh to Catholics, the Maze to Protestants; Derry to Catholics, Londonderry to Protestants; the six counties or the North of Ireland to Catholics; Northern Ireland to Protestants. Although both communities share a common first language, they both need what Alasdair MacIntyre describes as 'a second first language.' Padraig O'Malley, *Biting at the Grave*, The Blackstaff Press, Belfast, 1990, p. 185.
4. This was the second hunger strike after the first hunger strike broke down during Christmas 1980. Bobby Sands joined the IRA in 1972 and within six months was imprisoned for possession of firearms. He was released in 1976; however in September 1977 he was sent to the Maze/Long Kesh charged again with possession of firearms. He immediately went 'on the blanket', and from that onto the dirty protest.
5. Padraig O'Malley, *Biting at the Grave,* The Blackstaff Press, Belfast, 1990, p. 165.
6. I am indebted to Declan McGonagle for this information and many other insights through various conversations.
7. In conversation with Richard Hamilton, he recounted how he had seen the Orange marchers clash with the RUC in 1985 on TV when their traditional marching route through 'the Tunnel' at Portadown (a Catholic area in a Protestant town) was blocked by the police because of a ban on marches that were likely to cause a breach of the peace.
8. *Biting at the Grave,* op. cit., p. 109. Father Matt Wallace, a curate in the parish of Joe McDonnell's (one of the hunger strikers).

# MAINIE JELLETT AND IRISH MODERNISM

There is a popular belief that Mainie Jellett, together with Evie Hone and Nora McGuinness, introduced modern art into Ireland. This is not quite accurate, though, as they say, there is a lot of truth in it. The major exhibition of Jellett's work at the Irish Museum of Modern Art at Kilmainham, Dublin (December 1991–March 1992); its catalogue, and Bruce Arnold's *Mainie Jellett and the Modern Movement in Ireland* (New Haven and London 1991); as well as S B Kennedy's *Irish Art and Modernism 1880–1950* (Belfast, 1991) have helped to put the record straight.

A good deal of antagonism towards modern art, (particularly cubism and surrealism, but also fauvism and even post-impressionism) was prevalent in Ireland thoughout the first half of the twentieth century, particularly in circles connected with the Royal Hibernian Academy. This came from two not unconnected sources. On the one hand, there were the followers of Orpen, who regarded Modernism as an aberration and were waiting for it to go away; on the other hand, there were those who wanted to build up a national art based mostly on the principles of social realism (though its protagonists would have foresworn anything that savoured of Stalinist social realism). Undoubtedly they dominated the Irish art world until the introduction of the *Living Art Exhibitions* (inspired by Mainie Jellett) in 1943.

It would, however, be inaccurate to suggest that Irish artists were ignorant of what was happening on the Continent of Europe prior to World War I. I have (on long loan) a catalogue of an exhibition shown in 1912 at the Arts Club in Dublin. It included half-a-dozen Picassos and Matisses, a Vlaminck and other such pictures. Indeed, as Arnold and Kennedy say, Irish artists and the Irish art public were far more aware of what was happening in mainland Europe than their British counterparts.

S B Kennedy sets the scene for our discussion of Mainie Jellett and Modernism, and he also raises some questions, or forces us to raise them. The first is: what is to be regarded as Modernism? When did it begin? (These are not two questions.) The second is: is there such a thing as Irish Modernism, and, if so, what is it?

Kennedy casts his net rather wide and, in consequence, makes the discussion less interesting, since, for him, the modern movement includes impressionism, post-

In recent months, exhibitions and publications have focused on the development of modern art in Ireland. **Cyril Barrett** overviews the relationship between theory and practice in the crucial years.

*Mainie Jellett,* Portrait Study of Betty, *gouache on paper, 26.5 x 20.5. Private collection.*

impressionism, fauvism, cubism and everything after that up to that curious phenomenon known as 'post-modernism'. (Mercifully, we do not have to discuss that here, not that it is any more elusive a concept than Modernism.) Now, of course, if you stretch Modernism back that far, Irish artists come out rather well, as does awareness on the part of the Irish public. Whistler's work was exhibited in Dublin in 1884. In 1892 Roderic O'Conor had settled at Pont Aven and shared his studio with Gauguin. Post-impressionism must have reached Ireland about the time it reached Britain, and before it reached the United States. Although Roger Fry's Post-Impressionist exhibition of 1910 ante-dated Ellen Duncan's in Dublin by some months, and though the Dublin exhibition contained many works shown in Fry's, the fact that the two took place in such rapid succession shows that the awareness of post-impressionism in Ireland was at least contemporaneous with that in Britain.

But even if Modernism were confined to post-impressionism, the thesis that Irish artists, and certain sections of the Irish public, were aware of it as early as their counterparts in Britain is bought

cheaply. Though these exhibitions did not cause the same furore in Ireland as in Britain, they had just as little lasting impact in one country as in the other.

What we are talking about so far might be better described as 'avant-garde', a term Kennedy often uses in place of 'Modernist'. This will enable us to confine the term '*Modernism*' to cubism and post-cubism up to the late 1940s, which is all that is required for present purposes. It now becomes a question of the impact of cubist and post-cubist art on Irish artists and the Irish public, while still leaving scope for Irish artists like Mary Swanzy who are avant-garde though not cubist. With this limitation on the concept of Modernism we are still able to say that Ireland was abreast of the times in awareness, since Ellen Duncan's second exhibition, to which I refer above, contained cubist works by Picasso, Gris, Marchand and Herbin.

There matters rested, to all outward appearances, for a decade. Meanwhile an amalgam of cubism and its near neighbour, futurism, had developed in England, namely Vorticism. (It died out during the 1914–18 war). The next phase in our story belongs to Mainie Jellett, who, along with Evie Hone, had gone to Paris in 1921 to study under the cubist painters Andre Lhote (sometimes spelt L'hote) and Albert Gleizes. I shall postpone further discussion of this episode, save to say that it had a profound effect on the Irish artistic public, predominantly disturbing on the one side and defiant on the other. Continental Modernism continued, in one or other of its denominations, to be exhibited in Ireland annually from the early 1920s on. In 1923 the New Irish Salon was formed. It lasted until 1928 and put on six exhibitions. In 1924 Lhote and Gleizes were shown. There was an important exhibition of continental painters, *Loan and Cross-Section of Continental Paintings* which included the cubists, Braque, Derain and Gris; and also the 'metaphysical' painter, de Chirico. Even during the war, continental Modernists continued to be shown. With the first *Irish Exhibition of Living Art* in 1943 one might say that the exhibition of continental Modernism had become institutionalized.

All this may give the impression that the artistic public in Ireland were intensely interested in, and favourably disposed towards, Modernism. Nothing could

## MAINIE JELLETT AND IRISH MODERNISM

be further from the truth. The most that can be said is that it was *made* aware by a small group, a coterie, of zealots. But, for the most part, they did not like what they saw. In 1947, I witnessed this for myself, when I made my first direct contact (as distinct from indirect, through reproductions) with Modernism at Victor Waddington's *French Exhibition*. The prevalent reactions were bewilderment and derision. Even the critics were, for the most part, hostile. One of the merits of Kennedy's book is that he gives us choice snippets from those early reviews.

The most perceptive and best reasoned of these were by George Russell (AE). Of the artists in Ellen Duncan's 1911 exhibition, he said they were 'not decadent, but decrepit', although he exempted Gauguin, Denis and Signac. Of Signac, however, he said, quite rightly, that his work was 'an unemotional and cold application of science to art'; he was more scathing about Jellett and her mentors. Thomas Bodkin was another hostile, but not imperceptive, critic. In 1911 he dismissed Matisse as 'a mere artistic charlatan'. As for Picasso, he continued his polemic against him throughout his life. More balanced views were offered by Thomas MacGreevy and Edward Sheehy.

However unsympathetic was the critical assessment of continental Modernism, it clearly had a small but discriminating number of patrons in Ireland, otherwise there would not have been so many works available for inclusion in exhibitions. Public patronage was another matter. Indeed the lack of awareness of continental and, later, British, Modernism verged on the farcical. Even in the 1950s the Municipal Gallery of Modern Art in Dublin looked as though the twentieth century outside Ireland had passed it by, and, perhaps, that is how its purchasing committee wished it to be. But the greatest farce of all was the rejection of a Rouault and a Henry Moore, offered to the Gallery by the Friends of the National Collections of Ireland. The first was considered blasphemous (though Maynooth College gladly accepted it on loan) while the latter was considered obscene! (It should be said that the Friends, founded in 1924, with a view to donating works of Irish artists to public collections, extended its scope, in 1944, to include works by continental artists).

One of the great merits of Kennedy's book is that he devotes a whole chapter to The White Stag Group whose importance in the history of Irish Modernism has not been fully appreciated. Some of the most prominent artists in the movement – Jellett, Hone, Patrick Scott, Nano Reid, May Guinness, Ralph Cusack, Thurloe Conolly – belonged to it at some time. Founded in Bloomsbury, London, in 1935 by a Hungarian emigré and psychoanalyst, Basil Rakoczi, and an Englishman, Kenneth Hall, its exponents were interested in subjectivity in the form of creative psychology, with special reference to art – the white stag is, apparently, a Hungarian symbol of creativity.

The White Stag group was pacifist, so, in 1939, when they saw war looming, they absconded to neutral Ireland and headed

*Mainie Jellett, Figures in a Landscape, 1921. Oil on canvas, 66 x 85cm. Private collection.*

for the west. In 1940 they gravitated to Dublin and continued their interrupted business with lectures on creative psychology and held their first exhibition which included works by Jellett. The life of the Group was short. When the war was over the non-indigenous members left the country, but not before they had put on, in January 1944, an exhibition of *Subjective Art*. Apart from the *Irish Exhibition of Living Art* held the previous year, it was the most important exhibition from the point of view of Irish Modernism, held during the war. Herbert Read was to have opened the exhibition and to lecture. He could not come, but his lecture was read and he wrote an introduction to the catalogue. This did not set the seal on Irish Modernism, and, indeed, gave it little more than a condescending and ill-informed pat on the back, but his support added weight to Modernism in Ireland. Far more interesting were the exchanges in the press as recounted by Kennedy. The most interesting is the divergence of opinion between a letter writer to the

*Evening Mail* who spoke of 'A veil of imbecile mystery, to cover up paucity of inspiration' and an editorial which began: 'Properly speaking all art is subjective art', and went on to defend the right of any artist to find his emotion away from naturalistic representation and to paint as the spirit moves him. Just as there is a rich mine waiting to be explored in the criticism of the time, so also in the art columns of the press.

Kennedy's book is very thoroughly researched, with excellent and interesting footnotes, a full bibliography and index (except for the exhibitions) and useful appendices. Its shortcomings are that its chronology is sometimes difficult to follow. (In a book of this kind it is not necessary to give potted biographies of the artist in the text). Also, apart from reservations about the use of 'Modernism', the distinction between academic and avant-garde artists in Ireland is not as clear-cut as Kennedy sometimes suggests.

I turn now to Bruce Arnold's book, the exhibition at the Irish Museum of

Modern Art, Kilmainham, and its catalogue. Bruce Arnold was instrumental in having the exhibition mounted, and it is not difficult to see why, apart from the cynical suggestion that it would be advantageous towards the sale of both his book and Jellett's work. There has, until now, never been a major retrospective exhibition of her work, and Arnold was surely right in suggesting that within a half-century of her death, it was time that we should have the fullest possible exposure of her work and the most up-to-date appraisal of it.

From an early age Jellett proved herself to be competent at drawing and, in her teens, at painting in the French style favoured by Norman Garstin. Although she fell under the spell of William Orpen, both at the Metropolitan School of Art and at his house in Howth, she never completely succumbed to his style. Garstin's influence prevailed until she went to London where the influence of Sickert was to become permanent for her. This was the first of what she called her three revolu-

*Mainie Jellett, Achill Horses, 1939. Oil on canvas, 61 x 91 cm. National Gallery of Ireland, Dublin.*

# MAINIE JELLETT AND IRISH MODERNISM

tions. (The other two were brought about in 1921 by André Lhote and Albert Gleizes). In the catalogue, Paula Murphy questions the revolutionary nature of these changes of style. Speaking from a feminist point of view, she sees these changes in Jellett's style as merely adapting herself to a dominant male. Be that as it may, contact with these three males revolutionized her style, even if her style did not, thereby, become revolutionary. Sickert gave her more supple and free use of paint. Lhote gave her paintings freedom in another sense – freedom from naturalistic representation, freedom to construct pictures (as in *Figures in a Landscape* of 1921) primarily with regard for composition. He also gave her a cubist sense of mass. Gleizes gave her a taste for abstraction, the *El Dorado* of Maurice Denis and his successors, 'colour and shape on a flat surface.'

In my opinion, revolutionary or not, it was a disaster both for her own art and for Irish Modernism, that she went to Gleizes. Both Lhote and Gleizes were academic, but, of the two, Lhote was the less pernicious. While under his influence, Jellett produced some splendid nudes and compositions of nudes – besides *Figures in a Landscape* there are *The Three Graces* and various standing and seated nudes, mostly female, but also a few extremely muscular males. Also on display were some fine cubist portraits, including *Girl in Blue* and *Portrait of a Young Woman* (both of which, it is to be hoped, will eventually find their way, along with *Figures in a Landscape*, into a public collection).

By the time Jellett was painting in France, cubism had progressed beyond the Cézannesque cubism of Lhote to pure abstraction, and Jellett foolishly wanted to follow it. She felt a need to be up with the avant-garde, though, by 1921, it had moved beyond even abstract cubism. Heresy usually catches up with orthodoxy and by the time she and Evie Hone reached Gleizes's studio, even abstract cubism was entombed in academic exercises. But Gleizes had two things to offer Jellett – a method of painting and a method of teaching.

Jellett was gifted, intelligent, humane, profoundly Christian, and, for those days (the inter-war years), something of an evangelist. She wanted to convert, in this case to Modernism. In 1923, back in Ireland, she exhibited at the New Irish

*Mainie Jellett*, Religious Composition. *Gouache on paper mounted on board, 22.5 x 17.25 cm. Private Collection.*

Salon and the Society of Dublin Painters. The reception of her work was mixed, the mixture predominantly unfavourable. Jellett exhibited two paintings and two drawings, all abstract. The reviewer in *The Irish Times* expressed bafflement – 'an insoluble problem'. The same newspaper published a reproduction of one of Jellett's pictures above a photograph of an onion shaped like a brooding bird with the caption 'TWO FREAK PICTURES – ART – AND NATURE'. But it was left to AE, writing in the *Irish Statesman*, to say the harsh word. Having praised Harry Clarke lavishly, he turned to Jellett and wrote: 'We turn from Clarke's pictures and find Miss

Jellett a late victim to Cubism in some *Sub-section* of this *malaria*. (Elsewhere he described Cubists as *"bacteria".*) She seems as heartily as any of the cubists to have adopted as motto Fuseli's famous outburst, "Damn nature. She always puts me out." . . . . We hope the visitors will not be led away . . . (by) the *sub-human* art of Miss Jellett.' And he goes on: 'The real defect of this form of art is that the convention is so simple that nothing can be said in it. It is as impossible to be subtle in this convention as it would be to write poetry if the poet was limited to use fifty words, the same words, no matter how many poems he wrote or moods he wanted

# MAINIE JELLETT AND IRISH MODERNISM

*Mainie Jellett,* The Ninth Hour, *1941. Oil on canvas, 86 x 64 cm. Hugh Lane Municipal Gallery, Dublin.*

ture was entitled 'Cubism and Subsequent Movements in Painting'. Abstract cubism, she said, did not renounce nature but endeavoured to penetrate nature, to discover its natural laws and create according to them, making all the forms interdependent like the organisation of the universe itself.

Towards the end of the decade, her abstracts take on the suggestion of religious representation. It was her contention that spirituality could best be expressed in abstract or, at least, non-figurative, art. This, as she saw it, was the tradition of Cimabue, Duccio and Fra Angelico, which had been interrupted by the introduction of perspective. There is a timelessness in these pictures, as in the Byzantine tradition, due not only to absence of naturalism, but to the two-dimensional way in which the figures are represented. I should like to note that Jellett's somewhat mystical belief in the spiritual values of abstract art was not shared by many of her fellow artists either at that time or since.

Throughout the 1930s, Mainie Jellett continued to campaign on behalf of her own brand of modern art and also to take part in important exhibitions in Paris. (Constant contact with Gleizes was probably responsible for this.) She exhibited at the *Salon des Surindépendents* in 1930, *Abstraction-Création* from 1932 to its demise in 1936, and at the *Salon d'Automne* in 1938. She and Hone exhibited at *Abstraction-Creation*, in 1932, when the only British artist was, surprisingly, Edward Wadsworth, whose title to being an abstract painter was largely due to applying cubist 'deconstructive' techniques to the camouflage of naval ships. At the next exhibition, Nicholson and Hepworth were represented. So during the pre-war era, Irish modernist artists (the tiny few) were up with, if not ahead of, the game.

To return to Ireland, the greatest triumph of Jellett's short life was the establishment of the *Irish Exhibition of Living Art*. The story has been so often told that it hardly seems necessary to repeat it here. Nevertheless, some further light is thrown by Arnold's account, written from Jellett's point of view. For instance, when asked to report on the RHA exhibition of 1942, she wrote: 'this year's Academy seems to suffer even more from the faults I have mentioned last year . . . The RHA must not shut its doors to life,

to express. In fact, what Miss Jellett says in one of her decorations she says in the other, and that is nothing.'

This sparked off a controversy that was to persist up to 1950 and beyond. A friend, Maude Ball, was the first to take up the cudgels. In letters comparing the harmony of colour in painting to that of sound in music, she quoted Rameau and Stanford on Mozart. Thomas McGreevy lent his support, while Thomas Bodkin continued his polemic against Modernism in general and cubism in particular. McGreevy concentrates on harmony of colour and added that 'the freedom from subject, from painted psychology, from

symbolism, has heightened the aesthetic value of her work'. As Arnold points out (p 82), Jellett was ten years ahead of Ben Nicholson in consistently producing pure abstract compositions, though it is not entirely accurate to say that she was the *only* painter in the British Isles that was doing so. In the 1920s, for example, Evie Hone was also doing so.

In 1925 Jellett exhibited abroad with the London Group and at Versailles in the *L'art d'aujourd'hui* exhibition, with Evie Hone and May Guinness. In 1926 she began the series of lectures on modern art that she was to continue for the remainder of her life. Her first public lec-

# MAINIE JELLETT AND IRISH MODERNISM

otherwise it will of necessity die of senile decay.' And she went on: 'This present exhibition is, with very few exceptions, an all Irish exhibition, therefore we are in a position to take stock of what academic art is and what it stands for in this country — let us open our eyes and our minds and form our own honest opinion and ask ourselves, is this what we want as Irish art? If it is then there is nothing more to be said.' (p 195).

But Jellett was most interested in young Irish artists. In 1941 Louis le Brocquy had a painting rejected by the RHA, and in 1942, two: *The Spanish Shawl* and *Images of Chaos*. It has been said that they were technically flawed (a limb not quite right, etc) but they were outstandingly imaginative and even in the best sense (ie giving food for serious consideration) disturbing paintings, products of disturbing times! It was time for some sort of change. The result was the setting up of an alternative exhibition: the *Irish Exhibition of Living Art*.

It has been claimed that the title had been thought up by Sybil le Brocquy. Perhaps; who knows? But I agree with Arnold that it sounds more in keeping with Jellett's call not to shut the doors to life. We all know how the Living Art impulse revitalised Irish art, and how it progressed. What we are not aware of is the vital role played by the academics in this transference of power. As Arnold recounts it, not only did Dermod O'Brien, the President of the RHA from 1910, become a patron, but he also exhibited in the first exhibition, as did Sean Keating and Laurence Campbell. It was not an I and thou, us and they, exhibition.

This is an important point to remember when talking about Irish Modernism. The *Irish Exhibition of Living Art* was not a home for exclusively Modernist artists (any more than the *Oireachtas* exhibitions were a home for nationalistic art or the RHA for academic art in the old sense). Although much is said about the divide among Irish artists in the mid-twentieth century, it never really existed, in the way it did in Britain and elsewhere.

Whoever thought up the name, one thing is certain — when the committee for the Irish Exhibition of Living Art was formed, Mainie Jellett was Chairman. Unfortunately, she was too ill to attend the exhibition which opened on 15 September 1943. It was well received.

*Mainie Jellett, I Have Trodden the Wine Press Alone. Oil on canvas, 76 x 56 cm. National Gallery of Ireland, Dublin.*

However, Dr A J Leventhal was not slow to detect a compromise between, as he put it, the academy, and the independents as represented by the *Salon d'Automne*: 'the Salon half-heartedly rejected Academicism and lacked the courage to ally itself with the prevailing modern tendencies'. How Jellett would have replied to this criticism we can never know. Arnold's view is that she would probably have concurred, 'while at the same time knowing that for Irish Living Art to succeed it was necessary to avoid being opposed to the academic tradition' (p 197). This seems right. So much for Irish Modernism.

Bruce Arnold's final chapter on the dying of Mainie Jellett is most moving, particularly his account of her conversations with her life-long friend Elizabeth Bowen, the novelist. The most pathetic moment in her dying days was when she said to her sister, Babbin (Rosamund), 'You know, I have a wonderful picture in my mind, I wonder will I ever be able to paint it?' That, where Mainie Jellett is concerned, is the eternal question. Would she have been able to paint that picture?

There is no question but that Bruce Arnold has done a considerable service to our knowledge of twentieth-century Irish

art through his book and his contributions to the Mainie Jellett exhibition. As a historian and a political correspondent, he is sensitive to the political, social and religious background into which she was born and through which she lived. I am not convinced that the amount of historical and social background he offers us is necessary to an understanding of her work, or of the modern movement in Ireland (to quote the title). Kennedy does this more economically. My only criticism, as ever, is that Arnold seems to have little sense of chronology and is slipshod on facts. It is excruciatingly difficult to get clear the order of events, much less dates. (Mercifully the catalogue of the exhibition provided the necessary information). As for the aberrations in dating, I do not know whether Arnold or his editors (Yale University Press, no less) were responsible for the countless and repeated errors and inconsistencies — Roderic O'Connor for O'Conor, dates contradicted by illustrations, eg 21:1917 for 1918. These criticisms aside, this is a most valuable piece of research and a tribute to a valiant Irishwoman. As Arnold says, the title of one of her last works, *I Have Trodden the Wine Press Alone*, would offer a worthy epitaph for this courageous woman.

Finally, the exhibition and its catalogue. The exhibition itself was splendidy selected and splendidly hung. In what I call the main gallery (the broad corridor of the old, seventeenth century, Royal Hospital) the main development of Mainie Jellett's art was clearly and sensitively laid out, culminating in her impressive and central work *Homage to Fra Angelico*, the picture which above all sums up her life and work. In the side 'cubicles' — once the bed-sitting rooms of military pensioners — were more intimate pictures related to those outside.

What emerges is rather curious. First, the catalogue does not offer dates unless they are (a rare occurrence) attached to the signature. However, the works are grouped in periods of less than a decade, and sometimes of as little as two years. (Eventually approximate dates were added to the picture labels.) But this is a trivial criticism. What the exhibition made clear was the ease with which Mainie Jellett learned to paint and how this ease persisted throughout her life. Then, and this is far less pleasant, it showed how persistently she succumbed to

# MAINIE JELLETT AND IRISH MODERNISM

masters who, to my mind, cramped her style. And, thirdly, it demonstrated how she adopted an artistic ideology that was alien to her artistic character.

First, her almost effortless style. There is a watercolour, which she painted at the age of fourteen of sand dunes at Wimereux in France (cat. no. 1) that has both freshness and simplicity together with complete competence. About the effect of the painting techniques taught in the Metropolitan School, Dublin by Orpen and Tuohy, I shall say no more, than that, in spite of their restrictive practices, Jellett produced a delightful oil painting, freely painted, of her sister, *Babbin with the Pot-Pourri* (cat. no. 6). During her stay at Westminster, under the influence of Sickert, she produced a number of stunning watercolours of students in life class, two of which were in the exhibition (cat. nos. 17 and 18). Alas, my favourite *Girl with Ribbons* of 1917 was not shown. Even under the influence of Lhote and Gleizes, she continued to paint spontaneously. There is a charming watercolour of her sister, Bay, in a boat *Boat, Plocton* (cat. no. 43) painted in 1921, and an oil of *Trees* (cat. no. 85) painted in 1926. Admittedly *Trees* lacks the spontaneity of the early watercolours, as do other landscapes of the period (eg *Cotswold Landscape,* Arnold, p 91).

The point is that, while she was doing her cubist exercises in abstract art, she was still making representational paintings, albeit in a stiff cubist manner. Spontaneity returned slowly from the mid-1930s, especially under the influence of the Royal Academy, London, *Exhibition of Chinese Art,* but most remarkable of all are her very last works — those freely prancing *Achill Horses* (cat. no. 130) of 1941, and, above all the sketches of female nudes in her notebooks (cat. nos 138–143) which take us right back to 1917, (particularly, cat. no. 142, *Seated Female Nude,* which so closely resembles *Girl with Ribbons.*)

How her art would have developed had she lived longer (she was only forty-seven when she died) is hard to tell. The exhibition demonstrates that her artistic development was not a progression, as it was with, say, Mondrian. There was always a tension between intellect and sensibility. While her intellect drove her into

*Mainie Jellett,* Seated Female Nude, *1922. Oil on canvas 56.3 x 46.2 cm. Ulster Museum, Belfast.*

the mainstream (or mainstream minus one) of Modernism, her sensitivity her in a side stream of a sensuous form of drawing all her own.

The result was that Mainie Jellett, for the last twenty-odd years of her life, produced works which are delightful to look at, most decorative, but, with rare exceptions, lacking in depth. They were not even cubist in any strict sense of the word. They were sensuous in form as well as in colour. One has only to compare her break-down of Betty or her *Abstract Study* (Arnold p 73) with Gleizes's diagrams from *La peinture et ses lois* (cat. p 31) to see this. Gleizes is, for the most part, geometrical, while Jellett is always sensuous, her lines curved. This is not too important, but it is sad that she sold her birthright for a mess of ideological pottage. What is important, and might be considered a disaster, is that she thought that in so doing she would lead younger Irish artists kicking and screaming into the twentieth century.

Walking along the corridor and through the 'cubicles' looking at those abstract compositions, I was delighted by the beauty of the colouring and subtlety of the compositions. There is room in this

world for art that is purely decorative. Jellett may have regarded them as experimental, not intended to be decorative. Experimental or not, they are beautiful in their own right, some stunningly so.

Beautiful they may be and experimental also, but it is hard to see how her later, religious, works are made more effective, emotionally and spiritually, by being semi-abstract. But this was what she believed should be. She believed that abstraction and two-dimensionality were the proper vehicles for religious representation. *The Ninth Hour* and *I Have Trodden the Wine Press Alone* are impressive paintings. That they are so because they are semi-abstract is not obvious. One is conscious of the art rather than the subject. Even the colouring — predominantly blue in one case and predominantly red in the other — though effective, is unsubtle. (It might have worked better in stained glass).

Mainie Jellett could have done worse than follow her friend, Evie Hone, into stained glass. Already under the influence of Gleizes, she had gone into design, designing rugs, advertisements, popular murals and stage sets. But, no doubt, her painting would also have developed in the direction of her dying vision. But that is, alas, idle speculation.

What is beyond dispute is that Mainie Jellett brought Modernism, albeit of a limited and didactic kind, to Ireland in a peremptory way. It is equally beyond doubt that the Irish *cognoscenti* and *literati* were well aware of it long before Jellett. But Jellett's missionary zeal shook a wider audience into awareness of what was going on in the artistic world beyond Ireland's shores. I leave the last word with Paula Murphy, quoting from her essay in the exhibition catalogue,

> *Mainie Jellett has very specific relevance for the study of twenetieth century art in Ireland and it is through an examination of her art and ideas in context that the very real contradiction inherent in the term 'Irish Modernism' can be understood.*

> Cyril Barrett

Cyril Barrett has long been in the Department of Philosophy at the University of Warwick. His work over the years has been in the contemporary art field, with a specialization in kinetic art.

# GRACE HENRY

**James G Cruickshank** outlines the four stages in the development of Grace Henry's painting career.

Among the last exhibitions celebrating Dublin as Cultural Capital of Europe 1991, the Hugh Lane Municipal Gallery (HLMG) showed paintings by Paul and Grace Henry in November and December[1]. It was a revival, as we approach the end of the century, of what was at least an annual event, in some years both in Belfast and Dublin, between 1904 and 1926 when Paul and Grace Henry held joint exhibitions, in addition to showing with the Society of Dublin Painters and the Royal Hibernian Academy(RHA). The 1991 exhibition was immensely popular, if measured by public attendance and media reviews, and most of the paintings discussed in this article are to be found and described in the exhibition catalogue[1]. However, the exhibition once again emphasised the imbalance in public recognition between the two Henrys. Paul Henry's work has been available to a wide public through prints, posters and books, and through his two autobiographies[2], in which he omits any reference to his wife Grace. Also Paul is the subject of a substantial article[3] and continuing research by Dr S Brian Kennedy of the Ulster Museum in Belfast.

In contrast, no major article or book has been devoted to the life and work of Grace Henry. It is very difficult to find any source material as Paul Henry made a conscious effort to exclude her from his writings and to destroy any material referring to her. There were no children and surviving relatives have not been found. Grace is still unknown in Scotland, or even in her home region around Aberdeen. It is the intention here to look closely at the scant information available on her life and evolving painting style, and to attempt to produce an assessment of Grace Henry the artist. She was born Emily Grace Mitchell on 10 February 1868 near Peterhead, Scotland, and died Grace Henry, artist, HRHA, on 11 August 1953 in Dublin. She had a long life involving many spectacular changes of personal experience and opportunity as an artist. Born a Scot, she lived and worked mainly in her adopted country, and is buried in Mount Jerome Cemetery in Dublin.

There are four clear periods of development in Grace Henry's painting as a landscape artist, from the time of her marriage to Paul in 1903 and her death in 1953. Before these are examined in detail, it seems appropriate to reflect on her early

life in Scotland. Emily Grace Mitchell spent a significant period of thirty-two years in her parents' home or in Aberdeen, a period marked by its settled, domestic character, and in which there was very little sign of a future career as a professional artist. She had been born into the family of a Church of Scotland minister, the second youngest of ten children. For all of her early life up to the age of twenty-seven in 1895, the manse at Kirktown St Fergus, five miles north of Peterhead, Aberdeenshire, Scotland, was home to Grace Mitchell. The house was a large, traditional two-storey building of classical appearance. It was large enough for a household of about fifteen, including servants. It would have been a centre of social activity and the site of the private education of the children. Grace Mitchell's parents both came from aristocratic families of considerable wealth. Her minister father was known to be a controversial character, a politician in the Church of Scotland, someone almost of the status of a celebrity.[4] For Grace, her early life was one of comfort, security and continuous company. She was educated by a governess at home, but also probably attended a finishing school in London. Through her mother, Jane Garden of Piccadilly, she had many relatives in the city. A relative of her mother was later to pay for her training in painting after she left the Aberdeen area.

All this came to an end in 1895. Father, Reverend John Mitchell, retired that year after forty years in the parish of St Fergus. At the age of seventy, he moved into the city of Aberdeen and died later in the same year. Grace Mitchell was on her own for the first time, and was at the start of the wholly unsettled, almost itinerant, period of her life. After having one abode for twenty-seven years Grace spent the years from 1895 to her death in 1953 moving almost every year, with no fixed abode. Initially, she can be located at two addresses in Aberdeen,[5] when she exhibited with the Aberdeen Artists' Society in 1896 and 1898. These are her first recorded exhibits. There were around four hundred exhibitors in the exhibition on each occasion. Grace Mitchell's paint-

ings were *Portrait*, *Primrose* and *Italian Boy*, all three priced at the bottom of the range at three guineas only. None of Grace Mitchell's Scottish paintings can be located now. Almost certainly, Grace left Aberdeen in 1899, and it is remarkable that no image or symbol from her Scottish years appears in her later painting. The door to the past seemed to close when in 1899, she went travelling through Holland, Belgium and northern France on her way to Paris. She exhibited for a third and last time in the Aberdeen Artists' Society exhibition of November 1900 from the address 16 Rue Boisonade, Paris. This time there are four paintings, landscapes from Holland, Belgium and Picardy, now priced at five guineas.[5] On the way to Paris, there had been some reason for an increase in her artistic confidence and she has been reported for a few months at the Blanc Garrins Academy in Brussels. It is probable that it was well into the year 1900 before Grace arrived in Paris, and it is thought that Paul Henry left there in the same year or early in 1901.[3] She had arrived only just in time for the most significant rendezvous of her life, the meeting with and subsequent marriage to Paul Henry.

When they met in 1900 Grace Mitchell and Paul Henry were 'birds of a feather', at least socially, if not also in their artistic achievement. They were far from home, if either had anywhere to call home. Lonely, poor, apprentice artists, they came from similar Protestant church families, on the northern edge of the British Isles. Their family backgrounds were very similar, as was their situation in Paris. Paul Henry was quite established, even holding a small job in Whistler's Académie Carmen, and his interest in the painting style of James McNeill Whistler has been frequently discussed.[3] It now seems that the influence of Whistler, in modulated colour, simplified composition, and nocturnal subjects, was adopted very early by Grace Mitchell through her Paris connection with Paul Henry, and used by her in most of her painting in the first decade, 1905-15, of her life as a professional painter.

Grace became Mrs Paul Henry when they married at St Peter's Church, Bayswater, London on 17 September 1903. For the following seven years, the Henrys lived in or near London. They had various homes, all for short periods and often living with friends. Guildford and

*Grace Henry, The Long Grey Road of Destiny, (1913—14),*
*Oil on canvas, 25 x 19 cm. Private collection, Belfast.*

*Grace Henry, Stephen Gwynn or The Orange Man, (1918—19).*
*Oil on linen, 60 x 50 cm. Limerick City Gallery of Art.*

Southampton have been recorded as places where they lived just outside London, and while Paul Henry found employment drawing black and white illustrations for publications, Grace started her career in oil painting. Possibly three paintings of hers from the period in England, 1903-10, are known. One is a very simple Whistler-like composition, a nocturnal scene of the moon's reflection in a lake, framed by Wiseman's of 54 Above Bar Street, Southampton, a company in business at that address from 1898. The second is what is likely to be a self-portrait in a blue artist's smock, possibly her only self-portrait, painted on a canvas bought in St Ives and showing a woman in her late thirties with blue eyes and fair hair.[6] The third painting is *The Girl in White,* now at the HLMG, which was first exhibited from an address in London, and whose subject is the same girl as in the putative self-portrait.

All three paintings, though very different in subject, are similar in style and carry identifications of English origin. In all three, the mood is quiet and controlled, composition is simple and almost geometric. Colour range is limited and muted. Paint is not used thickly, nor required to work on its own. The Whistler influence is very strong in the nocturnal landscape. If any other paintings from this early London period are discovered, it is likely that they will be in a similar style, this being the first of the four phases of Grace Henry's painting, which continued after 1910 when the Henrys moved to Ireland and to Achill. That major move of home and lifestyle is well documented, as are the eventual different reactions of Grace and Paul to their life on Achill.[3] Initially, both seemed to adapt quickly and successfully to this new environment, one in such stark contrast to London, Surrey, Paris, Aberdeen or Belfast. The important point about Grace Henry's painting on arrival in Achill is that most of her work was done by moonlight, and the nocturnal or evening scenes continue the mood, muted colour and simple composition of Whistler. Grace Henry is still remembered in Achill for painting outdoors at night, often at the old bridge at Dooagh, in painter's smock and easel set up under the moonlit sky.[7] In a joint

exhibition held in Belfast in the spring of 1916 and entitled, *Pictures of the West of Ireland,* seven of the ten Grace Henry paintings discussed in a newspaper report are described as evening or moonlit subjects.[8] Included was the painting *The Long Grey Road of Disting* ('Disting' now thought to be a much-repeated error for 'Destiny') which was subject of an article on 'Nationality in Art — the work of Paul and Grace Henry', published in the *Colour* magazine of London in April 1918.[9] The author remarks with surprise that both painters have caught the personality of the west of Ireland, despite their alien backgrounds in Belfast and Scotland, but notices that each is individual and different in approach. Grace Henry is again noted for her attempts to simplify her subjects and to use subdued colour, lilac, grey, purple, Prussian blue and underlying black. This phase of dark painting and sombre moods comes to an end about 1915—1916. It had been a period of landscape painting, sometimes with figures in the landscape.

In the same volume of *Colour,* (Vol. 8 1918), the second period of the evolution

# GRACE HENRY

of Grace Henry's painting is marked by a print of *The Black Shawl* (present whereabouts unknown). It is very similar in subject, composition and colour range to the well-known painting *Top of the Hill* in Limerick Art Gallery, and both must date from about 1915. Suddenly everything has changed. Colour, composition and form become strong. There is broadening of subject matter to include figurative subjects, single figures and groups. Groups of local people with their donkeys returning from the fields, sometimes in arrangements that suggest the Holy Family. Professional groups are also included. Portraits are painted seriously, with great sensitivity and skill, particularly in the case of *Stephen Gwynn* or *The Orange Man*. The sad and beautiful girl figure in a colourful landscape, *Mallaranny*, appeals to a whole range of emotions.[10] Landscapes such as *Country of Amethyst* are notable for their harmony of colour, colour that is realistic and descriptive. Often in other paintings it depicts Paisley shawls of peasant clothing. Paint is applied more thickly and starts to work on its own, giving texture to the paintings. There is a new sense of freedom in the paintings, seagulls being used as an image of that freedom. The early, tightly-written signatures of *E G Henry* and *E Grace Henry* of the first period are now replaced by a casual *G Henry* with a following dash, a style which persists for the rest of her career. The signature *Grace Henry* over-rides both the first and second periods, but is probably not used much after 1925.

There are relatively few paintings known from this second period, and, since none of Grace Henry's paintings are dated, it is a matter of conjecture and using related dates that allows us to assume that we are dealing with paintings from the late Achill period from 1915 to 1920. The paintings from this period previously discussed are all reproduced in *Colour* magazine between 1918 and 1921, so it is fair to assume that they were painted one or two years prior to these dates. They include some of the most ambitious and-most acclaimed paintings of Grace Henry's career. She is now painting the people of Achill, not working or returning from work, but dressed in their traditional clothes, the colourful Paisley shawls. Subjects are now well-lit and include both interior and outdoor scenes. Colour, composition and subject are all

*Grace Henry, Spring in winter, (1922—23). Oil on canvas, 51 x 61 cm. Private collection, Belfast.*

equally strong. Her painting style is breaking free, becoming more expressive and establishes a fluidity in the use of paint that continues for the remainder of her career, allowing us always to identify a Grace Henry painting by that means. Her painting technique in brushwork is consistently the same from about 1915 until her death in 1953.

Grace Henry had started to loosen the bond with Paul Henry in this period, although her introduction of white cumulus clouds in the backgrounds of her paintings of about 1915 must have been influenced by his work of the same time. The Henrys returned to Dublin in 1919, and continued to work together for a time and were both involved in establishing the Society of Dublin Painters.[3] Around 1920, Grace had a romantic association with Stephen Gwynn and shortly after, went travelling with him in France and Italy. This decade of the 1920s coincides with her third period of painting. This is marked by the greatest freedom and looseness in her use of paint, by her use of colour to depict atmosphere and weather, or simply for its own sake, as in a Fauvist style. It was the period of even more experimentation in style and subject matter. Atmosphere and movement enter her paintings. Subjects now include *Spring in Winter* and *The Storm*, where clouds, of unnatural green and reddish brown colours, are sent hurtling across the sky. More and more seagulls are introduced to increase the sense of freedom. Trees are bent in the wind. Water appears to flow out of *Floods at Ennis*, and the *Kerry Sunset* is a blaze of red. Subjects do include very

loosely painted flower-pieces, where flowers mix with background and vases almost flow down on to the table. Commissioned portraits continue, but portraits of her own choice are more often caricatures employing Fauve-like colour. Her landscape subjects are still largely from Ireland, but have moved from Achill to Galway, Clare and Kerry. They are highly colourful, but few people are ever included. In every sense, this was a very disturbed period in her life, in her personal life and in her painting style. Grace Henry parted permanently from Paul Henry in 1927 (see Kennedy[3]), but they were never divorced. Paul Henry married Mabel Young as his second wife only after Grace had died.

The fourth and final period of her changing style was built around Grace Henry's travelling in France and Italy in the 1930s. She made several visits to the south of France and to the Adriatic coast of Italy, to Venice and to Chioggia. The brilliant light of the Mediterranean is reflected in the intensified colour of her paintings; more red, magenta, alizarin, cobalt, orange and white are introduced in particular. Colour is sought in her choice of subjects which are now mainly of boats, elaborate sails of complex and colourful designs, canal scenes, shorelines and coastal villages. Grace Henry now adopts a more conventional, more realistic approach in the representation of houses, villages, boats and harbours. Much more architectural detail is included in the line of a roof, window, shutters, paths and steps. In the studio, Grace continued to paint flower arrangements, as she did throughout her career. There are few portraits, except commissions, but they are sympathetic, and there are only a very few interiors. France and Italy, where she lived continuously from about 1935 to 1939, inspired some of her most colourful and most decorative canvases. The paintings from the village of Mougins (near Nice), in particular, and sails in Chioggia, are some of the most flamboyant, pleasing and confident of her career. Paintings of this period featured very largely in her London exhibition of 1939,[11] and dominated again in the 1991 exhibition at the Hugh Lane Gallery.

Grace Henry returned to Dublin in 1939 at the age of seventy-one. This was effectively the end of her career, although she continued to paint and to exhibit. For her last years, she moved around friends

*Grace Henry, Reflection of the Moon, (1904–05),*
*Oil on canvas, 46 x 52 cm. Private collection, Belfast.*

*Grace Henry, Top of the Hill, (1915–16).*
*Oil on linen, 60 x 50 cm. Limerick City Gallery of Art.*

*Grace Henry, The Red House at Mougins, (1935–36).*
*Oil on board, 27 x 35 cm. Private collection, Belfast.*
*Exhibited Irish Women Artists (NGI 1986) and Paul and Grace Henry (HLMG 1991).*

# GRACE HENRY

and cheap hotels mainly in the Dublin area. She was a sad and lonely figure, usually found sitting in hotel lounges waiting to talk to anyone passing by. Her work, always of variable quality was now poorer. She was limited to painting from memory or painting still-life.

Despite the very wide range of subjects she tackled and her experimentation with many different techniques, the paintings of all her four periods have a consistency of style, mood and expression. She was more a landscape painter than anything else, and these four periods relate mainly to her landscapes. These paintings were serious, professional works, but they had features which revealed the artist as a passionate, poetic, frivolous, extravagant, emotional and volatile woman. Though her work included some of uneven quality, her career covered a period of over fifty years, and at times, reached levels of artistic ability and creativity close to that of the Scottish Colourists, who were her immediate contemporaries and painted very similar subjects on the continent.[9] Grace Henry's paintings always demonstrate the artist's special sensitivity with colour, which is used to convey mood, atmosphere, light and movement. After her Achill period,

*Grace Henry*, Horse drinking at village pond, *(1912–13)*, Oil on wood, *28 x 36 cm. Private collection, Belfast.*

she used paint thickly and in sweeping brushstrokes so that her subjects seemed to flow together and sometimes almost seemed to move. She used lines in the same way throughout all her paintings, to draw the eye inward to a focal point. Often there were lanes or roads or paths leading inward, usually with irregular contours converging and diverging, concentrating and releasing energy. Lines along hedges or walls were never straight. Sudden, un-

predictable rises and downward plunges conveyed excitement to the subject. They conveyed also the feelings and personality of the artist.

Grace Henry may not be ranked among the greatest of painters in Ireland, but she had a distinction over a wide range that few can match. She was possibly the first, even before Swanzy, Hone and Jellett, to experiment with 'modernism' in her few early attempts to create abstractions of the landscape. Her Achill paintings include examples moving in the direction of abstraction. In the work of her three later periods, her use of paint and fluid brush work are distinctive. Most of all her paintings carry her particular stamp as a professional artist, able to create a unique style combining brushwork and use of colour to convey mood and an excitement that works powerfully on the emotions of the viewer.

*James G Cruickshank*

*James G Cruickshank, formerly of the Queen's University of Belfast, is the author of books and articles on Irish geography, and as a native of Aberdeen, Scotland, and amateur artist, has become a researcher of Grace Henry and a collector of her works. He gave one of the lectures during the 1991 Paul and Grace Henry exhibition.*

## NOTES

1. The catalogue of *The Paintings of Paul Henry and Grace Henry*, 26 November – 31 December 1991, HLMG, Exhibition Curator and Cataloguer – Antoinette Murphy. Details of most of the paintings discussed here may be found in the catalogue.
2. Paul Henry, *An Irish Portrait*, London, Batsford, 1951 and Paul Henry, *Further Reminiscences*, Belfast. Blackstaff Press, 1973.
3. Brian Kennedy, 'Paul Henry: An Irish Portrait', *Irish Arts Review*, Yearbook 1989–90 pp. 43–54, should be used for further background and quotations from correspondence referring to both Paul and Grace Henry. This should be used as a source of information on the private lives of the two Henrys, as no new material for the period of their marriage will be included here.
4. Church of Scotland records, *Fasti Ecclesiae Scoticanae*, Six Synods of Aberdeen and Moray, Aberdeen, 1926, provides a full family record of births and deaths, and an outline of the career of father John Mitchell.
5. Emily Grace Mitchell lived at 72 Ashley Road, in 1896, and at 50 Stanley Street, Aberdeen in 1898. Her paintings sent from

Paris in 1900 to the exhibition of the Aberdeen Artists' Society were *Kirk-Zutfen, Holland, Canal in Dordrecht, Josef* and *Apple Blossom in Picardy*. The last became a recurrent subject in later years.
6. Mairin Allen, 'Contemporary Irish Artists – Grace Henry', *Father Matthew Record*, November 1942, p.4, provides this physical description of the artist and reviews her painting of the 1930s.
7. Personal communication from John McNamara, Dooagh, Achill, which provided information about the reports of Grace Henry's night-time painting, passed through the two previous generations of his family.
8. Paintings exhibited in *Pictures of the West of Ireland*, Paul and Grace Henry, Underwood Typewriter House, Belfast, 23 March – 8 April 1916. Newspaper review is to be found in the *Northern Whig*, 23 March 1916, p.8
9. *Colour* was an art magazine published from 53 Victoria Street, Westminster, London, from 1912 until about 1925 (or later). It gave attention to colourful paintings and printed many of them. Five of Grace Henry's paintings and three of Paul Henry's are

included. *Colour* appeared to consider these of similar importance and colour interest to paintings by the Scottish Colourists, and artists like Laura Knight, Augustus John, Orpen, Sickert and Bevan. Paintings by these were all featured about as frequently as those of the two Henrys. *The Long Grey Road, to Disting or Destiny* was in Vol. 8, 1918, *The Black Shawl* in Vol. 8, 1918, *Mallaranny* in Vol. 10, 1919, *The Orange Man (Stephen Gwynn)*, in Vol. 14, 1921, and *Country of Amethyst* in Vol. 14, 1921.
10. Comment in *Colour*, Vol. 10, 1919, on the painting *Mallarany* included, 'there is a great deal of Ireland packed into this picture . . . it explains why there is an Irish question? The implication is that the artist was making a political statement.
11. Possibly the most acclaimed exhibition of Grace Henry's work was that at the Calmann Gallery, 42 St James's Place, London, 11–31 July 1939. Of the thirty-four paintings on show, most painted abroad in the 1930s, ten were included in the 1991 exhibition in HLMG.

# JAMES DIXON

The story of my first meeting with James Dixon has often been told. I was painting a harbour scene on the island one Sunday morning and, when the islanders came out of mass, several of them stopped on their way home to watch me. 'I could do better than that', said James and rather naturally I asked him why then he didn't do it. 'No materials', he said — so I promised to provide him with paper, which he mostly liked painting on, and paints. He refused brushes saying he could easily make his own out of his donkey's tail. That is how it all began, though later Jimmy showed me a bird he had painted and also a *Crucifixion* scene he had painted with old tin left-overs of paint on top of a calendar.

As far as I know his first attempt, after our meeting, produced the remarkable *Harbour Scene* that Bruce Arnold reproduced in his book on Irish painting. Naturally I bought the picture, now part of the Glebe Gallery collection, and from that moment there was no holding him. This must have been in 1956 or 1957.

Tory Island, a rock three miles long and about a quarter of a mile wide, has no trees and sits in the middle of the Atlantic. John Berger once described the inhabitants as people from a wreck rowing desperately for the shore but with no hope of ever getting there. The island he felt, when he visited it with me, was about to fall over the cliff-edge of Europe. Nothing except the fabled Hy Brasil between it and the setting sun.

I don't think when James commented on my picture he meant to criticise my possible technical ability at representational detail. Luke Batterham wrote in a thesis on Dixon 'it was just that the studied, restrained pictorialism employed by Hill to represent the island bore little relation to the Irishman's own experience of the place on which he had spent almost his entire life'. Most of Dixon's pictures, apart from the few portraits, are related to the island and what goes on during its daily routine. Proportions, perspectives and topographical accuracy have no part in his work. Animals may appear larger than people and a rather disconcerting aerial view may suddenly be added to a normal flat landscape. He uses dark and sombre colours with white flecks applied for waves or gulls. Browns and blues are mixed and they help to make the greys.

Once, to a local newspaper man, he said 'You don't get all that much colour here,

James Dixon, although untrained, gained recognition as a natural painter, and examples of his work are in several public collections. **Derek Hill** describes the emergence of the artist.

*Derek Hill, Portrait of James Dixon Oil on canvas 74 x 89 cm.*

except the blue and greys of the sky and the glistening of the sea. There is nothing romantic about little boats fighting with crashing waves and winds.' The islanders do fight hard for survival and may through the school of painting that followed Jimmy's example, have achieved this. A long struggle against governmental wishes to evacuate the island.

Shipwrecks were often chosen as subjects by Jimmy, the most famous being the sinking of the *HMS Wasp* in 1884. The boat had come from Sligo it seems, to collect island rates long overdue and the inhabitants are said to have turned a cursing stone for its demise. Whatever happened, the lighthouse is alleged not to have been functioning that night and the loss of over eighty lives was the result. There are several pictures of the sinking of the *Titanic*, something that had always made a great impression on Jimmy as a boy. His rival, James Rogers, one of the other island painters, depicted the *HMS California* — the ship that is said to have disregarded the *Titanic* and its signals and that, far later, was wrecked on the island when cruising gently out beyond the West Town harbour.

Some people talk of an early Dixon or a late one, but there's really little difference to be seen in technique between the dates when he was at work. The dates he often wrote, with the titles, on the corners of his pictures are not always accurate. He just painted his own feelings towards a subject, and that was that. Apart from the sea pictures and scenes of islanders herding cattle or attending dog

races — something I admit I never saw on the island — he painted birds and flowers and a very occasional portrait of them — as he imagined them. Ellen Ward was already in her late nineties and then he painted her posthumously. He also painted the Queen, titled *To the Queen wishing you the Best of Luck,* and Winston Churchill, whom he greatly admired. His picture of the Queen was sent to her and a courtier replied that Her Majesty wished him many years ahead for his good work. Lady Churchill was given the picture of Winston but its whereabouts can only be surmised, alas, after the destruction of Sutherland's magnificent portrait. He also painted myself, as a present, a Union Jack in hand, wearing a suit and a tie — something I'd never do on the island — and beside me a landscape and a flower picture to demonstrate the things I loved. A typical Englishman! Any true likeness to the subject was not achieved.

Apart from the HMS Wasp's sinking, Jimmy painted *The First Steamship* — also, of course, from imaginatioin. The picture is almost entirely of the sea, with great variety of paint surface. Underneath he writes 'The first steamship that ever passed Tory Island Sound. The Tory islanders sent after her thinking she was on fire when they saw the smoke of her when they were tired out they had to turn back killed out and one of them said she is as far away now as ever. by James Dixon Tory Island 12/2/64.'

Dixon's brush strokes often overlap so that the sea, the land and even the boats make an inseparable unit and each element is in constant conflict with the other. To the islanders the sea is not merely a means of their fishing livelihood but is also often a reason of their death by drowning.

The other island painters may achieve island views and scenes but none of them — not even Alfred Wallis in Cornwall — have ever depicted the dramatic and restless natural elements or the reality of storm conditions in the way that Dixon has.

*Derek Hill*

*Derek Hill is well-known for his portrait and landscape paintings, many of which interpret the Donegal coastline near his home. Hill donated the Glebe Gallery Collection, Donegal, to the nation. As he recounts above, he encouraged James Dixon, (1887–1971) the naive painter.*

ILLUSTRATIONS OVERLEAF
'DIXON ON TORY' BY PAUL MULDOON
ON PAGE 182.

*James Dixon, The 'Ave Maria', The First Motor Boat on Tory, 1968.
Oil on paper, 57.2 x 76 cm. Private collection.*

*James Dixon, Mary Driving the Cattle Home Across the Sands of Dee, 1964.
Oil on canvas, 57 x 71 cm. Collection the Arts Council of Ireland.*

*James Dixon, Sinking of the Titanic, 1966.*
*Oil on paper 56 x 76.2 cm. Private collection.*

*James Dixon, HMS Wasp Foundering on Tory, 1968.*
*Oil on paper, 57.2 x 76 cm. Private collection.*

# WORD AND IMAGE

### Dixon on Tory

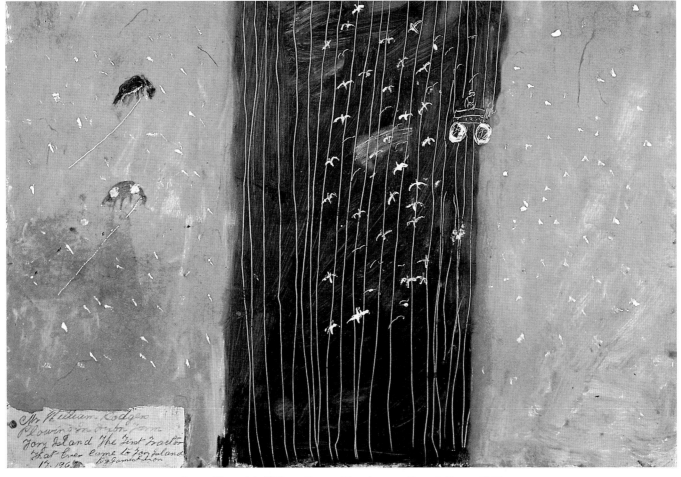

*James Dixon*, Mr William Rogers Ploughing in Dixon's Farm, *1967.*
*Oil on paper, 57.2 x 76 cm. Ulster Museum, Belfast.*

*Inscribed*, Mr William Rogers Ploughing in Dixon's Farm Tory Island,
the First Tractor that ever came to Tory Island.

*Incorrigible these beginnings,*
*The first flagstaff that was erected*
*On Ardlarin Point by Lloyds*
*For signalling to ships and the first*
*Tractor that ever came to Tory.*

*These representative lives*
*Steered between the rocks of sea and land.*
*And these other uncluttered journeys*
*The Wild Goose leaving after*
*A good dance in Tory Island hall,*

*The Queen on her Royal Yacht Britannia*
*Miss Rodgers driving the cattle home.*
*The easy telling of these endings*
*The Wasp wrecked on back of the lighthouse*
*The Rothy Bay of Greenock*

*On the rocks near the east end,*
*The Fairholm on the rocks beside Alarin.*
*Ninety people have been drowned*
*Under this weight of oil and canvas*
*Though one survived by clinging to the brush.*

Paul Muldoon

Reprinted from *Knowing My Place*, (Ulsterman Publications, 1971), by kind permission of the author.

# WILLIAM CROZIER

Ireland first became aware of William Crozier in the round when his large retrospective exhibition toured Ireland and Britain in 1990–1991; it was seen, in a truncated version, at the Crawford Gallery in Cork and later in full at the RHA Gallagher Gallery in Dublin (see *Irish Arts Review* Yearbook 1991–92, pp. 237, 240, 241). His large, almost aggressively colourful paintings made an immediate impact on the Irish public, who previously had seen only occasional works by him in group exhibitions. They were mainly landscapes, but they combined this with a rich, tapestried, almost abstract sense of colour orchestration.

Crozier is Scottish by birth and training, but he has been an Irish citizen for many years and spends part of each year in West Cork, whose landscape – including its Atlantic coastline – figures prominently in his recent work. He does not identify himself with the New Wave of Scottish painting which gained so much publicity in the mid-1980s and says that he likes being an exile – 'it gives you a special energy for working, and a perspective on things.'

Apart from Britain and Ireland, he has exhibited in the US and Canada, France, Germany, Spain, Italy, Poland, and Denmark, and is hung in many museums and collections – though not yet in public collections in Ireland. Recently, one-man exhibitions of his work have been seen at the Taylor Galleries in Dublin and at the Scottish Gallery in London, now restyled as the William Jackson Gallery. In the opinion of many people, he has painted better since the mid-1980s than he has ever done, which may at least partly reflect his gradual easing out from his art-teaching responsibilities at Winchester.

Crozier was born in Coker, a working-class suburb of Glasgow, in 1930, of mixed Irish and Huguenot descent. He says that he has always felt Irish – 'when you grow up in Glasgow in an Irish family, you automatically feel yourself to be Irish.' He got his training as an artist there and made a long visit to Paris while still in his 'teens. During the 1950s he was in London, where he mixed with the Soho set which included Bacon and Freud, as well as his fellow Scots Colquhoun and MacBryde ('the two Roberts'). During that decade he also lived in Dublin, where at one stage he painted stage sets for a living, and was familiar with the McDaid's Bar

Critics have noted a new vitality and authority in William Crozier's recent work. **Brian Fallon** explores Crozier's relations with international art.

literati, including Patrick and Anthony Cronin (who, incidentally, opened his retrospective in Dublin). He is married to Katharine Crouan, an art historian.

Though Crozier admires the seriousness and power of the best contemporary British artists, he does not easily fit into a British context. At a time when Continental – and particularly German – Expressionism was ignored or despised in Britain, he discovered the qualities of artists such as Schmidt-Rottluff and Nolde. He says of German Expressionism in general: 'I like its immediacy, and it expanded the emotional language of painting, so that it could have psychological overtones.' This explains why, in spite of his uninhibited admiration for French art, there are elements in his style which are remote from French taste. France is his favourite country, though he also has links with Spain and visits it nearly every year with his wife. Crozier describes himself as 'mainly a landscape painter', but says also: 'I never found the language to do so, but I would like to paint some great classical pictures.' He has a special reverence for the European 'Grand Style' as exemplified by Claude and Poussin.

FALLON: *You have a definite sympathy with Expressionism, which must have been unfashionable in Britain at that time.*

CROZIER: There was a huge Munch exhibition in 1948, which only went to Glasgow. That was my introduction to Expressionism. There was nothing in English about it in those days. Only that little Penguin –

FALLON: *I know it – I still have a copy somewhere. It was written under an alias – 'Peter Thoene', or something like that.*

CROZIER: There were only a few things in colour, the rest was black and white. But the impact Expressionism made on me at that time was overwhelming. I remember going into the gallery in Hamburg and every artist had a room of his own – I had never experienced such a wealth of emotion. I also remember going up to see the

Nolde Museum in Seebüll. I think what he had was an obvious primitivism that touched the Germans very deeply. They didn't see it as 'modern art', a barrier to get through. They felt it was a common German language of art.

FALLON: *Yet your main loyalty seems to have been to Paris and French art.*

CROZIER: I went to Paris because I thought that it was the centre of things. Some of that was a hangover from what I had read about it before the war. Picasso, Braque, Matisse were simply what modern art was supposed to be about. But I also saw the generation of Hartung, Soulages, etc and I realise now they influenced me much more than I thought at the time.

But as I grow older, I find that I feel closer and closer to classical art. For instance, I have never found an older artist who admires Klee much, or is even interested in him, but younger painters seem to rediscover him all the time. I find Rembrandt much less interesting than I did. If you were to take ten or so of the portraits and self-portraits, I think you have the man in his essence. There is something artificial about the big compositions, however much you admire them. You don't get that in Claude or Poussin, who are always looking out at something over the hill or beyond the horizon . . . I have been looking a lot at Courbet – you know *The Studio*? That is a work which is a kind of summing-up. You have to have something magisterial you can measure yourself against, some central work.

FALLON: *When I looked at it last, I felt that it must have darkened a lot from what it looked like originally.*

CROZIER: If you could only paint pictures that were old when you painted them! I would actually like to show a painting only when it was at least twenty years old, or even 200. If a picture looks too new, it loses one of the richest qualities that it can have.

Have you seen the Sistine Chapel restoration? I saw it at about the halfway stage, and it was like losing a continent. Nobody will ever know it in the old way again. What they have taken away is the age of the paint. If you look at cathedrals, they have all been destroyed by people restoring them.

*William Crozier,* Yellow Strand, 1989, *oil on canvas, 61 x 76 cm.*

*William Crozier, English Night, 1990, oil on canvas, 107 x 114 cm.*

# WILLIAM CROZIER

FALLON: *Can we ever really understand the art of the past, in that sense?*

CROZIER: If you got someone from, say, the year 1400 to draw that bottle there, he would draw it differently from you and I. And the difference would not be in the drawing alone, it would be something he put into the drawing.

As I mentioned to you before, I am doing this big picture about exile. I have been working on it for some time now, and it has been going through several stages. At the moment, it's a triptych.

FALLON: *How do you feel about, say, conceptual art?*

CROZIER: I want an art which engages every part of me, but all these people seem to engage only a single part of me. I hate the sort of art which is some kind of visual pun. I think you do need great art — I don't necessarily know what that is, but you do need the 'Grand Style'.

I looked at the Cecily Brennan show in TCD. I admire her, as an artist, but I cannot see how she did these things — waterfalls and so on — without much imaginative output into them. I believe that you cannot do that, really.

FALLON: *Tell me more about your triptych.*

CROZIER: I call it *The Green Fields of America*. There is a bit in it of the pictures which interest me — a bit like Courbet, a bit like Claude . . .

I think it is time that Irish painters should look forward, without that look back over the shoulder, as if they were thinking of a 500-year-old tragedy. I would like them to be more revolutionary — it's something to do with dumping modern '-isms' and finding the future.

FALLON: *You have lived, or at least stayed, in New York, haven't you? I think you said before that you didn't like it much.*

CROZIER: I had a studio in New York — it must hve been about 1964 — no, it was about 1970. I had it for a year in all, but only worked in it for about seven months. No, I have grown to like New York much more than I did. I think some cities are easy to find the measure of — you step in, but you could get done very badly if you didn't get the pace right. We tend to get disoriented in New York. After all, it looks the wrong way — we tend to look to the sunset. But one thing New York has — if you are alive at all, it is impossible to walk up Fifth Avenue and not to feel exhilarated.

FALLON: *When you went there first, what particularly interested you?*

CROZIER: When I went there, it was Abstract Expressionism which interested me. I even went to the Cedar Tavern, where they used to drink. But I remember going to the Met, and the French Room was so sensational, that when I went out I had forgotten where I was and was surprised to find that I was in New York.

FALLON: *What else — apart from Abstract Expressionism — impressed you there?*

CROZIER: The only big show I saw was called *New Image* or something like that. It was an art historian's attempt to show how the commonplace subjects had moved into art. There were these two little Légers which were just glowing off the walls.

FALLON: *You are known as a disciplined, regular worker with a large output — I think you have estimated it at about ten thousand paintings. What are your working methods — for instance, since your colours are generally so luminous, do you start with a white ground?*

CROZIER: It has to be a white ground, I cannot work any other way. I have to draw it on the canvas until I have the balance of the sections absolutely right. If I leave a bit not quite right, the picture will never be complete. That is something I have to start out with.

It is in the middle period that the picture is slowly achieved. But then comes the part in which there is a sense of freedom and you don't have to make choices — the choices are made for you. But certainly, the first part is absolutely crucial — I could not start without that part being absolutely right.

FALLON: *What about your media — for instance, do you like acrylic paint as well as oils? Of course, you have also painted a lot in watercolour . . .*

CROZIER: I find that with acrylic paints, I try to 'bend' them to make them like oils. Or else I use them rather like watercolour. A lot happens in that area which does not happen with oils.

I would not be in the least surprised if in a few years people refused to buy oils for health reasons. Experience in America shows a strong pressure against the dangers of working oil paints. But it is still the medium I love best. Somehow, they got it right early on — the Venetians, and the others, Titian, Rembrandt. There is a fantastic sense of tradition in the medium.

The tradition of the independent, personal, maker of oil paints is dying. Winsor and Newton now make nearly all the paints. I used to use only French paints, for a while, but I think that particular firm has now been taken over by Winsor and Newton too. The old range was about forty colours, now it is about twenty or twenty-five. That is because the situation is dominated more and more by amateur painters.

When I make up a black, I love the ash from peat. You add a little of that to your other colours, and you get a marvellous quality.

FALLON: *You know the international art world and its workings, yet you have managed to stay independent and apart from it. What do you think of it today, in view of the so-called recession, and so on?*

CROZIER: I used to hear people talking about something called 'the League'. That meant that if you sold a picture for about £1,000,000, or so, you were in that league. Now that is all gone, they no longer get those prices, and only the kind of people who see nothing but the Emperor's clothes — only that kind, who pushed it, could tell you what it was about.

FALLON: *Your big picture The Rowan Tree is a favourite of mine. I had assumed for a long time that it was a rural scene or subject — perhaps something you had seen down in West Cork — but I have read since that the actual setting was a stretch of public park in London, between Wood Green and Palmers Green.*

CROZIER: And in the background were these big chestnuts, so voluptuous! It was one of these pictures in which the symbolic idea corresponded exactly to the reality.

*Brian Fallon*

*Brian Fallon is Chief Critic of* The Irish Times.

# MICHAEL HEALY'S STAINED GLASS WINDOW OF 'ST VICTOR'

**David Caron** discusses
one of Dublin's most intriguing
and beautiful windows by the
Irish stained glass artist,
Michael Healy (1873 - 1941)
in St Catherine's and St James's
Church, Donore Avenue.

For several decades following its foundation in 1903 in Dublin by Sarah Purser, An Túr Gloine (The Tower of Glass) Stained glass Studio employed artists, in particular Michael Healy, Wilhelmina Geddes and Evie Hone, who produced some of the finest windows created anywhere this century. Along with Harry Clarke, who worked in the family firm, these artists designed hundreds of stained glass windows of considerable merit which can be found in every county of Ireland and in four continents.

Of the principal artists of the Irish stained glass movement, Healy, Geddes, Hone and Clarke, it is Michael Healy (1873–1941) who is the least well known. This is partly due to the fact that he lived his life as a virtual recluse, signed any of his windows only very occasionally, and almost never participated in exhibitions; in effect, Healy actively avoided any action which might have brought attention to either himself or his work. Nowadays Healy is probably better remembered in the public eye as the creator of charming deft watercolour studies of Dublin street characters; this would surely displease him since he made these studies as a diversion while on his lunch break from An Túr Gloine, and he purposely destroyed many of them before his final illness.

Healy is also less well known as a stained glass artist because his artistic style is not as easily immediately to identify or categorise as those of, say, Hone or Clarke. Throughout his nearly forty-year career as a stained glass artist, Michael Healy employed a variety of styles. To an extent these styles evolved sequentially, although they do not altogether develop neatly one after another; rather Healy oscillated between a range of styles, particularly in the second half of his career.

The common thread that runs through all Healy's windows is the quality of his sensitive draughtsmanship. Indeed, as a student at the Dublin Metropolitan School of Art he was recognised for his drawing and it was this marked ability which led John Hughes, the modelling teacher, to recommend Healy to Sarah Purser when she was looking for her first recruit to An Túr Gloine.[1] The influence of Healy's stained glass instructor, A E Child, himself a student of the great Christopher Whall, is readily apparent in Healy's earliest windows.

*Michael Healy, St Catherine of Alexandria, (for St Catherine's and St James's Church of Ireland, Dublin), 1923. 22.2 x 8.2 cm, watercolour on paper. (NGI 18,357)*

Italian Renaissance painting clearly inspired Healy — the legacy of an eighteen month sojourn in Florence at the turn of the century — and it is possible to identify this pervasive influence throughout his career. Byzantine mosaics also appear to have made a significant impression on Healy and several of his windows of the late 1920s and 1930s are treated in a manner suggestive of this style.

Michael Healy, like Clarke, revelled in detail. Many of Healy's most successful works are single-light windows of modest proportions which could be closely inspected by the viewer. These commissions afforded Healy the possibility of including little vignettes, often incorporating his favoured aciding[2] technique, which would form a stunning border to frame the primary subject. Not only did they serve a decorative purpose but these little scenes could also enhance the narrative quality of the window by including, for instance, significant scenes relating to a saint's life.

Of all Healy's stained glass windows, the work that contains by far the most fascinating and abstruse imagery is that of 'St Victor' in St Catherine's and St James's Church of Ireland, Donore Avenue, Dublin. It is also a remarkably beautiful and enchanting window which captivates the viewer's attention on a variety of levels; from the erudite series of historical vignettes which challenges the intellect to piece together the sequence, to the simplicity of the innocent dancing child leading a seemingly endless line of meandering animals.

'St Victor' was erected in memory of Mrs Hannah Bailey (née Messer), principal of St Catherine's Girls' School from 1890 to 1923, who died on 13 June 1929. The order for the window was placed at An Túr Gloine by the rector of St Catherine's and St James's, Canon Hugh Thompson, and it was he who selected the various subjects to be incorporated in the window. The imagery in the window reflects Canon Thompson's abiding interest in the parish's history and as he died while Healy was undertaking the commission, 'St Victor' can almost be viewed as a memorial to the canon himself.

Hugh Walter Brownlow Thompson was born in 1872 in Co Donegal, a son of the rectory. (In due course Canon Thompson's own son was to take Holy Orders). In 1906 Mr Thompson was appointed curate of Holy Trinity, Rathmines. Signi-

# MICHAEL HEALY'S STAINED GLASS WINDOW OF 'ST VICTOR'

ficantly, in 1909, Michael Healy was commissioned by a local family, the Tarletons, to erect a four-light window to their parents' memory in Holy Trinity Church. This impressive window, Healy's largest and most ambitious commission to that date, depicts 'Saints Philip, Peter, Paul and Andrew'. Mr Thompson must surely have been impressed by this sublime window with its resonant colours, tracery incorporating symbolic subjects, and delightful vignettes in the predella panels.

In 1912 Mr Thompson left Rathmines to become rector of St Catherine's, Thomas Street, and its daughter church, St Catherine's Chapel-of-Ease, Donore Avenue. Two years later, on the recommendation of Mr Thompson and the Select Vestry, St Catherine's Chapel-of-Ease was renamed St Victor's. The name was selected to revive a link with the twelfth century Abbey of St Thomas, which stood on the site of St Catherine's Church, and was occupied by a community known as the Canons of the Congregation of St Victor.[3] Vignettes illustrating these historical developments are featured in Healy's 'St Victor'. (In 1969 the church was renamed again and is now known as St Catherine's and St James's).

During Canon Thompson's incumbency, three single-light stained glass windows by Michael Healy were commissioned for St Catherine's and St James's Church. Although Healy's final window of the trio, 'St Victor', is definitely the most intriguing of these, before examining it in detail, it is worthwhile noting the other two.

In 1915 Healy executed 'Hope', and this commission is one of the rare examples of an allegorical figure by Healy. Unlike A E Child, Kitty O'Brien, Ethel Rhind and Wilhelmina Geddes, Michael Healy appears to have positively steered away from commissions featuring allegorical figures. 'Hope', robed in emerald, is depicted gazing at a bud opening at the end of a dry branch. She rests against an anchor while crocuses flower at her feet. Healy, who was a much more innovative and dynamic artist than Child, surprisingly has taken his cue in terms of colour, composition, and imagery from an insipid window of the same subject exected in 1905 by his teacher.[4]

'Hope' has a timeless appearance, though her costume appears to be loosely based on those of the Middle Ages. This

St. Victor. *Detail of 'St Victor' window.*

Adam of St. Victor, *Detail of 'St Victor window, centre left.*

Thorneycroft's statue of Baron Plunkett, Archbishop of Dublin, in Kildare Place. *Detail of 'St Victor' window, lower right.*

feeling of period is reinforced by the treatment of a broad border of two-dimensional decorative architecture which encases the figure, and which does *not* feature in Child's window. The border is a fanciful mixture of turrets, tiled roofs, crenellations, pointed and curved arches, leaded dormer windows and latticed panels. The colours, mauve roofs and warm plasterwork with the occasional glimpse of an intense midnight-blue sky, are calculated to suggest a continental cityscape. Despite the charming border, 'Hope' is generally an uninspiring work and is not representative of the exciting stained glass Healy was beginning to produce by this date.

An infinitely more successful work than 'Hope' was the second window which Healy made eight years later for St Catherine's and St James's, 'St Catherine of Alexandria'. Executed in 1923, it was erected in memory of Miss Jane Elizabeth Matthews, who was for twenty-eight years assistant teacher in St Catherine's Girls' Day School and Sunday School. Among the Memorial Committee were Canon Thompson and Hannah Bailey[5] (in whose memory 'St Victor' would be erected). Healy depicted St Catherine as a handsome, almost matronly figure, with several of her traditional attributes. The draughtsmanship of St Catherine and the boy at her feet is superb, but the principal joy of this window is the series of small panels which form a border to the left and right of the saint. Among the several panels, some of which are totally abstract, are two distinct groups which are interspersed.

A group of four depicts a segment of a meandering river which is composed of azure, blue, mauve and emerald glass. Since St Catherine's birthplace was Alexandria, one could be excused for assuming that this represented the Nile. In fact, Canon Thompson's idea of inserting the river panels arose from the proximity to the church of the Poddle, one of Dublin's ancient and historic waterways. He was, however, eager to point out that the inclusion of four rivers also had a theological basis; the four flowing rivers are an early Christian symbol of the writings of the Four Evangelists whose words of life fertilise and enrich human life.[6] There is no staining, no aciding and only economic painting in these vibrant panels.

In dramatic contrast to these areas of flat intense colour are another group of panels which are uniformly stained and painted in such a manner as to suggest that the im-

*Michael Healy, St Victor,
1930. St Catherine's and
St James's Church of Ireland,
Dublin.*

# MICHAEL HEALY'S STAINED GLASS WINDOW OF 'ST VICTOR'

ages have been beaten into dulled bronze. Among the figures depicted in these five stunning panels are a Christian soldier, a rhetorician, and a philosopher.

When Hannah Bailey died in 1929, Canon Thompson was eager that a permanent memorial of her life's work among the parish's young people should be forthcoming.[7] In due course Canon Thompson placed an order at An Túr Gloine for a window to be designed by Healy depicting 'St Victor' which was to be inserted in the aperture to the right of 'St Catherine'. Of course, at that time the church was named 'St Victor's'.

Canon Thompson had by now developed into one of An Túr Gloine's staunchest and most influential supporters. As editor of the *Church of Ireland Gazette* he ensured that virtually all new windows produced at An Túr Gloine received at least a paragraph, often a detailed description, in the weekly periodical. Windows designed at the other Dublin studios, such as Clarkes and Earleys, only occasionally received a mention. The effect was that An Túr Gloine almost appeared to take on the stature of stained glass studio by appointment to the Church of Ireland.[8]

When Healy received the commission for 'St Victor' he first (as was the standard procedure) executed a pencil and watercolour sketch design for the window scaled at one inch to one foot. The sketch design was submitted to Canon Thompson and the Vestry for approval and then to the Archbishop of Dublin for sanction.[9] The composition of 'St Victor' is very similar to that of 'St Catherine'; a full-length representation of the subject in the centre, surrounded by a broad border incorporating a variety of vignettes. Despite the fact that some details of the sketch design are (mainly due to the small scale) not clearly identifiable, the spirit and composition of the window as executed closely resembles the sketch design.

St Victor, a Roman soldier who suffered martyrdom under Emperor Maximian, is shown in armour, complete with helmet, sword and shield. The wide border surrounding the saint depicts a series of small vignettes; the subjects of these minute scenes are of two distinct themes which alternate (similar to the treatment of the vignettes in 'St Catherine'). One series of six illustrates a passage from Isaiah,[10] the other series depicts seven different episodes of varying degrees of obscurity relating to the history of St Catherine's

'. . . and a little child shall lead them' (Isaiah 11:6). Detail of 'St Victor' window, bottom right.

Apse of St Catherine's church and memorial panel. *Detail of 'St Victor' window, bottom left.*

Sir Peter Lewis. *Detail of 'St Victor' window, lower left.*

and St James's and its parent church of St Catherine.

Commencing at the bottom left, a meandering line of wild and domestic animals including a bear, ram, goat, lions, wolf, calf and zebra make their way up the side of the window, over a bridge at the top and down the right side.[11] Leading the procession is a young child delicately painted on an irregular shaped piece of milky white translucent glass which is positioned at the base of the window so that the cavalcade of animals almost becomes a continuous chain.

Interspersed among the procession, though not ordered in chronological sequence, is the series of vignettes connected with the church's history.

One vignette near the dancing child depicts a silhouette of Thorneycroft's well-known statue of Baron Plunkett, Archbishop of Dublin, in Kildare Place. Archbishop Plunkett had, from 1884 to 1896, been manager of the Church of Ireland Training College (now demolished) which was located in Kildare Place. His inclusion in this window is significant for more than one reason; first, he was manager of the college where Mrs Bailey trained, and secondly, because he laid the foundation stone of St Catherine's and St James's Church in 1896.

In the bottom left of the window Healy includes a little scene of the neo-classical apse of St Catherine's Church (1796), Thomas Street, the parent church of St Catherine's and St James's. Various educational institutions were closely connected with St Catherine's Church and parish: the first Sunday School in Dublin (and the second in Ireland) was founded in the parish in 1786, and the Church of Ireland Training College also had its commencement in the parish.[12]

Directly above the vignette of St Catherine's apse is an extract from St Paul's First Epistle to Timothy: 'Fight the good fight'. In keeping with this strong exhortation Healy has rendered the text in dominant gold sans serif letters set against a refulgent ruby background. The quotation is particularly apt in a window which celebrates a soldier saint.

In another panel Sir Peter Lewis (or Lewys), the first post-Reformation vicar of St Catherine's Church is represented. Canon Thompson (the thirty-third incumbent of the same position) had a particular interest in Lewis and lectured on the subject.[13] Healy's representation of Lewis is an amalgam of two similar cut

# MICHAEL HEALY'S STAINED GLASS WINDOW OF 'ST VICTOR'

stone panels in the National Museum;[14] a full-length bearded figure in a flowing Geneva gown, carrying a resting animal – probably a rat – in his right hand.[15] Above and below Peter Lewis is the following inscription in Latin: 'Petro Lewys Clerico, domus nostrae dispensatori: hujus operis,Praesidi.' which can be translated as 'Peter Lewys, Clerk, steward in our household, president of this work.' This inscription originally appeared in two vertical columns on the better preserved of the two stone panels.

Mid-way up the left hand border, Healy depicts in wood-cut fashion, 'Adam of St Victor', who was the Abbot of the Abbey of St Thomas in 1290.[16] Adam of St Victor is shown, quill in hand, working industriously at his desk. This vignette is related to the panel in the same position on the right border.

Directly opposite Adam of St Victor, rendered in the style of an illuminated manuscript, is the following: 'Cum beata Catharina doctos vinceret doctrina', which is an extract from Adam of St Victor's *Hymn on the Martyrdom of St Catherine.*

High up on the left hand side, there is a small monotone vignette depicting the Becket Chapel in Canterbury Cathedral. This alludes to the fact that St Thomas's Abbey was named in memory of St Thomas à Becket, Archbishop of Canterbury.

The vignette in the right border corresponding with that of the Becket Chapel shows two angels spinning what appears to be an armillary sphere (a model of the presumed orbits of the sun and planets). It is captioned 'Science of the Middle Ages' and alludes to the fact that the congregation of St Victor 'became famous for Science and Profound Learning'[17] during this period.

At the top of the window there is a bridge over which the procession of animals cross. The bridge is a stylized depiction of Lewis's nine-arched Bridge of Athlone which he built over the Shannon in the years 1566–7. Lewis was an accomplished architect and master mason. In addition to the Bridge of Athlone, Lewis is also accredited with rebuilding the crypt of Dublin's Christ Church Cathedral of which he was precentor and proctor subsequent to his period at St Catherine's.

Beneath the centre arch of Healy's representation of the Bridge of Athlone is a minute acided figure of a man on horseback wading across the Shannon. His identity would almost certainly seem to be that of the Dutch general, Godard van Reede de Ginkel, who was commander of the Williamite forces in Ireland. On 30 June 1691, after a protracted siege against the Jacobite army in Athlone in which control of the bridge was the key factor, General Ginkel finally gained the walled town when a picked force of two thousand men traversed the river on a ford just south of the bridge.

In a panel positioned directly beneath the River Shannon, Healy has depicted the body of St Victor being guarded by two lionesses.

An Túr Gloine sent the bill (£108) for 'St Victor' on 28 November 1930, which indicates that the window had been completed by this date.[18] This was almost exactly six months after the commission had received sanction from the Archbishop of Dublin. It is likely that Healy would have spent much of this period working on 'St Victor' though we know that he also executed a somewhat smaller and less detailed window for a New Zealand crematorium chapel during the same six months.

'St Victor' represents one of the finest windows of Healy's middle period when he mainly executed modestly sized single-light windows crammed with beguiling detail. From the mid 1930s onwards most of his commissions were for clerestory windows, often of several lights, which, because of their distance from the viewer, precluded the detailed vignettes which characterise windows such as 'St Victor'.

*David Caron*

David Caron was educated at the National College of Art and Design, Dublin (BSc in Visual Communications), Pratt Institute, New York (MS in Communications Design), and Trinity College, Dublin (PhD). The subject of his PhD was 'An Túr Gloine and Michael Healy (1873-1941)'. He is the author, along with Dr Nicola Gordon Bowe and Dr Michael Wynne, of Gazetteer of Irish Stained Glass. He currently lectures in Graphic Design at Limerick School of Art and Design.

## NOTES

1. C P Curran, 'Michael Healy: Stained Glass Worker 1873–1941', *Studies*, vol XXXI, March 1942, pp. 70–1.
2. Aciding is a technique employed on flashed glass, that is glass in which one layer of coloured glass is fused to another (usually white glass) in a molten state. Aciding is the process by which, using hydrofluoric acid, the layer of colour can be removed from flashed glass.
3. *St Catherine's and St James's Church – Seventy-fifth Anniversary Year Book*, Dublin, 1972, p. 8.
4. Child depicted 'Hope' in the right light of 'Faith, Hope and Charity' (1905) for the Church of Ireland, Howth, Co Dublin.
5. H W B Thompson, 'The Memorial to Miss Matthews', *St Catherine's Parish Magazine,* June 1923, p. 2. (Copies of the parish magazine are preserved in the Representative Church Body Library, Churchtown, Dublin).
6. W B Thompson, 'The St Catherine Window', *St Catherine's Parish Magazine,* January 1924, p. 3.
7. H W B Thompson, 'Obituary of Mrs Bailey', *St Catherine's Parish Magazine,* July 1929, p. 1.
8. The number of C of I clergy and laity patrons who commissioned from An Túr Gloine far exceeded Catholic patrons, and Canon Thompson's championing of the studio must have been a significant factor in attracting many C of I orders.
9. The pencil and watercolour sketch design for 'St Victor' is in the collection of the National Gallery of Ireland (NGI cat no 18,396). It measures 23.5 x 9.1 cm (9¼" x 3½"). A note on the sketch design indicates that it was sanctioned by the Archbishop of Dublin on 23 May 1930.
10. 'The wolf shall dwell with the lamb and the leopard shall lie down with the kid, and the calf and the lion and the fatling together, and a little child shall lead them . . .' (Isaiah 11:6).
11. Most of the animals are listed in Isaiah, though in the case of the goat and zebra, Healy has exercised artistic licence.
12. 'St Catherine's Church', *Church of Ireland Gazette*, vol LIII, 28 July 1911, p. 651.
13. H W B Thompson, 'The First Vicar of St Catherine's'. A transcript of this lecture,
originally delivered at a public meeting of St Catherine's Association on 2 March 1914, is among Canon Thompson's papers which are housed in the Representative Church Body Library, Churchtown, Dublin.
14. The panels depicting Lewis originally featured on the Bridge of Athlone (which had been built by Lewis), until the bridge was taken down in 1730. Healy would have sketched the panels in the crypt of the National Museum where they are still preserved.
15. The identity of the animal, a subject of controversy, is examined in detail by the Rev John J Joly in his work *The Old Bridge of Athlone*, Dublin, 1881, pp. 56–70.
16. St Catherine's Church stands on the site of the Abbey of St Thomas.
17. Thompson, 'The First Vicar of St Catherine's', *ibid.*
18. An Túr Gloine work journal, no 2, p. 74. Basic details relating to all commissions (dimensions, cost, etc.) are contained in the studio work journals which are preserved in the National Gallery of Ireland.

# PAINTING ON PORCELAIN

**Kevin Curry** discusses the artist, Herbert Cooper, and the Queen's Institute (1870–1907) in Molesworth Street.

Saint Valentine's day 1870, saw the beginning of a small but important industry in Dublin. Its importance was such that it attracted gentry, nobility even royalty, who it could be said beat a path to its door in order to purchase its wares. The industry was the Queen's Institute Painting on Porcelain school situated at 25 Molesworth Street, Dublin, a location which forms part of Buswell's Hotel.

The inspiration to start a Painting on Porcelain school came from an energetic Dublin man W H Kerr,[1] who, despite being of gentleman stock, had begun a business career managing his father's retail china shop at 114 and 115 Capel Street. One of his duties was to travel to England to visit suppliers. It was on one such visit to the factory of Chamberlain and Co. at Worcester that he met and fell in love with Caroline Louisa Chamberlain. Her father Walter Chamberlain, was director of the Royal Porcelain Works at Worcester. The factory had gone into decline due to heavy financial losses, having inherited financial problems partly due to the style of wares produced. Its troubles were added to by Walter Chamberlain's failing health. When they announced their intentions to marry, Walter Chamberlain asked Kerr if he would consider coming to Worcester to take over the running of the factory. Kerr agreed, and in 1850 he left Dublin and his father's business to take up his new position at Worcester.

Kerr embarked upon an immediate rebuilding programme at the Royal Porcelain Works, employing, in the main, the skills of Irishmen. One of those involved in the work was a young architect, Robert Williams Armstrong, who was to remain

*An unusual shaped cup (c. 1870) probably from Worcester's quality porcelain range which was influenced by Limoges. (Private Collection).*

*Porcelain tea tray, decorated in 1870, inscribed on reverse W H Kerr, Q I, Dublin. (Private Collection).*

*Comport with rare gilt and jewelled border, centre panel painted by Herbert Cooper 1871. Unmarked. (Private Collection).*

*Scent bottle manufactured at Worcester c. 1845. (Private Collection).*

*Cabaret plate manufactured in Staffordshire and painted in the Queen's Institute by Herbert Cooper, 1880. (Private Collection).*

*Staffordshire vase painted by Cooper c. 1885 (National Museum of Ireland).*

# PAINTING ON PORCELAIN

a life long friend of Kerr's and who was later to become Art Director at Belleek.[2] Kerr had long since recognised the quality of the local clays around Belleek and, on moving to Worcester, had arranged for a shipment of Belleek clay to be sent to the Royal Porcelain Works. His reasons for this were twofold. As a nationalist in the truest sense, he promoted Ireland and Irish materials whenever possible. Also with the advent of the Great Exhibition (London, 1851) he experimented with the clays from Ireland in an attempt to produce a new porcelain body in order to try to regain their lost share of the porcelain market. Although Kerr failed to make any significant impact on the Great Exhibition, it is nonetheless widely accepted that he saved the Royal Porcelain Works from certain ruin. The 'Shakespeare' service, designed by a young Dublin sculptor, William Boyton Kirk and exhibited at the Dublin Exhibition 1853 was the start to a most successful period which was to last up to his retirement in 1862. In that same year, he returned to Dublin to manage the family's retail china business in Capel Street. He and his wife moved into the family home at Strandville House, Clontarf.

In 1861, a group of concerned citizens founded the Irish Society for the Employment of Women. The society commenced from humble beginnings in rooms occupied for the purpose at 43 Grafton Street, its total funds amounting to thirteen shillings and fourpence.[3] Within a few months, it had outgrown its small surroundings and moved to more adequate premises at 25 Molesworth Street. It later became known as the Queen's Institute for the training and employment of educated women. Its purpose now was to train gentlewomen of limited means for employment in the Post Office and the professions. However, as the demand for the training of women grew, so too did the number of courses on offer. By 1865, it was known as the Queen's Institute of Female Professional Schools.

W H Kerr, through his association with the Belleek Potteries and its Art Director, Robert Armstrong, arranged for the Queen's Institute to design many important commissions for Belleek. It was probably due to the success of these moulded designs that Kerr also decided that the pupils at the Queen's Institute could be taught how to paint on porcelain. There was already a kiln in situ at no 25 and his

retail shop offered a guaranteed outlet for decorated wares of high quality. He had received several commissions from members of the royal family when he was in Worcester, and he still continued to be favoured with royal patronage in Capel Street.

The Board of Trustees readily granted the enterprising Mr Kerr permission to proceed with his plan to set up a school for Painting on Porcelain. To manage the school he had in mind one Herbert Cooper, who attended the school of Design, at Worcester. Cooper was known to Kerr during his time at Worcester and had shown a natural aptitude for painting on a ceramic surface.[4] In 1869, Kerr travelled to England to find Cooper and eventually did so with more than a little difficulty, as Cooper was an itinerant miniaturist travelling from place to place painting miniature portraits of members of important families. When Kerr offered him the position of manager, of the Queen's Institute Painting on Porcelain school, Cooper accepted and returned to Dublin with Kerr.

The task of finding the money to pay for the new kiln lay squarely on Kerr's shoulders. In the meantime, Cooper made use of some of the undecorated porcelain objects in Kerr's possession. Kerr had discovered quantities of porcelain in the white when he had arrived in Worcester in 1850. One such piece was a beautiful scent bottle. It was manufactured at Worcester about 1845 during the Chamberlain period. Its importance is heightened by the fact that Chamberlain's exhibited a scent bottle with floral motifs in the Manchester exhibition of 1845/46, and a similar pair without the floral decoration are in the Victoria & Albert Museum. The scent bottle illustrated, however, is unique in so far as it was decorated by Herbert Cooper in 1869 and fired in the old kiln in the Queen's Institute. It bears the painted marks *H C* (Cooper's initials) and *Q I* (for Queen's Institute).

Whilst Kerr continued to extract money for the new kiln from friends and persons associated with the Queen's Institute, Cooper was exhibiting paintings on porcelain at the Royal Hibernian Academy.[5] Contributions for the new kiln fell short by a sum of £45, this Kerr contributed from his own pocket.[6] By the end of January 1870, the new kiln was completed.

## First Period 1870–71

Newspapers of the day proclaimed successful the experiments with the refiring of decorated porcelain in the new kiln at the Queen's Institute. Both Kerr and Cooper were delighted with the results, and on 14 February 1870, the first period of Painting on Porcelain at the Queen's Institute commenced. During the first period, all porcelain decorated at the Queen's Institute was manufactured at Worcester. The illustrated teatray was decorated in 1870. The painted inscription on the reverse: *W H Kerr, Q I, Dublin* is overglaze. All marks or inscriptions of the first period include Kerr's name; not all pieces are marked. In the cases of services, one or two pieces might have an identification mark. Cooper is associated with flower painting more than any other motif; however, it would seem that he was equally proficient at painting fruit.

A surviving example from Kerr's early days at Worcester is an unusual shaped cup with its matching saucer. The shape of the cup is probably influenced by an earlier Limoges example. There is an example of similar design (although more squat) in the Heraldic Museum, Kildare Street. It, however, is made from Worcester clay, whereas the one illustrated is made from Belleek clay. The gilt decoration on the already ostentatious handle tends to be heavy and flat in appearance. The finely painted flowers in the ellipse panel are obviously the work of a master of his art. His work as a painter in miniature stood Cooper in good stead in executing this finely detailed subject. The painted inscription on the base of the cup, apart from Kerr's name and the Queen's Institute mark, bears the word *Manufacturer*. Although the title *Manufacturer* was used by many decorators of fine ceramics, this confusion could not be attributed to Kerr, as he was a manufacturer during his time at Worcester, where this cup and saucer were made. This is believed to be the only known example where the word *Manufacturer* is used on porcelain decorated at the Queen's Institute.

Kerr's association with the Queen's Institute ensured that he was favoured with royal patronage. In 1870, Queen Victoria ordered a Belleek breakfast service from Kerr's of Capel Street, who in turn commissioned a design from the Queen's Institute.[7] The design which they produced – moulded sea-motifs on unpainted ware

— shows the success of that section of the school too. The Board of Trustees were delighted with this success, as also with the extra revenue generated by the Painting on Porcelain section of the school, and the important members of society which it attracted. A decision was taken to include works by the pupils of the Painting on Porcelain School in the annual exhibition, held each year in December. It proved to be a most fruitful decision since the exhibition sold out. Many important services were commissioned, despite the fact that Kerr had large stocks of Queen's Institute decorated porcelain at his Capel Street premises. Everybody was delighted; everybody, that is, except Mr Kerr, who had intended that all porcelain decorated at the Queen's Institute should be sold through his retail outlet.

Kerr began to hatch a new plan on which Herbert Cooper agreed to collaborate. In their own interests they decided to transfer the Painting on Porcelain school to Kerr's Capel Street premises. W H Kerr was to carry out major renovations to his shop, the cost of which was to be borne entirely by him. Their plan was to have a grand opening of the Capel Street shop to coincide with the opening in December 1871 of the Exhibition of Arts, Industries and Manufacturers now planned to be held in Capel Street. Cooper, at Kerr's request, agreed to accept a master gilder into the Queen's Institute to teach him the modern techniques of gilt decoration. It is not known who the master gilder was; most probably it was someone from Worcester. The combined work of the unknown gilder and Cooper the artist is recorded on a part Worcester dessert service in a private collection. It is equal to, if not better than, the finest specimens being produced at the time in England. Cooper painted different varieties of wild flowers on each individual piece which is enhanced with a rich gilt and jewelled border against a purple band. The plates bear the Kerr/ Queen's Institute mark, some are painted in puce and others in black whereas the comports are devoid of any mark. It would be difficult to guess what a service such as this one would have cost, but, in 1871, a pair of vases decorated at the Queen's Institute and purchased from Kerr's of Capel Street would have cost between one hundred and five hundred guineas.[8]

The exterior of Kerr's premises was

*Staffordshire cup and saucer c. 1880.*
*(Private Collection).*

completed in August 1871, the entire works having been carried out according to plans by Mr John McCurdy, Leinster Street. Kerr's importance can be gauged by the fact that a royal party made a special visit to his Capel Street showrooms coinciding with the completion of the exterior of the building, and several orders were received from members of the royal party.[9]

Kerr was in the process of installing a magnificent suite of apartments at nos 114 and 115 when something went drastically wrong to halt his plans. Cooper had taken umbrage to the presence of a stranger (the gilder) overseeing his work, and he asked Kerr to have him removed. Kerr, a man who was used to getting his own way, refused to accede to Cooper's request. Cooper, in turn, refused to cooperate with the transfer of the Painting on Porcelain school. In short, the two men fell out. The suite of apartments was never completed by Kerr who sold the family home at Strandville House to offset the huge cost of the Capel Street project. He did, however, exhibit on a small scale at the 1872 Dublin exhibition. So too did the Queen's Institute. Kerr and Cooper had gone their separate ways, their relationship had ended, and so too had the first period of Painting on Porcelain at the Queen's Institute.[10]

### Second Period 1872–1883

In the wake of Kerr's departure, Herbert Cooper began making pottery on a small scale at the Queen's Institute. This was probably from necessity rather than choice, as he sadly missed the volume of sales generated by the influential Mr Kerr. He was joined by Frederick Vodrey, a china and glass merchant with an address

at Moore Street.[11] The partnership lasted about a year after which Cooper concentrated solely on managing the Painting on Porcelain school. During the second period, there is a marked change in Cooper's style; he seems to express himself more fully through his paintings of his favourite subject — 'flowers from nature'. Painted cabaret plates are signed *H Cooper* either on the front or the reverse. His finest works are signed and dated, whilst other pieces are signed with initials only.

Worcester porcelain was no longer used by Cooper; it is quite likely that Kerr used his influence with the factory to stop supplies of blanks to the Queen's Institute. During the second period, items of bone china and glazed earthenware, from various Staffordshire factories, have been identified. Exquisite examples of jewelled borders are no longer in evidence, yet in terms of decorative quality it produced consistently superb examples. To appreciate the difficulties in achieving such a high standard it should be understood that, unlike painting on canvas, the ceramic artist uses enamel colours, that is to say metallic pigments mixed with powdered glass and applied to a glazed surface. The colours are then fused by firing in a kiln at high temperatures. Since all colours do not fuse at the same temperature several firings may be necessary. This involves building up layers of enamel and ensuring that each subsequent firing is at a lower temperature than the previous one. A further problem which must be overcome is the alteration of colours during the fusing process in the kiln. The illustrated cup and saucer, depicting 'flowers from nature' against a pale green ground, displays the artistic refinement evident in all examples of decorated porcelain from the Queen's Institute. However, on close inspection, the enamel colours partly project as though in relief from the flat surface, full absorption into the glaze has not been achieved. It is either an apprentice piece, or the work of more than one pupil who had not fully understood, or did not allow for, the alteration of the colours during firing, thereby necessitating too many firings at less than the desired temperature.

The Queen's Institute held an exhibition of painted porcelain annually at its premises at 25 Molesworth Street. Public interest however, had gradually declined. In direct contrast to the halcyon days dur-

# PAINTING ON PORCELAIN

ing the first eighteen months, the school had now resorted to painting on ceramic tiles and including them in its exhibition. It must have been evident to all concerned that the school's existence was to be of limited duration. Other departments of the Queen's Institute must have been experiencing difficulties too, because on the 14 February 1883 a meeting was held for the purpose of receiving the report of the committee of investigation. It dealt with the liabilities and assets of the Queen's Institute. The liabilities were found to be in excess of those stated in the report, but the committee believed that they could be met if the building was put up to auction and its effects realised.[12] This was the beginning of the end of the Queen's Institute, the death knell had been sounded, and in a matter of months it ceased to exist. Herbert Cooper moved into new premises a mere two doors away (no 27) where he opened his own Painting on Porcelain studio.[13]

## Third Period 1883–1907

Herbert Cooper was manager of the Painting on Porcelain school during his time at the Queen's Institute. On moving to no 27, he referred to himself as artist and manager. The following year, he was known as Professor of Porcelain Painting. Whether his title was conferred or assumed matters little; his work speaks for itself. Over a century later, it tells us that he excelled himself in his chosen profession. During the early part of the third period, Cooper painted an excellent Staffordshire vase. It is one of the most beautifully decorated pieces during this entire per-

iod. The ground colour is a light shade of green, a colour favoured by Cooper throughout his career. The floral painting is of superb quality. The gilding is applied sparingly, which tends to support the view that Cooper had learned from his early years not to use heavy gilt decoration, as it tended to overshadow the painted floral designs. This signed vase is in the collection of The National Museum of Ireland.

It is to his credit that on opening his studio at no 27 he allowed some of his students to sign their names on the reverse of plates and the bases of cups. One such pupil and the first to be afforded the distinction of signing her work was Alice Elwood, who came from Lackafinna, Co Mayo, to study under Cooper. Her initials are to be found on the reverse of plates exquisitely painted with flowers; some bear the date 1884.

In 1887, the firm of Hammersley and Company was established at the Alsager Pottery, Longton. It, like many other porcelain manufacturers sold plates, tiles and other wares as blanks for decoration outside the mainstream ceramics industry. From 1888, to its date of closure, Cooper's studio at 27 Molesworth Street, not only decorated the wares of Hammersley and Company n the white, but also added further decoration to the finished products of the pottery, in many cases with the addition of a date.

A plate painted with flowers signed H Cooper, Dublin and dated 1893, together with the factory mark of Hammersley & Co, is one of two in a private collection. The other is signed 'Fanny Moran' and dated 1905, and also bears the factory mark. The latter is the latest known dated

example before the demise of Cooper's studio which closed in 1907. Ill-health forced him to abandon the work he loved so much. He retired to his home at 7 Vergemount Avenue, Clonskeagh; the third period of Painting on Porcelain had ended.[14]

Herbert Cooper died in 1916 during the midnight of Ireland's misfortunes. Apart from family and a few close friends, it mattered little to the rest of Ireland that a seventy-two year old man had departed this life; on a global scale it mattered less. Yet, he had left to Ireland and the world, a legacy of great beauty through the countless pieces of porcelain painted by him and his pupils over a period of thirty-seven years. Neither the Queen's Institute Painting on Porcelain School nor the name Herbert Cooper are to be found in any of the accepted books on porcelain marks. It is hoped that from this article a situation which has prevailed for too long will finally be redressed and the schools and studio at 25 and 27 Molesworth Street, will be given credit long overdue for the magnificent specimens of painted porcelain, so exquisite in their varied designs and so perfect in their execution.

*Kevin Curry*

*Kevin Curry has spent many years researching English porcelain of the eighteenth and nineteenth centuries.*

### ACKNOWLEDGEMENTS

The National Library, Dublin; The Gilbert Library; The Berkeley Library, Trinity College, Dublin; The National Museum, Dublin; The Civic Museum, Dublin; The City Museum and Art Gallery, Hanley, Stoke-on-Trent; The Dyson Perrin's Museum, Worcester; Spode, Stoke-on-Trent and private collections.

## NOTES

1. The Ninth Annual Meeting of the Queen's Institute, 1871, Dublin, p. 14.
2. Mairead Reynolds, 'Early Belleek Designs', *Irish Arts Review*, Autumn 1984, p. 24.
3. *The Freeman's Journal*, 22 September 1871.
4. There is a misconception perpetuated by time that Herbert Cooper worked with Copeland's of Stoke-on-Trent. Not only did he not work with Copeland's, he never worked in any of the Staffordshire potteries. This is borne out by an unpublished manuscript in the City Museum and Art Gallery, Hanley, Stoke-on-Trent, in which there is no reference to Cooper. If he had been born, educated,

taught, worked or exhibited in Staffordshire one would expect his name to be included in the manuscript.
5. Ann M Stewart, *Royal Academy of Arts Index of Exhibitors, 1826–1979*. Dublin (1985) Vol. 1, p. 164.
6. The Ninth Annual Meeting of the Queen's Institute, 1871, Dublin, p. 31.
7. Mairead Reynolds, *Early Belleek Wares*, (National Museum, Dublin 1978).
8. *The Irish Builder*, 15 August, 1871, p. 210.
9. *The Irish Builder*, 15 August, 1871, p. 211.
10. Female ceramic artists from the first period include: Francis J White, Finglas, Dublin;

Matilda Stoker, Dublin and London; M W Weisse, Eccles Street, Dublin.
11. Aisling Molloy, 'Vodrian Pottery', *Irish Arts Review*, Spring 1987, p. 33.
12. *The Irish Builder*, 15 February, 1883, p. 48.
13. Women painters from the second period include: Josephine Webb; Francis M Brett, Booterstown, Dublin; Mary A McGee, Drumcondra, Dublin.
14. Women porcelain painters of the third period include: Fanny Moran; Alice Elwood, Lackafinna, Co Mayo; J E C Comiskey, Booterstown, Co Dublin.

# THOMAS FARRELL, SCULPTOR

**Paula Murphy** outlines the career of the distinguished nineteenth-century Dublin sculptor, Sir Thomas Farrell.

Thomas Farrell, (1827[1]–1900) was a retiring man, whose private life remains private. Described in 1864 as 'a most amiable and unassuming gentleman',[2] Farrell, the sculptor, is easily understood through his work, while Farrell, the man, is less easy to uncover. If the range of his subject-matter was limited, his sculptural output was nonetheless extensive and in a career that focused on portrait work, much of which was of a public nature, this sculptor, who might well be considered apolitical, found himself working in a political and controversial arena. The commissions he received would largely indicate nationalist leanings, and Farrell was born with Catholic Emancipation, into a Catholic family. However the family circumstances would prosper through contact with the Lord Lieutenant of Ireland, and it seems likely therefore that Thomas Farrell would have been raised with a respect for this particular office and a positive attitude to the Union.

Born into a sculptor's workshop[3] in the parish of St Bride in Dublin, Farrell was raised with the tools and materials of his profession and was the first of the sons in the family to be given a formal sculptural training beyond his father's studio. He was admitted as a student at the Modelling School of the Royal Dublin Society in 1842. This opportunity was not afforded to either of his elder brothers, perhaps because they did not display sufficient talent to be accepted, while in Thomas's case the ability was unquestionable. There can be little doubt that his experience in his father's workshop placed him well ahead of his fellow students. Thomas was a prize-winner in 1843 in the category 'Original Design in Clay' and awarded premiums by the Royal Irish Art Union in 1844 and 1846.

At the public distribution of prizes at the school in December 1843, Earl de Grey, as Chairman of the Royal Dublin Society, on the occasion of Thomas receiving his prize addressed him thus:

'Farrell, your name is not unknown to me, for I have had the pleasure of seeing other members of your family since I have become a resident in Dublin. At first I was not aware that you were the son of one of whom I have a very high opinion, but I am glad of it, and have great gratification in presenting you with this prize. I saw the figure for which you obtained it, and it struck me as a very clever piece of work, before I knew by whom it was executed. I

*Thomas Farrell, Captain John McNeill Boyd (1812–61) Marble. (1864) St Patrick's Cathedral, Dublin. Captain Boyd, RN, was drowned in a dramatic rescue attempt off Dun Laoghaire pier.*

*Thomas Farrell, Archbishop Daniel Murray (1768–1852), flanked by allegorical figures of Meekness and Prudence. Marble c.1855. St Mary's Pro Cathedral, Dublin.*

would, in conclusion, observe, that I never saw more civility, honesty and taste combined in one man, than in the head of your family.'[4]

Such public recognition from the representative of the Crown for the Farrell family, and for Terence and Thomas in particular, cannot but have helped the early development of Thomas's career.

Teaching at the Modelling School in the 1840s placed emphasis on drawing and modelling from the antique and, coupled with the considered importance of John Flaxman, this reveals a continuing interest in neo-classical theory. Farrell's First Year prizes were both Flaxman books, the *Anatomical Studies* and the *Illustrations of Aeschylus*. However as Farrell made his way from the north side of the Liffey, the new location of the family workshop since 1841, to the Modelling School, which was situated in Leinster House in Kildare Street, he passed through the centre of a city that boasted several monumental statues of English rulers, in a weighty and pompous late Baroque style, (all of which are now no longer in place), with Grinling Gibbons' equestrian statue of William III in College Green being the most publicly prominent.

A study of architectural sculpture in the city would have made Farrell aware of an interesting development that had taken place in the commission for pedimental sculpture for the new portico of the Bank of Ireland in College Green earlier in the century. Edward Smyth had been obliged to work to the designs of John Flaxman for his second set of figures, *Hibernia, Fidelity* and *Commerce*. This restriction to the commission exemplified new and serious insistence on an international neo-classical style while revealing a lack of confidence in the taste of native artists. The popularity of John Hogan, working out of Rome in the first half of the nineteenth century, is further evidence of classical interest and outsider status.

The neo-classical style found its roots in Ireland rather later than in the rest of Europe and, because of this, it merges almost imperceptibly into a Victorian style of classicism in the second half of the century. Farrell steps clearly into this classical camp in his early formative years, aligning himself stylistically, through the influence of John Flaxman, with the sculpture of the emigrant John Hogan and the local Thomas Kirk. Far-

# THOMAS FARRELL, SCULPTOR

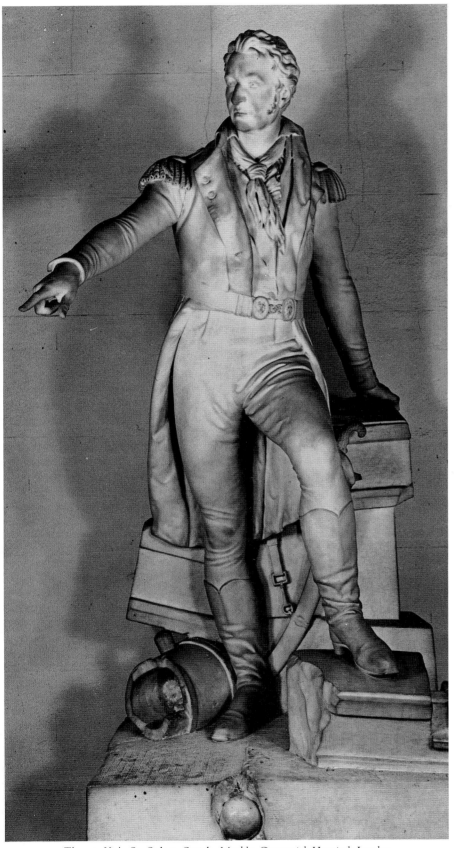

*Thomas Kirk, Sir Sidney Smith, Marble. Greenwich Hospital, London. Exhibited Royal Academy 1844.*

rell's indebtedness to Kirk, who had trained his father, is most marked in his statue of *Captain John McNeill Boyd* (1864), in St Patrick's Cathedral. Boyd, who had drowned in a storm in February 1861, while leading a dramatic rescue attempt off Kingstown (now Dun Laoghaire) pier, is shown conducting the rescue with an authoritative gesture. While more rugged than strictly classical, the work was directly inspired by Kirk's statue of *Sir Sidney Smith* for Greenwich Hospital, which Farrell had the opportunity to view on two occasions when the full-size model was shown in Dublin, at the Royal Hibernian Academy in 1844 and later at the Great Exhibition in 1853. In time Farrell was to slip, beyond the influence of Kirk and Hogan, under the metaphorical wing of Francis Chantrey and John Henry Foley, both major monumental sculptors of the nineteenth century.

The city's public spaces were gradually throughout the century to become peopled with significant but silent protagonists from the hands of Foley and Farrell, with national heroes confronting the more traditional and by then somewhat outdated royal monuments. At an early age Farrell must have been made aware of the politics of monumental sculpture, as in 1836 Grinling Gibbons' statue of William III was toppled from its pedestal in College Green by a politically motivated and specifically targetted explosion.[5] Although he was only nine when this event occurred, it must have been the subject of considerable discussion in the Farrell household and cannot have escaped the notice of the young Thomas.

The first half of the 1850s witnessed much activity in the artistic world with major exhibitions in Cork and Dublin. Farrell exhibited at both. At this stage his early promise began to draw important commissions for him. Shortly after the death of Daniel Murray, Archbishop of Dublin, in February 1852, it was decided to commission a commemorative monument to him for the Pro-Cathedral in Marlborough Street. A committee was formed and interested sculptors submitted designs. John Hogan and Thomas Farrell were amongst the applicants, and the former was considered the most likely to succeed. Hogan had returned from Rome, to work in Ireland in 1849 and actively promoted his presence in the country.[6] He was in receipt of continuous favour-

# THOMAS FARRELL, SCULPTOR

*Thomas Farrell, Waterloo. Bronze relief panel on Wellington Testimonial, Phoenix Park, Dublin. Completed 1861. A commission originally intended for Terence Farrell.*

able criticism in the press and it was therefore a considerable blow to the established sculptor to find that the commission was offered to the young and relatively inexperienced Farrell. Hogan must have had expectations for the commission, having carved a bust of Murray in 1844.

Farrell's design for the monument is no longer extant, but the finished carving of the kneeling Archbishop and the two allegorical figures, *Meekness* and *Prudence,* is strictly neo-classical, drawing heavily on Hogan and the Italian sculptor, Antonio Canova. Nothing distracts from the central focus of the work which is the devotional nature of the portrait. This commission, the first major Catholic church commission in the nineteenth century, must be recognised as the breakthrough for Farrell. It is at this stage that he can be seen to step beyond his position as simply one of a family workshop and to establish himself as an independent sculptor with a separate career. The commission in itself conveyed considerable prestige. Dr Daniel Murray had been a particularly prominent and active member of the Irish clergy, much loved and deeply mourned by the Catholic community. The fact that the commission was won in competition against such authoritative opposition as Hogan reinforced the significance.

Strickland points out that Farrell went to Italy to choose the marble for the Murray monument and that he took the opportunity to visit Rome and Florence.[7] While this may serve as another indication of the importance of the commission, it was, nonetheless, unusual for an artist to travel from Ireland to Italy for the specific purpose of choosing marble. Stone was normally ordered through an agent. It seems more probable that the opportunity for a short study trip to Italy was being offered to Farrell, as there was still an acceptance amongst many Irish sculp-

tors, up to and even beyond the mid-century, that it was important to view the work of the Italians, to experience the sculpture at first hand. J R Kirk, Constantine Panormo, John Gallagher, James Heffernan, Patrick McDowell and James Cahill, all travelled to Rome in the first half of the nineteenth century. Farrell was probably in Rome over the winter of 1853/1854. He may well have carried letters of introduction from Paul Cullen, the new Archbishop of Dublin, who had been Rector of the Irish College in Rome in the 1840s and had left the city only in 1850, and who was noted for his interest in sculpture. Back in Dublin by the summer of 1854, Farrell began work on the carving of the portrait statue of the Archbishop. It was completed and erected in the Pro-Cathedral in the following year.

Thomas's new prosperity resulting from the Murray commission led to artistic and domestic independence from his family. In 1856, he moved to the south side of the city, near the canal, in Warrington Place. This address seems to have been residential only, as Farrell continued to submit Gloucester Street as his studio address. In spite of a certain separateness and the obvious superior talent of Thomas over his brothers, the family, father and sons, was often described in terms of a single unit, such as 'The Messrs. Farrell'[8] or 'that eminent firm'.[9] Unlike his brothers he was to become actively involved in the Royal Hibernian Academy, being elected a full member under the new charter of 1860, by-passing the associate stage. Either the operation of this institution was of great interest to Farrell or alternately he was such a diffident and shy man that he was cajoled into taking various posts, probably a little of both, because he held several different positions at the Academy throughout the remainder of his life. Appointed initially Professor of Sculpture for the year 1862, this appointment was not renewed but passed at the end of the

year to J R Kirk. However, Farrell subsequently became a Council member on three occasions, Auditor for one year and Treasurer for twenty-two, until finally in 1893 he was rewarded for his sustained commitment to the Academy by being elected President. Two years later, somewhat ironically, the year after Kirk's death, Farrell was once more appointed Professor of Sculpture at the Academy, no more than an honorary merit at that stage in his life.

A second significant commission was offered to Farrell later in the 1850s, when he was invited to model one of the bronze panels, initially to have been the work of his father, for the Wellington Testimonial in the Phoenix Park.[10] Farrell chose to illustrate the Battle of Waterloo in one of its closing moments with the fall of the Earl of Uxbridge, an incident which ignited renewed energy in the English cavalry, who are shown charging the French soldiers. The Earl of Carlisle as Lord Lieutenant visited Farrell's studio in Gloucester Street to view the work in progress in August 1859 and was much pleased. The model was completed by March of the following year, and sent to be cast in London, at Thomas Potter's foundry in South Molton Street. Later that same year Farrell was invited to London to inspect the casting. However it appears that he did not make the journey, because he was shocked on viewing the bronze relief after its arrival in Dublin.

The casting was completed in February 1861 and on 1 April Thomas Farrell wrote to General Sir Thomas Larcom, explaining his delay in viewing the relief due to pressure of other work and indicating his outrage at Potter's lack of craft:

*It is the last thing that Mr Potter will ever cast for me, unless he improves very much, for it is without exception the most disgraceful piece of work I have ever witnessed — so battered and butchered is every part of it, that I had considerable*

# THOMAS FARRELL, SCULPTOR

*difficulty in recognising any of my own work at all — The outline of the figures of course could not be altered and that from the ground will produce a good general effect — Thank Heaven, it is gone up to such a height, for I would not for any consideration that it was seen on the ground as my work — I intend going tomorrow to try if I can do anything with it myself, for I see it is quite useless to ask Buckingham — he may know how to bolt or solder but he has as much eye for art as an oyster.*[11]

His poor opinion of the casting did not prevent Farrell, along with J R Kirk, who had also modelled a Wellington relief panel, trying to capitalize on this commission with a request to the Earl of Carlisle to seek patronage for them in London in the form of commissions for statues in the Houses of Parliament,[12] but this attempt to penetrate the English market failed. Nor did it deter Farrell from working with

bronze on other occasions, as witnessed in the relaxed standing figure of *William Dargan* (1863) outside the National Gallery of Ireland and the elegantly sophisticated seated *Lord Ardilaun* (1891) in St Stephen's Green, Dublin.

If Farrell seemed in the early 1860s to have been moving into the position of leading sculptor in Ireland, there was another rival poised to secure several important commissions in the next two decades. While John Hogan had not proved serous competition, John Henry Foley, who had left Dublin for London at the age of sixteen, in 1834, had made a considerable reputation for himself there, and was much sought after in Ireland. He received many commissions for monumental work of a public nature in Dublin, while his private patrons were largely English and/or Protestant. Farrell was not ignored by the Protestant community, but

he now added to this already active nucleus of patronage an emerging Catholic clientele. Catholic Emancipation had instigated a new freedom and given a certain confidence to the Catholics in Ireland. New churches were built to reinforce the strength of the religion and these required decorative and commemorative sculptural work. Catholics began to be recognized for their talents rather than ignored for their religious beliefs, and Farrell received commissions for statues and busts of prominent Catholics, clergy and laity. Amongst this latter group can be found very apt examples of the new patronage — a statue (1884) of one of the first Catholic barristers to take Silk, Richard Lalor Shiel; another statue (1886) of the first Catholic Chancellor since the reign of James II, Thomas, Lord O'Hagan, both for the Main Hall of the Four Courts, in Dublin;[13] a bust (1866) of

*Thomas Farrell, William Dargan (1799–1867). Bronze. 1863. National Gallery of Ireland, Dublin. Dargan was a railway magnate whose financial support for the Dublin Exhibition of 1853 helped found the National Gallery.*

*Thomas Farrell, Lord Ardilaun (Arthur Edward Guinness, 1840–1915). Bronze. 1891. St Stephen's Green, Dublin. Erected by public subscription in gratitude for his having organised the opening of the Green as a public park.*

# THOMAS FARRELL, SCULPTOR

the second Catholic appointed to the Irish Bench, Judge Nicholas Ball;[14] another bust (1899) of the only Catholic to be appointed Resident Commissioner of National Education in Ireland, Sir Patrick Keenan, for Tyrone House (now the Department of Education) in Marlborough Street, Dublin.

Commissions received by Farrell for portrait statues of the Protestant community were frequently of a particular type and seem related to his being an Irish Catholic. Many of these commissions were for portraits of people who had a particularly active interest in Ireland. Examples are the statues of Sir John Gray, (1879), for O'Connell Street, Protestant nationalist, proprietor of *The Freeman's Journal*, and active member of Dublin Corporation, who, against considerable opposition, worked hard to improve water facilities in Dublin; Sir Alexander Mac-Donnell, (1878), for the forecourt of Tyrone House,[15] a seated portrait of an ar-

*Thomas Farrell*, Sir Patrick Keenan (1826–94), *the only Catholic Resident Commissioner of Education. Marble. Unveiled 1899. Dept of Education, Marlborough St. Dublin.*

dent Protestant from Belfast, educated in England, who, as Resident Commissioner of Education in Ireland through the mid-century, showed a particular concern that the young people of Ireland be instructed in their own religion; Sir Robert Stewart, (1898), for Leinster Lawn, an important figure in the world of music, who had a strong interest in ancient Irish music; William Smith O'Brien, (1867), for Carlisle Bridge,[16] a Protestant and revolutionary nationalist.

This last mentioned was particularly significant in terms of both the person and the site. The statue commemorates a descendant of the Protestant nobility turned nationalist revolutionary, who received a death sentence, later commuted, for attempted insurrection, and who had died in 1864. Although there is no evidence that Farrell was a politically motivated person, this was a very political monument. The figure, shown in the stance of one commanding the attention

*Thomas Farrell, Sir Robert Stewart (1825–94). Marble. 1898. Leinster Lawn, Merrion Square, Dublin. Stewart was a renowned organist and Professor of Music.*

*Thomas Farrell, Sir John Gray (1816–75). Marble. 1879. O'Connell St, Dublin. Gray was proprietor of* The Freeman's Journal, *and MP for Kilkenny, but commemorated for the Vartry scheme which improved water facilities in Dublin.*

# THOMAS FARRELL, SCULPTOR

of a crowd, arms folded, displaying a very real confidence, inspired reverence and hatred alternately in the population of the city; reverence in those who remembered Smith O'Brien as a committed nationalist and hatred in those who viewed the statue as a commemoration of a misguided terrorist. It is not of colossal size and was designed to be positioned at an angle between d'Olier Street and Carlisle Bridge, (now O'Connell Bridge). It was already known that the O'Connell monument would, at a future date, be placed at the top of Sackville Street, (now O'Connell Street), on the far side of the Bridge and the only other monumental statue in the immediate vicinity was that of Nelson, somewhat 'skied' in comparison. Bringing these Irish heroes closer to street level made them, appropriately, much less remote than the Nelson figure. The unveiling of the Smith O'Brien monument proved a somewhat contentious occasion with differing opinions being aired in the speeches. John Martin, a follower of Smith O'Brien, invited to unveil the monument, noted that this was the first time for many years 'that a monument had been erected in a public place in Dublin to honour an Irishman whose title to that honour was that he devoted his life to the Irish national cause'.[17]

If this monument was controversial, it was because of Smith O'Brien's particular brand of politics and the methods he adopted. However the real sculptural controversy of the mid 1860s was the awarding of the commission for the O'Connell monument.[18] The monument committee advertised a competition in 1864, prior to which there had been considerable support for Thomas Farrell receiving the commission, in the form of letters to the committee and to the newspapers, and recommendations to visit his studio and see his work in progress.[19] The whole idea of a competition was controversial for differing reasons. On the one hand it was believed that sculptors of major standing would not trouble themselves to submit designs, considering it a waste of their time.[20] On the other hand great importance was attached to the nationality and residence of the sculptor who was to receive this commission, the majority of people preferring an Irishman resident in Ireland, and the fear that an internationally advertised competition would

*Thomas Farrell,* William Smith O'Brien (1803–64). *Marble. Unveiled 1870. O'Connell St, Dublin. O'Brien was a Protestant Nationalist revolutionary, sentenced to death for high treason, 1848. The sentence was commuted; he was exiled and subsequently pardoned.*

attract submissions from outsiders was very real.

However the competition went ahead and sixty designs were received by the committee for exhibition in the City Hall. Amongst these were four Farrell sketch models, with Thomas and his brothers, James, Joseph and John, all submitting work. Thomas's design was for a three-tiered monument with O'Connell seated on top of a pedestal, which had reliefs illustrating significant moments in the Liberator's career. Four allegorical figures were shown seated around the pedestal – *Erin, Law, Patriotism* and *Eloquence* – and situated beyond these

figures around the base of the monument were semi-reclining personifications of different aspects of *Liberty*. The modelling of the figures in the Farrell design was described at the time as 'spirited'.[21] The designs submitted by his three brothers were somewhat similar in conception.

None of the Farrell designs, nor any of the other fifty-six submissions, were considered acceptable by the O'Connell Monument Committee. A second competition was no more successful. Subsequently, amidst much controversy, the commission was offered to John Henry Foley. This ignored the public appeal for the commission to be given to an Irish artist living and working in Ireland, and can be seen as an interesting example of the continuing Irish lack of confidence in local or, perhaps some saw it as parochial, talent. Foley had a huge reputation in London, whereas Farrell had only proved himself on Irish soil. The type of person, who could suggest anonymously in a newspaper article[22] that an Irish artist would produce a ludicrous monstrosity instead of a work of art, had won the day.

Although the monument was not erected in Sackville Street until 1882, the same year that Farrell's statue of Cardinal Cullen was unveiled in the Pro-Cathedral, Foley had sent a model of his work for exhibition in the City Hall in 1867. Such had been the controversy surrounding the work that surely every sculptor in the city must have viewed the model. Farrell particularly noted Foley's use of a drum with relief figures, a design feature which he made use of in his monument to Cardinal Paul Cullen, in the Pro-Cathedral, Dublin, fifteen years later in 1882. The Cardinal is positioned on top of a carved drum, which takes the place of the more usual, and frequently uninspiring, pedestal. The drum is used to illustrate the various religious institutions, social, medical and educational, founded by Cullen. The Murray and Cullen statues face one another across the nave of the church and, in these works, Farrell can be seen to have received the two most significant Catholic Church commissions of the nineteenth century. Where Murray, dedicated to the spiritual growth of the Church in Ireland, is shown kneeling in prayer, Cullen, a powerful figure, equally dedicated, and the first Irish prelate to be created Cardinal, is portrayed as an authoritative standing figure,

# THOMAS FARRELL, SCULPTOR

*Thomas Farrell*, Monument to Members of the Irish Republican Brotherhood. *Symbolic figures of Erin, Patriotism and Fidelity. Marble. 1886. Glasnevin Cemetery Dublin.*

*Thomas Farrell, Cardinal Paul Cullen (1803–78). Marble 1882. St Mary's Pro Cathedral, Dublin. Cullen was the first Irish Cardinal. The drum figures represent scenes from his life.*

commanding respect. The very scale of the monuments and their respective attention to detail is different. Both however have accessory figures for the purpose of revealing more about the individuals than can be captured in their portraits alone.

When Farrell had been invited to carve a tomb monument for Richard Whately, the late Protestant Archbishop of Dublin, for St Patrick's Cathedral in the 1860s, he had chosen a completely different format. Making use of a recumbent effigy lying on a tomb-chest, the sculptor was showing an awareness, not simply of the setting for the work, but also of the new theories being expressed about the design of Church memorials. Criticism of the lack of piety found in many monuments led to a desire

for the dignity and simplicity of medieval recumbent effigies.[23] Certainly this required dignity and simplicity is present in Farrell's Whately monument, which is carved with an elegant and mature hand. Farrell may have been familiar with the writings of Pugin, who in his *Contrasts* (1836), recommended the addition of supporting angels at the head of the recumbent effigy, for he incorporated these in a subsequent tomb monument commemorating Cardinal McCabe, (1887), in Glasnevin Cemetery.

Farrell received commissions for a number of tomb monuments throughout his career. This was inevitable due to his association with the Farrell and Son Marble Works at the gates of Glasnevin Cemetery, which was probably owned by

his uncle. Several of these monuments were wall tablets executed in relief format, or including a bust of the deceased. However, in his later career, on two occasions, Farrell stepped beyond the portrait aspect of the memorial into symbolism. Both of these works are in the cemetery at Glasnevin. The first of the monuments commemorates members of the Irish Republican Brotherhood, with representations of *Erin, Fidelity* and *Patriotism.* Yet again Farrell was in receipt of a commission that was politically controversial. The year was 1883, the named members of the IRB were already buried in the plot. However the monument was not put in place until 1933. This was not a reflection on Farrell's celtic nationalist imagery, but the inscription on the monument, referr-

# THOMAS FARRELL, SCULPTOR

ing to Fenians who had died for Ireland, was deemed unacceptable. The IRB monument was outlawed for some forty years.

The second symbolic memorial by Farrell in Glasnevin Cemetery commemorates Ellen Palles, the wife of Christopher Palles, the Lord Chief Baron, who died in 1885. This work makes use of religious rather than celtic symbolism, with Farrell indicating the new spiritual, rather than the late material, aspect of the deceased, in his representation of the flight of the soul, illustrated by a draped female ascending into heaven. This is a three-dimensional variant of a very popular subject, which had its nineteenth-century origins in John Flaxman's *Monument to Agnes Cromwell*, in Chichester Cathedral. Thomas' father, Terence, had incorporated this theme into his monument to the Countess de Grey, in Flitton, Bedfordshire.

While working on tomb memorials and monumental statuary, Farrell continued, throughout his career, to receive commissions for bust portraiture, some of which were portraits from life, others posthumous busts. Farrell recognised the importance of the bust portrait in keeping 'the sculptor's art from being extinguished in Ireland'.[24] Members of the nobility, the religious communities, the medical, legal, academic and artistic professions and the political platform, Catholic and Protestant, were all portrayed in stone, with Farrell employing different styles and different types of dress for his busts.

*Thomas Farrell, 'Sursum Corda'. Monument to Ellen Palles (1839–85), wife of Lord Chief Baron Christopher Palles. Marble. c. 1888. Glasnevin Cemetery, Dublin.*

Some of these were modelled in connection with monumental statues, but most were independent works. In one case Farrell was invited to portray three members of one family. He carved a portrait bust of Mother Teresa Ball (1862), the founder of the Loreto Order in Ireland, her sister, Mrs Anna Maria O'Brien (1872), a devoted social worker and co-founder of the Irish Sisters of Charity, and their brother, Judge Nicholas Ball, who died in 1865. The type of sculpture required a considerable amount of contact with people, this being particularly necessary in the case of a bust of a deceased person. While there are examples of Farrell working variously from paintings, photographs and death masks, he would also discuss the personality of the deceased with family or friends.[25] The fact that Farrell, through his work, was relatively familiar with a wide social group is no indication that he was an outgoing person. His father had been described as 'modest, unassuming, diffident' by Earl de Grey[26] and Thomas seems to have inherited a similar character.

Thomas Farrell did not marry, nor did any of his brothers, and we know nothing of his friends or connections. In fact, he had such an extensive career that he may have been something of a workaholic, with little time or use for anything outside of his sculpture. The obituary in *The Irish Times*[27] suggests that he was a perfectionist, illustrating this view with an anecdote about Farrell rushing from the building, in a sudden lack of con-

*Thomas Farrell, Archbishop Richard Whateley (1787–1863). Marble. 1865. St Patrick's Cathedral, Dublin.*

# THOMAS FARRELL, SCULPTOR

fidence, at the moment of unveiling of one of his most important works. A retiring and modest man,[28] he was probably made uncomfortable by the lavish banquet that occasionally accompanied an unveiling ceremony and by the speeches made in his honour. The presentation to the Royal College of Surgeons in Dublin in 1886 of his seated statue of William Dease, an eminent surgeon, was followed by such a banquet, as was the unveiling of the portrait statue of Sir John Gray in Sackville Street in 1879. One newspaper report[29] of the latter occasion states that Farrell had himself made a humorous speech, while another reporter[30] gives a resumé of the text of the speech which simply confirms the diffident and shy nature of the man.

While Farrell's talent seems to have forced him into a public position, he remained self-effacing. Nonetheless his work was much admired in his own day. Favourable reports continued to appear in the newspapers after each unveiling. In fact, it might be said that public opinion revealed a greater confidence in his work than Farrell had himself. From the mid-1870s until his death in 1900, his position as leading Irish sculptor was largely unchallenged. J H Foley's death in 1874 removed the significant competition. J R Kirk and James Cahill were active up to the 1890s but hardly serious competition, and the younger generation of sculptors headed by John Hughes and Oliver Sheppard would not begin to make an impact until around the turn of the century. Thomas's father had died in 1876, but it seems likely that Thomas had already been at the head of the family workshop for a number of years. He was, however, never a wealthy man and had frequently to request initial payment to begin work on a commission and seek the balance of his account when the work was completed.[31] Just three years before he died, even as President of the Royal Hibernian Academy, while working on the statue of Robert Stewart in 1897, he was so out of pocket that he had to request money from the committee.[32]

Farrell's continued interest in the institutions of art saw him appointed to the Board of the National Gallery of Ireland in 1876 where he remained a member until the end of his life. During the 1870s he also received his first major commissions for work outside Dublin, when he was invited to carve two standing figures for the

*Thomas Farrell,* William Dease *(c. 1752–98). Marble. 1886. Royal College of Surgeons, Dublin. Dease was an eminent surgeon and co-founder of the College.*

# THOMAS FARRELL, SCULPTOR

forecourt of the Cathedral of the Assumption at Tuam. One of these statues commemorated William Burke, a benefactor of the Church, and the other portrayed John MacHale, the Archbishop of Tuam. Apparently something of a bigot, MacHale was openly anti-English and pro-denominational education in Ireland. Farrell, therefore, found himself once more in the hands of an ardent nationalist. Although Farrell received a number of commissions for work outside the capital in the form of bust portraits, tomb monuments and some monumental statues, he remained very much a Dublin sculptor. It is impossible to know how much he travelled either within the country or further afield. It might be assumed that the receiving of a particular commission for, say, Tuam or Wexford, would necessitate a visit to the site. But his monumental statues are often of such a type that they could be placed anywhere and they do not always reveal a special awareness of their final position. Certain-

*Thomas Farrell*, Mother Teresa Ball (1794–1861), *founder of the Loreto Order in Ireland. Marble. 1862. Loreto Abbey, Rathfarnham, Dublin.*

ly, the majority of his commissions were for locations in Dublin, which largely removed the necessity for frequent travel.

At the close of 1880s Farrell was working on a commission for architectural sculpture, which was new territory for him. The new Science and Art Museum and National Library was being built in Kildare Street, to the design of Thomas Deane. The design incorporated much sculptural detail on the facade at roof level, statuary groups, single figures and urns. A plinth to support and feature the statuary groups was included in the architectural detailing of the building. Farrell received the commission for these groups and when the building was opened in August 1890, four of them were already in place showing *Painting, Sculpture, Architecture* and *Poetry.* A drawing of the building by T Raffles Davison indicates that there were to be several other groups. *Music* and *Drama*, for example, would presumably have formed part of the series. However the original design was curtailed

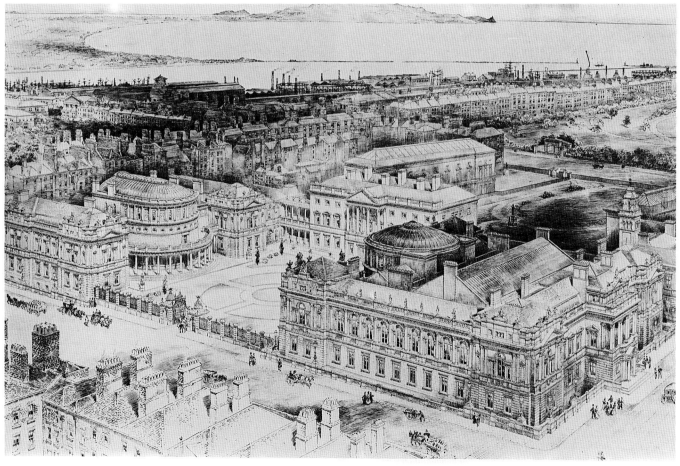

*T. Raffles Davison*, National Museum and Library Complex, Kildare St. Dublin, *showing statuary groups at roof level, the commission for which went to Thomas Farrell. Drawing in possession of the National Museum of Ireland.*

# THOMAS FARRELL, SCULPTOR

due to lack of money,[33] and only the initial four groups seem to have been completed. The sculptural work remained in place on the building for a very short time, less than twenty years; the Board of Visitors, in their report for the year 1909–1910,[34] noted the removal of the statuary groups due to decay and requested their replacement as an integral part of the design of the building. Farrell was dead by the time the groups were taken down and there appears to have been no attempt to commission any replacements.

In the last decade of his life, Farrell continued to receive a significant number of commissions for portrait work. Amongst these were busts of Cardinal Newman (1892), for University Church, and Sir Charles Cameron (1893), a very active President of the Royal College of Surgeons. There were three commissions for monumental statues in this decade. In the case of the Robert Stewart statue, the Committee invited six sculptors to submit estimates for the work, with Farrell the only resident Irish name amongst the group. It was in these last years of his life that Farrell was to receive what must have been the crowning accolade to his career. On 13 October 1893, he was elected President of the Royal Hibernian Academy, and in May of the following year he was knighted. Farrell had been a constant exhibitor at the Academy and was the first sculptor elected to the presidency. In a speech delivered in 1896,[35] he indicated what he considered to be the objectives of the institution, which were the gratuitous education of young artists and the promotion and cultivation of public taste by the Annual Exhibition of the works of living artists. He drew attention to the lack of commercial prosperity in Ireland at the time, which was not good for the Academy. However he felt that its civilizing and refining influence was ever present for the public good. Farrell was a concerned President and his interest in the proper training of young artists is evident in the strenuous efforts he made to secure an increased Government grant for instruction in draughtsmanship and painting in Ireland.[36] Adequate sums were not forthcoming and when he pointed out that 'the Academy has had to contend with the most adverse circum-

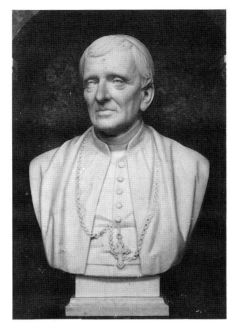

*Thomas Farrell*, Cardinal John Henry Newman (1801–90). *Marble. c. 1891.*
*University Church,*
*St. Stephen's Green, Dublin.*

stances',[37] this must surely be one of the problems to which he was referring.

It is certainly the case that Farrell was a conservative and traditional administrator and it comes as no surprise therefore to find other members of the Academy actively involved in more progressive ideas. The desire to see what was considered to be a more modern range of art, British and Continental, was instigated by newspaper articles in September 1898. George Russell, in a letter to the *Daily Express*,[38] indicated the need to see a loan exhibition of modern art in Ireland, because the paintings exhibited at the Royal Hibernian Academy were bad. The Editorial reply to this letter suggested that Dublin was 'now a desert waste of philistinism' and highlighted the diminished attendance at the Academy. While many members of the Academy were clearly in agreement, there was opposition from the more conservative members and the name of the President is nowhere to be found in any of the reports about the forthcoming exhibition.

Although Farrell's commissions remained just as plentiful in the 1890s as they had been in previous decades, it is in-

teresting to note that he returned in these last years to the creation of ideal works, an area he had rather neglected since the early stages of his career. In fact, he drew attention to the neglect of what he termed 'poetic or imaginative sculpture' in this country, in favour of memorial work.[39] This seems to indicate a certain regret at having devoted his artistic talent almost exclusively to portraiture and perhaps even to suggest that this talent cannot have been wholly fulfilled within this limitation.

The Farrell sculpture-yard remained at Gloucester Street, while Thomas had moved from his house in Warrington Place to Mountjoy Square in 1881, and in 1895 to a large house in Stillorgan, formerly owned by and named after Lord Redesdale, a former Lord Chancellor. When Thomas Farrell died in Redesdale House on 2 July 1900, his three remaining brothers were living with him. He left instructions that there would be no elaborate ceremony. The diffidence and retiring nature of this man in life was to be respected in death. At Farrell's own request, he was to be dead three days before there was any notice placed in the newspaper.[40] This wish was respected. However, a funeral service was held and was attended, particularly by fellow artists.[41] His obituary in *The Irish Times*[42] paid tribute to a 'great genius', the successor of Foley and Hogan, whose death left a gap which it would be hard to fill. The Royal Hibernian Academy held a meeting on 18 July 1900 at which was recorded their deep sense of loss at the death of her President. They acknowledged the admirable characteristics of Farrell, who was considered to have been honourable and straightforward, courteous, kindly and endearing. The report continued: 'The Academy regrets that family arrangements precluded its members from exercising the privilege of paying the last tribute of respect to the deceased, by accompanying his remains to the grave, and publicly testifying by their presence on that occasion the honour and esteem in which they held him.'[43]

*Paula Murphy*

*Paula Murphy is a Lecturer in History of Art in University College, Dublin.*

# THOMAS FARRELL, SCULPTOR

## NOTES

1. The date of the birth of Thomas Farrell is problematic. Strickland in his *Dictionary of Irish Artists* notes his year of birth as 1827. The Parish Records of the Church of St Andrew, Dublin, record the baptism of a certain Thomas Farrell on 13 May 1827. However the parents' names are entered as Terence and Anna, while Thomas's mother's name was Maria. Further problems arise if we approach his birth-date from the year in which he died, 1900. His obituary in *The Irish Times* states that he was born in 1829 and the records of Glasnevin Cemetery, where he is buried, indicate that he was seventy years old when he died. However, the age at death, given probably by a member of the family, may not be accurate. I propose to take 1827 as the year of birth.

2. Quoted in a letter from Daniel O'Connor, Bishop of Saldes, to Father John O'Hanlon, April 1864. Ms Ch 6/2 City Hall.

3. For further information on Terence Farrell, other members of the family and the family background see Paula Murphy's article, 'Terence Farrell, Sculptor', in *Irish Arts Review Yearbook*, 1991–1992, pp. 73–79.

4. *Proceedings of the Royal Dublin Society*, 1843–1844, No 80, Appendix V, p. ci.

5. The sculpture was reassembled and proved subsequently to be a frequent target, until fatally damaged in 1929 and removed.

6. *The Freeman's Journal*, 8 May 1852.

7. Walter Strickland, *A Dictionary of Irish Artists*, Maunsel & Company, Ltd, Dublin and London, 1913.

8. *The Dublin Builder*, June 15 1861.

9. *The Dublin Builder*, June 1 1860.

10. For further information on the Wellington Testimonial see Larcom, Ms 7778, National Library of Ireland.

11. Ibid. The price agreed with Potter for casting the reliefs in bronze included fixing them in position on the Wellington Monument. The name Buckingham, therefore, must refer to the man sent from the foundry in London to carry out this installaton.

12. Ibid.

13. These two statues were destroyed when the Four Courts was burnt in 1922. C P Curran's photographs of the carvings and his manuscript with related notes, in The Irish Architectural Archive, are an invaluable record.

14. The whereabouts of the bust of Judge Nicholas Ball is unknown.

15. The statue of Alexander McDonnell was removed from its position outside Tyrone House in the 1950s, following the destruction, for political reasons, of other monuments in the city. It is currently stored in Daingean, Co Offaly, with the overflow of works from the National Museum.

16. This monument was moved, due to traffic congestion, in 1929, It is now positioned in the centre of O'Connell Street at the junction with Abbey Street.

17. *The Irish Times*, 27 December 1870.

18. Dublin Corporation Archives in the City Hall, Dublin, have in their possession a number of manuscripts relating to the O'Connell Monument, in particular Ms Ch 6/1, the Record and Minute Book of the O'Connell Testimonial General Committee, and Ms Ch 6/2, The Newspaper Cuttings.

19. Ms Ch 6/2, City Hall.

20. John Henry Foley, in a letter to J R Kirk, indicated that neither he nor other men of his position in the art world would think of entering for a competition. The letter was published in *The Freeman's Journal* and noted at the O'Connell Committee meeting, 4 November 1863. Ibid.

21. *The Dublin Builder*, 15 February 1865.

22. *The Freeman's Journal*, 27 May 1964.

23. Nicholas Penny discusses the new interest in the recumbent effigy in the nineteenth century in his *Church Monuments in Romantic England*, (1977), and draws attention to J H Markland's 1840s publication *Remarks on English Churches and on the Expediency of Rendering Sepulchral Memorials Subservient to Pious and Christian Uses*.

24. This quotation is taken from Farrell's reply to the toast drunk in his honour at the banquet to mark the unveiling of the Father Reffe memorial in Blackrock College on 17 December 1896. Father Reffe Memorial Booklet, 1896.

25. A letter from Daniel O'Connor, Bishop of Saldes, to Father John O'Hanlon, April 1864, tells how Farrell had invited him to view a posthumous bust of Dr Yore in preparation, because O'Connor had been acquainted with the deceased. Ms Ch 6/2, City Hall.

26. *Proceedings of the Royal Dublin Society*, 26 January 1843, Appendix III, p. xiix.

27. *The Irish Times*, 5 July 1900.

28. 'The Institution which I so unworthily represent' said Farrell, as President of the Royal Hibernian Academy, addressing the Reffe Ceremonial Banquet. See note 24.

29. *The Irish Times*, 25 June 1879.

30. *The Freeman's Journal*, 25 June 1879.

31. This happened in the case of the commission for the Wellington Testimonial when Farrell wrote to Larcom, 3 June 1861, requesting the balance of his account, which stood at 31 pounds. Ms 7778, National Library of Ireland.

32. 'Though I know that under the terms of the agreement I am not entitled to it, still if the Committee will kindly stretch a point to let me have sixty pounds from the 4th of October I will esteem it a great favour.' Letter from Farrell to the Stewart Memorial Committee, 28 September 1897. Ms 23 H46, Royal Irish Academy.

33. *Reports by the Directors and Officers of the Science and Art Museum, the Botanic Gardens, Glasnevin, and the Metropolitan School of Art, Dublin, 1883–1893*.

34. *National Museum of Science and Art and Royal Botanic Gardens, Dublin, Report of the Board of Visitors*, Dublin, 1910.

35. Father Reffe Memorial Booklet, 1896.

36. *The Irish Times*, 5 July 1900.

37. Father Reffe Memorial Booklet, 1896.

38. *The Daily Express*, 10 September 1898.

39. Father Reffe Memorial Booklet, 1896.

40. *The Irish Times*, 5 July 1900.

41. *The Irish Builder*, 1 August 1900.

42. *The Irish Times*, 5 July 1900.

43. *The Irish Builder*, 1 August 1900.

# KREMLIN GOLD – THE ART OF THE ORTHODOX CHURCH

Last year, as part of the Dublin 1991 European City of Culture celebrations, the Irish Museum of Modern Art hosted a significant exhibition of Russian decorative art and painting. The exhibition subtitled *Russian gold and silverworking and jewellery from the 12th to the 20th century*, was a selection of 97 works of art from the Armoury collection of the State Museums of the Moscow Kremlin.

The scope of the exhibition was broad both in terms of the time span and the type of work displayed. The earliest exhibit was a gold bracelet of the fourth century and the latest a Fabergé model of 1904; and the range of arts/crafts represented included metalwork, jewellery, enamel painting, icon painting, gem carving and embroidery. The individual items in the exhibition were clearly chosen to be very representative of their period and type. One of the most striking aspects of the exhibition as a whole was the high proportion of religious, as opposed to secular, works of art. This imbalance is indicative of the enormously important position which the Orthodox Church had in Russian society for centuries. The vast majority of the precious objects exhibited were made especially to serve the needs of the Orthodox church, with a collection of altar crosses, icons, gospel covers, chalices, patens and other utensils of church liturgy forming the basis of the exhibition. There was also a significant proportion of works of religious art produced for the private devotional needs of the tsar, his family and other wealthy individuals. Among these were miniature painted and carved icons made from a variety of materials including carved gem stones, wood and bone in elaborately ornamented precious metal surrounds, as well as a number of richly decorated gold and silver pendant crosses.

## Pre-Mongolian Jewellery

Many of the earliest works in the exhibition were items of female headdress jewellery made after the conversion of the Russians to Christianity, and before the Mongol invasions of the thirteenth century. These pieces represent the first flowering of identifiably Russian jewellery and served to illustrate the style, and particularly the techniques, popular among the jewellers of the eleventh and twelfth centuries. These included granulation (the soldering of tiny balls or grains

Thousands marvelled at the golden treasures from the Moscow Kremlin on show at the Irish Museum of Modern Art in autumn 1991. **Wanda Ryan-Smolin** sets these magnificent works in their cultural and artistic framework.

*Chalice, Novgorod, 1329, gold with jasper bowl set with almandines, amethysts, sapphires and pearls. Height 23.2 cm, diameter of bowl 12.8 cm.*

of gold or silver on to a metal surface); filigree (open-work ornamentation made of thin gold or silver wires usually twisted and soldered to a metal backing); cloisonné enamel (enamel poured into cells formed by metal bands on a metal ground); chasing (the surface tooling of metal with hammer and punch to produce relief ornamentation); and *niello* (the application of a black alloy of silver, copper and lead on engraved metal). Almost all of these techniques were to remain popular with Russian gold and silversmiths until well into the nineteenth century and, indeed, are still used today in Russia in the commercial production of souvenirs.

Equally many of these techniques were used in much earlier times but, while the origins of Russian jewellery and metalwork are very old, its birth and that of Russian art in general is usually regarded as coinciding with Russia's conversion to Christianity which took place in 988 or 989.

The story of Russia's adoption of Christianity as described in the chronicles[1], illuminates the early development of Russian art. The pagan Grand Duke Vladimir of Kievan Russia (ruled from 978 to 1015), following approaches made to him by learned men of various religious faiths, sent envoys to different lands to study the style of worship in each. The most impressive accounts brought back to him were of the splendour and beauty of the Greek churches which his envoys visited in Constantinople. Shortly afterwards Vladimir laid siege to the Greek city of Kherson[2] and subsequently used it as a pawn in securing the hand in marriage of the Byzantine Princess Anna, sister of Basil II and Constantine VIII. Basil and Constantine agreed to the marriage on condition that Vladimir converted to Christianity, which he duly did[3].

Vladimir's conversion and that of his subjects, whom he forced into mass baptism in the River Dnieper, had far reaching consequences. The most immediate of these was in the area of education, with the introduction of the Cyrillic alphabet, and in the artistic sphere with the sudden development of monumental church architecture and its decoration. Vladimir set in motion an extensive church building programme in Kiev for which he engaged architects, artists and craftsmen from Constantinople and other Greek cities including Kherson. The Greeks introduced into Kiev the fully developed art and architecture of the Byzantine Empire. Native craftsmen and builders were employed alongside, and trained by, the Greeks and so the new style was quickly assimilated into the existing culture. The churches, palaces and monasteries of Kiev became the models for other Russian cities and within a century of conversion a new and distinctly Russian aesthetic had been formed.

## Fourteenth Century Metalwork

With the coming of the Mongol hordes and the fall of Kiev in 1240, artistic production of all types was severely curbed, and in most areas made completely impossible. The only important Russian centre to escape this fate was Novgorod which, since the mid eleventh century

# KREMLIN GOLD – THE ART OF THE ORTHODOX CHURCH

had been an apanage principality of Kiev. Novgorod had an independent republican style of government which was largely the result of its strong economic and advantageous geographic position. It was a merchant town with established commercial links with the areas to the North and West of Russia and in particular with the German cities of Bremen and Cologne. The twelfth century witnessed a tremendous growth in the religious and cultural life of the city with the construction of more than sixty new churches. While Kiev is credited with the introduction and fostering of early Russian art, Novgorod is recognized as the birthplace of the national style.

During the thirteenth century Novgorod maintained its independence from the Mongols by paying a yearly tribute which left them without the money for any major building programmes. The decorative arts, however, faired much better, with standards of craftsmanship being maintained throughout the century and into the next, though with an understandably reduced output. An example of both the high standard of Novgorodian craftsmanship and the rarity of metalwork from this period is the chalice of 1329, which was the only fourteenth-century piece in the exhibition. The chalice is silver-gilt with a bowl of carved red jasper and the shape, proportions and combination of materials used point to a knowledge of Western European metalwork of the twelfth century while the ornamentation is typically Novgorodian. Characteristic of Novgorodian filigree are the s-shaped scrolls with offshoots used in the gem-studded band beneath the lip of the chalice and around the foot. The engraving of the saints around the broad rim of the chalice was influenced by contemporary trends in icon painting, while the interlace ornamentation surrounding the saints is similar to that of early fourteenth century illuminated manuscripts of Novgorod.

According to its engraved inscription, the chalice was made for the Archbishop of Novgorod, Moisei, in 1329, and as it is more lavish in its use of gem stones and wealth of decoration than was normal for Novgorod at this time, it is thought that it may have been made to commemorate the visit of Ivan Kalita in the same year. Ivan Kalita's appointment as Grand Duke of Moscow by the Mongolian Great Khan in 1325 heralded the beginning of

*Crown from the framework of the Virgin of Bogolyubovo Icon, Moscow, late 14th/early 15th century, gold set with sapphires, almandines, tourmalines, emeralds, turquoise and pearls. Individual sections 11.5 x 8 cm.*

the unification of the Russian lands and the rise of Moscow above all other principalities. About the same time the head of the Orthodox church in Russia, Metropolitan Peter, transferred his see from Vladimir to Moscow. With the move, Moscow and particularly its Kremlin (fortified citadel) became the spiritual centre of the Russian lands.

Most of the works on show at IMMA came from either the cathedrals or the treasury of the Moscow Kremlin and many of them were made in its workshops. The most important of these was the Armoury (first mentioned in the chronicles in 1547) which chiefly produced weapons and armour but also employed icon, fresco and miniature painters who were engaged in decorating the palaces and churches of the Kremlin. Other associated royal workshops produced gold and silverware, saddlery, bedding, clothing, embroidery and lace. The gold and silver workshops reached the height of their development in the second half of the seventeenth century.

In 1700, both workshops were closed and the master craftsmen were transferred to the new capital, St Petersburg. In 1727 the Armoury was merged with the state treasury and the other remaining workshops to form the Workshop and Armoury Palace which became home of the Kremlin's treasures. The Armoury was turned into a museum at the beginning of the nineteenth century.

## Fifteenth Century Metalwork

From the end of the fourteenth century or beginning of the fifteenth century came two exhibits of Moscovite workmanship, a crown and a *tsata* (collar) both originally part of the framework of the *Virgin of*

*Bogolyubovo Icon.* The crown is noteworthy not only because of its aesthetic appeal, but more especially because of the light it sheds on the development of Russian victory over the Mongols at Kulikovo in 1380.

What is instantly obvious is the crown's close stylistic and technical affinity with the jewellery of the pre-Mongolian period. The background decoration of freely applied filigree spirals coupled with the expressive use of multicoloured stones (precious and semi-precious) firmly link it with the work of the twelfth century.

The craftsmen who created the Bogolyubovo crown were not merely continuing the forms and techniques handed down to them by their forefathers but were also purposefully seeking to emulate the achievements of the independent pre-Mongolian era. After years of stagnation and oppression artists and craftsmen were attempting to express their national identity by turning anew to native sources of past centuries for inspiration.

The *Virgin of Bogolyubovo Icon* was for centuries one of the most sacred icons of the Kremlin's Annunciation cathedral. It was removed from the cathedral during Napoleon's occupation of Moscow. Parts of the frame were later recovered, though the icon itself was never returned and was presumably destroyed having had, at the time, no intrinsic monetary value.

## The Sixteenth Century: Jewellery

The majority of exhibits on show at IMMA were of the sixteenth and seventeenth centuries, a fact which reflects the flourishing state of the Kremlin workshops during these centuries.

The Mongol hold over Russia was finally broken in 1480 and a period of great cultural activity ensued; the Kremlin walls and towers were rebuilt and the most notable cathedrals and churches were built. Ivan III, through his marriage with the Greek princess Sophia Palaeologa, had gained direct access to Italian culture since Sophia had been educated in Rome as a ward of the Pope. Shortly after her arrival in Moscow, Ivan sent emissaries to invite Italian architects and craftsmen to build new churches and palaces in the Kremlin and to instruct native craftsmen in Renaissance techniques.

The result of Ivan III's initiatives in the cultural field are very evident in the style of the sixteenth century Russian jewel-

# KREMLIN GOLD – THE ART OF THE ORTHODOX CHURCH

lery exhibited at IMMA. One *panagia* (an icon worn like a pendant by senior members of the Orthodox clergy) is of particular interest. It was made in the Kremlin workshops in 1589 for Tsar Fëdor Ioannovich (1557–82) and his wife Tsarina Irina Fëdorovna (1563–1604), for presentation to Iov, who became the first patriarch of Russia in that year. The cameo in the centre of the *panagia* is of a two layered onyx[4] and the subject is the *Crucifixion* with Christ on the cross between the disproportionately small figures of the Virgin and St John. The inscriptions are all in Greek but the method of carving employed and the uniformly low relief of the images suggest that it is a twelfth century Italian work though strongly influenced in its iconography by Byzantine models, possibly ivories[5]. The reverse of the stone is carved in intaglio[6] with full length figures of Saints Constantine and Helena. They stand together holding a cross between them dressed in imperial costume. Both the Emperor Constantine and his mother Helena were frequently represented in the art of the orthodox church because of their crucial roles in the establishment of Christianity in the Roman empire. The simplicity of style and the severity of the frontal depiction of the two saints indicate that they were a later addition to the cameo and presumably date, like the *panagia* itself, to 1589. The gold setting is decorated with a stylized plant motif in enamel filigree[7] in which the influence of the Italian Renaissance can clearly be discerned. The *panagia* is further embellished with rubies, sapphires and strings of pearls in a manner characteristic of the best of Russian jewellery of this period.

## Icons

The painting of icons[8] which is so readily associated with the culture of Russia has a history in the Eastern church dating back to at least the sixth century although little has survived from this early period due to the devastating effect of the iconoclasm[9] of the eighth and ninth centuries. Following the defeat of iconoclasm, icons came to be regarded not only as visual counterparts to the religious texts but also as sacred objects to be venerated in their own right. This idea stemmed from the belief that icons of Christ and the Virgin were copies of original portraits from life. In many ways

*Panagia, Moscow, 1589, gold set with sapphires, rubies and pearls. Cameo, Italy? 12th century, onyx, 15 x 8.8 cm.*

this accounts for the totally different approach taken by painters of both churches to similar subjects.

In Byzantine and later Russian painting, the emphasis was always on refinement through repetition rather than invention. Despite this, specific styles did emerge.

The first style of icon painting introduced into Russia was Byzantine, with the direct importation from Constantinople and other centres, of icons and icon-painters in the eleventh century. The art was quickly established in Russia, first at Kiev and subsequently in the Novgorod, Vladimir-Suzdal and other areas. Throughout the twelfth and thirteenth centuries however, Byzantine models like the *Virgin of Vladimir*[10] remained influential. In the troubled thirteenth and fourteenth centuries, with the breaking of trade links with the East, Russian painters became more self reliant and a native style began to emerge. As with other art forms, Novgorod was an important haven for its development. From the mid-fourteenth century came a resumption of contact with Byzantium and the arrival of a new wave of Greek artists, the most influential of whom was Theophanes the

Greek (Feofan Grek) a fresco and icon painter who worked in the Byzantine cities of Galata and Chalcedon before arriving in Russia. Although none of his Moscow work[11] has survived, his style, characterised by the small heads, delicate features and subtle tonal modelling of the figures together with a very personal impressionistic use of white highlights, proved inspirational for many Russian painters including Andrey Rublev. Rublev (1360/1370–1427 or 1430) was a monk of the Trinity-St Sergius Monastery at Zagorsk and later of the Andronikus Monastery, Moscow. His most outstanding works are the *Old Testament Trinity* icon painted for the Father Superior Nicon and the *Deesis* icons of the Zvenigorod Cathedral. These are considered to be the finest examples of Russian icon painting[12]. Rublev, whose style differs so much from Theophanes' despite their close association (they worked together in Moscow in 1405) is contemplative and spiritual in mood and marked by a delicate use of line and well balanced, uncluttered compositions.

In the second half of the fifteenth century, with the emergence of Dionysius (1440/50s–after 1504), there came a definite move away from Byzantine tradition with the abandonment of all traces of Hellenistic illusionism in the treatment of volume and spatial recession. Dionysius was a lay painter of the Moscow school, his style being characterized by extreme elongation of figures, a clear sense of rhythm and a light palette. He is known chiefly from the icons and frescoes he did for the St Therapont Monastery Cathedral of the Nativity of the Virgin on Lake Beloye.

The work of all three of these artists continued to exert considerable influence on icon painting throughout the sixteenth century. With the growth of the centralised state, icon painting became more standardized. Moscow became the focal point for all artistic activity, with artists being drawn from all the regional centres including Novgorod whose artists were moved *en masse* to Moscow after the fire in the capital in 1547. The term *mixed style* is used to describe the work of those sixteenth century artists who drew on the traditions of both Moscow and Novgorod. Other styles co-existed and as a result it is difficult to establish any clear pattern of development. However it is possible to make some generalisations about the six-

# KREMLIN GOLD – THE ART OF THE ORTHODOX CHURCH

teenth century style which may serve as an introduction to an examination of those icons from the Annunciation Cathedral exhibited in the Kremlin Gold exhibition.

Many icons painted during the reign of Ivan the Terrible[13] (as these were) had a more clearly didactic role than before and thus the drawing became sharper, the compositions more geometric and the colouring decorative. These features can be seen in the Annunciation Cathedral icons along with additional elements which firmly place them in time, such as a sense of quiet sadness in the facial expressions, a lack of direct eye contact between the figures and the viewer[14] and a muted colour scheme dominated by olive greens and yellowish ochres.

The nine panels included in the Dublin exhibition came from two of the four side chapels (*Entry into Jerusalem* and *Synaxis of the Virgin*) of the Annunciation Cathedral. The cathedral (the Royal chapel of the Russian Tsars) was built by Pskovian master builders between 1484 and 1489. Originally a small structure roofed with three domes, it was enlarged in the 1560s by the addition of four single domed chapels. All the available evidence suggests that the icons were made specially for the iconostasis of the new chapels in the 1560s. An iconostasis is a screen of icons that separates the sanctuary from the naves in Orthodox churches. The iconostasis as a form originated in Russia from the custom of hanging icons along the altar rail; this system of display developed into a more permanent structure comprising three tiers of icons. The central tier was the most important and was reserved for the *deesis* icons with Christ in the centre flanked by the Virgin and St. John the Baptist. The upper tier depicted some or all of the twelve major church feasts and the lower tier accommodated local saints and normally incorporated three pairs of doors. The central doors, called the royal doors because only the priest and tsar could enter the sanctuary through them, were decorated with scenes depicting the four evangelists, the *Annunciation* and the Divine Liturgy.

Iconostases from the fifteenth and sixteenth centuries frequently included a fourth and sometimes a fifth tier of icons above the church festive tier and in the seventeenth century a sixth tier was occasionally added. As the iconostasis is made up of separate panels it can easily be dismantled and reassembled in a new location as frequently happened in the past, this practice adding to the historian's difficulties as their provenance is so often lost. Another feature of the iconostasis was the tendency gradually to expand it to accommodate all the available space. Thus it is not uncommon to find icons of vastly differing periods arranged together in one structure[15].

The icons exhibited in Dublin from the Annunciation Cathedral iconostases were all of the same period and were in fact linked together, with scenes from two tiers being combined on one panel; so that instead of eighteen panels there were only nine. The panels exhibited at IMMA were arranged as shown in the diagram.

The *deesis* tier, being the most important, is much larger than the festive tier and includes Christ in Majesty surrounded by the symbols of the four evangelists. He is encircled in a mandorla with floating circles of seraphim[16] signifying heaven. The red diamond within the mandorla represents the light emanating from His divine being while the red rectangle beyond the mandorla represents earth. Other panels of the *deesis* tier depict the Virgin (always referred to as the

| Nativity | Presentation in the Temple | Baptism of Christ | Raising of Lazarus | Entry into Jerusalem | Transfiguration | Crucifixion | Descent into Hell | Ascension | Descent of the Holy Ghost |
|---|---|---|---|---|---|---|---|---|---|
| St Basil the Great | Apostle Peter | Archangel Michael | Mother of God | Christ in Majesty | | St John the Baptist | Archangel Gabriel | Apostle Paul | St John Chrysostom |

*Icons from the side-chapels of the Cathedral of the Annunciation, Moscow, 1560, tempera and silver gilt on wood. Central panel 143 x 64.5 cm, side panels 134.5 x 34.5 approx.*

# KREMLIN GOLD – THE ART OF THE ORTHODOX CHURCH

'Mother of God' in Russia), St John the Baptist, the Archangels Michael and Gabriel, the apostles Peter and Paul and the saints John Chrysostom and Basil the Great. The later two saints are deeply revered in Russia as fathers of the Greek church and hence their important positioning in the iconostasis. The scenes from the church festive tier are all ultimately based on Byzantine prototypes and, while most of them appear in a similar form in western painting of the mediaeval period they are rare in the sixteenth century and some of their details are unique to the Russian Orthodox Church. In the *Entry into Jerusalem*, for example, the donkey has been replaced by a horse (the donkey being unknown in Russia in early times)[17] which Christ rides side-saddle in the Eastern manner rather than astride. A small child in white spreads out his cloths before Christ and the city fathers and other inhabitants of Jerusalem hold out olive branches in greeting to Him. *The Descent of the Holy Spirit*, is of a type exclusively associated with the Eastern Church and shows a patriarchal figure of a bearded man who personifies the world in the centre of the apostles. This motif is of Byzantine origin though there he is normally shown holding the twelve scrolls of the gospels in twelve languages while here the apostles

are seen holding the scrolls. The scrolls replace the tongues of fire, and the bearded man replaces the Virgin of typical western interpretations of the event. The Virgin is generally absent in representations of this scene in the Russian Orthodox Church as it traditionally highlights the role of the apostles rather than of the Virgin. The two-dimensional graphic style of these icons with its extremely stylised mountains and trees, is typical of icon painting of the period. The rich decorative effect created by the silver-gilt surround ornamented with stylised plant motifs (worked in the *basma* or repoussé technique) which extends into the picture space is also characteristic, and at the same time illustrative, of the level of collaboration common between artists and craftsmen at the time.

## Seventeenth Century Metalwork

During the seventeenth century this type of collaboration in the production of icons became more pronounced as the desire for ornamentation increased. Two works in the exhibition, in particular, displayed this tendency, the *Jerusalem Virgin Icon* and the *Trinity Icon*.

The *Jerusalem Virgin Icon* is dated to the first third of the seventeenth century and comes from the Archangel Cathedral in

the Kremlin. As the burial place of the Grand Princes of Moscow and later the Tsars of Russia, the Cathedral of St Michael the Archangel (designed by an Italian architect Alevisio Novi and built between 1505 and 1509) was particularly well endowed with lavishly decorated icons. The *Jerusalem Icon* was, according to the cathedral inventories, kept on a lectern close to the places where Tsar Alexei Mikhailovich (1629–1676) and his elder son Tsar Fëdor Alexeevich (1661–1682) were buried. It is thought that it came to the cathedral at the time of one of their deaths.

The icon is mounted in an elaborate gold case with doors that can be closed over. On the inside of the doors are engraved images of the Archangels Michael (left) and Gabriel (right). The frame of the interior of the case is heavily chased with a border of stylised plant motifs which is set with five blue sapphires and seven *niello* medallions. The medallion scenes relate to the Virgin and her life and represent (clockwise from the top right corner) the *Birth of the Virgin*, the *Presentation of the Virgin in the Temple*, the *Meeting at the Golden Gate*, the *Virgin Orans*[18], the *Intercession of the Virgin*[19], the *Assumption* and the *Annunciation*. The icon itself is of the Virgin and Child. The Jerusalem Virgin is a variant of the *Virgin Hodegetria*

*The Jerusalem Virgin Icon, Moscow,*
*first third of the 17th century, Icon, tempera on wood.*
*Case, gold set with emeralds, rubies, sapphires and pearls,*
*26.3 x 36 cm (open).*

*Trinity Icon, Moscow, between 1676 and*
*1682. Icon, tempera on wood. Frame, gold*
*with enamel and set with diamonds,*
*28.8 x 22.8 cm.*

('She who shows the Way') in which the Virgin gestures in the direction of the Child. The type originated from an icon believed to have been painted by St Luke and blessed by the Virgin herself, which was sent by the Empress Eudocia from Palestine to Constantinople in 438 and placed in the church of the Hidegoi ('Pointers of the Way') in the imperial palace. Although the original *Hodegetria* did not survive, it was widely known through many Byzantine copies. The Jerusalem version differs from the original severely frontal representation of the Byzantine type in that a degree of intimacy has been introduced by the slight inclination of the Virgin and Child's faces towards each other. Much of the painted surface of the icon is hidden from view by the strings of pearls hung across its lower half and by the splendid haloes and crown of the revetment which, like the frame, is chased and studded with sapphires, rubies and emerald. The ornamentation of the frame, haloes, and crown are a development of stylistic trends already present in Russian jewellery in the sixteenth century, while the more delicate *niello* work on the slim section of the framework to the right and left of the Virgin points to the growing influence of middle eastern and in particular of Persian art. Also characteristic of this period is the use of table cut stones alongside the older smooth cabochon stones.

The *Trinity Icon*, made between 1676 and 1682, is quite different in style. The gold frame (*oklad*) covers practically the entire surface of the icon with only the heads, hands and feet left exposed. The goldsmith replicated every detail of the underlying icon in *repoussé* with the finer details engraved and highlighted in enamels. The wealth of narrative detail and the appealing manner in which the material world is described in the icon, is an indication of the general secularisation of Russian art which manifested itself towards the end of the century. The painting style of the icon is representative of the period in its use of dark brown for the flesh tones imitating the darkened condition of the highly revered icons of earlier centuries. The practice of covering icons with a metal frame was to continue into the eighteenth and nineteenth centuries though it became increasingly common for painters to execute only the parts which were visible and not the

Crown 'Monomakh's cap', Constantinopole?, late 13th/early 14th centuries, gold set with rubies, emeralds and pearls.

entire hidden composition as in the *Jerusalem Virgin* example. The subject of the icon, the Old Testament Trinity, is common in the Russian Orthodox Church where Old Testament scenes and especially those that prefigure the Incarnation and Passion of Christ are important. The primary figures rendered in the icon are the three angels who appeared to Abraham in the desert beneath the oak at Mamre. They prophesied that a son (Isaac) would be born to Abraham's wife Sarah. The angels were seen as a symbol of the Trinity and in this case Christ may be identified with the angel on the left because of the blue colour of His garment, and His gesture of acceptance in response to the central angel (God the Father) who alludes to the future sacrifice of Christ by extending his hand over the dish containing a calf's head; the Holy Ghost is represented in the angel on the right. The scene also includes Abraham who brings food to the table, Sarah in the background and a small boy killing the calf in the foreground. The killing of the calf symbolises the sacrifice of Isaac and the ultimate sacrifice of Christ.

In addition to the framed icons described above, the exhibition also included several other fine examples of the work of seventeenth century Russian goldsmiths. Outstanding were a censer in the shape of a Russian Orthodox church, and a tabernacle also of a form reminiscent of church architecture, spectacularly decorated

with a large pink tourmaline. Both of these pieces are characteristic of the best of Russian church gold of the period. Of the secular works of decorative art produced in the seventeenth century those commissioned by the tsar and his family were naturally the most splendid, and a selection of ceremonial tablewares illustrated this. Most impressive were the *kovshi* used for drinking mead and wine which were regarded as important symbols of status and merit. The prototype of the *kovsh* was the carved wooden scoop or ladle in the shape of a wild duck which has been used in Russia as an everyday utensil for thousands of years.

Of great historic interest is the small crown used for the coronation of Peter the Great (1672–1725). Peter was only ten years old when he became Tsar of Russia, along with his brother Ivan Alexeevich. Because of his mental and physical ill health Ivan was considered unfit to rule, but, as the elder brother he had many supporters, and a compromise was reached whereby both brothers were crowned together. Ivan was crowned with the so called 'Monomakh's Cap', a crown which had been used since the fifteenth century for the coronation of the Grand Princes of Moscow and Tsars of Russia. It is called 'Monomakh's Cap' because of a fifteenth century legend which claimed that it was a part of a gift of royal regalia sent by the Byzantine emperor Constantine IX Monomachus to the Kievan Grand Prince Vladimir Monomakh. The crown which dates to the late thirteenth or early fourteenth century and is of oriental workmanship, is also in the Armoury collection (although it was not included in the Dublin exhibition). Peter's crown, which is referred to in contemporary documents as 'Monomakh's second dress cap' in order to distinguish it from the original, was made specially for his coronation in 1682. It is made from eight sections of sheet gold riveted together (the wire rivets camouflaged by bevelled ribbing), and surmounted by a hemisphere of beaten gold set with precious stones and a cross decorated with pearls. In shape, layout of the stones (with one stone and three or four pearls to each of the eight sections) and settings (in particular the raised settings on the dome of the cap), it is almost identical to the original crown. The only significant difference between them is in the elaborate filigree ornamentation which covers the

# KREMLIN GOLD – THE ART OF THE ORTHODOX CHURCH

entire surface of the first crown. Although the design of the two crowns is very similar, the lack of profuse ornamentation on Peter's crown (conceivably the result of hasty execution) gives it a clarity and a strength which sets it apart from its prototype and places it firmly at the beginning of a new era. Great importance was attached to the coronation of tsars in Russia by both church and state, as the tsars like the Byzantine emperors before them were believed not only to receive their authority to rule from heaven but also have temporal supremacy over the church.

Apart from the various ceremonial pieces a number of decorative works of a more utilitarian kind were also included in the exhibition. Many of these were representative of the extraordinary growth and development of filigree enamel alongside a newly adopted technique of enamel painting. The source of these works was Solvychegodsk in the northern province of Vologda, which was the major centre for the production of painted enamel wares in the seventeenth century. Solvychegodsk enamels or Usolye enamels as they are sometimes called (because of the fame of the Usolye workshops) can be easily recognized by their bright colours, large-scale floral designs and various representational motifs which include depictions of figures and animals. The overall treatment of the motifs, especially the use of cross hatching in the application of the colours, is at times strikingly reminiscent of Italian majolica of the late Renaissance.

## Eighteenth and Nineteenth Century Jewellery and Metalwork

Peter the Great's reign is viewed as a watershed in the history of Russia, not least because of his opening up of Russia to western influences. The consequences of his actions and in particular his founding of St Petersburg had a major impact on the development of art in Russia. Numerous items in the exhibition illustrated how Russian jewellers and metalworks adapted the various western styles of the eighteenth century to their own needs. The best of these were a paten (1789) and chalice (1795) commissioned by Catherine the Great from the St Petersburg firm of Ivar Buch and executed in the neoclassical style.

The nineteenth century exhibits point-

*Crown 'Monomakh's second dress cap', Moscow, 1682, gold set with sapphires, emeralds, rubies, tourmalines, cornelians and pearls. Height 20.3 cm, circumference 61 cm.*

*Cross by Ovchinnikov, Moscow, 1885, gold with enamel and set with diamonds and emeralds, 13.4 x 11.9 cm.*

ed to the complete integration of Russia art and craft with the mainstream of European culture. In Russia, as elsewhere, historicism was in vogue with the emphasis on a return to the country's national historic style. The Ovchinnikov cross, a replica of a pectoral cross which belonged to Peter the Great, is an excellent example of Russian revivalist jewellery. It was made in 1885 in Moscow by the firm of

Pavel Akimovich Ovchinnikov (1830–1888). The firm, which remained in business until 1916, was one of the largest and most successful producers of gold and silver in Russia, receiving numerous awards at home and abroad. The cross is of cast gold set with brilliant cut diamonds and emeralds, and painted in enamels. Diamonds superseded other gems in the eighteenth and nineteenth centuries, as cutting techniques became more skilled and the decorative quality of diamonds became more apparent. The reverse of the cross is painted in a scrolling pattern of acanthus leaves and flowers in a combination of chiefly pink, black and green enamels.

The chief competitor and contemporary of the Ovchinnikov firm was the firm of Fabergé, founded by Gustav Fabergé in St Petersburg in 1842, and made famous by his son, Peter Carl, who took over the firm in 1870. Although educated in St Petersburg, Peter Carl Fabergé travelled extensively in Europe and served his apprenticeship as a goldsmith in Frankfurt, thus becoming familiar with the fashionable European revivalist jewellery of the period. He first achieved international acclaim for his copies of Scythian treasures, made in 1882 and exhibited in Moscow and Nuremberg. He became official goldsmith to the Imperial court in 1885 and the firm soon expanded, opening branches in Moscow (1885), Odessa (1890), London (1903) and Kiev (1905). By 1900 the firm employed a staff of over 500 who, under the artistic direction of Fabergé, designed and produced a wide range of decorative articles including cigarette cases, photograph and miniature frames, animal and figure hard-stone statuettes, clocks, desk sets, jewelled flower arrangements and Easter eggs. The main characteristics of Fabergé products were a high standard of execution, a preference for enamels and semi-precious rather than precious stones, and originality and novelty in design.

All of these attributes are present in the Model of the Moscow Kremlin exhibited at IMMA. It was made in 1904 for the Emperor Nicholas II and is one of a series of Easter presents, the first of which Fabergé produced in 1885 for Alexander III who gave it to his wife Marie Fëodorovna. Alexander thereafter commissioned one annually for Marie Fëodorovna. His son, Nicholas II, continued the practice, ordering two annually for both his mother and his wife, Alexandra Fëodorovna. As Easter gifts, they were designed in the shape of an egg which could be opened to reveal a surprise. The design of many of the eggs was derived from eighteenth century French examples in the Hermitage collection to which Fabergé was allowed special access. The surprises inside the eggs were generally of Fabergé's own invention and inspired by themes from the lives of the imperial family. They included miniature models of the Royal yacht (the Pamiat Azova), the coronation carriage (1897), Gatchina Palace (1901) and cameo portraits of the imperial children (1914) to name but a few. The Model of the Moscow Kremlin differs from many of the other imperial eggs in that the egg itself, which is based on the architecture of the Assumption Cathedral, is incorporated into the centre of the piece rather than enclosing the composition within its shell. The surprise element is not, however, lost in the design which, in addition to being a stylised model of the Kremlin's walls, towers (based on the Spasskii and Vodovzvochii towers) and main cathedral, also contains a concealed musical box.

The cathedral of the Assumption (or Dormition) was designed by the Italian architect Rodolfo Fioravanti[20] between 1475 and 1479 and although influenced by Renaissance concepts was based on the twelfth century cathedral of the Assumption in Vladimir. The Grand Prince of Moscow, Ivan III, chose the Vladimir cathedral as a prototype because he wished to underline the supremacy of Moscow over other Russian cities and in particular over Vladimir which it superseded as capital of the Russian lands. Cubic in form and built on a square plan, it is surmounted by five domes resting on wide drums. The cathedral of the Assumption, being the seat of the Metropolitan of Moscow, was the primary church in Russia. It served as the burial place of the Metropolitans and later of the Patriarchs

*Model of the Moscow Kremlin by Faberge, St. Petersburg, 1904, gold painted with enamel on an onyx base, height 36.1 cm, base 18.5 x 17 cm.*

and was the church where all the major state ceremonies were set. Because of its central role in the religious and secular life of the country, it was frequently copied and eventually came to be regarded as the most acceptable model for traditional orthodox churches all over Russia.

The Model, which is set on a hexagonal block of onyx, is of cast engraved gold decorated in enamels. The guilloche technique (of working the underlying enamel ground with lathes to produce varying patterns) in which Fabergé excelled is here used to enhance the realistic appearance of the buildings, the green

enamel of the roofs revealing an underlying tile pattern and the opaque white of the egg a delicate brick pattern. The Model is one of only ten remaining imperial Easter eggs in the Armoury collection. The complete collection (which included more than forty eggs) was sent in crates together with the contents of the palaces at Czarskoje Selo and Gatchina to Moscow after the Revolution. The crates were opened after Lenin's death and the majority of the eggs were sold off to western dealers in 1925.

Fabergé also produced less elaborate eggs for non-imperial clients and a whole series of miniature eggs which were often collected and worn together as a necklace. The tradition of giving gifts of Easter eggs (made from a variety of materials including, wood, papier-maché, porcelain, hardstones and precious metals) was very strong in Russia because of the importance attached to Easter by the orthodox church. The Fabergé Easter egg, the Ovchinnikov cross and a host of other nineteenth century works of religious significance highlight the major influence which the Orthodox church continued to have on Russian society throughout the nineteenth century and right up to the time of the Revolution. The Kremlin Gold exhibition finished appropriately with Fabergé's model which, like Fabergé himself[21] and the monarch for whom it was made, mark the end of an era in Russian history and culture.

*Wanda Ryan-Smolin*

*Wanda Ryan-Smolin is a graduate of the Jagiellonian University, Cracow with an MA in the History of Art. She was for many years on the staff of the National Gallery of Ireland.*

ACKNOWLEDGEMENTS

I would like to thank the following people for their assistance in the preparation of this article. In Dublin, Philomena Byrne of the Irish Museum of Modern Art and my husband, Boris Smolin. In Moscow, Irena Bobrovnitskaya of the State Museums of the Moscow Kremlin and Demitry Czyzoff.

NOTES OVERLEAF

# KREMLIN GOLD – THE ART OF THE ORTHODOX CHURCH

## NOTES

1. The chronicles were at first simple lists of yearly events produced by the newly founded monastic institutions of the eleventh century. By the twelfth century they had developed into systematic historical studies. The complete collection has been published as *Polnoe sobranie russkikh letopisei* (Akademiya Nauk, Leningrad, 1843–1929).

2. Chersonesus

3. See S. H. Cross, *The Russian Primary Chronicle* (Cambridge, Mass., 1930). This account appears in the *Russian Primary Chronicle* which records the very early history of Russia. However as the Chronicle was not written contemporaneously with the actual events but in the early twelfth century it is likely that much of the descriptive detail is more legendary than historical. That aside, it still stresses the importance in the minds of the Russians of the purely visual and sensuous qualities of the Greek Church as the chronicle suggests that it was the art and architecture of the Byzantine Empire more than anything else that convinced Vladimir and his contemporaries of the superiority of Greek Orthodoxy over other religions.

4. The semi-precious stones sardonyx, cornelian, agate and onyx have for centuries been those most frequently chosen for glyptics. Sometimes precious stones were used, including emeralds and sapphires and even diamonds, though these were of course much more difficult to work. An example of a sapphire cameo was included in the Dublin exhibition (cat. no. 2).

5. See I.A. Mishakova, *Gemma iz Panagii patriarkha Iova, Drevnierusskoye iskusstvo. Zarubiezhnye sviazi.* (Moscow, 1975), pp. 45–54.

6. In intaglio the design is sunk into the stone, while in cameo the reverse is the case, with the design appearing in relief.

7. In this technique the enamel is enclosed in borders of applied filigree.

8. Icons are religious images painted on panel. Traditionally icons were painted in tempera on wooden panels made up of one or more pieces of wood joined together by wedges slotted or in the back. The centre of the seasoned panel was hollowed out leaving a raised border around the sides and often lined with a piece of linen (*pavoloka*) followed by a layer of gesso (*levkas*). The finished painting was covered by a final layer of oil (usually linseed) to brighten the colours. This last layer tended after some time to have a darkening effect of the icon which led the painters of the seventeenth and later centuries to use particularly dark palettes in imitation of what they thought were the intentionally dark icons of earlier times.

9. The iconoclasts (image breakers) ruled that only the cross and ornament based on plant forms were permissible in church decoration. Eventually in 843 orthodoxy triumphed when the rule was reversed by the iconodules (image veneraters).

10. An early twelfth century Greek icon now in the Tretyakov Gallery, Moscow.

11. Since the restoration of these icons in 1918 most art historians have regarded them as the work of Theophanes the Greek who is documented as having painted an iconostasis for the cathedral in 1405 but for various reasons, including its size which would have made it too big for the original church, and the fact that the interior decoration of the church was destroyed by fire in 1547, it is now recognized that the present iconostasis was originally painted for a different church at a slightly earlier date. They remain, however, among the best examples of icon painting in existence and because of their affinity with the Novgrodian frescos of Theophanes, many Russian scholars now think 'they are the work of an outstanding (though anonymous) Byzantine master working within the mainstream of the same artistic trend'. See E. Smirnova, *Moscow Icons of the 14th to 17th Centuries*, (Leningrad, 1989), pp.12–14, 262–263.

12. All of these are now in the Tretyakov Gallery, Moscow.

13. Ivan IV (1530–1584), better known as Ivan the Terrible, became the first Tsar of Russia in 1547.

14. The penetrating gaze of religious figures is perhaps the most memorable and moving aspect of the earlier icons while here none of the saints look at us directly and even Christ, who is represented in the severely frontal manner that the subject dictates, seems to look not at us but at some point beyond us.

15. For a discussion of icon painting in the service of the iconostasis, see M A Alpatov, *Early Russian Icon Painting*, Moscow, 1987, pp. 33–39.

16. Seraphim, who, along with cherubim, surround God in perpetual adoration, are the first in the hierarchy of angels as classified by the fifth century Pseudo-Dionysius in his *De Hierarchia Celestii*. The seraphim are here depicted in the customary manner with heads only and two pairs of wings.

17. See D. and T. Talbot Rice, *Icons, The Natasha Allan Collection Catalogue*, National Gallery of Ireland catalogue, (Dublin 1968), p. 59.

18. The *Virgin Orans* called the *Virgin Blacherniotissa* in Russia because the type originated from the image of the Virgin in the mosaic in the apse of the church of the Blahernae, Constantinople. It was among the most popular types of the Virgin in which she appears with her arms raised in the antique gesture of prayer and with a medallion image of Christ Emmanuel on her breast.

19. The intercession of the Virgin, called the *Pokrov*, in Russia derives from the legend of the Miracle at Blachnea when the Virgin appeared in the church during a service and spread her cloak or *pallium* over the congregation and interceded for their salvation. In the miniature *niello* version on the Jerusalem icon case, the virgin is in the upper register while below her in a pulpit is the Byzantine poet, Romanus the Melodist and St Andrew from whose *Life* the subject is described. For a discussion of this subject, see A. Grabar, 'Une source d'inspiration de l'iconographie byzantine tardive. Les cérémonies du culte de la Vierge', *Cahiers archéologiques*, 25 (Paris, 1976).

20. Rodolfo Fioravanti (c.1415–c.1485/6) of Bologna was called Aristotle by the Russians because of his wide learning and varied abilities.

21. In 1917 the firm was taken over by a workers collective, Fabergé emigrated in 1918 and died in Switzerland in 1920.

# MARGARET MACNAIR STOKES (1832–1900)

*Lord Walter FitzGerald,* Miss Margaret Stokes Sketching The High Cross of Moone.
*Date unknown. Photograph of a b & w photograph 11.5 x 14.3 cm.*
*(Alexandra College Magazine, December 1900. Alexandra College, Milltown.)*

Anyone who undertakes a study of the Irish high crosses, will quickly come across the name Margaret Stokes, one of the pioneers of Irish art and archaeology. At a time when the study of such things was completely dominated by men, particularly gentlemen-scholars, Margaret Stokes stands out as an exceptional figure. Her contributions to Irish art and archaeology were largely due to the privileged life she led and they were inspired by the discoveries of the nineteenth century, such as the Cross of Cong, the Tara Brooch and the Ardagh Chalice. She was born in York Street, Dublin in 1832, the eldest daughter of William and Mary Stokes, the same William who later became the president of the Royal College of Surgeons. As there was no suitable establishment where young girls could be educated in Ireland, she was taught by governesses. Thus she had no formal education but was very accomplished in art and music. Her father nurtured her love of study and it was through that close association that she met the people who were to have an enormous influence on her, chiefly George Petrie (1790–1866), Frederick William Burton (1816–1900) and Edwin Quinn, the third Earl of

The world of Irish art and archaeology is greatly indebted to the scholarship of Margaret Stokes. Her pioneering work is described by **Janette Stokes.**

Dunraven (1812–1871). A combination of these and other antiquarians and artists, plus her father's precise training, instilled a deep passion for archaeological investigation, which became evident in the work she later accomplished.

George Petrie probably had the greatest influence on Miss Stokes. In 1833 the Government sponsored the Ordnance Topographical Survey, on which Petrie, John O'Donovan and Eugene O'Curry were employed. Due to lack of funds, the survey ended in 1839, but George Petrie kept on with his work, continuing to make summer expeditions around Ireland along with Dr Stokes, Burton, Dunraven and many more enthusiasts. In 1857 Miss Stokes accompanied her father, Petrie and others to the Aran Islands and went on summer expeditions from 1866–1869. When Petrie died in 1866 leaving his work on Christian inscriptions unfinished, Margaret Stokes completed the task;

she was familiar with his work and had an avid interest in the translation of inscriptions, so between 1872–79 she edited the two volumes of *Christian Inscriptions of the Irish Language.*

In 1871 Dunraven died leaving his monumental work on Irish architecture unfinished. Dunraven had seen Sir Samuel Ferguson's poem *The Cromlech of Howth* (1861), which contains some of the finest examples of Miss Stokes' artistic worth, styled after the initial letters from the Book of Kells, for which she was greatly admired. Dunraven believed her to be well suited to the task of editing his *Notes on Irish Architecture,* given the fine work she had done on editing Petrie's two volumes. According to Dunraven's son 'He would have felt much more distress at leaving matters in such a comparatively unfinished condition had he not been perfectly assured that, in entrusting the manuscript and other materials to Miss Stokes he was placing them in hands thoroughly competent and most desirous to do justice to them'[1]. These first publications were the result of her earnest desire to complete the labours of her friends.

Many years later, after death had remov-

# MARGARET MACNAIR STOKES (1832–1900)

ed those she took care of, and she herself was well past middle age, Margaret Stokes' real contribution to Irish art and archaeology began. She continued her journeys around Ireland and this resulted in two publications. In 1878, the same year her father died, she wrote *Early Christian Architecture in Ireland*. It was illustrated with woodcuts from drawings not only by herself, but also by Petrie, Burton and many others. The book outlines the history of Irish architecture from pagan forts up to the Romanesque. Miss Stokes uses her considerable knowledge of the saints' lives, not only to portray the period covered in each chapter but to highlight the way important religious traditions were expressed in architecture.

In the appendices her farsightedness is exemplifed under the heading of *The Preservation of National Monuments and Ecclesiastical Ruins*. At one point she comments 'It is one of the most hopeful signs of the present time that, . . . within the last fifty years a new interest has arisen in our ancient monuments . . .': but she goes on to give a warning '. . . lest our enthusiasm — religious, historical and artistic, should, if not duly restrained, do more for the destruction of these monuments than their preservation. To repair wisely may be a labour incurring a far great expenditure of time and thought, than to rebuild, or even to restore: yet when the importance of the work is duly weighed who will say that such is labour wasted?'[2].

In 1887 Miss Stokes wrote *Early Christian Art in Ireland*, presented as a manual of

Margaret Stokes, The Doorway of the Old Church at Temple Martin, Co. Cork. *Date unknown. Ink on paper, 17 x 12.6 cm. National Gallery of Ireland.*

the archaeology of Ireland through manuscript illumination, metalwork, stone cutting and building. In it we also learn of the deep gratitude and feeling she had for George Petrie. 'To the mere archaeologist antiquity is everything, and art nothing: but the mind of the great man who founded the Irish school of Archaeology, George Petrie, was one of wider grasp, and such a mind as his is required to perceive the qualities which form the essential elements of the individuality of Irish Art'[3].

She was obsessed with the individuality

of Irish art, and dedicated her research to exploring the artistic styles of our manuscripts and monuments. In 1876 she was elected an honorary member of the Royal Irish Academy. This was a rare occurrence and achievement for a woman at that time and, one that suggests her scholarly contributions to Irish art and archaeology had gained a sincere respect.

For the last ten or twelve years of her life she took a particular interest in high crosses, drawing them, taking rubbings and photographs, as she intended writing a book on the high crosses of Ireland. In the early 1890s she also made at least two expeditions to Europe, travelling mainly in France and Italy. These journeys are captured in her two books, *Six Months in the Appenines in Search of Irish Saints in Italy* (1892) and *Three Months in the Forests of France: A Pilgrimage in Search of the Vestiges of Irish Saints in France* (1895).

Both publications reveal her tenacity and natural curiosity, pursuing the lives of the Irish saints in a colourful and sentimental style without diminishing their scholarly aspect. Her writing style is one born out of a time in the nineteenth century that enjoyed the poetry of Keats and Tennyson and the art of the Pre-Raphaelites. Both Margaret's brother, Whitley, and her friend F W Burton were acquainted with the Pre-Raphaelite Brotherhood (1848) in London. Burton's most famous painting *The Meeting on the Turret Stairs* (National Gallery of Ireland) reflects the influence of the Pre-Raphaelites. With its bold colours and clarity of detail, this painting also shows

Margaret Stokes, The North Door of Cormac's Chapel, Cashel, Co. Tipperary. *Date unknown. Pencil on paper, 23.8 x 18.9 cm. National Gallery of Ireland, Dublin.*

Margaret Stokes, The Bell Tower and Church on Inis Clothnan, Lough Ree, Co. Roscommon. *Date unknown. Ink and pencil on paper, 25.5 x 35.5 cm. National Gallery of Ireland, Dublin.*

# MARGARET MACNAIR STOKES (1832 – 1900)

the impact of George Petrie's studies of early Irish architecture and medieval costume. Burton's painting was based on a Danish ballad, *Hellelil and Hildebrand*, translated by Whitley Stokes in *Frazer's Magazine* (1855), and was bequeathed to the National Gallery of Ireland by Margaret Stokes.

On returning to Ireland she continued her study of high crosses. In 1898 the Royal Irish Academy published her work on the high crosses of Castledermot and Durrow as a first instalment to the great work she was planning. It was while she was working on the other high crosses, that she had cause to complain about the Royal Irish Academy's treatment of her photographs. In rough notes called *Methods* (no date) she mentions that the Academy just wanted her drawings but she insisted that they use her photographs also to illustrate her work. She says 'It is not a matter of opinion but of fact that all that is written or carved on these ancient monuments cannot be revealed by bare photographs.' It seems that the Academy wanted to make the photographs look better but she felt this was not wholly honest. 'I have rubbed away the moss with my chamois glove till I found designs that seemed, before doing so, as crude and disconnected as W Westwood's T pattern. I have found such designs resolve themselves into perfect consecutive linear patterns, therefore when I show you these things, I speak what I do know and, if knowing the secrets hidden in these blotted defaced hands, I kept them secret, would my illustrations be as honest as they are? or contain as many truths?'[4].

Miss Stokes was the first person to study the cross of Moone in any detail. Her *Notes on Moone, Drumcliff, Termonfechin and Killamery* were published posthumously by the Royal Irish Academy, one year after her death.

*FW Burton,* The Meeting on the Turret Stairs, *1864, Watercolour on paper. 95.5 x 60.8 cm. National Gallery of Ireland.*

Margaret Stokes believed that in art the Irish had created something very different from the rest of Europe, and felt strongly about matters of preservation and restoration. About this she remarked 'We never can, indeed, restore the very buildings themselves, living spirit of which was an inseparable part of the religion, thought and manners of the past; but is it also true that we cannot revive that spirit? . . . we are bound to spare no effort to keep these works among us for centuries to come'[5].

*Janette Stokes*

*Janette Stokes is currently studying Art History at Trinity College, Dublin.*

## ACKNOWLEDGEMENTS

I am very grateful to Roger Stalley, Trinity College, for all his help and advice. For all their assistance I would also like to thank the staff of the National Gallery of Ireland, the Royal Irish Academy and Alexandra College.

## NOTES

This brief paper was given at the Roscrea Medieval Conference on Irish High Crosses in April 1991, as part of a session entitled 'The Debt We Owe To Three Women'.

1. Dunraven, 3rd Earl *Notes on Irish Architecture*. 1875. Vol 1, Preface.
2. M. Stokes, *Early Christian Architecture In Ireland*. 1878 Appendices "The Preservation of National Monuments and ecclesiastical ruins".
3. M. Stokes, *Early Christian Art in Ireland*. 1887.
4. Notes entitled 'Methods'. No date. Royal Irish Academy.
5. M. Stokes, *Early Christian Architecture in Ireland*.

## MAJOR WORKS BY MARGARET STOKES

George Petrie, *Christian Inscriptions in the Irish Language*. Edited by M. Stokes Dublin 1872 – 79 2 volumes;
Dunraven, 3rd Earl, *Notes on Irish Architecture*. Edited by M. Stokes London 1875 – 77. 2 volumes;
Adolphe Didron, *Christian Iconography*. Translated and edited by M Stokes. London, Volume 1 1851: Volume 2 1886;
Margaret Stokes, *Early Christian Architecture in Ireland* London 1878; *Art Readings for 1880* Dublin 1880, Alexandra Literary Society; *Readings on Archaeology and Art*, Dublin 1883; *Early Christian Art in Ireland*, 1887; *Six Months in the Appenines*, London and New York 1892; *Three Months in the Forests of France*, London 1895; *Notes on the Cross of Cong*, Dublin 1895; *The High Crosses of Castledermot and Durrow*, Dublin 1898; 'The Holed Stone Cross at Moon', *Journal of the Country Kildare Archaeological Society*, 1899; 'Notes on the High Cross of Moone, Drumcliff, Termonfechin and Killamery'. Edited by T Johnson Westropp. *Royal Irish Academy*, Dublin 1901.

# THE GONDO TUNNEL ON THE SIMPLON PASS C. 1829

*James Hore,* The southern entrance to the Gondo tunnel on the Simplon Pass.
*Watercolour, 18.2 x 26.3 cm. Private Collection.*

Through the rediscovery of a small corpus of his works, the relative quality of a talented Irish amateur artist may now be assessed.

James Hore, almost certainly, was the second son of Walter Hore of Seafield, County Wexford. The customary genealogical reference books give no date for either his birth or death, or indeed marriage, if in fact he did marry. How may one be sure that he was an amateur artist, or at least considered himself thus? On three of four pencil drawings executed in Rome in 1829 the artist duly inscribed 'drawn by James Hore Esqʳ'; these inscriptions are actually on the reverse of the original frames, but are clearly by the same hand which inscribed the reverse of the sheets with the title of the views delineated. The drawing in this example is described as 'The arch of Constantine and part of the Colliseum'. These very deliberate inscriptions surely indicate the fact that Hore considered himself not only an amateur artist but a gentleman. His cousin, Lady Charlotte Stopford, as Viscountess Stopford, wife of Viscount Stopford, heir to the Earldom of Courtown, had died in Rome on the 29 February 1828, and was buried in 'The English burying ground', the subject of another of the four draw-

**Michael Wynne's** examination of early nineteenth-century drawings sheds light on the career of the Wexford artist James Hore.

ings which reappeared together.[1]

Fisher mentioned drawings of Pisa and Corfu, but unfortunately they cannot be located at present.[2] It is very easy to envisage that such drawings could be connected with the Roman drawings, executed on a Grand Tour. More recently, a very fine *View of Piazza del Popolo, Rome,* in pencil and watercolour, has come to light. It is signed on the reverse, but not dated.[3] This sheet may also relate to the visit to Rome in 1829. All of the drawings seen by the writer display a mind primarily interested in architectural views, and show a remarkable degree of accuracy in both perspective and detail. More like a landscape is the drawing of *The English Burying Ground, Rome,* which naturally was a subject of family *pietas* for a young cousin who died at a tender age.

There were several ways by which the Grand Tourist could get to Rome. A transcontinental route, as opposed to a lengthy sea journey, frequently involved the use of

the Simplon Pass, which was a well worn route and a reliable one, dating back to Roman times.[4] The fact that it was used by James Hore is confirmed by his watercolour showing *The Southern Entrance to the Gondo tunnel on the Simplon Pass.* The sheet is both fully signed and monogrammed. This precise location was identified by Dr Bruno Weber of the Zentralbibliothek in Zurich, to whom the writer is gratefully indebted. His verdict is supported by two points, one dated 1820,[5] the second dated 1831.[6] Hore's watercolour was most probably done between the execution of these two lithographs, either on his way to, or on his return from Rome, where he is fully documented as a visitor in 1829.

Common to the two lithographs and Hore's watercolour is the distinctive little bridge, which dates from the Napoleonic improvement of the entire route. The bridge is there to this day and may be traversed, but the normal traffic is on the modern N7 national highway.[7] Both of the lithographs show rough, scraggy, and precipitous terrain, with stunted trees. Hore seems to have idealized the land around the bridge and tunnel entrance, replacing the trees and uneven ground with glacier-style formations. It is unlikely that this 'transformation' was due to the

# THE GONDO TUNNEL ON THE SIMPLON PASS c. 1829

*James Hore,* The Arch of Constantine and part of the Colliseum. *Pencil on paper, 18.8 x 26.2 cm. Private Collection.*

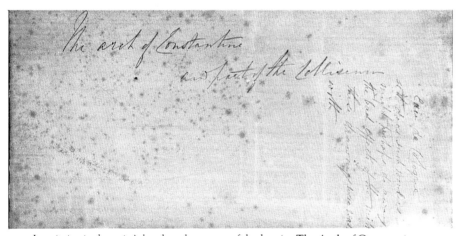

*Inscription in the artist's hand on the reverse of the drawing* The Arch of Constantine. *Also another inscription, 'Eau de Cologne, as it does such wonders, might perhaps do away the bad effects of the milk these drawings were washed with.'*

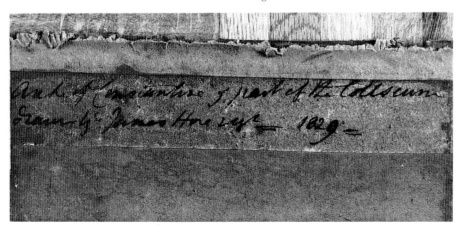

*Original inscription in the artist's hand on the reverse of the original frame of* The Arch of Constantine.

fact that the artist was travelling in the depths of winter which might have altered the prospect. Much more likely is the hypothesis that he made a quick sketch of the dramatic view, surrounding the essential features with planar sweeps, a solution that would appeal to an artist with an architectural bend; moreover, such an expeditious approach would also have had the virtue of not delaying unduly his travelling companions.

One group of drawings and watercolours fits into the pattern of a Grand Tour record in and around the year 1829. Quite different are three known oil paintings which were exhibited at the Royal Academy in 1837. These depict three of Dublin's most outstanding views: *The Four Courts from the Quay, the Phoenix Park in the Distance, Trinity College and the Bank,* and *A View of the Custom House, Dublin.* To these must be added another *View of the Custom House, Dublin,* taken from a vantage point not immediately opposite Gandon's masterpiece, but somewhat upstream. All four oils are very good examples of the work of a view-painter; many professional painters would be proud of them. Three of the four are signed and dated, but the 'Esq' is missing. No doubt the artist was still a gentleman, but that journey through the Gondo tunnel and an interval of eight years gave James Hore the professional confidence to submit to and have accepted by the Royal Academy three views of Dublin, for the exhibition of 1837.

*Michael Wynne*

*Dr Michael Wynne is the Keeper of the National Gallery of Ireland.*

## NOTES

1. At an exhibition held by Cynthia O'Connor & Co., Ltd., Dublin, August 1974. *Cf.* M. Wynne in *Studies,* Vol. 65 (Spring 1976), pp. 46-51.
2. S. Fisher, *A Dictionary of Watercolour Painters 1750–1900* (London 1972), p. 113.
3. M. Wynne, *Irish Arts Review,* Vol. 2, No. 1 (Spring 1985), p. 42.
4. P. Arnold, *Simplon, die vier Strassen: Römer, Mittelalter, Napoleon, Nationalstrasse* (Brig 1975), *passim.*
5. Lithograph in Cockburn and Harding, *Views to illustrate the route of the Simplon* (London 1822).
6. Lithograph in R. Céard, *Souvenirs des travaux du Simplon* (Geneva 1837).
7. P. Arnold, *op. cit.,* ill. p. 65.

# CULTURAL CONFERENCING

**Anne Kelly** reports on two recent conferences in Dublin: on managing the arts and on education in the cultural sphere.

Culture is no stranger to controversy and 1991 provided some opportunities for polemics, beginning with Dublin as European City of Culture and ending in the shredding of copies of a history of the Arts Council. In between were some interesting initiatives such as *The Art of Managing the Arts conference* and, on a less ambitious scale, the *Irish Heritage Education Network conference*.

Arts management provided the theme for a conference at the Irish Museum of Modern Art, organised by Patricia Quinn of the Arts Council with an organising committee which represented the Taoiseach's Department, the National Lottery and some key arts managers. The title of the conference presupposes that managing the arts is itself an art, and one now officially recognised as providing something of a 'hidden subsidy' to the arts because of the poor financial rewards for those involved.[1] The chance of inflating the ego which is often part of the package can be insignificant when other levels of nourishment are low. The conference, by highlighting the role of the arts manager and gathering enough of them together in one place, aimed 'to create a sense of constituency and common interest.'[2] However it was this very sense of solidarity which had the effect of creating a dichotomy between the managers and 'authority' in the final sessions.

The formal agenda was a wide-ranging one dealing in plenary sessions with such issues as 'Who's in charge of the arts?' and 'Who's paying for the arts?' as well as sessions on practical management issues like 'The manager and the market' and 'Commercial sponsorship.' Delegates found the usual conference mixed bag in terms of depth and quality of contributions by speakers and many found that the seminar sessions were most useful but too big to allow for real debate. As always on these occasions the full agenda and limited time were in competition with the need for discussion. Much of the chat was reserved for the social part of the conference, and this was at least as important as the formal agenda.

The old shibboleth of whether the arts should be managed at all or should be left to the artists, was frequently aired in sessions. That such a debate exists is healthy and the conference provided an opportunity (perhaps not enough, or not often enough, or not seriously enough) to air the question. It is interesting to speculate on how many other professional groupings are prepared to address the question of their own legitimacy and survival in such a way. But then the arts manager is often the artist manqué who can only survive in close proximity to the beloved in a sometimes incestuous way. The questioning also indicates that this is an area which survives on openness and dynamism and that it could never become the narrow 'conspiracy against the laity' predicted for other professional groupings.

Flashes of fire appeared from time to time at the conference when delegates and 'authority' as represented by the Arts Council, the Department of the Taois-each, or the platform in general, came into open conflict. This was particularly evident in the final plenary session when 'the climate of fear' privately expressed throughout the conference was finally made public. The notion that arts managers did not feel free to take openly opposing or controversial positions because of fear of losing their grants was vigorously rejected by the Director of the Arts Council. But whether justified or not, the existence of such a feeling reflects a suspicion that the relationship between the Council and its political masters had become too intimate. The arms-length principle on which the relationship was originally based was seen to be floundering, and the symbiosis which is fundamental to the health of the arts was thought to be endangered.

What this Open Forum indicated was that the 'sense of constituency' which the conference hoped to engender had already been in existence in latent form. It was reinforced and given expression by the conference. The irony is that had the final session come first, the agenda would have been set in a more satisfactory way in relation to later sessions. The organisers were aware that this was a desirable outcome of the conference. 'It was our hope that the actual agenda would be asserted at the event by conference delegates, and to a considerable extent this was what happened.'[3] However, since it happened, in the final session this precluded any real debate on some of the more important issues, such as the reality of relations between the arts and the state. The session was nevertheless cathartic for delegates and it accentuated the genuinely felt con-

*The National Gallery of Ireland, Dublin.*

*The Irish Museum of Modern Art at the Royal Hospital, Kilmainham, Dubli*

# CULTURAL CONFERENCING

cern among arts managers at the perilous state of many of the organisations. It indicated the differences that exist between the established and successful arts managers for whom marketing and other skills are stock in trade, and the smaller budding initiatives which are producing good work in desperate circumstances and which operate on the margins.

Training provision for Irish arts managers was outlined at the conference and the question was addressed in some detail after the conference by one of the delegates. Pat Cooke writing in *Circa*[4] on post-graduate education for art and heritage management suggests that this kind of specialist training in some way attempts to correct 'the blur of a "broad" education' which is traditional in the humanities or arts. This was the usual route to a career in the area before the emergence of specialist courses. From my own experience this danger can be overstated. What a good educational initiative tries to do is to deepen the educational experience, sometimes, but not always, arts-based at degree level, as well as to provide the functional skills required to manage a modern arts enterprise. Developing imaginative and visual skills and exposing participants to arts experiences should be a fundamental part of training and a mix of participants with both contemporary arts and heritage backgrounds facilitates this and helps to break down barriers. The rationale for the development of this kind of education is not to feed the undoubted hunger for 'credentials' identified by Pat Cooke, a hunger made all the more intense by competition for jobs today, but to answer a need in relation to the better and more efficient use of scarce resources in difficult times, as well as the provision of a good educational experience.

That such issues are now being debated in print and at conferences is a positive sign. Annual conferences of the Irish Museums Association address key issues and this body has now developed into an important professional association. One of the aims of the arts management conference was the formation of a profes-

sional association, something attempted many times in the past but without success in each instance. A standing conference on managing the arts has emerged from this conference, and an interim committee established. Its object is to examine all the issues involved in managing the arts, including the possibility of a professional association. The success of the conference may well be measured by such an outcome.

Another professional group representing education in the cultural sphere was established in 1989. The Irish Heritage Education Network (IHEN) is a thirty-two county museum education group which recognises the vital role of teachers in this area. Its brief is a wide one covering the activities of museums, galleries, and contemporary arts centres, and it aims to bridge the gap between these organisations and the public through workshops, seminars and the publication of information material. 'The changing face of Irish heritage' was the theme of the 1991 Autumn Conference at the National Gallery, and the keynote address on 'Broadening Horizons: Cultural Traditions in Northern Ireland' was given by Maurna Crozier of the Cultural Traditions Group. This is the title taken by a group of people 'who hoped to address the murderous diversity of life in Ireland through investigating the cultural expressions of all the communities involved.'[5] Through music, language, literature, oral history and sports it is hoped that social divisions can be both understood and worked through to a more tolerant future. A programme of conferences, debates, projects, awards and fellowships is being undertaken to this end. Peter Woodman of University College, Cork and the National Heritage Council spoke on networking within a museum service and on the need for local government to encourage the growth of museums relevant to their specific localities. One of the most important examples of this in Ireland, the Orchard Gallery in Derry, was represented by Pauline Ross who spoke of the Orchard's outreach workshops in hospitals and for other social

groups. The tourism potential of the heritage was dealt with by Sean Browne of Bord Failte in the language of 'markets' and 'targetted growth segments' more familiar to the arts management conference. Archaeological development and the Discovery Programme of the Office of Public Works was covered by Anne Lynch. This programme was launched by the former Taoiseach in 1991 as part of a project to communicate the picture of the past to experts and public alike. Finally Pat Cooke, using the example of the 'In a State' exhibition at Kilmainham Gaol in summer 1991, returned to the theme which concerns him regarding training. This is what he sees as the increasing tendency of 'heritage' and 'arts' to be conceived of as two almost mutually exclusive forms of activity, to the detriment of both. 'In a State', by engaging artists with a heritage amenity, accentuated its relevance to contemporary cultural life. In this way 'the past is not merely another country, but the one we happen to live in.'[6]

The existence of initiatives such as these conferences has greatly enhanced the level of debate of cultural issues during 1991. In spite of hard times for the arts in terms of funding and the lack of an infrastructure particularly in the heritage area, those involved continue to work and develop the cultural debate.

*Anne Kelly*

*Anne Kelly is Director of the Arts Administration Studies Unit at University College Dublin.*

NOTES

1. Colm O'hEocha, Chairman's Introduction, The Arts Council, Annual Report 1990.
2. Patricia Quinn, 'The Art of Managing the Arts, first conference responses', *Circa*, No. 61 Jan/Feb 1992, p. 38.
3. Ibid.
4. Pat Cooke, 'A modern disease, art and heritage management' in *Circa, op. cit.* p. 30.
5. Maurna Crozier, 'Broadening Horizons: Cultural Traditions in Northern Ireland'. IHEN conference paper 1991, p. 1.
6. Pat Cooke, 'Cell Art: changing the image of a gaol.' IHEN conference paper 1991.

# W J LEECH'S BRITTANY

William Leech first visited Concarneau in Brittany in 1903 and his experience there was a turning-point in his development. **Denise Ferran** describes the important elements, both personal and artistic, of this vibrant period in his career.

*You cannot possibly do better than choose Concarneau in Brittany as a pitch for your easel. Whether you intend to paint marines, landscapes, interiors or figures, that is the place for you; if you want, on the other hand, to laze away a month or two, Concarneau affords you every facility for so doing. You may reckon on finding pleasant artist companions, both English and foreign, in the town, and at the village of Pont-Aven ten miles off. Then again, you will live right royally at a cost of five francs per diem, or even less.*[1]

This advice by Frank Emmanuel was given in 1894 in *The Studio* magazine and was read and acted on by many artists.

Leech first went to Concarneau in 1903. He became involved in its established artistic colony, and began painting this fishing port and its surrounding countryside in the open air, but his style of painting remained traditional in composition and sombre in palette.

In Dublin, Walter Osborne had been Leech's teacher when he attended the Royal Hibernian Academy School from 1899 until 1901. In later years he recalled Osborne's teaching with admiration:

> *He had enthusiasm and could teach. It was about then that I first saw French painting, the Impressionists etc, what a sudden revelation! Doors and windows thrown open and the darkness invaded by light and air; it was the beginning for me.*[2]

However it was to be some years before the influence of Impressionism became evident in Leech's work.

In November 1904 Leech was able to see in Dublin the exhibition of paintings collected by Hugh Lane, which included the works of Courbet, Degas, Nathaniel Hone, Augustus John, Lavery, Manet, Monet, Roderic O'Conor, William Orpen, Walter Osborne, Pissarro, Renoir, Steer and Whistler.[3] Many of these artists, particularly Whistler, Lavery and Orpen, were to have a great influence on Leech in the subsequent years. It must have inspired Leech to find that someone of William Orpen and Augustus John's age was already being included with the great moderns of France. He and his friend Sydney Thompson, a New Zealand artist, were in Dublin in 1904 recovering from typhoid fever which they had contracted in Brittany, and both of them would probably have seen these paintings. They had already had opportunities in Paris and London to see the work of

most of these artists. Nevertheless, Leech continued to paint in a formal academic manner, restricting his palette to earth tones until 1910 when his palette lightened and his brushwork became confident and fluid. It was his experience of painting in Concarneau that lightened his palette and freed his painting style.[4] He had begun to paint more freely, producing lighter toned paintings *en plein air*, while continuing to paint academically formal paintings in darker tones in his studio.

The influence of Whistler (especially his *Portrait of Thomas Carlyle*) (1872–73) can be seen in Leech's *Portrait of a Man with Bottle*. The pose of the figure as a dark form against the background and the quiet feeling of endurance in each sitter is similar. This Whistler portrait, which is comparable to his more famous *Arrangement in Grey and Black, No 1: The Artist's Mother*, shows the influence of Velazquez, an interest shared by many of his contemporaries which was to be prolonged by younger artists such as Orpen.[5] Whistler had studied at the Studio Gleyre in Paris in 1856 and that studio's dedication to Velazquez was pervasive.

In his *Portrait of a Man with Bottle* Leech, like Velazquez, uses strong *chiaroscuro* lighting on the worn face of the peasant sitting drinking in the bar. In his painting of 1904, Leech was still unaffected by the work of Monet, Renoir, Van Gogh or any other Post-Impressionist. One might contrast this with the work of Roderic O'Conor (1860–1940) who had progressed to painting *Portrait of a Young Woman Smiling* (1902) and *Breton Girl* (1903) using strokes of pure colour, not only in the face of his subject matter but also in the background.[6]

In Leech's painting, the light on the face and hands is strongly contrasted against the raw umbers and 'vandyke' browns of the shadowy clothes of the man. He sits, in profile, forming a diagonal with his head and shoulders and

dividing the canvas into thirds on the vertical plane. His outstretched hands create divisions in a similar way on the horizontal plane. The dark glass of the bottle of wine sitting on the table forms an upright, echoing the plane of the man's shoulders and head. Because of the tonality of the painting and the lack of colour, emphasis is concentrated on the rugged face and toil-worn hands.

In this portrait, Leech seems to have been influenced by the social realism of Courbet and by Courbet's influence on the work of Whistler. Whistler, as a student in the 1850s, was a frequent visitor to the Louvre. There he met Fantin-Latour who introduced him to the work of Courbet.

In Leech's *The Green Room – Interior of a Café*, dated 1908, the same figure of the old peasant is included in the detailed interior with figures painted in a style reminiscent of an early Orpen.[7] The walls are in deep green, toning with the brown and ochre of the wood of the bar surround, tables and chairs. Though relieved by glimmers of warm toned grey highlights, the work shows little influence of modern French painting or of the light created by the Impressionist palette. The old peasant is sitting becapped at the extreme left of the painting, drinking a cup of coffee with two of his friends, one of whom has a small liquor glass on the table in front of him. All three look toil-worn, their shoulders rounded by work, with bent backs and expressively boned hands. The lighted areas form strong contrasts, throwing the three faces engrossed in conversation into dramatic *chiaroscuro* against the brown shadows which verge into black. Sunlight bursts in from an area in the lower left of the picture plane and appears to come from an open door opposite, admitting the light into the dim interior and illuminating the area on the left in a flood of white. It falls on the traditional wooden rush-seated kitchen chairs which tone closely with the light pine frames. To the right, enveloped in shadow, is the figure of a fourth man, who waits, leaning on the counter, seeking service. Like the other men, he is dressed in a woven suit and cap and with traditional clogs on his feet. Above his head, well-stocked shelves of bottles and china cups glisten in the refracted light and shine under the brass lamp. In the background the gentle, withdrawn figure of a young girl is sil-

# W J LEECH'S BRITTANY

W J Leech, The Market, Concarneau, *oil on board, 22 x 16.5 cm.*
*South Tipperary County Museum & Art Gallery, Clonmel.*

*CONCARNEAU. — Le Marché. — LL*

*Contemporary black and white photograph of The Market Concarneau.*

houetted against the lacy curtains of the lighted window; she stands, reading a book. She is glimpsed through the open door leading from the bar and is framed in a series of rectangles formed by the window frames and the door frames. The well-stocked bar suggests that of the Hotel des Voyageurs where Leech was staying at the time. None of the group of peasants is perturbed by being observed by the artist, since this hotel housed many artists and they were a common sight. The foreground space of this picture heightens the volume of the room and places the people within a proscenium arch. On the wall to the left, the framed picture of the head and shoulders of a young red-headed woman indicate the form that Leech's painting style was to take in future. The simplified bold areas of paint, the lightened palette and the strong play of light depart from the darker, more academic treatment of the interior of the room.

The café was, and still is, an important social centre in French society and would have been a natural meeting place for artists, including William Leech and his friend Sydney Thompson. There Leech was able to observe and engage in the local community and became an acceptable part of Concarneau life, unimpeded in his painting and observation. Another familiar aspect of French village life is the barber's shop; it too has a place in the community. The contrasts of light and dark of *Interior of a Café* are repeated in Leech's *Interior of a Barber's Shop*, painted a year later in 1909. The foreground of

mirrors reflects the shelf immediately in front and the two windows behind in strong rectilinear shapes. Reflected figures are silhouetted in spaces bathed in light, similar in manner to the figure of the lady in the background of *Interior of a Café*. To the left, the stooped figure of the barber leans over the seated figure of the balding man being shaved in the barber's chair, his shoulders covered in a pink towel. The back of the barber is shown in the mirror in front of him. The figure of another man contained in the second mirror may be the artist caught capturing the scene. This is an early indication of Leech's interest in the use of mirrors — also an interest of Orpen and, earlier, of Velazquez.

Soft greens and warm ochres contrasted against more sombre browns and dark greens are a feature of both paintings. The brushstrokes in *The Barber's Shop* are bolder and the paint more fluid, applied with greater painterly freedom than in the smoother, more formal execution of *Interior of a Café*. A new freedom has been introduced into this loosely painted small interior. The colour is softer but still does not herald the acid yellows and greens of *A Convent Garden*, of about two years later.

In Leech's *The Fair, Concarneau*, a caravan fills the area on the right. A woman dressed in Breton peasant clothes stands beyond the wooden steps leading up to the caravan. Barrels and containers clutter the area to the right, but details are eliminated as Leech paints the subject in

a bold, simplified rendering of traditional composition.

The large weekly and smaller daily markets were held outside the Hotel des Voyageurs. The women were then resplendent in their traditional Breton costumes, the more affluent the wearer, the more elaborate these were. Contemporary photographs detail the rich pattern and movement of the bustling scene and capture the fascination and uniqueness of the subject matter for the artist.

*The Market, Concarneau*, records a similar subject. This time, the high horizon line of the composition encompasses a lively scene of white-bonneted Breton ladies, clustered around a market stall. The figures are depicted simply, with the foreground broken by the shadows of the tree which are formed as patterns on the ground. *The Market, Concarneau* would more than likely have been painted *en plein air* since its dimensions conform with those of the box with six slots in which Leech carried his small wet oils on board. These small works were painted with no preparatory drawings and helped develop Leech's free painterly technique which aided the use of pure colour in his work. These *plein air* studies form a bridge between his early academic painting and his later, more freely painted, impressionistic work.

The harbour became a popular subject for Leech, who mainly painted empty boats moored in the water at sunrise or at evening time. *A Sunny Afternoon, Con-*

W J Leech, Portrait of a Man with Bottle, *1904, oil on canvas, 49 x 50.8 cm. Private Collection.*

W J Leech, The Fair, Concarneau, Brittany, *oil on canvas, 33 x 46 cm. Private Collection.*

*W J Leech, The Green Room – Interior of a Cafe, 1908, oil on canvas, 74 x 84 cm. Private Collection.*

*W J Leech, Interior of a Barber's Shop, 1909, oil on canvas, 30.5 x 51 cm.
The Crawford Municipal Gallery, Cork.*

# W J LEECH'S BRITTANY

*carneau* is an unusually busy harbour painting which depicts rows of freely painted houses along the quayside forming a top border. Women gather on the quay to watch and help as the sardine boats come into harbour. There is a feeling of activity as the fishermen busily unload the boats. Sydney Thompson recalled how the harbour used to come alive with the arrival of the fishing fleets, and wrote in his memoirs that: 'sometimes in one day two or three hundred tunny boats would arrive and that meant between fourteen hundred to two thousand fishermen from all parts of the coast living crowded on the wharfs and in the cafés. Men excited by having made a big catch or not having caught anything'.[8]

Leech has used soft tones of blues and greys to depict a gentle panoramic view of the harbour with the tunny boats pulled up in the Pénéroff Basin, alongside the quay of the main street. With the influence of Whistler, his palette had lightened. Leech also painted *Fishing Boats, Concarneau* which shows a small upright section of the harbour with the boats preparing to go fishing in the early light of dawn. A lone woman leans against the cream gable wall of a quayside home which is reflected in the water of the foreground. Blues and greys and earth tones give a gentleness to the painting. Leech's brushstrokes are assured and fluid and drawn on the spot. Reviewing the Royal Hibernian Academy Exhibition of 1909 in *The Freeman's Journal*, Thomas Bodkin wrote about Leech's work, mentioning his *Sunny Afternoon, Concarneau*:

> In landscapes as well as in portrait, Mr W J Leech, RHA distinguishes himself in this exhibition. His Sunny Afternoon in Concarneau is charming for its atmospheric clearness, good perspective and other artistic points, which almost make the spectator think he is looking at a real scene instead of a picture . . .[9]

*Sunny Afternoon, Concarneau* was bought by Nathaniel Hone the Younger. This was an important approbation for Leech as, years later, in 1950, he was able to recall to Leo Smith: 'I remember another picture of mine bought from the Academy by old Nathaniel Hone of the Quay at Concarneau, a long picture . . . about the first picture I sold'[10].

By 1909, at the age of twenty-eight, Leech was established in his career as an artist. He had been made an associate of

*W J Leech, The Secret Garden, oil on canvas, 114 x 86 cm. Private Collection.*

the Royal Hibernian Academy in 1907 and was to become a full Academician in 1910. He continued to send work to the Academy of scenes painted in Concarneau.

*A Convent Garden, Brittany*, painted about 1911, combined the influence of post-impressionist technique with the subject matter of impressionism. Leech poses his companion, Elizabeth Kerlin, as the young contemplative novice, dressed in a traditional Breton wedding dress nd starched lace coiffe. He uses his brush and draws with decisive strokes in fluid paint to capture the flimsiness of the lace of the wedding gown which contrasts with the heavier folds of the white cotton robes of the nuns walking in the background. A dark border highlights the upturned face of Elizabeth which is in full sunlight and throws into focus the lace details of her elaborate coiffe. The lovely garden of lilies which Leech painted and called *The Secret Garden*, and which he exhibited at the Royal Hibernian Academy in 1920 and at the Royal Academy in 1921 under the title *Lilies*, was used as the foreground of *A Convent Garden*. It was a secret garden, hidden behind high stone walls across in the old walled town of Concarneau, overlooking the bustling har-

bour. Why did Leech paint Elizabeth as a young bride in a convent garden? At that time they were planning to marry but firstly Elizabeth had to obtain a divorce. This would preclude their marriage taking place in a church, with the usual splendour of the bride in white, that was accorded to most weddings, especially Breton weddings.

Furthermore, earlier, in 1904, Leech had spent some time in this convent garden convalescing from typhoid fever. He probably painted *La Soeur du Saint Esprit*, which depicts a young nun sitting with a book on her lap, beside a lighted window, at this time. It is in his academic dark style. When it was exhibited at the RHA in 1913, the reviewer in the *Irish Independent* wrote;

> Soeur du Saint Esprit, which shows a nun sitting with folded hands beside a window, captures both interest and affection. Handled broadly but with masterly confidence, this study in browns and off-whites is reminiscent of the Dutch Masters in its suggestion of peace and repose, and is to my mind the gem of the exhibition.'[11]

The later painting, *Les Soeurs du Saint Esprit* or *A Convent Garden, Brittany*, was painted at least six years later, probably from studies of nuns in the garden which Leech made at the time. Elizabeth poses as a novice, praying with book in hand, in the foreground. It was popular among artists in Brittany to paint young virgins in white bridal gowns, and First Communicants as they carried the statues of the local saint, during the religious festivities of The Pardons. Leech would probably have known *The Arrival of the Pardon of St Anne at Fouesnant*, by Alfred Guillou, the Concarneau painter, which was painted in 1887 and is in the collection of the Quimper Museum. In this painting the local procession is arriving in boats with the first boat containing young women who are dressed in traditional white wedding gowns, bringing with them banners and the statue of St Anne.[12] Guillou dramatically recorded this highly spectacular, colourful and religiously moving occasion. Hirschfeld, Leech's artist friend in Concarneau, painted *Procession de Notre-Dame-des-Flots*, around 1900, capturing the flowing white robes of the brides and First Communicants in accurately painted details of lace and starched coiffes.[13] The traditional bridal dress worn by Elizabeth in *A Convent Garden* is similar.

# W J LEECH'S BRITTANY

Leech painted Elizabeth in many roles, which seem intent on capturing the different facets of her character. *A Convent Garden* glows with light and colour. In the background shadows of the tree-lined avenue of the walled garden are 'Les Soeurs du St Esprit', or 'Les Filles du Saint Esprit' (Daughters of the Holy Ghost), the sisters who ran the hospital and the school in Concarneau. The garden is still there to-day but the hospital has become a home for the mentally retarded which is no longer run by the nuns. Their mother convent was, and still is, in St Brieuc, in northern Brittany.[14]

There is theatricality in Leech's 'Convent Garden'. Elizabeth is captured in a spotlight of sunshine, on the stage of life with the nuns as a dark frieze in the background. Leech was not interested here in realistically capturing religiosity. Rather this painting is a statement of love and devotion to the woman he married in 1912.

When Leech exhibited this painting at the Paris Salon in 1913 he called it *Les Soeurs du St Esprit*. In 1915, he exhibited a painting with the same title at the Royal

W J Leech, La Soeur du St Esprit, *oil on canvas, 44.5 x 28 cm. Private Collection.*

Hibernian Academy but the low price quoted in the catalogue suggests that this was probably a smaller study. Leech had painted the earlier study of a nun sitting in a window seat reading, which he exhibited at the second exhibition of his work at the Dawson Gallery in 1947, entitled *La Soeur du Saint Esprit*. It was common practice for Leech to exhibit paintings in France, at the Paris Salon, with titles in French, and then subsequently to exhibit the same painting in Ireland or England with an English title. *The Convent Garden* was also exhibited at the Royal Academy in London in 1921 as *Nuns and Lilies*, but was titled *Réligieuse* when shown in the *Exposition d'Art Irlandais*, at the Musee d'Art Ancien, in Brussels in 1930. *The Sunshade* belongs to the same artistic period as *A Convent Garden* and Elizabeth is again the model. As background Leech re-used his painting of a garden of lilies, entitled *The Secret Garden*, which he had exhibited at the Royal Hibernian Academy in 1920 and at the Royal Academy in 1921. It gives the impression that the model is posed in a garden, rather than in a studio. The

W J Leech, La Dame Aux Irises, *oil on canvas, 66 x 86.5 cm.*
*Private Collection.*

W J Leech, The Sunshade, *oil on canvas, 81 x 65 cm,*
*National Gallery of Ireland cat. no. 1246.*

*W J Leech, A Convent Garden, Brittany, c. 1911, oil on canvas, 132 x 100 cm.*
*National Gallery of Ireland, cat. no. 1245.*

*Alfred Guillou, The Arrival of the Pardon of St Anne at Fouesnant, 1887,
Musee des Beaux-Arts de Quimper, France.*

# W J LEECH'S BRITTANY

strength of light is similar to *The Goose-Girl* and *The Convent Garden*. Sunlight bursts in strongly from the left of the painting and highlights Elizabeth's face and hands. The cadmium yellow of the cardigan vibrates against the viridian green of the umbrella which casts green shadows on to the model's shoulders. These strong yellows and greens are repeated in the tall lilies in the background with additional colour introduced in the reds and purples of her hat. The handle of the parasol forms a strong diagonal which runs from the bottom right to the top left. Leech has used thick, impasto paint to represent the texture of the woollen cardigan which is in contrast to the smooth painting of the face and hands and the umbrella. Elizabeth is also the model in *La Dame aux Irises*. She poses, fashionably dressed in a black, vee necked, dropped waist dress with a turban style hat and bright red lipstick. One of the irises, in a jug beside her, becomes a flower to the side of her hair. The petals are painted in rich cerises and purples with shadows in blue. Their position to the extreme right of the picture plane is a daring compositional arrangement and is reminiscent of the figure of Elizabeth as the novice, moving out to the right of *A Convent Garden*. The brushwork in this painting is fluid and confident, put on with a creamy consistency and heralds the painting technique of future Leech work. The canvas is filled with a light that is different from the exterior light of *The Goose-Girl* or *The Convent Garden*. It is light that has shone in through the window and which patterns the wall behind.

When Elizabeth ceased to be his model, a productive, exciting and varied artistic period ended. She was replaced by new subject matter in new locations but vibrant colour, light and freedom of paint handling, remained. Ending his marriage with Elizabeth also terminated his long association with Brittany, its landscape and its people and with these changes Leech adopted a different approach to his painting; 'I used to paint very quickly, had to, because of my interest in passing effects. But after some years I decided that perhaps I ought to go more deeply into things.'[15]

*Denise Ferran*

*Denise Ferran, a graduate of the Courtauld Institute, and holder of the Silver Medal and the Watercolour Prize at the Royal Ulster Academy, is Art Education Officer at the Ulster Museum. She is completing a Ph D thesis at Trinity College Dublin and is author of the monograph* W J Leech *(Dublin 1992) in the series, Lives of Irish Artists.*

## NOTES

1. Frank L Emmanuel, 'Letters to Artists, Brittany as a sketching ground,' *The Studio*, IV, 1894, p.180.
2. Letter to Leo Smith from W J Leech, 16 February 1967.
3. S B Kennedy, *Irish Art & Modernism, 1880–1950.* p.9. published for The Hugh Lane Municipal Gallery of Modern Art, Dublin by The Institute of Irish Studies at The Queens University of Belfast.
4. Julie King, *Sydney Lough Thompson, At Home And Abroad*, Robert McDougall Art Gallery, New Zealand, 1990, p.34.
5. Bruce Arnold, *Orpen: Mirror to an Age*, Jonathan Cape, London, 1981, p.145.
6. Roy Johnston, *Roderic O'Conor, 1860–1940*, exhibition catalogue, Barbican, London; Ulster Museum, 1985, pp 79–81.
7. Julian Campbell, *The Irish Impressionists*, National Gallery of Ireland, 1984, p 260, illus b&w.
8. King, *S L Thompson*, op cit p.53.
9. Review, unsigned, by Thomas Bodkin, *The Freeman's Journal*, 31 March 1909, p.5, col.5.
10. Letter from W J Leech to Leo Smith, The Dawson Gallery, 2 November, 1950.
11. Review initialled 'P H G', 'Artist Reveals Vivid Descriptive Powers' *Irish Independent* Wed., 21 May 1947.
12. Catalogue, *Post–Impressionism*, Royal Academy of Arts, 1979, p.86, illus, b&w.
13. *Concarneau, de Pas en Pas*, Ville de Concarneau, 1987, p.214, illus, b&w.
14. Information kindly given by Françoise and Jean-Michel Gloux, Concarneau, September 1991.
15. Letter from W J Leech to Leo Smith, The Dawson Gallery, 17 May 1967.

# CLEMENT McALEER

Through his masterly handling of the intangible, Clement McAleer slipped in the early 1990s unnoticed to prominence. McAleer, born in Co Tyrone in 1949, paints wind and water, air and spray with solid conviction. When faced with a recent painting by McAleer, one is tempted to call for one's greatcoat and one's umbrella, like Fuseli before a canvas by Constable.

Since 1978, when he became the Junior Prizewinner at John Moores XI exhibition, McAleer has been living and working in Liverpool. This physical detachment from Ireland has induced a tension in his recent work. Although his shoreline subject matter may be prompted by more than his experience of the Irish coast, it holds nevertheless an undertow of melancholy, a tangible remembrance of things past.

During his period as a student at Canterbury College of Art (1972–75) and the Royal College of Art (1975–78), McAleer explored the paradoxes of the painted window frame or doorway. His John Moores prizewinning work, *Reflection on a Day in April* (91 x 183 cm), painted at Canterbury in 1974, is a triptych of views through a ruined, roofless shack standing apparently deserted in a field. The passage of time, from morning to afternoon as the painting is read from one side to the other, is indicated by the changing quality and direction of the light. The particularly compelling aspect of the work, however, is the series of spaces that McAleer invents within it, spaces which open and close, reveal and then just as suddenly close themselves down again. Time and narrative, suggested by the passage of the light, is marked further by the viewer's journey within the pictorial space, and by the sudden, startling appearance of a tiny watching figure in the background of the right-hand canvas.

This was a student work, but its maturity impressed the John Moores' judges. Nearly twenty years after it was painted, it is clear that *Reflection on a Day in April*, with its pictorial device of painted frame and open window plundered from artists as various in time and place as Friedrich, Hopper and Diebenkorn, was an early step on what McAleer has called his 'interior journey'.[1] McAleer's paintings became larger in scale when he moved to Liverpool, freed from the restrictions of student life. *Coastline* (1980-84, 167 x 243

The development of the richly metaphoric work of the Co Tyrone-born painter, Clement McAleer, is traced here by **James Hamilton**.

*Clement McAleer, Coastline, 1980–84. Oil on panel, 167 x 243 cm. Private Collection.*

cm), an extensive, even idealistic view of a river's mouth, had Merseyside as its starting point. It was, however, over-painted many times, and as it progressed to completion, became for McAleer much more of an Irish siubject with its damp greens and feeling of light and space. The expanse of the painting, the slow, winding river and the low horizon echoes Ruisdael; its shifting light, and its panache and loose-wristed handling, suggests Wilson Steer. In the diminutive, distant church tower on the right, there is even a reference to Constable — though this is no bosky Dedham Vale, but the sunstruck, flatulent Irish Sea coast, with shacks, outfall pipes and churned-up sand beside.

With *Coastline* McAleer began his journey from the anonymous stage property of *Reflection* to a living landscape. Instead of looking through a window, as in the earlier painting, he was now outside it — though only just. In other paintings of the late 1970s, McAleer's imagery becomes more complex, with a richness and an accumulation of reference and texture building up over a period of time. The structure of his paintings becomes surer too, *Sandhills* (1980) having a relentless X-shaped grid beneath the independent romping of the dunes.

In 1981, McAleer's working pattern received some welcome structure of its own when he won a major award from the Arts Council of Northern Ireland, near enough a year's salary, to enable him to paint full-time. The two projects that he

began and brought to completion with the help of this award took him back to Ireland — the first to Belfast, the second to Dublin — both being journeys into and around these Irish cities.

The painting made in Belfast, a panorama of the city, *Black Mountain, Belfast* (1981–82, 121 x 605 cm, on five panels. Coll: City Hospital, Belfast), was the largest he had attempted, and was a natural extension of the earlier landscapes which stopped short of the panoramic. To paint *Black Mountain*, McAleer took a flat in Ashley Avenue with a 180 degree view of the city. The mountain dominates the painting, lowering over the endless lines of terraced houses, whose dark blue roofs lie like strips of insulating tape horizontally across the landscape. Historical parallels include not only the diminutive but visionary eighteenth century bird's eye townscapes of the brothers Samuel and Nathaniel Buck, but also nineteenth century city panoramas whose existence was due as much to the nerve of the artists undertaking a risky balloon flight, as to the drama of the subject itself.

In Dublin, McAleer was invited to take part in the *Ulysses Project*, an exhibition of six artists' responses to *Ulysses* at the Douglas Hyde Gallery, organised as part of the James Joyce Centenary celebrations in 1982. McAleer contributed a series of six paintings suggestive of six episodes in the book, making not a geographical but a narrative panorama of the events of Bloomsday, 16 June 1904. Three of the paintings, *Telemachus: The Martello Tower, Sandycove, Hades: Prospect Cemetery, Glasnevin* and *Ithaca: Childman Weary* use a circular motif to symbolise the cyclical nature of the single day in the *Ulysses* narrative. The circle of the Martello Tower, seen from the air in the painting, is echoed in the mandala-like structure of the aerial view of Glasnevin Cemetery, while in the Ithaca episode we see from above, as if through the wrong end of a telescope, Bloom and Molly in bed together. Bloom has been reflecting on the Earth's movement through space and on 'the heaventree of stars hung with humid nightblue fruit.' As he falls asleep curled in the foetal position, he becomes, 'the childman weary, the manchild in the womb. Womb? Weary? He rests. He has travelled.'[2]

McAleer's pictorial handling of Joyce's narrative is free interpretation rather

*Clement McAleer, Easter, 1992. Acrylic on canvas, 183 x 175 cm. Collection of the artist.*

*Clement McAleer, Stormy Sea, 1992. Acrylic on canvas, 183 x 175 cm. Private Collection.*

# CLEMENT McALEER

than illustration. Echoing Bloom's journey across Dublin and his observation of the city and its inhabitants, McAleer's paintings inspect the city as if through a set of six different lenses. In addition to the aerial views already mentioned there is a map of Dublin at 3 pm, whose roads and railways are likened to veins and arteries; an apparently ordinary pictorial view, *Lestrygonians: The City Streets at 1 pm*; and finally *The Sixteenth of June* with the flickering images of countless sights seen, recalls 'the day's events and changing moods in fragments and flashes of memory, places visited and people encountered.'[3]

In the autumn of 1982, once the *Ulysses Project* was firmly behind him, McAleer embarked on a personal Odyssey when he flew to the west coast of America. Developing the format of the multiple image that he used to effect in the *Ulysses Project*, McAleer encapsulated his American experiences in the painting *American Journey: The West Coast*, breathlessly noting down landscapes traversed, and conveying in a series of snapshot flashbacks on a double canvas, 'the sense of time on the road, the feel of space, light and movement viewed through flashes and fragments of colour and detail.'[4] Through his unwillingness, or even inability to commit himself to a

single image in *American Journey*, McAleer kept himself separate from this alien landscape of long, straight, interminable roads, wide horizons and abrupt coastlines.

On his return to Liverpool, McAleer began to edge his work towards abstraction, though he has never been able to bring himself to engage fully with the abstract. The stiller his images might be, indeed, the more detached he seems to be from them, in motion himself and just passing through. These may be sea shores, railway embankments, quarries, or pathways, but the common factor remains that these are all places of transition. When he himself stands still before an image, however, its elements seem to erupt around him, wind, water, air and paint in turmoil, as if it is only through his own constant journeying that his world is kept in place.

To meet this elemental challenge, McAleer's brushstrokes became more gestural, even calligraphic at times in the mid 1980s. He began to paint in acrylic on large sheets of paper, rather than in oil or canvas or board, and this both restricted his vision in one respect, and freed it in another. Although the standard size of the paper (101 x 121 cm) forced him to work to a particular scale and use a particular gestural radius, it sharpened his in-

stinct for the selection of those fragments of the world that he sought to paint, and his intentions in choosing them. Grand though his panorama of Belfast may have been, it lacked a point of view.

The titles of his works, sometimes hurriedly invented a few days before an exhibition opening, have a new abstracted quality – *Nightfall* (1985), *Flood* (1985), *Sand Drift* (1986) – and mark McAleer's flight from subject-matter. Beneath the tossing of the brushstrokes, however, there remains a structure to these works, just as there is a bottom to the sea. The composition of *Sand Drift*, for example, is held together by flowing diagonals which may be read either as rivulets in the sand or, through a teasing shift of scale, as a pattern of roads seen from the air. In a later painting, *Shoreline* (1991), there is no 'land', no longer any sense of where you are, but the horizontal tendencies in the central area give the work a point of balance, while the central void with its vertical drips reminds us that in the end this is just a painting.

Works such as these, painted in a small ground floor studio with restricted natural light, are a mix of memory, invention, imagination and metaphor. McAleer sees them as experimental, even transitional. 'They don't mean I will necessarily go on to be an abstract

*Clement McAleer, Ulysses Series. Hades: Prospect Cemetery, Glasnevin, 1982. Oil on canvas, 167 x 152 cm. Collection of the artist.*

*Clement McAleer, John Clare Series. Asleep on a Bed of Clover, 1989. Oil on canvas, 183 x 183 cm. Collection of the artist.*

# CLEMENT McALEER

painter. I may go back to description.' The dynamism of the recent paintings results directly from McAleer's use of acrylic, and this is a quality that he brings back to his oil paintings when he returns to oil.

From time to time, McAleer is drawn to subject-matter that is specific, even literary, 'something I can hold on to,' as if too long an exposure on the fringes of abstraction breeds an insecurity. He spent the summer of 1988 painting a triptych at The Deeps, Co Wexford, in a large, haunting garden with crumbling walls, overgrown weeds, flowers and trees — everything rapidly returning to nature. *The Deeps (Wexford)* was painted out in the open, directly from the subject with the canvas leaning against the garden wall and moved into an old shed between showers. In it, McAleer captures that moment of transition, the moment before nature takes back the man-made world for good.

A further, deeply considered group of paintings is his *John Clare Series* made in 1989. McAleer based these six works on John Clare's journal of his journey in 1841 from the Asylum in Essex, where he had been held for five years, to his native village of Helpstone, Northamptonshire in search of his childhood sweetheart. As in the *Ulysses* series, the *John Clare* paintings flash from one viewpoint to another, inspecting Clare's story, and the world, from six different angles and through six different lenses. *Asylum, High Beech* is an unsettling, vertiginous composition, reflecting Clare's own restlessness and his obsession with Mary Joyce, whom he imagined was now his wife. Just as Molly and Bloom were observed from above in *Ulysses*, so now *Asleep on a Bed of Clover* looks down at Clare: 'I lay down with my head towards the north to show myself the steering point in the morning.'[5]

There is an intense vitality in the four central paintings in the *John Clare Series*, those canvases which show Clare to be momentarily free of the restriction of the

Clement McAleer, Sand Drift, 1986.
Pastel and acrylic on paper, 121 x 101 cm.
Private Collection.

asylum at the beginning, and the reality of his life in the final canvas. Here, the poet arrives home to find nothing and 'no Mary — her & her family are as nothing to me now though she herselfwas once the dearest of all — & how can I forget.'[6] The sense of escape in the central sequence, the sense of both the poet and painter relishing the freedom of 'the grass below — above the vaulted sky', is as tangible as the final tragic arrival is inevitable. McAleer's *John Clare Series* has the power of good cinema.

Having woven an extensive body of work around the kind of landscape which encloses man, or with which man has interfered, McAleer is now not so scared to do things that are 'beautiful'. He recognises a new lusciousness entering his colour, particularly in the exuberant group of large acrylic paintings (183 x 175 cm) such as *Easter*, *Stormy Sea* and *Red Blossom*, exhibited in January 1992 at the Kerlin Gallery, Dublin. In these, painted as a result of several recent visits to the West Coast of Ireland, he edges towards the vividness of the kind of abstract expression seen in the work of the American painters Sam Francis or Clyfford Still. In McAleer's work, however, the constant presence of metaphor is unmistakeable. Words of Gerard Manley Hopkins,[7] which gave the title to his painting *Glass Blue Day* (1991), may stand also for McAleer's struggle to paint the unpaintable:

> The glass-blue days are those
> When every colour glows,
> Each shape and shadow shows.
> Blue be it: this blue heaven . . .

James Hamilton

*James Hamilton has organised and written catalogues for many exhibitions, and now writes full-time. His biography of Arthur Rackham (1990) was followed by a biography of William Heath Robinson (Pavilion Books, 1992). He is currently writing a history of 20th century British wood-block printmaking, to be published by Barrie and Jenkins in 1993, and contributes to The Spectator.*

### ACKNOWLEDGMENTS

*I am grateful to Clement McAleer and Clare Stracey, Director of Midlands Contemporary Art, for their help in preparing this article.*

### NOTES

1. Sheila McGregor, *Clement McAleer*, catalogue introduction, Atkinson Art Gallery, Southport, 1987.
2. James Joyce, *Ulysses* Penguin edition, p. 658.
3. Artist's statement in poster/catalogue of *The Ulysses Project*, Douglas Hyde Gallery, Trinity College, Dublin, 1982.
4. Clement McAleer. Statement in exhibition catalogue: *Clement McAleer Paintings and Drawings*, Arts Council of Northern Ireland, 1984.
5. John Clare, *The Journal; Essays; The Journey from Essex* (ed. Anne Tibble), Carcanet New Press, Manchester, 1980, p. 118.
6 *Ibid*, p. 117.
7. Gerard Manley Hopkins, 'The Blessed Virgin Compared to the Air We Breathe', *Poems and Prose of Gerard Manley Hopkins*; Penguin, 1953, p. 54-8, lines 83-6.

# SOME EARLY O'MALLEY PORTRAITS

**Vera Ryan** considers the importance of his portraiture in Tony O'Malley's early development as a painter.

Tony O'Malley is not a portrait painter. He is primarily a landscape painter, a painter of place. Although deeply rooted in observation, his paintings are mainly non figurative. Born in 1913, he started painting in Ireland in the forties and went to Cornwall in the next decade, where he developed his characteristic style. He is a prolific artist and portraits represent a very small proportion of his output. Yet the evolution of his work cannot be appreciated without an understanding of the early portraits. In them he achieves a feeling and a synthesis of observation and interior contemplation which marks his best work. They chart his sense of identity at a very crucial stage in his life as an artist.

He had started painting while in a TB sanatorium; the long bouts of isolation endured by him from 1945 to 1950 brought him to painting and held him with it. Like many artists of his generation he never went to art school, and so had no sustained training in life drawing. In the sanatorium he sketched many fellow patients, as he was to in a St Ives hospital in 1961. None of these sketches developed into a portrait.

His early portraits are in general the

Tony O'Malley, Portrait of the Artist's Mother, c. 1953. Oil on board, 29 x 18 cms. Collection Jane O'Malley.

wrought works of someone seeking an understanding of their familiar or intimate world rather than the polished accomplishments of someone commissioned to capture a likeness. None are commissioned works.

When he left the sanatorium in 1950, O'Malley felt that his attempts at art were unlettered and that he had as yet 'no central insight into the nature of art'.[1] But there was no doubt about his commitment to the painting: 'my obedience, my turning to painting excluding other things, came very soon after finally leaving the san.'[2]

Although he had to resume his job in the bank in order to make a living, 'I never let myself away with light allusive stuff — the paintings were heavy with intention'.[3] A serious self-taught artist, he exhibited in Dublin in the *Oireachtas* and *Living Art* in 1951, 52 and 53 and received some recognition.

*Self Portrait Outside the Studio — Arklow* of about 1953 is a strongly frontal composition showing the artist standing outside his studio hut in the garden of his lodgings in Arklow on a moonlit night. The sage, lavender and grey tonalities, so frequent in his later paintings, are here

Tony O'Malley, Self Portrait Outside the Studio — Arklow, c. 1953. Oil on paper, 38 x 56 cms. Collection Jane O'Malley.

*Tony O'Malley, The Gardener, 1957–1960. Oil on board, 46 x 60 cms. Private Collection.*

*Tony O'Malley, Van Gogh, Winter, From a Dream, 1961. Oil on board, 60 x 69 cms.*
*Collection, University College, Cork.*

# SOME EARLY O'MALLEY PORTRAITS

worked with the strong rectangular shapes of door, figure and bench creating an eerie atmosphere. 'Strong shapes give endurance';[4] there is a Munch-like staccato feeling to the image of O'Malley's stiff skeletal silhouette in the ghostly light.

We do not see the self as likeness here, partly because it's a night picture. We see the clean shaven self as linked with the studio, as in many of the later self-portraits or studio interiors. The importance of the studio to O'Malley at this stage related to privacy, to the necessity of the possibility of contemplation. He had a small hut in the sanatoria, where he could paint and write his journal, and had worked in fairly extreme isolation during his illness in the forties. Back working and living in lodgings with a half dozen or so other lodgers, he often used his bedroom as a studio. 'You'd use the mirror in the wardrobe door for your Self-Portrait'.[5] He had very little time to himself and 'an unfortunate comment would often block you'.[6]

The poet Paul Durcan, though much younger than O'Malley, has captured the plight of the artist as misfit in Ireland in the 1950s and later, in his Daddy, Daddy (1990). Despite O'Malley's personal popularity and amiability he felt an outcast. As an artist he was on a path taking him away from the set forms of Irish society, which could have fossilised him. A studio was creative territory, even if it was often dark before he got there. The hut in the back garden in Ferrybank, Arklow, gave him some creative freedom, symbolised perhaps by the open door in O'Malley's picture. Despite the unfortunate comment or two – 'I didn't see you at Mass on Sunday'[7] for example – he regarded the three or four years (1953–1957) in Arklow as positive. We can sense the simultaneous hope and tension which the artist experienced at the time in his Self Portrait outside the Studio – Arklow.

When working in Enniscorthy and Arklow respectively in the early fifties, O'Malley used to drive over to Callan on Sundays, to see his mother who was bedridden with liver or spine problems. She had nursed him at home during his early convalescences until the doctor saw that she was too old for nursing and got Tony a bed in the sanatorium in Kilkenny. Gerry O'Malley, Tony's cousin, wrote about her 'Aunt Margaret was a gentle demure woman with an exceptionally beautiful singing voice'.[8]

She died in 1954. O'Malley painted a number of small but important pictures of her in bed. She did not pose for them although the artist often sketched her in her room. An ordinary country man didn't easily sit in front of his mother and draw her. Making a portrait was a furtive business. The paintings were done from memory. For O'Malley 'realism comes from the power of memory, memory creates a reality'.[9] One portrait was done ten years after the memory of her sitting up in bed saying the rosary.

The earlier one, Portrait of the Artist's Mother of around 1953 painted rather dryly on board in a light colour range of blue, yellow, pink and white has been described

Tony O'Malley, Portrait of Lizzie Sweeney, 1957–1960.
Oil on board, 39 x 39 cms. Private Collection.

Tony O'Malley, Self-Portrait – Winter, Heavy Snowfall at Trevaylor, Cornwall, 1962/63. Oil on canvas, 46 x 35.5 cms.
Collection Jane O'Malley.

# SOME EARLY O'MALLEY PORTRAITS

by Brian Fallon as 'a small masterpiece'.[10] In it we look at the figure as if seeing it through a membrane or perhaps a window, the blue of whose frames is thrown onto the scene. This cross light, filtering into the room, shifted by cars passing on the street gives a strong structural sense to the picture, and establishes a subtle distance between viewer and sitter. Mrs O'Malley seems to be sitting up in bed, and her half-length figure is painted at an almost three-quarter angle. She is probably just lifting up the bed clothes although her hands are not visible. Perhaps she is about to get out of bed. She turns full face towards the viewer, eyes lowered, revealing no awareness of being observed. Her head forms a magnificent strong oval shape in the centre top of the composition. The hair is richly painted. This strong head shape expresses the dignity of the figure. The artist has used white to bracket the head in diagonal parallels of pillow and sheet. There is white too under the flatter yellows and pinks of the shawl or bedjacket. The central section is the most volumetric section of the picture, which flattens out into marvellous, almost swirling, rich, pinks, blues and whites at the bottom and is disciplined, on the other hand, by the strong horizontals and verticals on top. The transitions between foreground and background are beautifully handled. The pictorial ambiguities — is she about to get out of bed, what are the blue traceries — are expressed with restraint; it is an entirely ungestural picture, an intimate picture of the mother of the forty-year-old artist.

The autobiographical element in O'Malley's portraiture is particularly strong in the early fifties. *Portrait of Mattie* also of about 1953 is a fine head of his younger brother whose sudden death in 1958 devastated the artist. In this picture Mattie, whom O'Malley painted more than once, smokes the customary cigarette which probably led to his death from heart disease at the age of thirty-nine. The head is amply modelled and set against a window. Cold blues and browns dominate, and give a rather lonely feeling to the picture. Like the *Portrait of the Artist's Mother*, *Portrait of Mattie* is a small intimate work, done from memory. It's about 'the calling up of Mattie. I couldn't look at Mattie and do that'.[11] There is a subdued echo of Matisse's *Portrait of Derain* (1905) in this picture and of

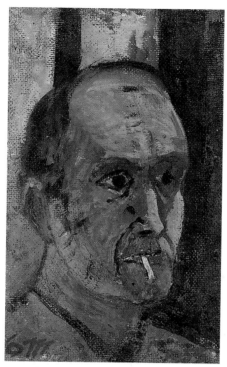

*Tony O'Malley, Portrait of Mattie, c. 1953. Oil on board, 29 x 18 cms. Collection Jane O'Malley.*

Matisse's *The Green Stripe* (1904) in the *Portrait of the Artist's Mother*. But it is the quality of feeling in O'Malley's work which makes these two pictures important, whereas in Matisse formal innovation is the significant factor.

During the fifties O'Malley also sketched and painted portraits of people from outside his family. He moved to New Ross in 1957, and this was his last bank posting. A year later, in 1958, he retired from the Munster and Leinster Bank on a very modest pension. He stayed in New Ross until 1960, at last a professional painter. His paintings gained in momentum during this period, despite his grief over Mattie's death. His friend Gabriel Lalor was a carpenter and made him an easel and some picture frames. Once again, the portraits he painted are few in number but they include the exceptional *Portrait of Lizzie Sweeney* and *The Gardener*.

Lizzie Sweeney was an old lady who fascinated O'Malley. Her husband was long dead, and she had no children. She would go for a 'nip' at eleven in one of the pubs in New Ross, usually with money donated unsolicited by the people who passed her by. Lizzie, whom O'Malley

knew and liked, was probably sketched from the Austin Seven van in which the artist used to sit to paint. He painted her against the background of a New Ross Street, rendered in blues and pinky rusts. She is very much to the forward plane of the canvas, separated from the houses by a snowy street. Blue in the ribbon of her hat links her with the street and houses, while the V-shape of her shawl brings the figure forward and down. Lizzie's expression is not easily readable, although her eyes turned to the side suggest that she is thinking. Her coarse features are painted quite coldly in blue over pinks. The shawl, by contrast, is very warmly painted. Nothing in the portrait suggests that Lizzie was a rather marginalised member of the community as indeed she was. For O'Malley, she was an important part of the New Ross Community. Her presence is sturdy. The device of the foreground figure, seeming to contemplate the background, is one which appears later in *Van Gogh, Winter, From a Dream* and *Landscape with Figure, Clare Island*. Around this time also, he painted a portrait of another old lady, Nanny Moore.

These old ladies were part of the visual life of small town Ireland in the late fifties. The artist might look out the window and see them standing in the street. The streets were often empty, due to the emigration of the forties and fifties and he particularly liked these slightly separate people, who had little awareness of their image, but were intensively individual, and dignified.

In New Ross, O'Malley had many supportive friends, notably Mrs Lalor and Mrs Ronan. Madame Elsa Smith, a Swiss painter, who used to invite him to lunch some Saturdays, and Mrs Hennessy, a lady painter in the town, shared his interest in painting. His painting *The Gardener* is probably a fusion of a memory of an old gardener whom he used to watch in the green house of Lamberton Hall, Arklow, years earlier and Mrs Hennessy's gardener, Kelly. He did drawings of the gardener in Arklow, and carried away an image of him, which he mulled over. The image is distilled in *The Gardener*. We think of Cézanne's gardener, Vallier. O'Malley's portrait is a half-length, the sitter's clasped hands and impassive gaze make for a rather impassive portrait. The treatment of the hands recalls the carved hands of an apostle by O'Tunney in Jer-

# SOME EARLY O'MALLEY PORTRAITS

point Abbey, the Cistercian Abbey near Kilkenny which meant so much to O'Malley. The hatted figure is painted in the same blue and ochre colours as Lizzie Sweeney, but the background of the shed is rich and magical in contrast with the coolness of the New Ross street. The plants stretch their tendrils over the glass and their mobile energy seems to complement the sculptural quality of the gardener. The window and plants create a pattern which frames the sitter. Window backgrounds recur in many of the portraits. *The Gardener* is a symmetrical picture, with the line of the shoulders of the gardener almost coinciding with the window sill, and the line of the brim of his hat coinciding with the window frame. Two pots on the right balance the figure of Kelly to the left. The paint handling of warm and cold tones of pinks and browns, blues, greens is remarkable. *The Gardener* was painted between 1957 and 1960.

During this period, O'Malley tried painting a girlfriend but found himself dissatisfied. She was too lovely. He couldn't catch the perfection of a young woman then, although much later, his wife Jane Harris appears in many of his pictures. There was a dread of having to flatter a young woman, then, and also a reluctance to respond to anything remotely fashion-conscious.

As O'Malley was almost as interested in literature as in painting, a gift in the sanatorium of Eliot's *Four Quartets* had meant almost as much to him as the legendary box of paints. He listened to Padraic Fallon's plays on the wireless and later got to know the poet, whom he frequently sketched. He also painted a picture, *Dream of W B Yeats*. In Cornwall, he drew W S Graham, the poet, and the painter Bryan Winter. But the creative spirit who turned out to be his most important subject was Vincent Van Gogh.

When O'Malley settled in Cornwall in 1960 he did not see himself as abandoning Ireland – it meant too much to him – but 'either you massaged the national ego by doing Finn MacCool, or you were isolated'.[12] He opted to be in the artistic community of St Ives, which he first visited on holiday in 1955.

O'Malley's studio was in the St Peter's Loft Art School run by Peter Lanyon and Bill Redgrave. O'Malley, who had been painting seriously for ten years, was respected as a mature artist. 'Peter was very respectful of his work. He wouldn't dream of trying to teach him'.[13]

Some of the most powerful works done in Cornwall in the early sixties are pictures of departure, of self-questioning. *Van Gogh, Winter, From a Dream* was probably done in 1961. Van Gogh's head is set against a background of bleak snowy enclosures with two bare trees and a high horizon. We see only the head, with the distinctive red hair and beard almost elbowed out of the bottom of the picture by the gnarled tree. The space is steep, and the sense of enclosure strong. In the dream which led to the picture, O'Malley sensed these walls or enclosures as the trap which held Van Gogh until he was released by painting. The enclosures are based on a back yard in Arklow. O'Malley had done many snowy landscapes in Arklow, Wexford and New Ross and these probably contributed to the success of this picture. The sky is reminiscent of early Van Gogh drawings, much admired by O'Malley. Again, he uses blues as well as whites and browns to give an intensity to the picture and to focus on the bottom of the composition. Van Gogh's expression is introspective rather than confrontational. It is winter the winter of the spirit, the winter of discontent. We feel O'Malley's empathy with the great Dutchman who, like himself, came late to painting and endured misunderstanding. O'Malley did other portraits of Van Gogh, but none are as potent as this.

O'Malley confined himself to the same colour range of browns, whites, blues and blacks in his *Self Portrait in Trevaylor, Cornwall* (1962 or 1963), a small oil on canvas which shows the now bearded artist in front of a very richly-painted window wearing the St Ives fisherman's jersey. O'Malley has spoken about the sense of stimulation he felt in Trevaylor, a beautiful mansion near Penzance where he was Mary Redgrave's lodger from 1962 to 1966. He also enjoyed the company of the painter Nancy Wynne Jones, who owned the house and the poet W S Graham, who lived across the way. But there is a sense of tightness or constriction to this fine self-portrait which suggests that the artist was still in a period of anxious self-examination.

There is an element of expressionism in a few of O'Malley's portraits of the fifties and sixties which exists less in the landscapes and still-lifes. In *Landscape with Figure, Clare Island* of about 1962, the expressionist influence of Munch seems to be fused with that of the mystic El Greco. Like *Self Portrait Outside The Studio*, this is on paper.

The high horizon with the figure in the foreground is reminiscent of the Van Gogh picture and O'Malley once again re-

*Tony O'Malley, Portrait of the Artist's Parents, 1962. Gouache on paper, 59 x 91 cms. Private Collection.*

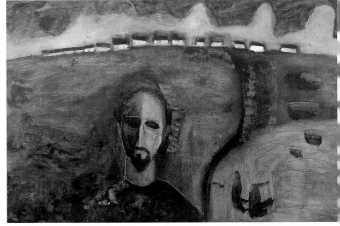

*Tony O'Malley, Landscape with Figure, Clare Island, 1962. Oil on paper, 57 x 89 cms. Collection Betty Rock-O'Malley.*

# SOME EARLY O'MALLEY PORTRAITS

tains a sense of the intensity of the background. The figure is clearly a self-portrait, one of the hundred or so executed by O'Malley. The flatly painted black bearded artist has a gaunt iconic quality and the use of outline is strong. The strong volumes which expressed the head in the earlier pictures have flattened out. He uses the hatching strokes of Byzantine art. The scoring may be a fusion of the influence of Ben Nicholson in Cornwall, where the painting was done and the memory of the marks drawn into some of the stones in Jerpoint. It is another picture of departure, testing the artist's sense of identity.

Clare Island, off Co Mayo, was the home of his father, and O'Malley's sense of identity is bound up with his island origins. Significantly, when he left the sanatorium in 1950, he went to Clare Island on a visit, and in 1970, on one of his most important return visits to Ireland prior to his marriage, he did 'a completely compulsive series of drawings'[14] there. He still visits the island. If *Van Gogh, Winter, After a Dream* is about O'Malley's artistic identity, *Landscape with Figure, Clare Island* is one of his most important pictures dealing with cultural identity.

The parallel use of warm and cool palettes, seen in the seventies and eighties in his Bahamian and Callan/Cornwall pictures respectively, has always existed in his work. It is seen in the warm orange-reds and the use of black and white which give a sombre rich effect to the self-portrait, similar to that achieved in *Portrait of the Artist's Parents* of around 1962. Again there is a Byzantine feeling to this picture where the heads of his father Pat O'Malley (1873–1936) from Clare Island and his mother Margaret O'Malley (née Ryan) (1870–1954) glow like religious icons. Pat O'Malley worked for Singer Sewing Machines and was 'a poetic man, a dreamer . . . a man of strong political views'.[15] His own father and uncle had been drowned off Clare Island. He himself was reared there, settling in Callan after his marriage. For O'Malley, the energy to paint those who were dead had to be established in the artist in the sitters' lifetime. 'We are all spirits with outward appearances. Trying to catch the phantasmal side of a person interested me, but it was like dice throwing. Sometimes I could haul up an image of a

*Tony O'Malley,*
Portrait of the Artist's Mother in 1953, 1963.
*Oil on canvas, 41 x 30.5 cms.*
*Collection Jane O'Malley.*

person'.[20] Usually when he did so, the painting was an amalgam of images of the person, a distillation of years of familiarity. He then felt witness to their essence, rather than creator of their portrait. This is the case in the portrait of his parents.

The strongly commemorative side to his portraiture is an intriguing feature of O'Malley's work. Many of the best portraits are of people close to death or are, as in the case of *Portrait of the Artist's Parents, Portrait of the Artist's Mother in 1953, Van Gogh, Winter, After a Dream* and *Hawk & Quarry in Winter, In Memory of Peter Lanyon* (1964), reflections on people already dead. In the latter the memory of the man is respected through place not portrait. There are at least two important early sixties portraits of his mother. *Portrait of the Artist's Mother in 1953* was done in Trevaylor, nine or ten years after her death. It is a small tender oil on canvas, in which we see his mother saying the rosary in bed, and is not at all morose. Beautiful and subtle uses of yellow are a feature of it. It has a wonderful surface reality. O'Malley's interest in painting deceased family and friends is the result of an introspective nature seeking through painting to make connections between past and

present. It has to do with his sense of painting being about the relation too between inner and outer worlds, those of appearance and those of essence. He once said, 'I have no interest in portraiture. I'm only interested in a self asking who and what are you'.[16] In that quest, painting is not bound by sequential time. 'With me, painting has no time'.[17] Portraiture for O'Malley in the fifties and sixties was largely about finding out who and what he was and was based on a subtle inter-relationship between memory and observation.

'Once I discovered the essential in abstraction, I moved away from these kinds of paintings. They were important because calling myself an artist meant coming to terms with the human'.[18] 'The element which makes painting live is the psyche. I identified with Knut Hamsin, the Norwegian provincial who wrote the unconscious life of the mind in *Women at the Pump* and *Hunger*. In Ireland then the psyche had to be clean or forgiven . . . I moved more towards essences, and tried to fuse the elements of place and people through abstraction'.[19] The early portraits are an important part of his journey in quest of these essences.

*Vera Ryan*

*Vera Ryan is a lecturer in Art History at the Crawford College of Art and Design, Cork.*

## NOTES

1. Interview with the artist 27 June 1991.
2. Ibid.
3. Ibid.
4. Interview with the artist 15 July 1991.
5. Ibid.
6. Ibid.
7. Ibid.
8. Gerry O'Malley, 'Man making his Mark', *Sunday Tribune*, 3 September 1988.
9. Interview with the artist, 27 March 1987.
10. Brian Fallon, *Tony O'Malley*, (1984), p. 60. Fallon's excellent catalogue is the authoritative work on O'Malley.
11. Interview, 27 June 1991.
12. Ibid.
13. Nancy Wynne Jones, 29 September 1991.
14. Brian Fallon, *Tony O'Malley*, (1984), p. 99.
15. Gerry O'Malley, 'Man making his Mark', *Sunday Tribune*, 3 September 1988.
16. Interview, 27 March 1987.
17. Ibid.
18. Interview with the artist, 10 February 1992.
19. Interview with the artist, 10 February 1992.
20. Interview with the artist, 27 June 1991.

# THE PADRAIC O CONAIRE COMMISSION

In Eyre Square in the centre of Galway city is located one of Ireland's best known statues, that of Padraic O Conaire (1883–1928), Irish writer and story-teller. He was the first modern writer to earn his living writing exclusively in Irish. The figure (140cm high) carved in limestone is surrounded by other monuments of varying types. These include a statue to the 1916 leader Liam Mellows and a striking piece of modern sculpture representing a Galway hooker. Yet it is the O Conaire monument which is regarded in popular affection as the city's favourite landmark. Local children play around it and climb over it, visitors like to be photographed beside it. Much of its charm lies in its accessibility to passers-by. Unusually the figure is presented not on a high plinth but seated on a low wall: a wall reminiscent of those dotted through the Connemara countryside lying to the north-west of the city. The statue is almost at the spectator's eye level and appears to inhabit the same space. However its approachability also lies in the very informal treatment of the figure itself. O Conaire, a gentle unassuming poet-writer and alcoholic, is depicted as he presented himself in life, wearing a shabby crumpled suit and shirt with loosely tied bowtie, his hat worn back to front. Balanced on one knee is an open copybook in which he appears to be writing and, while one hand holds the pen, the other is grasping his lapel. The pose is one of quiet concentration and his facial expression is meditative. At his feet, nestling in foliage, are a small bird and rabbit. An inscription 'Slan leis an Samhradh' is placed beneath[1].

The history of this sculpture is worth exploring as it offers an insight into the efforts made by one Irish artist, Albert G Power RHA, and his patrons, the Galway members of the Gaelic League,[2] to produce a work of art which articulated the cultural and political aspirations of newly Independent Ireland. Its artistic significance in relation to the unusual treatment of a sculpted literary figure is also worth noting.

The project began in 1929, one year after the death of the writer. Some of his friends in the Gaelic League, Galway, met to consider erecting a monument over his grave. With this object in view a circular was sent to members of the League and others interested in its activities. In response to this initial appeal about £200 was raised[3]. However by the time the

The history of one of the best known statues in Ireland, the Padraic O Conaire monument in Galway, by **Sighle Bhreathnach-Lynch**.

*O Conaire Monument as originally erected in 1935. Reproduced from postcard.*

*O Conaire Monument as it appears today. The monument was relocated in the square in 1966 but the wall was not rebuilt exactly as Albert Power had arranged it.*

money was raised a new and more ambitious plan had been decided upon. It had occurred to the committee that the empty pedestal in Eyre Square on which a bronze statue of Lord Dunkellin, of Portumna Estate, Co Galway had earlier stood, would provide a splendid base for a statue of O Conaire[4].

The sculptor chosen to carry out the work was Albert G Power RHA (1881–1945). Power had trained in the Dublin Metropolitan School of Art at the beginning of the century, and under such teachers as William Orpen and John Hughes his years there were distinguished by many awards, prizes and scholarships. In 1912 he had set up business in Dublin. The scope of this venture was wide and included the production of monuments and architectural work in marble, stone and bronze, altars, statues and tombstones. Some of his religious work demonstrated Power's strong desire to produce a distinctive Irish art in its choice of native materials and use of Celtic motifs. He also showed considerable talent as a portraitist and, from early in his career, his portraits were prominent in the RHA annual exhibitions. Many of these were of major figures of the literary revival: W B Yeats, James Stephens, Lord Dunsany, Tom Kettle and Arthur Griffith. Through his friendship with the writer and physician Oliver St John Gogarty, an important influence on Power's career, he was given some important government commissions both on behalf of the Free State Government and later de Valera's Republican Government. Other republican factions throughout the 1920s and 1930s also employed him. By 1930 he was already regarded as one of Ireland's leading sculptors. Because of the political character of much of his work as well as its distinctly Irish vein, he was perceived as an artist capable of expressing in sculpture the new cultural and political objectives of the nation.

Early in February 1930 Power attended his first meeting with the committee in Galway and produced some sketches from which a choice could be made[5]. At this stage he estimated that the statue would cost about £280, if the pedestal belonging to the earlier statue of Dunkellin was available free of charge. It was immediately agreed that a delegation would approach the Galway Urban Council to see if this could be arranged, and the Chairman and Treasurer Thomas Concannon,

# THE PADRAIC O CONAIRE COMMISSION

Secretary Liam O Buachalla and committee members Professor O'Briain and Dr Dylan were elected to carry out the negotiations. It was also proposed to circulate notice of the League's activities to the main bodies of the city: the County Council, Galway City commissioners, the Mechanics Institute and the local Chamber of Commerce. The League was anxious that the honouring of O Conaire would not be a partisan affair but one celebrated by all those who represented different strands of city life[6].

Some weeks later O Buachalla informed Power that the comittee had been granted permission to use the Dunkellin pedestal, and was now forging ahead with collecting the sum necessary to bring the project to completion[7]. With this in mind he notified Power of the intention of having photographs taken of his drawings for the monument. Blocks were to be made in order to reproduce the proposed design in all papers and magazines throughout Ireland and the United States 'as a means of propaganda and to initiate fund raising'[8]. Power was requested to prepare and submit to the committee a detailed estimate for the work as soon as possible. However Power, renowned for delays in matters of business, was to take some months before submitting the estimate. A typed letter finally arrived to Liam O Buachalla dated 3 July. It read

> I propose to execute in limestone a portrait figure of the late Padraic O Conaire as per sketch and to erect same on the existing pedestal in Eyre Square, Galway. For the sum of £350 (three hundred and fifty pounds). The work to be finished before St .Patrick's Day in March 1931[9].

A handwritten note to O Buachalla in Concannon's writing at the bottom of this letter is worth recording. It indicates that Concannon in fact had probably extracted the estimate from Power himself while on a visit to Dublin! However it also reveals Power's own enthusiasm for the project. The note read:

> At long last we have the estimate. I spent most of the day with Power. He is obviously fully committed to the job. His devotion, his loyalty and regard for Padraic will be seen in the statue.

It ended with the heartfelt plea 'In the name of God let us get on with work'.

Once Power's final estimate was known and approved, much effort was expended raising the amount needed for the monument[10]. The reaction of some of those appealed to is interesting. Lady Gregory, for instance, while willing to subscribe to the fund, had some private misgivings. These she voiced in her journal:

> Thomas Concannon writes in Irish asking me to subscribe toward a statue of O Conaire that is to be put up in the square in Galway in place of poor Dunkellin who . . . had worked so hard for Galway for the making of a packet station. I must subscribe for the sake of Thomas. But I have looked again through those gruesome stories of his (O Conaire) and do not like them. His poems I hope are better. I am glad respect should be shown to a writer; those monuments are not for politicians and fighting men only[11].

These views are very different from those generally associated with the Gaelic League in this period. Because she herself came from the same class of society as Dunkellin, Lady Gregory did not automatically perceive him as a 'hated landlord' and, although deeply interested in the revival of the Irish language, she clearly showed some independence of judgement in her unwillingness automatically to laud the work of anyone writing in Irish, even if only in the privacy of her journal. Her final remarks also indicate an awareness of the common assumption that only those involved in political struggles of one kind or another were worthy of commemoration in stone.

A second lukewarm reaction was openly voiced by a Mr Gregory who had sent a cheque for one guinea to the committee. In his letter of thanks Concannon wrote 'Let me begin by saying that our obligation to you is increased since you have sent us this help, in spite of your disapproval of the Memorial idea' . . .[12]. He then went on to agree that while Gregory's idea of the Memorial taking the form of an edition of O Conaire's works was a good one it would be quite beyond the resources of the committee. His hope was the monument to the writer would hasten the day when 'some progressive publisher will bring out such an edition as would satisfy your, and our desires'. Gregory had also suggested that the young O Conaire should be depicted and not the man of later years, physically wasted by his addiction to alcohol. Concannon was reassuring on this point:

> . . . it was the latter that we knew best in Galway, and we took for our starting point the photo Padraic himself gave me together with an account of his life the year we appointed him for the first time to give a couse of lectures in Spiddal College — I feel that Albert Power is sufficient of a poet as well as an artist to grasp the revelation of the real Padraic and while he will give us the Wanderer of the Crann Geagach [a character in O Conaire's writings] he will not forget the poet and the gentleman that Padraic always was.

Among those who subscribed to the project enthusiastically was Dr Tuohy, father of the artist Patrick Tuohy who had recently committed suicide. Concannon, clearly touched by Dr Tuohy's generous response to the appeal in spite of this tragedy, wrote by return of post:

> I cannot tell you how moved I was to get your beautiful letter this morning and your generous cheque towards the Padraic O Conaire Memorial. We appreciate very much your kindness in sending this and we appreciate it all the more since the immensity of your own recent loss might well have rendered you unresponsive to other appeals. This has not been so and your warm Irish heart in its grief for your own dear son, has not forgotten poor Padraic O Conaire[13].

Concannon was aware that Dr Tuohy was probably acquainted with Power. His son had known the sculptor well since their student days in the art school. Taking advantage of this fact he continued:

> I wonder could we burden you with another little commission. I suppose you know Albert Power who is to do the statue? I think it would please him if you called to see how the statue of Padraic is progressing. If you tell him I asked you to call I think it will serve a useful purpose in keeping him up to time.

It is clear from these remarks that Concannon was worried that Power might not complete the commission on time. His instincts were to prove to be correct because the monument was not to be ready before St Patrick's Day 1931. In fact it was to be four more years before it was finished.

The first delay was caused by difficulties in finding a suitable block of limestone. Both the artist and the committee were united in their insistence that only the most perfect piece of stone would do; if necessary they were prepared to wait for one to be found. A schoolteacher friend of Concannon, Padraic Savage, was asked to look out for such a block and, when it materialized, to purchase it. He lived near Durrow Quarry, Co Laois which produced

# THE PADRAIC O CONAIRE COMMISSION

an excellent limestone and Power, anxious to use a native material in this most Irish of monuments, was determined to have the quarry's most flawless piece. Savage wrote to Concannon in July 1931 to inform him that he had already been to the quarry and had talked to the owner, Luke O'Brien, who assured him that the first suitable stone would be put by for Power. He expected one to turn up within the next few weeks[14]. However four months later no such block had materialised and Savage wrote to Concannon:

*Every fortnight since I came home I have visited the quarry and O'Brien has the same story – there is no suitable stone there, and I saw with my own eyes that this was the situation. Last Saturday O'Brien took out a stone which was quite large but it was not suitable. There were lines or streaks through it and he said that Power would not use it and that he would not give it to him. I said to O'Brien that the committee were doubtful if he was at all serious. He then showed me a letter from another man, accusing him of the very same thing. 'Would you not write to the committee telling them they would have a stone before Christmas?' 'If they don't have it before Christmas they will never have it', he replied. It's not my fault. Hang on. Be certain I won't leave him alone[15].*

A disconsolate letter followed two months later:

*I was at the quarry and have no good news. I have been speaking frequently to O'Brien since I wrote. He got three or four big stones but they were all faulty. Some of them had to be split and the only one which was sound was 10 inches too short. I don't know how to advise you. O'Brien is opening another corner of the quarry and there is nothing at present to be found there but in another fortnight or so there is a chance he may find bigger stones, something suitable but that is only his own opinion. I am sorry about all this but there is nothing I can do about it[16].*

The following May, Savage wrote to Concannon to reassure him that he had not forgotten about purchasing the stone. He had visited the quarry every fortnight since Christmas and he was personally certain that no stone had slipped through unknown to him. During that time O'Brien had examined one stone which he had thought might be right but had discovered that it was not sound and, feeling sure that Power would not use it, rejected it[17]. However four weeks later a block had been located and Savage wrote to Concannon:

*At long last O'Brien has a stone. Power saw it a week ago. It is very large and will have to be reduced according to a sketch from Power showing how to dress the stone, and the quarry, with their heavy instruments, can do in a week what would take him a month[18].*

But Savage's worries were not over yet. O'Brien, he went on to report, had stated that it was very difficult to get Power to pay his bills promptly. He already owed him £200 for the last six months for limestone purchased for other commissions, and so far had paid out only £50. The quarry owner had implied to Savage that he would not hand over the stone before payment (this was to come from funds already paid to Power by the committee). Two weeks later he reported:

*I was speaking to O'Brien. He is unwilling to give any more credit to Power. He is writing to him tomorrow asking him to send a cheque before he gives the stone. He says that he knows that Power has been paid for the statue in Gort and therefore that he should pay him the money for the stone before he gets it. I'm sending the bill which he gave me a few days ago to you. Power asked us to dress the stone further and that will cost a little bit more but it is not worth talking about the difference. I hope Power sends him the cheque before too long[19].*

Savage's next letter one month later reported that O'Brien had now gone looking for the money owed him for the Gort commission while on a trip to Dublin. When he visited Power's house he was informed that Power was already in Gort but would be visiting the quarry on his return journey to Dublin[20]. The letter also indicated that the sculptor had not, in fact, visited the quarry as stated. In order to impress upon the Chairman the seriousness of the matter he recounted the conversation he had with the quarry owner on the matter:

*I said to him [O'Brien] 'would you not give the stone if you get the price from Concannon?' 'I will not', he said, 'because if Power gets the stone I won't get as much as a penny out of the monies owing by him to me'. There was nothing I could say but ask him to promise me that he wouldn't part with the stone.*

The letter concluded with a rueful comment on Power's inability to feel any sense of urgency

*Power saw the stone five weeks ago and he knew perfectly well that we were waiting for it for about a year and you would think he would do his best to get it. He is an odd sort of fellow without any doubt.*

Within weeks Savage was once more writing urgently to Concannon. Not only was the sculptor delaying payment for the block (£18.10.0) but he had not yet sent measurements. Savage pleaded, 'For God's sake write to Power asking him what kind of messing he is up to. He would wear the patience of Job'[21]. However a letter written in October indicates that Power had finally been persuaded to hurry himself along and Savage told Concannon that the stone was now in Attanagh station awaiting delivery by rail to Dublin. 'You have no idea of the anxiety I suffered because I knew two or three other people were looking for a stone of that sort', his letter concluded[22].

Power finally began the carving of the statue in November 1932. In June of the following year, because of the prolonged delay in getting the project underway, Concannon was obliged to write to Galway Urban Council to reassure its members that all was well and that the work was now in progress. He informed them:

*the artist does not expect to have his masterpiece complete for another twelve months. We are giving him his own time. But we hope that before 1934 is out Galway will be in possession of a monument which will be a work of artistic beauty, such as , we venture to say, no other town in the Irish provinces possesses[23].*

However it was to be February 1935 before the work was finished. During the previous year it appears that a discreet eye was being kept on Power to make sure he did not let up on the commission. A letter to Concannon from Owen Larkin a stone mason from Ballinasloe, who was to be involved with the monument at a later date, reads:

*I expect to be going to Dublin again soon and will send you a further report of the progresss made since I saw it. He [Power] certainly has a very happy way of punishing his sincere friends and I can see no hope of him changing. However he seems most enthusiastic over this job and I have every confidence he will execute it satisfactorily. I will keep at him every time I go to town[24].*

These lines articulate what everyone who had business dealings with Power felt about him. He was an easy-going, pleasant person to deal with but he had no business acumen and in particular lacked any sense of urgency. He tried the patience of all he came in contact with, yet

# THE PADRAIC O CONAIRE COMMISSION

each and every one was agreed that he was an artist of some considerable talent and for this reason his failings were tolerated.

His absence of business flair caused him undue financial worries throughout his career. Not surprisingly, therefore, while he was carrying out this commission, he appealed to the committee on several occasions to advance him money on account. Two letters written by Concannon in 1934 reveal his tact and diplomacy in dealing with Power on this issue. In May he wrote:

My wife gave me such a good account of the progress you are making with your magnum opus of poor Padraic that I am encouraged to send you a cheque for £20 on my own responsibility which I hope the committee will approve of when I bring them together, which I hope will be soon[25].

Power contacted the committee again in October. Concannon's reply was prompt and again courteous. This time the committee had been adamant about not advancing any more money. Concannon reported that, although it was his opinion also that no funds should be sent to Power,

I was sure you would not . . . send us such an urgent SOS and with such a "crack of the whip", were it not that you were in urgent need of it. This reasoning on my part had its effect and my committee have authorized me to send you the sum of £75 and to say to you that this is entirely a matter of grace on their part. A cheque for the authorized sum is sent you herewith[26].

Concannon also showed diplomacy in getting across to him the views of O Conaire's relatives on how their illustrious relative should be depicted. In the letter written in May in which he enclosed £20 to Power he commented:

I told Padraic's uncle today, Canon Conroy of Oughterard, and his aunt, Mother Magdalen of the Mercy Convent Galway, of your progress and both were delighted the Canon remarking 'I hope he will not show him with his pipe in his mouth'. I assured him that whatever way you treat him it will be a magnum opus. It is well at any rate that the family feelings with regard to the pipe would be respected[27].

In February 1935, when the figure was ready, Power attended a meeting of the committee[28]. Owen Larkin from Ballinasloe was also present. He was to be in charge of building the foundations for the erection of the monument. At this meeting Power announced that he would not be using the Dunkellin plinth after

all and Larkin was instructed to build a replica of a Connemara wall[29]. Why the sculptor had rejected the plinth was to become clear in a report of the Connacht Tribune two days later. The newspaper's special correspondent reported:

Albert Power with whom I had a long talk last evening, spurned the idea of placing this seanachie high upon the black marble pedestal that once carried Foley's famous Dunkellin. It would have been grotesque, bizarre, altogether absurd. Padraic's place in the memories of his people for now and for all time was in his native setting. Therefore he will sit and write eternally in the immortality of Irish limestone upon a rubble Connemara wall twelve feet in width[30].

On the other hand a reporter from the Irish Independent wondered about the placing of O Conaire's hat back to front. Power answered simply ' "Its the way he wore it. I saw him going up the other side of the street there one day, walking all hunched up", and he crouched down sideways and took a few steps about the yard to illustrate how O Conaire had walked, "and he had his hat on back to front". This triumphantly'[31].

It was also noted by the same writer that the boots were carelessly laced and Power's reply was likewise. The reporter professed amazement at the lifelike qualities of the figure and wrote in almost poetic vein:

Below the hat swept the immense brow. The eyelids drooped above the fine, strong nose and the delicate, sensitive, almost effeminate mouth and chin. The head was bent in thought over the copy book on his knee, and the pencil in the hand seemed actually to move. The whole pose bespoke half-drowsy contemplation, a spirit wandering in the land of fantasy. Thus must O Conaire have sat many a time on the wall and banks of the fields throughout Ireland, while his muse inspired him to write as none other has written Gaelic of the things around him. I became conscious that I was waiting for the lifting of the heavy eyelids, for the sluggish, gradual movement of the dreamer coming awake. It was inconceivable that it could have been wrought in stone.

A letter writer to the Irish Press, E Bloxham of Gorey, who had also been to see the statue in Power's studio, also waxed lyrical about it. He felt that the figure:

belonged to the Hidden Ireland where poets and scholars did not stand aloof on pedestals of self-importance. They lived and moved among the common people, and their genius flashed out as naturally and erratically as

does sunshine through the rain clouds of his native Connemara. The genius of the Hidden Ireland was uninfluenced by any standard of art save its own. Mr Albert Power's work is of the same order. His inspiration is native. From a rock of Irish limestone he has fittingly and worthily commemorated Padraic O Conaire[32].

Albert Power himself seems to have kept a close eye on the many reports about the work in the nation's newspapers. In January he took the Editor of the Irish Press to task, and wrote a letter which was subsequently published in the readers column. It read:

I have seen the announcement in the Irish Press about my figure of Padraic O Conaire. While the general impression which it conveys is correct, yet it requires some adjustments to enable the matter to be brought into better focus, and reveal what the work signifies. First of all, I would like to mention that this is not the first attempt of a Portrait sculpture in Irish limestone — a medium the possibilities of which in this domain have been quite overlooked in Ireland.
Irish limestone lends itself particularly to sculpture, it is native of the soil, harmonises with our climate, and its warmth of colour gives life to a figure carved from it, which is seldom seen in imported white marble. In other words our Irish crystalline limestone is our own White Marble. Incidentally it is not correct to say Padraic O Conaire is depicted wearing a rather damaged hat and baneen; very great care and thought were given to this part of the work.
The essential theme is the poetic thought of the Gael which I hope is depicted through the native stone[33].

The unveiling was set for Whit Sunday, 9 June 1935. In the weeks leading up to what promised to be a great event the committee was busy making final arrangements. At a meeting early in March it was decided to invite Eamonn de Valera to perform the ceremony[34]. As political leader of the country and a man passionately interested in promoting the Irish language as the mother tongue of all Irish men and women, it seemed doubly appropriate. De Valera was delighted to accept the invitation. Long an admirer of both O Conaire's writings and of Albert Power's work, he himself had been to Power's studio to see the work in progress[35]. It was arranged also to have the proceedings broadcast on 2 RN the national radio station, and Professor Liam O Briain, a member of the committee, was to give the commentary in Irish.

# THE PADRAIC O CONAIRE COMMISSION

A list of special guests was drawn up, arrangements were made to have extra trains laid on for people from outside Galway who wished to be present at the ceremony. A band and choir were invited to be present and a special lunch was to be held in Albert Power's honour before the unveiling ceremony at 3.30 p.m.

On Saturday 8 June, Eamonn de Valera arrived in Galway to unveil the monument. He was to spend the weekend with Thomas and Helena Concannon. That same afternoon he was received at University College Galway, and presented with an address of welcome by the staff and students. Next morning, having attended mass and visited the Convent of the Poor Clares and the Magdalene Asylum, he proceeded to the Great Southern Railways Hotel where the lunch for Power was being held. Before the meal addresses in Irish were presented to de Valera by the Urban Council and other public bodies. Its emphasis set the theme for the rest of the day's speeches: the monument would serve as a reminder of O Conaire's fame not only in Galway but in every place where the Irish language was prized by the Irish people[36]. The content of de Valera's address is worth noting because it demonstrates what the monument itself stood for in the eyes of the Fianna Fail leader. It was symbolic of his passionate desire for an Irish speaking Ireland, and, accordingly, he seized on the occasion of its unveiling to remind Irish people of their duty to the language. The *Irish Times* reported:

> He said that Galway was in a position to do much for the Irish language. It was the capital of the Gaeltacht and it was on the big towns of the future that the Irish language would depend. The language had not died out of the City of Galway and the people of that city could make it the language of their business and everyday life. By doing that they would make Galway not alone the first city of the Gaeltacht but of the whole of Irish-Ireland.[37]

The occasion was also used to hint at future government objectives relating to the arts in Ireland. In reply to the toast to him by Thomas Dillon of UCG, de Valera said that he hoped that they would soon have an opportunity to devote more time and attention to the development of the Irish language, literature and the arts, to which they had not been able to devote so much attention during the last twenty years[38].

John Hughes, George Salmon 1904. From Paintings and Sculptures, *Trinity College Dublin* Anne Crookshank.

The event too seemed an appropriate one to point out the difference between the public monuments already in existence throughout Ireland and Power's one. Mr Justice Meredith who spoke to the toast proposed by de Valera to Albert Power stated:

> the memorial was a reminder of how far they had travelled along the road of progress from the days of the Nelson Pillar and Wellington monuments. They had in Dublin some statues of which they were proud and which won the admiration of visitors, great works by Hogan and Foley, but they were works of men who had lived under an alien tradition and alien culture. Those works, in fact, splendid as they are, might have been produced by a fellow like Michelangelo, but Michelangelo could not have produced this monument to Padraic O Conaire. Mr Power had produced a work of great force and distinction, a work full of Irish spirit and tradition, and one that would be of lasting credit to the City of Galway. It was tribute alike to their sense of responsibility and discretion that the people of Galway should have selected Mr Power for this work.[39]

After the lunch the guests of honour walked out onto Eyre Square where the unveiling was to take place. The statue lay under a tarpaulin. Unknown to most of the crowd was the fact that, not many hours before, the figure of O Conaire had been discovered dressed up in a blue shirt by some local policemen. Some students from Galway University who were

members of the Blueshirt movement had decided to make a rather striking political protest to de Valera! The reason behind the protest was their strong feeling that the country was rapidly heading for a one-party State, one ruled by the Fianna Fail party. This was based on the fact that many of their meetings were being regularly broken up. It was hoped therefore that when de Valera unveiled the statue the discovery of the shirt would make him feel somewhat ridiculous. Much to their disappointment it was not to be.[40]

When the statue was unveiled it was greeted with great enthusiasm and its lifelike qualities were particularly commented upon. The recollections of one person present at the ceremony gives an intimation of this:

> The similarity to the real O Conaire gave us a pleasant shock. It was as if O Conaire had never left us. People said the statue was the 'dead spit' of Padraic, Padraic in a steille bheatha . . . we got a surprise to find Padraic in a sitting position but we were quite pleased with it. It's a pose, I think, that suits a writer and lover of the natural scene[41].

Power's success with his depiction of the writer was recognized immediately for the statue's ability to conjure up the man as if still alive and sitting on a wall, recording his thoughts. He had been a familiar figure around the city during his last years and his distinguishing features were readily identified. The lack of formality in the work was also admired. People were used to seeing sculptures of 'great men' placed high above them in an attitude of aloofness. This seated figure on a low wall seemed so much more approachable. The fact too that the general shabby air of the writer had been faithfully rendered was another point in its favour. It was how he was remembered in real life. Power's accurate but markedly compassionate representation is in fact informed by O Conaire's own attitude to others in his writings. He had been renowned for writing sympathetically about very ordinary people whose lives were not marked by success but rather by mistakes and failures of all kinds. The stories were realistic but tinged with pity and tenderness for people who seemed weak in their dealings with others, and it is this understanding which underlines the unusual treatment of the figure.

When the statue is compared to others

# THE PADRAIC O CONAIRE COMMISSION

of the same kind it becomes obvious that this work is an innovative example of the genre. Two fine precedents of seated figures were known to Power. One was the impressive bronze of Sir Benjamin Guinness by John Henry Foley (1863) outside St Patrick's Cathedral. Its subtle variation of still contemplative pose, yet rhythmic treatment of the drapery, raised it above the level of a stereotyped formula. John Hughes' statue of George Salmon in Trinity College (completed 1904) also offered an exciting variation of the seated figure. Whereas the former was depicted in quiet meditation, Salmon was represented leaning forward slightly as if to engage with the students passing by. The O Conaire monument, however, goes beyond the variations in these two works and brings to the category of the seated figure a new novelty. Its insistence on placing what was regarded as an important man of letters on a simple stone wall and rendering it without any sense of rhetoric or moral example breaks with the conventions of this type of monument. The fact that Albert Power was a conservative academic sculptor in matters of style and interpretation makes this break all the more noteworthy.

*John Henry Foley, Sir Benjamin Guinness 1863. From Irish Sculpture from 1600, Anne Crookshank.*

Yet when this work is understood in the context of his personal artistic beliefs, the individuality of the interpretation becomes clear. From his earliest student days Power had believed in the production of an Irish art. For him it encompassed not just an art of the highest technical quality and the use of Irish materials where possible. Above all it meant an art produced by those having what he termed a 'national outlook' and he believed that only such artist could treat Irish subjects in a suitably sympathetic fashion[42]. This was a work which was to celebrate a man of Irish letters who symbolised for many what being Irish meant in the Ireland of the 1930s. Thus Power went beyond the conventions of academic art because he wanted to express in a native stone something new and distinctly Irish.

In spite of a radical shift in modern Ireland's cultural and political goals, this work has managed to remain a popular one. With its deliberate lack of conventional treatment, and strong elements of unsophisticated informality, it remains a monument with an enduring artistic appeal.

*Sighle Bhreathnach—Lynch*

*Sighle Bhreathnach-Lynch lectures in the History of Art at University College, Dublin and is an occasional lecturer and guide at the National Gallery of Ireland. She has completed a PhD thesis on the sculptor Albert Power, RHA.*

## NOTES

1. These lines 'Goodbye to the Summer' are from a well-known work of O Conaire.
2. The Gaelic League, founded in 1893, was dedicated to the 'de-Anglicisation of Ireland' through its work in the revival and preservation of Irish language.
3. University College Galway Archives, LS Breise 38, Memorial fund appeal leaflet. I am indebted to Mr C Townley of Galway for making me aware of this valuable source of information.
4. The family seat of Lord Dunkellin was Portumna Castle. A life-size bronze statue by Henry Foley had been erected in Eyre Square in 1873 and was popularly believed to have been subscribed for by his tenants against their will. It was later thrown into Galway Docks during some disturbances, retrieved and smelted for its bronze. The pedestal was of marble.
5. O Buachalla Papers, Minutes 2 February 1930. I am indebted to Tom Kenny of Galway for allowing me access to the papers of Liam O Buachalla, a former member of the committee. These include the Minutes (incomplete) which were written in Irish and some letter. I would also like to thank Maire Ni Mhurchu, formerly Reference Librarian RTE, for her generous help in translating these and other appropriate documents.

6. Ibid
7. Ibid., letter 22 February 1930
8. Ibid., see Minutes, 12 February 1930
9. Ibid., letter 3 July 1930
10. UCG Archives, LS Breise 38. Judging from the volume of Concannon's correspondence during 1931 he appears to have been particularly busy in this regard.
11. *Lady Gregory's Journals*, Vol 2. Bks 30-44, p.575 Edited by Daniel J. Murphy (Gerrards Cross, 1987).
12. UCG Archives *op. cit.*, letter 2 February 1931
13. Ibid., letter 7 January 1931
14. Ibid., letter 17 July, 1931
15. Ibid., letter 17 November 1931
16. Ibid., letter 2 January 1932
17. Ibid., letter 18 May 1932
18. Ibid., letter 1 June 1932
19. Ibid., letter 13 June 1932. Power had not long before purchased a block of limestone from O'Brien which had been used for a pedestal for an Italian marble statue of Christ the King, later erected in the town square of Gort Co. Galway.
20. Ibid., letter 23 July 1932
21. Ibid., letter 18 August 1932
22. Ibid., letter 9 October 1932
23. Ibid., letter 5 June 1933
24. Ibid., letter 24 April 1934
25. Ibid., letter 12 May 1934

26. Ibid., letter 5 October 1934
27. Ibid., letter 12 May 1934
28. O Buachalla Papers, Minutes 17 February 1935
29. This is not mentioned in the Minutes of 17 February 1935 but was reported by the *Conacht Sentinel* two days later. Its editor had been approached by those present at that meeting.
30. *Connacht Sentinel* 19 February 1935, p.3
31. *Irish Independent*, 12 April 1935, p.5
32. *Irish Press*, 4 February 1935, p.6
33. *Irish Press*, 22 January 1935, p.6
34. Minutes, 2 March 1935
35. Information kindly supplied by Terry de Valera, letter 10 December 1987.
36. See full reports in *Irish Times*, *Irish Press*, of 10 June 1935 and in *Connacht Tribune* of 15 June 1935.
37. See *Irish Times*, 10 June 1935 p.8
38. Ibid.
39. Ibid.
40. I would like to thank Mr Patrick Lindsay, one of the students involved in this escapade, for his frank and highly entertaining account of the episode.
41. Recollections of Professor T P O Broin.
42. See *Wolfe Tone Weekly*, Vol. 1, No. 36, 7 May 1938.

# GRAHAM KNUTTEL

I was born in Dublin, in March 1954. My parents came to Ireland in 1947 from Bedford in England where my father had served with the RAF. His father, Adolf Knuttel, was a stone quarry owner in Dresden but my father and his mother came to England after the First World War.

My father is a strange eccentric man, but had nothing on his mother. I met her only once when I was four or five but the memory will never leave me. She was very tall and thin with a hook-like nose not dissimilar to my own. Her cheeks were hollow, whitened with powder and highlighted with rouge. She was dressed all in black, except for a white lace frill at her neck. The sight of her beside my father's huge dark wardrobe sent me into a state of total hysteria. There being no one else in the room, she tried to lock me in the wardrobe. I can still hear her cackling and feel her long white claws at the back of my neck.

I often look at my drawings of birds with which I have had a long obsession and I wonder. I am glad that I managed to find some sort of humour in what I firmly believe was a very close call. I think she might easily have strangled me and possibly eaten me had not my cries been heard.

**Graham Knuttel's** recent exhibition prompted this revealing autobiographical statement.

She was returned that same day to Margate where she lived in a guest house surrounded by her collection of stuffed animals until her death in 1962.

In her final weeks of life she changed her religion several times in an obvious display of panic buying.

My mother's family were more normal. Many of my summer holidays were spent in their house in Northampton, then a small market town.

My grandfather had been shell-shocked in Flanders in the First World War but the only manifestations of this that I could discern were a tendency to shout in his sleep all night and to cross roads as if he were in a trench, holding his hat, knees bent, gripping the wall firmly on the other side.

He would take me to see my Uncle Freddie who was a municipal painter. Part of his brief was to maintain the various coats of arms and painted war memorials throughout the town. We would sit in the sun for hours watching him paint his

bright rich reds and blues, and his fine and important gold leaf highlights.

We went to England two or three times a year and I remember the atmosphere of that journey very well. We took *The Princess Maud*, a steam-ship notorious for its creaking and rolling, packed as it was in those days too, with emigrant faces. We made the journey at night with a three hour wait at dawn in Crewe station for a connection. Under the grime and soot it was a magnificent building with its ornate brick work and cast and wrought iron. In many ways the scenes were reminiscent of the air-raid drawings of Henry Moore. To-day when I draw people, I draw in caricature railway porters I have seen asleep on mail bags, weary worried men and women busy and intent on that awful survival.

I had a happy childhood; I did all the things horrid boys do. My brother and sister were ten years older than me so I was left very much to follow my own destiny. I suppose my parents realised that children never turn out to be any thing other than what they want to be.

I wanted to be an artist from the earliest stage and although it was certainly an ambition viewed with dread by my mother and distaste by my father, there was good

*Graham Knuttel*, Semaphore. *Acrylic on canvas, 122 x 122 cm.*

*Graham Knuttel*, Opening Night, Closing Night. *Acrylic on canvas, 122 x 122cm.*

# GRAHAM KNUTTEL

provision of paper and paint and space at the dining-room table.

My brother when he was sixteen started at the National College of Art in Kildare Street and there was a smell of oil paint from his room that fascinated me.

My earliest memories of my own work are of battle scenes: columns of soldiers advancing and retreating by the use of my rubber, explosions caused by splashes of red ink, generals promoted and demoted by addition and subtraction of medals.

My school days were not those of a model student. In fact, few of them were spent at school at all. With my schoolbag safely hidden in a neighbour's hedge, many mornings and afternoons were spent sampling the café society and pubs of Dublin and exploring the rocky coastline of Dublin Bay.

As my interest in formal education waned, my absorption in drawing and painting grew. When I was eighteen years, I started at Art School. My years of training had given me an insight into the possibilities of bohemian life and Art School suited me very well. I had always had interest in figurative work, in the portrayal of the human condition, and from an early age I was familiar with the work of Van Gogh, Cézanne and Picasso. In Art School I was attracted to the life-drawing room where I determined to develop my skills as a figurative painter. I found myself to be an intuitive painter. I had little patience with the intellectual processes and conclusions which were involved with abstract and conceptual art. For me, to paint what I saw or felt or imagined around me should be a simple affair, painted from the gut.

In my last year of study, some new tutors, arrived, fresh from postgraduate studies in America, and proved to be a dangerous lot altogether. They were rabid abstract expressionists to whom artists such as Barnett Newman assumed god-like status.

My difficulty then was that I was isolated as a figurative painter and should I decline to imitate a transatlantic culture, I would certainly be doomed to failure.

I found it pragmatic therefore to stop painting temporarily and adjourn to the sculpture department for my final year.

My tutor there was an elderly sculptor who had seen trends come and go over the years and who emphasised to me the qualities of the older painters Cézanne,

*Graham Knuttel,* The Artist's Father, *Acrylic on canvas, 91 x 122 cm.*

Goya, Rembrandt. From his lifetime of carving wood and stone he was able to tell me something of the way that light revives form and how a paint can break the light into colours. It was a valuable year for me.

In 1976 I received my diploma for my exhibition of sinister, moving, wood constructions, a wooden bird, a portcullis, a shield, wooden machines reminiscent of medieval times, just as solidly built as my father's wardrobe.

I developed a love for sculpture at this time and for some years worked hard in carving and construction. However, through drawing and using colour in my sculpture, I gradually found myself returning to painting. Nowadays I work as both a painter and a sculptor. For a young artist, the initial years are extremely tough and hazardous. The bohemian life can be often dangerous too. My observations of humanity led me down some very dark alleyways, indeed, during my wilderness years, and, like my grandfather, I am also prone to shout in my sleep at my memories. At the beginning of 1987 I realized that I must mend my ways. I had a serious drink problem and ten years of my work was now in the hands of irate publicans and landlords.

I changed from being an alcoholic to a workaholic overnight with sensational results. Nowadays painting is an obsession

for me. I have a strict discipline and I work from first light every morning until darkness, and beyond. As I work, I use as source matter my experiences as a younger man. I like to paint the human predicament as I have seen it. My figures appear in an urban landscape of which I am part. I try to use colour and form to express the emotion of my figures. I have recently developed this course to include portraiture which I find exhilarating. I prefer a nightmare world full of shadows where danger and savagery is always close to hand.

My own doubts and fears and hopes are expressed on the faces that appear in the bars and backrooms in my work. Mr Punch is my *alter ego*. He reflects my moods. We fight the same battles from the same cupboards.

I return in my work constantly to still life as a source of inspiration. Its potential for simplicity and invention and its deep roots in tradition bring me back to my student studies of Cézanne and Picasso.

I try not to concern myself overly with intellectual reasoning or planning in my work. As a hard-working painter, my concerns are mainly technical, practical and immediate. My concern is to paint the picture first and think about it afterwards. That way I can progress in a proper manner. Above all I try to speak with my own voice and see with my own eyes.

*Graham Knuttel*

*Graham Knuttel was born in Dublin, Ireland, in 1954, of German and English parentage. Among his mother's family were several noted architects and artists including Thomas Cooper Gotch who co-founded the Newlyn School of Painting. He mentions also his great Uncle Archie Leach, better known as Cary Grant. His father's family roots are 'cloaked in secrecy' and he considers himself to be Irish or, more specifically, a Dubliner.*
*Initially renowned for his large wooden mechanically-animated sculptures, Knuttel has more recently emerged a painter with a rapidly growing international reputation. He is represented in many important collections in Europe and the USA as well as many public collections in Ireland.*
*He is a prolific worker spending up to fifteen hours a day in his studio every day. His life style could be considered as eccentric and in recent years he has become reclusive and attaches great importance to the privacy of his private life.*

*Reprinted from* New Works *by Graham Knuttel, catalogue of an exhibition in the New Apollo Gallery, Dublin, April—May 1992, with thanks to Mr Hugh Charlton.*

# THE GENIUS OF IRISH SILVER

Through the courtesy of John D Davis, who had the responsibility of organising this exhibition, I was fortunate enough to be able to see this collection before it was mounted on display and to examine the individual articles. In all, it presented an impressive array of high-quality pieces giving a very representative cross-section of the varied products of Irish silversmiths and of the different styles in vogue over a period of almost two hundred years, from around the mid-seventeenth century to the mid-nineteenth century. The main categories on show were drinking vessels such as the tankard and two-handled cups; vessels used in serving food, drink and condiments such as bread baskets, jugs, teapots, salvers and casters; ceremonial silver such as the mace and freedom boxes; tableware; candlesticks and accessories. Although the collection does include a number of articles made in Cork and Limerick, the vast bulk of the pieces are, as might be expected, of Dublin manufacture, and represents the work of celebrated masters — Thomas Walker, Robert Calderwood, John Hamilton and Thomas Bolton, who was Lord Mayor of Dublin in 1716—17, and there are others.

Articles considered as most typically Irish were also on show: the harp-handled cup, so-called because the handle resembles the neck and forepillar of a harp; the dish-ring, believed to have been used as a stand for a hot-dish; and the helmet-shaped jug, which was popular in Ireland from the 1730s to the 1770s.

A pair of sleeve or cagework cups made in Dublin 1696—98, the first entry in the catalogue, is one of the rarities of the collection and is of particular significance because of the structure which the word 'sleeve' pretty aptly describes. The term derives from the fact that the cups proper, which are plain, are contained within detachable cylindrical shells or sleeves. The latter are richly and beautifully decorated, following the manner of the late seventeenth century, in piercing with naturalistic foliate and floral patterns and with horn-playing and harping cherubs. The harp depicted is indeed most interesting for, although stylised, its form closely resembles that of the Irish harp of the period, a unique instrument recognised by its deeply curved forepillar and the method of playing in which the right hand was used to play the bass or longest strings.

John Teahan describes a special exhibition of a Texas private collection at the De Witt Wallace Decorative Arts Gallery, Williamsburg, Virginia, USA January 10 — October 12 1992.

*Pair of sleeve or cagework cups, Dublin 1696—98. Probably by James Thompson. 24 cm high.*

*Bread basket, Dublin c. 1755. James Warren. 35 cm overall length.*

*Selection of eighteenth-century freedom boxes in silver, gold and silver-gilt, length av. 8 cm.*

Another fine piece on exhibition was an octofoil salver, measuring twenty four inches in diameter. It was made by Thomas Williamson in 1734—35. The early eighteenth century was a period when relatively plain silver was popular, shape and proportions being relied on for variety and attractiveness. In the 1730s, however, symmetrical forms of chased and engraved decoration were introduced.

A bread basket, number 36, made by James Warren of Dublin about 1755 is a superb example of the rococo mode which was popular in Ireland after 1740. The style was of French origin and can be identified by its asymmetry which imbues it with a certain vigour and which gives a sensation of life and movement. Its subjects were both naturalistic and stylised. This basket is decorated in piercing and chased work depicting flowers, foliage, fruit, swirling scrolls and human masks.

One of the more historically interesting elements of the exhibition is the large number of freedom boxes — twenty-three in all. Those boxes were made to hold or to accompany the document granting the freedom of a city or guild to some distinguished non-resident or non-member. They were generally beautifully and exquisitely engraved with the name or with the coat of arms of the freeman and of the body by whom the freedom was conferred. The person who received the freedom of the city became an honorary citizen or freeman of that city and might be exempted from local taxes and tolls. The person who received the freedom of a guild became an honorary member of that guild. The boxes on show refer to grants of freedom by Dublin, Cork, Drogheda, Carrickfergus, Limerick, Derry (Londonderry), New Ross, Waterford, Wexford and Youghal and by the Corporations of Weavers, Sheermen, (Shearers), Hosiers, Cooks, Barbers, Smiths and, appropriately, the Dublin Company of Goldsmiths.

The accompanying catalogue by John D Davis, with its introduction and 118 entries, is an attractive, informative and well-illustrated production. It provides a commentary on the general styles and on the form and decorative details of individual pieces and sets the whole exhibition in its historical perspective.

*John Teahan.*

*John Teahan is Keeper of the Art and Industrial Division, National Museum of Ireland.*

# COLLECTING IRISH IN THE NEW YORK SALEROOM

**Homan Potterton**
reviews the sales of Irish
paintings and antiques in
New York last year.

Irish paintings, furniture, silver, and other decorative arts appear regularly – although not in any great quantity – in the New York auction rooms. Most items appear to have been in the States for some time, witness to the fact that for decades Ireland provided rich pickings for collectors and dealers from overseas. However, there is ample evidence that many of the Irish artworks which today appear at auction in New York find Irish buyers, telephone bidders (by satellite from Dublin, Cork or elsewhere in Ireland?) frequently winning out over those bidding in the saleroom and prices often greatly exceed the pre-sale estimates.

There were two quite spectacular examples of this during 1991. At a relatively minor sale of paintings in Sotheby's on 27 February 1991 (lot 276) a fairly typical (although good quality) Paul Henry landscape in the West of Ireland fetched $23,000 (about IR£14,000) against an (admittedly ludicrous) estimate of $3,000– $5,000; and over on Park Avenue, at Christie's, on 9 October 1991 (lot 4) a large and dramatic signed George Barret landscape that was estimated at $10,000– $15,000 was knocked down for $92,400 (IR£57,000).

Both works were being sold by institutions. The Barret was sold by the Youngstown Club, Youngstown, Ohio, to which it had been presented, as part of a collection of paintings, in the early 1960s. It was the only picture by Barret in the collection. Paul Henry's *Near the Twelve Pins, Connemara*, had been bequeathed to the Frick Collection by Artemise Redpath presumably with the intention that it would be sold (The Frick does not, as yet, feature masterpieces of Irish art!) and it must have been in America for some years – possibly even since the time Henry had exhibitions there around 1930. As a composition, it was more elaborate but somewhat similar to the *Lakeside Cottages* of the late 1920s in the Hugh Lane Municipal Gallery.

In the same sale at Sotheby's a beautiful society portrait by John Lavery (lot 210) sold for $16,000 (estimate $8–$12,000). It represented Miss Julia McGuire (in a ravishing apple-green dress) and had been exhibited at the R A in 1926 where it was widely praised.

Classical landscape *by George Barret.
Signed. (179.1 x 189.8 cm.) Sold at Christie's,
New York, 9 October 1991 (lot 4) for $92,400.*

Breton Girl *by Aloysius O'Kelly. Signed.
(42 x 33 cm.) Bought in at William Doyle
Galleries, New York, 17 April 1991 (lot 2).*

Respite from the Midday Sun, Brittany *by
Aloysius O'Kelly. Signed. (81.2 x 100.4 cm.)
Sold at Christie's New York, 23 May 1991
(lot 216) for $6,000.*

St Paul's from Waterloo, London
*by John O'Connor. Signed and dated 1879.
(83.8 x 135.9 cm.) Sold at Christie's,
New York, 21 May 1991 (lot 188) for $8,800.*

Paintings by Aloysius O'Kelly have turned up in New York auctions several times during the year and it seems at least possible that they all come from the same source. O'Kelly settled in New York in 1909 and remained there until his death in 1926 so it is not surprising to find his work in the New World. The pictures that have been sold during the past year have all been Brittany subjects which O'Kelly continued to paint throughout his life and most were fairly modest works. The first to appear was a small head-and-shoulders study of a *Breton Girl* at the William Doyle Galleries on 17 April 1991 (lot 2). With an estimate of $3–$5,000, it failed to sell. Then at Christie's (23 May 1991, lot 216) a much finer canvas, *Respite from the Midday Sun, Brittany* with an estimate of $10–$15,000 was knocked down for a very reasonable $6,000. Again at William Doyle (6 November 1991) two further works by O'Kelly appeared (lots 28 and 29): a seated *Breton Girl holding a Flower* and *By the Hearth*, a study of three Breton women sewing. With estimates of $1–$1,500 and $2–$4,000 respectively, the pictures sold at $4,500 and $5,700 and, however prized O'Kelly might be, neither painting was worth the money.

Among a sale of Nineteenth Century paintings at Christie's on 21 May 1991 (lot 188) was a signed-and-dated (1879) canvas by the Derry-born landscape and theatre-scene painter, John O'Connor, who had a successful career in London. This was a striking view of the *Thames looking towards St Paul's from Waterloo Bridge*. Strickland records a drawing of the same subject by O'Connor in the British Museum. The picture sold at Christie's for $8,800.

Within the field of Old Masters, two pictures of Irish interest passed through New York sales during the year – *A Portrait of a Knight in Armour* by the Florentine painter Cristofano Allori (1577–1621) that had been in the collection of the Earls of Milltown at Russborough (Sotheby's, 11 April 1991, lot 73) and a ravishing *Portrait of Lady Mornington* by no less an artist than Madame Vigée-Le Brun (Christie's, 22 March 1991, lot 654). Lady Mornington was, in fact, French but in 1794 she married the elder brother of the Duke of Wellington, Richard Colley Wellesley, 2nd Earl of Mornington having already borne him several children. But by the time Mornington became Viceroy of Ireland the couple had separated so perhaps the portrait (which, at $781,000, was probably

# COLLECTING IRISH IN THE NEW YORK SALEROOM

well out of reach of the National Gallery's Shaw Fund) was only peripherally Irish.

The embossed-paper pictures invented by the eighteenth century Dublin artist, Samuel Dixon, feature regularly in New York sales. Two pairs of them in typical japanned frames, catalogued as 'In the manner of Samuel Dixon', were included in a Sotheby sale of 'English Furniture and Decorations' on 18–20 April 1991 (lots 264 and 265). Against pre-sale estimates of $6–$8,000 for each pair, both lots fetched $7,000.

Good Irish furniture has been rarer in New York during the past year and the most interesting piece, a Gothic giltwood side table with a *scagliola* top (Sotheby's, 19 October 1991, lot 242) had been offered in the same rooms only last year when it was bought in at $100,000 (See Irish Arts Review Yearbook 1991–92, p. 226). This time round, when bidding climbed only to a miserable $60,000, it again failed to sell. In the same sale (lot 343) an attractive Irish George II walnut tea-table of about

*Mirror chandelier, late 18th century, signed by the Dublin maker John Aykboum. Sold at Sotheby's, New York, 19 October 1991 (lot 350) for $35,000.*

1735–40 fetched $7,250 against an estimate of $4–$6,000 while a beautiful and rare George III mirror-chandelier (lot 350) signed by the maker John Aykboum, whose business was on Grafton Street, Dublin went for $35,000 (estimate $12–$18,000). This was of the typical Irish type with an oval glass framed by facetted glass studs and a two light *girandole* hanging before the mirror from the top. At Christie's sale the same week (12 October 1991) a handsome George II Irish mahogany side table – quite plain but with a carved human mask centering the frieze (lot 82) – went for $9,900 (estimate $10 – $12,000). A pair of side tables in the same sale (lot 96) were catalogued as 'possibly Irish'. With black marble tops supported by lion monopedia supports, these were of the Italianate type made in Dublin about 1820 by Del Vecchio and other makers; but similar pieces were also made elsewhere – notably in Italy and indeed in America – so the exact origin of the tables was by no means certain. They

*George II Irish walnut Tea Table. Sold Sotheby's, New York, 19 October 1991 (lot 343) for $7,250.*

*George II Irish mahogany Side Table. Sold at Christie's, New York, 12 October 1991 (lot 82) for $9,900.*

*One of a pair of mahogany pier tables, possibly Irish, early 19th century. Sold at Christie's, New York, 12 October 1991 (lot 96) for $11,000.*

*Dublin Delft blue and white dish, c. 1755, possibly by Henry Delamain. One of two dishes sold at Sotheby's, New York, 18 April (lot 84) for $900.*

*Irish Delft blue and white bottle. c. 1755. Sold at Sotheby's, New York, 18 April 1991 (lot 99) for $1000*

*Irish Delft blue and white charger, 1760–70. Sold at Sotheby's, New York, 18 April 1991 (lot 91) for $900 (together with a Bristol plate).*

# COLLECTING IRISH IN THE NEW YORK SALEROOM

fetched a modest $11,000 (estimate $12 – $18,000). A pair of George II Irish mahogany side chairs in the same sale (lot 143) failed to sell (estimate $5 – $7,000). Irish eighteenth century Delft featured strongly in a sale at Sotheby's on 18 April 1991 but there were no bargains to be had. The most unusual item was a blue-and-white delft bottle of about 1755 (lot 99) which had been exhibited at the important exhibition of Irish delftware at Castletown House in 1971. The maker has not been identified but nevertheless the bottle – almost ten inches high – went for $1,000 (estimate $400 – $600). Two attractive blue-and-white oval dishes (lot 84) which had some stylistic similarity to the work of the most famous Dublin Delft maker, Henry Delamain, sold for $900 (estimate $400 – $600); a large platter in the 'Broken Scroll' pattern (lot 90) went for $1,400 (estimate $500 – $700); and a charger of about 1760 (lot 91) that was sold together with a Bristol plate fetched $900 (estimate $500 – $700).

Irish silver – some of it exceptionally fine – is always in good supply in New York but one of the rarest objects on offer during the past year – a dressing-table mirror by the Dublin maker John Humphreys 1991 (lot 337) failed to sell. Estimated at $30 – $50,000, it was 28 inches high and weighed 38 ounces with a shaped pediment surmounting an ogee-moulded frame. It was engraved with the coat-of-arms of Thompson impaling Wilmot and had come originally from the collection of Lord Swaythling. Another item of particular interest was a gold freedom box made

*Gold Freedom Box engraved with the arms of Castlebar. Irish, dated 1789. Sold at Christie's New York, 30 October 1991 (lot 113) for $15,400.*

in Dublin in 1789 and engraved with the arms of Castlebar and an inscription recording the grant of freedom to George Shea in that year. Just three and a half inches long, it sold at Christie's (30 October 1991, lot 113) for $15,400 (estimate $10 – $15,000).

Other silver prices during the year were as follows:

**William Doyle Galleries, 23 January 1991:** Pair of salvers probably by Charles Lemaitre, Dublin, approx 18 oz. ($1,500); Urn by Thomas Jones, Dublin, c.1781, 31 oz. ($1,100).

**Christie's, 18 April 1991:** Three-piece tea-service by Richard Sawyer, Dublin, 1808 and 1817, 37 oz. (B.I.); Tankard by Thomas Jones, Dublin, 1783, 44 oz., engraved with the arms of Carter ($6,600).

**Sotheby's, 19 April 1991:** Silver-gilt Claret Jug by James Fray, Dublin, 1836, 34 oz. ($2,000); Salver by Walter Archdall, Dublin, c. 1715, 17 oz. ($3,000); Two-

handled cup and cover by James Fray, Dublin, 1829, 40 oz. ($1,600); Pair of mugs by Joseph Walker, Dublin, 1696 – 98, 13 oz. ($2,750).

**William Doyle Galleries, 15 May 1991:** Coffee-pot, possibly by John Moore, Dublin, 16 oz. ($1,000); Sauce boat by William Townsend, Dublin, 7 oz. ($500).

**Christie's, 30 October 1991:** Cake basket by James Fray, Dublin, 1839, 51 oz. ($3,300); Meat dish by William Nolan, Dublin, 1820, 135 oz. ($7,700); Cake basket by Samuel Beere, Dublin, 1824, 51 oz. ($2,200); Pair of sauce boats by Charles Townsend, Dublin, c.1775, 21 oz. ($2,750); Pair of candlesticks by William Williamson, Dublin, 1737, 29 oz. ($6,050); Salver by Robert Calderwood, Dublin, c.1745, 57 oz. ($3,850); Silver-gilt dish probably by Richard Williams, Dublin, c.1770, 16 oz. (B.I.); Pair of waiters by Richard Garde of Cork, Dublin, 1832, 43 oz. ($1,760).

**Sotheby's, 31 October 1991:** Sauce boat by Richard Williams, Dublin, 1780, 23 oz. ($3,200); Four table candlesticks by William Williamson, Dublin, c.1750, 66 oz. ($6,000); Twelve pistol-handled cheese knives by Robert Calderwood, Dublin, c. 1740, 60 oz. ($9,000); Chalice probably by Isaac D'Olier, Dublin, 1729, 6 oz. (B.I.); Salver by Thomas Sutton, Dublin, 1741, 68 oz. ($5,000); Pair of two-handled cups by Richard Williamson, Dublin, c. 1750, 27 oz. ($3,750).

*Homan Potterton*

*Homan Potterton was Director of the National Gallery of Ireland from 1980 until 1988.*

*Silver tankard by Thomas Jones. Dublin, 1783. Sold at Christie's, New York, 18 April 1991 (lot 302) for $6,600.*

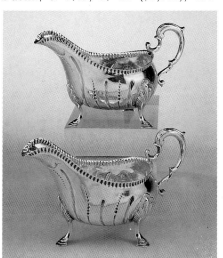

*Pair of silver sauce boats by Charles Townsend. Dublin, c. 1775. Sold at Christie's, New York, 30 October 1991 (lot 216) for $2,750.*

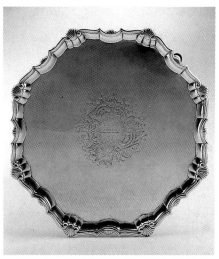

*Silver salver by Robert Calderwood. Dublin, c. 1745. Sold at Christie's, New York, 30 October 1991 (lot 235) for $3,850*

# IRISH ART IN THE LONDON SALEROOM

**Gertrude Prescott Nuding** reviews an interesting year in the London Salerooms, when Irish art prices began to stabilise.

Last year when contemplating this year's *Irish Arts Review Yearbook* article on the market for Irish art, it seemed that there would be little to write about — that is, in the traditional journalistic sense of 'newsworthy'. Christie's withdrawal from holding 'glitzy' evening sales within Ireland was a signal that expectations, both on the part of consignors and the auction house, had exceeded commercially profitable results. The unhealthy competitive pre-auction auctioning of reserves and estimates, that had been engendered by what was perceived as an aggressive effort to establish the London auction house on Irish soil, was about to outstrip the ready buying cash, given the general economic conditions. Indeed, speculators, both commercial and 'private', seem to have sat on their paddles for much of the year. And as the year progressed the heat was to be taken off the market — a healthy development in the eyes of long-term participants. Yet would enough quality works be enticed onto the market in order really to take a barometer reading of its state? And would evaluation of a particular work return to being based on quality rather than speculation against a previous price paid for any painting by X? Would leaner times reveal whether there was really an Irish market *per se* that was distinct from the general trends within the modern British market? Would misunderstandings arise from prices paid for 'Irish' works which had not been purchased for their 'Irishness'? And what would be the effect of unloading gallery stock during lean times?

One event of the year in the London market, which was both newsworthy and intriguingly revealing, was the sale of two eighteenth-century Irish landscapes by William Ashford, PRHA (1746—1824) at Christie's on 12 July 1991. Consigned by a private owner and appearing with hefty estimates of £120—150,000 and £100,000 —£120,000, *A Punt on the River Clodiagh at Charleville Forest, Co Offaly* and *Figures by a Weir on the River Clodiagh at Charleville Forest, Co. Offaly* sold respectively for £120,000 and £100,000. (Charleville Castle is a fine Gothic-revival castle, the creation of Charles William Bury, first Earl of Charleville, 1765—1835). Apparently bidding against the reserve (the room was noticeably still, with participants in the Irish market watching intently), London dealer Libby Howie purchased the paintings for a private Swiss collector; the buyer evidently was attracted to the paintings as examples of fine eighteenth-century landscapes available at what, in comparison to European landscapes of the period, appeared an attractive price. (To set the record straight, there was no truth to the post-sale rumour that the paintings were purchased for a Japanese collector of British art).

But observers of the Irish market were surprised that Christie's had, in the words of one dealer, been able to deliver what had been promised—an almost unheard-of price. The record for an Irish eighteenth-century landscape had been set at Christie's in New York on 15 January 1988 when a wooded landscape by Thomas Roberts the Elder sold for $230,000 or £130,000. The most recent auction price paid for an Ashford landscape was IR£8,000 (£7,692) paid at James Adam & Son on 17 May 1990 for a classical scene with cattle drovers and caravans. According to rumours which could not be substantiated, the trade had earlier offered a lower amount for the same Ashford paintings which Christie's had bettered subsequently in their estimate and suggested reserve, thereby winning the consignment.

On the back of the July success, Christie's then offered two Ashford landscapes in their 15 November sale: *A Mill near Lucan* (the more major work) and *Orpheus and Euridice in a Classical River Landscape* with estimates respectively of £50—80,000 and £6—8,000. Quite clearly the estimate for *A Mill near Lucan* (a subject which did not have the importance of the Charleville Castle paintings) had nonetheless been set with the July sale in mind. Previously it had been bought-in at the Irish auction house of Mealy's in Castlecomer, Co. Kilkenny, on 30 May 1991 at IR£37,000 against a more modest estimate of IR£35—40,000. Not only did the painting fail to attract specifically Irish buying once again, in crossing over from another segment of the art market it failed to secure a buyer at all, being bought in at £38,000. The second,

*William Ashford, PRHA, (1746—1824) A Punt on the River Clodiagh at Charleville Forest, Co. Offaly. Sold for £120,000, Christie's, London, 12 July, 1991.*

*William Ashford, PRHA, (1746—1824), Figures by a Weir on the River Clodiagh at Charleville Forest, Co. Offaly. Sold for £100,000, Christie's, London, 12 July, 1991.*

more minor painting also failed to sell at £3,800.

Thus, the prices paid in July for the Ashford Charleville Forest landscapes were understandable only when seen against the general market for eighteenth-century European paintings. Without an 'outside' buyer entering the specialised Irish market, high prices for any Ashford landscape could not be sustained.

At Christie's on 6 March 1992 an unexpectedly strong sale of Modern British and Irish Paintings, Watercolours and Drawings brought some cheer to art market participants, while escaping the general press's notice. Sir William Orpen's *In Dublin Bay*, a portrait of his wife Grace painted in 1909 standing on the windswept cliffs of Howth, was purchased by an overseas buyer for £125,000 ($231,375). Although larger, it is thematically a companion to *A Young Man from the West*, a self-portrait also painted in 1909, sold at Christie's on 8 November 1990 for £110,000 ($214,500), which also portrays a windswept, scarved half-length subject against a similar background. Alan Hobart of Pyms Gallery drew my attention to the fact that the two paintings had hung in the same collection until they were purchased by different buyers at Christie's in 1973; indeed, when Jonathan Horwich checked Christie's records, it transpired that both paintings had been purchased in 1909, by Francis Williams from the Goupil Gallery, although one in July and the other in December. In the 1973 Christie's sale the portrait of Grace had also secured the higher price (£6,500 or $17,063) with the *Self-portrait* (£4,200 or $11,025).

Two early Jack B Yeats's paintings from a series of twelve executed in 1913 as illustrations to George Birmingham's *Irishmen All*, sold to the Pyms Gallery — *The Police Sergeant* (estimate £20—30,000) for £44,000 ($75,108) and *The Minister* (estimate £20—30,000) for £45,000 ($76,815). In Christie's 9 June 1990 sale, two other paintings from the series sold to the Pyms Gallery, for a slightly higher average, indicating that some heat has come off the market: *The Greater Official*, estimate £18—24,000, sold for £48,000 ($75,840) and *The Exile from Erin*, estimate £20—30,000, sold for £58,000 ($91,640). The following week on 11 March at Sotheby's, a lovely Paul Henry

*Sir William Orpen, In Dublin Bay. Sold Christie's, London, 6 March 1992 for £125,000. (Companion to A Young Man from the West, see Irish Arts Review 1991—92, p. 233.)*

*Jack B Yeats, The Police Sergeant, 1913. Sold Christie's London, 6 March 1992 for £44,000.*

view of farm cottages with foreground detail and sailing boats sold for a solid price of £25,000 (estimate £6—8,000) again to the Pyms Gallery.

Buying was healthy elsewhere in the Modern British section of Christie's 6 March sale, where the quality and freshness of works justified interest. For instance, *Old Newlyn* by Stanhope Alexander Forbes sold to an anonymous buyer for £46,000 ($78,200), overseas telephone bidding competed for three John Singer Sargent watercolours (all estimated at £6—8,000) selling eventually to the same paddle for £13,000, £10,500 and £29,000. Spinks was the successful bidder, against the room and telephone, for Duncan Grant's *Portrait of Vanessa Bell* (recto) and *A Corner of the Inn, Kings Lynn* (verso) at £32,000 (estimate £14—18,000). John Nash's *Yarmouth Docks* (from the Estate of the late Cyril Franklin) sold over the telephone for £27,000 against an estimate of £10-15,000. At the time of the March sale, the Irish painting market was thus holding its own within the Modern British painting field. Indeed, the disappearance of the investment contingent has allowed the market for Irish paintings to stabilise without crashing and has opened the way for dealers and private collectors to make attractive purchases.

However by May some uncertainty surrounded the Yeats market due to rumours circulating regarding a group of paintings which had apparently been in the stock of Trinity Gallery, Jersey. This gallery had previously specialised in Scottish paintings and had entered the Irish painting market in 1988. Handled by a third (but interested) party, around twenty paintings from Yeats's late period had been offered widely on the market for around six months; they were sold (contrary to some rumours) for apparently realistic and strong prices to a consortium (rather than to specialised Irish dealers) some two weeks before the May sale of Modern British and Irish paintings at Sotheby's. Nonetheless, the prices were probably lower than the high prices which the dealer had been known to have originally paid; these purchases (which sources suggested had been made with considerable loans) had helped fuel the market for Yeats's work to its peak. Observers were concerned about what would happen to the Yeats market if the group remained unsold, or sold at low prices, or if the pur-

# IRISH ART IN THE LONDON SALEROOM

chasers were to put the works back onto the market yet once more in the near future.

The separate business, Trinity Gallery Ltd in London, incorporated in June 1990 went into receivership on 27 January 1992. Its receiver placed lesser Modern British Works in a Bonhams Lots Road sale on 23 April; these were valued for the most part at less than £500 each. More important (non-Irish) works were to be included in Bonhams (Knightsbridge) regular sale of Modern British paintings on 15 July, after this article went to press.

This uncertainty apparently affected the prices paid at Sotheby's 13 May sale for works by Yeats consigned by other vendors. The large (24 x 36 inch) 1920 canvas *The 'Haute Ecole' Act*, estimated at £70—80,000, sold for £80,000; in a more confident market it might have fetched £120,000. *Dawn, Holyhead*, (1920) sold for £33,000 against an estimate of £30—50,000 — an estimate which might have been exceeded. *The Handcuff Queen* (1925), sold at the low estimate for £40,000. *The Sisters*, (c. 1923) appearing with a very high estimate of £20—30,000, given its small size and minor status, was justifiably bought-in at £14,000. (A spokesman for James Adam & Son observed that the May results showed that

*Jack B Yeats*, The 'Haute Ecole' Act, 1920. *Sold Sotheby's, London, 13 May 1992 for £80,000.*

Irish paintings 'are best sold on Irish soil'). All in all, the market for Yeats (defying some predictions) did not crash and seems to have held modestly, against the odds.

The Yeats prices may have been helped by the confidence engendered by a strong British painting section of the sale. To a room crowded with the important buyers within the Modern British market, three important paintings from the late Lord Walston's collection sold well (Edward Burra's *War in the Sun*, estimated at £80—100,000 sold to a telephone buyer for £180,000; Laurence Stephen Lowry's *Industrial Landscape*, estimated at £150—

200,000, sold in the room for £155,000; Sir Stanley Spencer's *Seated Nude*, portrait of his first wife Hilda, sold in the room for £220,000 against an estimate of £180—250,000. Towards the close of the sale, Spencer's *The Daughters of Jerusalem* sold to a telephone buyer for £350,000 (estimate of £250—350,000).

The decreased activity by speculators over the past year should provide the Irish art market with much-needed breathing space. A small market, it is highly susceptible to the presence and absence of single major buyers. The responsible development of the market will depend on the various players' sensitivity, and ability to read the signs sensibly and not simply be lead upward or downward by the published (or indeed rumoured) results.

*Gertrude Prescott Nuding*

*Dr. Gertrude Prescott Nuding has written on the art market for various publications, including* The Art Newspaper, Art & Auction *and* Apollo, *since 1988. She came to England in 1982 as a Fulbright Fellow, has held curatorial posts in the United States and England, and has lectured on the history of prints, photography and collecting. Her chapter 'Britishness and Portraiture' was published this year in* Myths of the English, *edited by Roy Porter (London, Polity Press). She is currently working on a history of the art market in recent decades, with an eye towards the approach of the twenty-first century.*

# ART SALES IN IRELAND

**Robert O'Byrne** reviews
sales of Irish art and antiques
around the country, and notes
some surprises.

*Sir John Lavery, Sok el Lechina (lot 78).
Sold for £19,000 (est. £12—15,000) at James
Adam, Dublin. 29 May 1991.*

If sales may be taken as an indication of the country's economic health, then Ireland has been in severe recession over the past year. Not only were the prices realised for work at auction sometimes substantially lower than those which would have been achieved in the late 1980s, but the quality of work submitted was also often quite evidently poorer. Coming together, these two factors have left the trade both less buoyant and more pragmatic, which, as some members would acknowledge, is not necessarily a change for the worse.

The year covered here began with one of several attractive house contents sales, at Alma in Monkstown, Co Dublin which had been occupied by several successive generations of the same family and therefore had the now-rare charm of furnishings acquired over a long period of time. The mixture of Georgian, Victorian and Edwardian items sold for a total of over £100,000 with the top price of £5,800 being made by a Victorian D-end dining table. A handsome Irish mahogany hunting table with drop leaves went for £3,800 — somewhat less than its top estimate of £5,000 — while a pair of Victorian burr walnut side cabinets reached £4,600 (estimate £2,500—3,500). Two major picture sales in late May — at Taylor de Vere and James Adam respectively — suggested that, provided the work on offer was of sufficiently high calibre, the market would remain buoyant. The artist whose paintings fared best in both auctions was Leech; until now it has seemed as though he has been overshadowed in the salesroom by more popular twentieth-century Irish painters such as Yeats and Lavery. At James Adam, the latter's charming *Sok el Lechina* made £19,000 (estimate £12—15,000) while Yeats' *And the Sky over it* reached its upper estimate of £12,000. But the day's top price of £21,000 was achieved by Leech for a fine oil painting *Fishing Boats, Concarneau;* two other pictures by the same artist sold for the very respectable figures of £14,000 and £10,000.

Perhaps it was the fickleness of fashion which determined that Nathaniel Hone's attractive *Cows at pasture, Malahide* failed to sell at its bottom estimate of £3,000 even though the picture was to be included in the National Gallery's forthcoming retrospective of the artist. Another artist due a retrospective later in the year, Mainie Jellett, was represented by a fine oil which went for £13,500. And Micheal

MacLiammoir's original design for the dustjacket of his 1952 book, *Put Money in Thy Purse,* which incorporated portraits of the author, Hilton Edwards and Orson Welles amongst others, made £2,500.

At the Taylor de Vere auction, Leech again achieved the day's top price of £17,000 for his *Sunlight in a Snow-covered Landscape,* painted in a more subdued palette than is usual for this artist. William Scott's *Green with Envy,* a four foot square canvas, estimated at between £20,000—30,000 failed to find a buyer, despite the resurgence in popularity which had followed his death a year earlier.

Another equally large picture, *Stormy Beach, Feathanair, Co. Kerry* by Maurice MacGonigal, whose retrospective opened at the Hugh Lane Municipal Gallery in July, made £12,000, while his *Cleggan* went for £8,200. And a sombre-hued Norah McGuinness, *Oyster Catchers,* which had been sent in by former Taoiseach Garret Fitzgerald, made £2,600.

In Belfast, John Ross's mid-July sale saw about one-third of the works on offer fail to find a buyer. Predictably, amongst those which did sell, the top prices were netted by Northern Irish artists, with William Conor's *Fair Day* reaching £10,000 while pictures by Colin Middleton and George Campbell made £5,800 and £5,300 respectively. Pictures were also included in an auction at Mealy's of Castlecomer which made a total of more than £400,000 in the day's sales. Not that all the deals were concluded at the auction; the two

best prices for paintings were actually the result of private buying later, when £16,000 was paid for Yeats' *Young Ass by the Lake* and £15,500 for Frank McKelvey's *A Grey Day.* Amongst the furniture, a rather extraordinary French carved giltwood and painted boat-shaped wine cooler/jardiniere made £10,000 and a fine George III mahogany and marquetry secretaire cabinet sold for only £1,000 less. Towards the end of July, Mealy's came to Dublin, hosting a sale of silver at the Gresham Hotel, where the total value of the day's sales was £138,000 for almost 400 lots.

Included amongst these were some excellent examples of Irish workmanship, such as a pair of George III sauceboats made by Collins Brehon in Limerick around 1765 and a pair of George III baluster-shaped armorial wine ewers or jugs, made by Richard Williams of Dublin probably around 1770; these made £8,250. A rare pair of silver-plated barrel-shaped wine coolers, originally from the Hely-Hutchinson estate at Knocklofty, Clonmel went for £2,200. The Co Tipperary town had a connection with the item which, although not silver, achieved the day's highest price. This was a 22-carat gold George III freedom box, engraved with the arms of Clonmel and inscribed to Lieutenant General Sir Eyre Coote, KB and KC; it sold for £9,500.

More silver turned up at James Adam's sale of period furniture and Victoriana in early July, when a snuff box by Nathaniel Mills reached £400 and a pair of oil lamps presented to the Earl of Wicklow by the Second Life Guards, £2,700. And at Thomas P Adams Dublin sales around the same time, a set of four George III table candlesticks made by John Carton in 1776 was sold for £4,000.

Later in the month, the contents of another country house went to auction as Mrs Reginald Farquhar sold up Ardsallagh, near Fethard, Co Tipperary, where she had lived since just after the Second World War. Best-known for its exceptional gardens, Ardsallagh also held a distinguished collection of pictures built up by Mrs Farquhar and her sporting relative, Van de Vater. In the event, many paintings — by overseas artists such as John Bratby, Marcel Ducret and Bertram Priestman — failed to reach their estimates, possibly because these names were unfamiliar to Irish buyers. On the other hand, a set of four Regency carved wood

# ART SALES IN IRELAND

and gilt lights made the day's top price of £13,200 (estimate £8,000) while a set of five early nineteenth century giltwood and plaster pelmets reached £4,000.

Another private house was the source for a fine collection of furniture by James Hicks of Dublin which Mealys auctioned at Castlecomer on 30 July. Bought directly from Hicks in the late 1940s, the items fetched a total of £56,000 with the day's best price going to a George II-style Irish mahogany 'mask' table, some six feet long; at £17,000, it sold for more than double its upper estimate of £8,000. A Chinese Chippendale-style carved gilt and gesso wall mirror also went well above its estimate to reach £14,200.

In early August, the 27th annual Irish Antique Dealers Fair opened in Dublin's Mansion House with about twenty-eight members represented. The single most expensive item was offered by Paul Cooke, whose stand held a magnificent Bossi inlaid marble fireplace from No 6 Merrion Square priced at £250,000. Kenyon's had a lead and gilt maquette by John Van Nost the Younger of his George II statue, first erected in St Stephen's Green in 1758 and, after many vicissitudes, finally blown up by the IRA in 1937. Kenyon's also offered two statues matching those outside the Shelbourne Hotel; these were bought by entrepreneur Harry Crosbie and relocated outside his Point Depot on the Liffey quays. After the event, dealers commented that while business was down on previous years, there had been an increase in private domestic buyers venturing back into the market.

Coinciding with the fair, Dublin's George Gallery had an auction of Irish art, where the highest price was made by George Campbell, whose *My Window, Palo* went for £4,250, while his *Musicians, Virginia* sold for £3,500. A curiosity of this sale was the inclusion of twenty-three pictures by George Campbell's younger brother Arthur, well-known in Northern Ireland thanks to his work for newspapers and magazines. Although far less familiar in Dublin, his paintings sold surprisingly well at prices ranging from £2—800.

After a relatively quiet August, Christie's hosted an auction in Belfast Castle on 18 September where 77 per cent of the approximately two hundred lots were sold for a total of £248,000 sterling. The star of the sale, a painting called *The Carnival* by John Luke, only mustered bids up to half of its £30,000 estimate and remained

*One of a pair of library chairs, early 19th cent. (lot 803). Sold for £38,000 (est. £4—6,000) at Clobemon Hall, Co. Wexford. Hamilton Osborne King. 11 September 1991.*

unsold. William Conor, always popular in Belfast, was represented by two works, one of which, *The Farmers Race*, went for £16,000 (estimate £12—15,000), the day's best price. The second biggest price was for a Rose Barton watercolour, *The Turkey Girl*, which made £13,000 (estimate £10,000). Four of the six Daniel O'Neill pictures offered for sale found buyers, the best at £4,800.

Later that month, Hamilton Osborne King disposed of the contents of Clobemon Hall, Ferns, Co. Wexford, the former home of Commander HFP Grenfell. At an auction where more than £500,000 was spent, a pair of mahogany framed library chairs in the style of Thomas Hope far surpassed their estimate of £4—6,000 to reach £38,000.

Indeed, estimates seemed to count for little, as a Regency mahogany dining table on three pods went beyond the upper expectation of £10,000 to make £22,000, just as a massive pair of Chinese export fish tanks mounted on carved giltwood stands sold for £17,000 (estimate £8—12,000). An original watercolour by Snaffles (Charlie Johnson Payne) called *Where ye'd be say sick wid leppin'* made £7,800. Meanwhile, at Roseboro House, near Naas in Co Kildare, Mealy's realised more than £300,000 in a house contents auction which included a superb George IV breakfront mahogany library bookcase

originally from the Coddington family's home, Oldbridge House. This made £12,000, although the top price of £15,000 was achieved by a seventeen feet long Aubusson tapestry depicting a hunting scene. An early eighteenth-century Irish portrait of Jonathan Swift made £7,000.

Yet another house auction, although on a more modest scale than those in September, was conducted by Mealy's on 1 October at Annagh Lodge near Nenagh, Co Tipperary. This really was an old-fashioned sale, with everything down to the farm machinery being offered to buyers. Indoors, a William IV mahogany breakfront library bookcase made £4,000, while a library table of the same period went for £4,000. On the same day, Taylor de Vere held its autumn picture auction where the best price was, once again, made by a William Leech, whose *Sunlight on Sails, Concarneau* went for £17,000. Niccolo d'Ardia Caracciolo's *Capel Street* sold for £5,500, believed to be a record for this artist at auction, but other paintings fared less well, many failing to find a buyer, most notably a fine Walter Osborne, *Roundstone Harbour*, which carried a pre-sale estimate of £15—20,000. On the other hand, a rather whimsical Osborne portrait of a little girl, *Miss Mollie*, went for £18,000 at the following day's James Adam sale, and made the best price of the auction. An early Le Brocquy watercolour of *Tinkers Camping* made £3,400, but a similar pair of pictures by the same artist failed to sell subsequently. A curious book illustration *Boy and Girl on Achill* by Norah McGuinness, clearly under the influence of Harry Clarke, went for £350, substantially less than its £6-900 estimate. But then her gouache of New York Harbour made £3,200 (estimate £2—2,500) and a Roderic O'Conor coastal landscape went for twice this top estimate of £5,000.

Further surprises lay in store at what was intended to be the highpoint of the autumn season, the auction of the contents of Castletown Cox, Co Kilkenny. These, together with the house itself, had been bought earlier in the year from Ulli de Breffny by London-based merchant banker George Magan. Although £500,000 was spent, the two finest pictures, a pair of oils by Peter Jacobs Horemans, estimated at £40—50,000, failed to secure a buyer. The day's top price accordingly, was just £15,000 for an

# ART SALES IN IRELAND

elaborate Venetian silver gilt and poly-chrome painted cabinet. Several other items of furniture testified to the Italian interests of the late Brian de Breffny, such as a pair of ornate marble plinths, origin-ally from the Villa Demidoff in Florence, which went for £13,000 and a North Italian giltwood side table, sold for £10,000. So much had been hoped for this sale, run jointly by Christie's and Hamil-ton Osborne King, that the many hun-dreds of visitors to Castletown Cox were inevitably surprised when the quality of items in the auction failed to match popu-lar expectation. Fortunately, expecta-tions were simpler and so more easily met at the next country house auction, that of Streamhill, near Doneraile, Co. Cork, the contents of which were sold in mid-October. Of the approximately 400 lots, the best price was made by a pair of George III satinwood and marquetry card tables, sold for £9,000 (estimate £4—6,000). A Regency brass inlaid centre table also went above its £3—5,000 esti-mate to reach £5,500. One curiosity of this sale was a Killarneywood work table by James Egan, which had been on display for a number of years at Muckross House in Killarney; this made its top estimate of £5,000.

The following month saw another house contents sale at Longford House, Co Sligo, home of the Crofton family. Bad weather was blamed for the poor turnout which led to more modest prices than had been hoped for by the auctioneers. A set of sixteen Hepplewhite-style ladderback dining chairs, including two carvers, sold for £11,000. A fine Edwardian inlaid rosewood chiffonier made £4,600, just under its top estimate of £4,800. More furniture came up at Mealy's of Castle-comer auction in mid-November, includ-ing a George III-style satinwood and marquetry Steinway grand piano; this went well over the £12,000 expected, to make £20,000. A Georgian-style carved-gilt and gesso wall mirror, which had been positively attributed to James Hicks, also did well to sell for £8,500. This contrasted sharply with a mere Hicks-attributed five-piece satinwood suite of seat furniture; despite its fine qualities, it made only £2,600.

At Sheppards of Durrow, Co Laois, mean-while, the November auction brought a top price of £3,500 for two separate items: a rather overly ornate walnut and mar-quetry kneehole desk and a Louis Quinze

*Snaffles*, Where ye'd be say sick wid leppin'. Sold for £7,800 at Clobemon Hall, Co. Wexford. Hamilton Osborne King. 11 September 1991.

*Nicolo Caracciolo*, Capel Street. Sold for £5,500 at Taylor de Vere. 1 October 1991.

*W J Leech*, A Crystal Morning. Sold for £21,000 (est. £18,000) at Taylor de Vere. 3 December 1991.

ormolu-mounted walnut and ebony *bureau plat*. Disappointing sales were realised by an auction of surplus contents from Emmel Castle, Co Offaly, held in Blackrock by Hamilton Osborne King, where some items had come originally from the Mala-hide Castle sale of 1976. These included an *English Portrait* of the Talbot family (sold for £1,100) and a Jack B Yeats wash, which fetched £800.

In Dublin's National Concert Hall, Taylor de Vere held its winter auction on 3 December, selling approximately two-thirds of the 142 lots on offer. Yet again, the top price was made by a William Leech oil; *A Crystal Morning* surpassed its upper estimate of £18,000, to reach £21,000, although another picture by the same artist, *Cedar Tree*, failed to attract bids near its £7—9,000 estimate and went unsold. Equally disappointing, Maurice MacGonigal's *Loading Turf* (estimate £5-7,000) also went down unsold, as did an example of Patrick Collins work. On the other hand, perhaps because of the retro-spective just opening at the Irish Museum of Modern Art or because of their pro-venance from the personal collection of the late Victor Waddington, all eight of Mainie Jellett's works on offer sold at prices between £1,400 and £4,200; the latter for her *Study for Achill Horses*. But despite the recent Edward McGuire retrospective at the RHA Gallery, his portrait of Eamon Morrissey (estimate £10—12,000) was another picture which failed to find a buyer. Similar problems were faced at the winter sale at James Adam a week later, when about thirty per cent of the work remained unsold. The day's best price was achieved by Walter Osborne's *A Breton Courtyard*. Despite some pre-sale doubt over its authenticity, it went well past a top estimate of £10,000, to make £28,000. Almost as good, a small Yeats, *Old Timers from Frisco* sold for £26,000 (top estimate £24,000).

Another French subject, *Breton Woman Cleaning Pans* by Aloysius O'Kelly did less well, just making it to the lowest esti-mate of £14,000. Maurice MacGonigal's *Charlemont Mall, Dublin* went for £3,800, well below its £5-6,000 estimate, while Louis le Brocquy's *Woman*, dating from 1957, which had been expected to reach up to £20,000, failed to sell at all. Mealy's held a pre-Christmas book auction in Dublin at which the most interesting item was an original manuscript of W B Yeats' poem *The Lake Isle of Innisfree*. The

## ART SALES IN IRELAND

National Library had been negotiating to purchase this, but in the end it went to a private buyer for £7,500, respectably above its £3-5,000 estimate. The National Library did manage to buy about thirty other lots, mostly manuscripts of Irish interest, while in London, the same institution paid stg£4,950 for a working 'prompt' copy of Brendan Behan's *The Quare Fellow*, dating from the play's first production at Dublin's Pike Theatre in 1954.

January 1992 saw the appearance of the main salesrooms' annual reports for the previous year; a consistent note of pragmatism was evident as James Adam's review explained that 'unlike previous years, few outstanding works were on offer due to a cautious approach on the part of vendors.' Similarly, Taylor de Vere's report spoke of 'inferior quality' and 'too many lots', but suggested a growing interest in contemporary Irish art, while James Adam emphasised the rise in popularity of women artists such as Mainie Jellett and Grace Henry, both of whom would obviously have benefited from the previous winter's retrospectives.

Meanwhile, the 1992 sale season opened quietly with an auction of silver at O'Reilly's of Dublin, where the top price of £4,500 was paid for a pair of George II cast candlesticks dating from 1736/7 and made by Dublin silversmith John Hamilton. A George II coffee pot, also from Dublin and manufactured around 1730, made £4,000. At the end of January, James Adam held its first furniture auction of 1992, not as had hitherto been the case in the basement of the St Stephen's Green house, but on the first floor where picture sales have always taken place. Approximately eighty per cent of the lots sold for a total of some £120,000, with the day's best price of £6,200 being made by a nineteenth century Irish hunting table, eight feet long and showing evidence of much good use but handsome nonetheless. A kingwood vitrine with Vernis Martin panels fetched £4,800, while a Victorian brass club fender, still with its original seating, made £2,500. At Thomas Adams of Blackrock in mid-February, a picture sale included a fine example of Frank McKelvey's work, *Lake Reflections* which went for £9,400, although it was beaten for top price, as had been expected, by an equestrian portrait by English painter John Ferneley, going for £10,500. Irish art respectably held its own: Patrick Hen-

nessy's substantial still life went for £7,000 and a typical Nathaniel Hone, of grazing cattle, made £4,000. Mealy's sale in late February offered a huge variety of items, many of them coming from Limerick's Presentation Convent. In the midst of much bric-a-brac, an eighteenth century continental parquetry cylinder *bureau de dame* made the day's best price of £4,750 — considerably better than its £2—3,000 estimate — while a George III-style inlaid mahogany display cabinet went for £4,000. A week later, Fleury's of Cahir, long-established as a successful antiques business, held the first of what is intended to be a regular series of auctions on its premises. From more than 460 lots, the best price was made by a Georgian Adam-style white marble fireplace. A nineteenth century boulle table went for £3,100 and a very fine Sevres bowl and cover made the very reasonable price of £2,900.

The first Taylor de Vere picture sale of 1992 came a day later at the National Concert Hall when, as was expected, an exceptionally good example of the youthful Mainie Jellett's work, *Bathers*, made £14,000 (top estimate £15,000). Another Irish woman artist, Norah McGuinness, was represented by *The Long Road*, sold for £5,200, while Grace Henry's *Achill Landscape* made £4,500. Yet another Nathaniel Hone Malahide landscape, complete with its customary grazing cattle, fetched £6,500, a price closely rivalled by Daniel O'Neill's *Sisters*, which went for £500 less.

O'Neill, predictably, turned up again at Ross of Belfast's Spring auction, though his painting of *The Bridesmaid* failed to find a buyer at the sale; seemingly, it was later sold privately for £5,000. Mildred Anne Butler's oil *Tramore Strand* did best, making £7,000 (estimate £4—5,000), while a classic Paul Henry Connemara landscape fetched £6,500.

Back in Dublin, James Adam's Spring auction of pictures turned up another Paul Henry which, despite its modest dimensions and thin painting, made £10,000. An exceptionally good Walter Osborne, *Potato Gathering*, did best at £33,000, but the most interesting painting in the sale was a view by James Hore of Dublin's Four Courts looking across the quays and dating from 1837. This fascinating piece went for £24,000, while another historical document — Flora Mitchell's watercolour of Parnell Square

— was bought by the Hugh Lane Municipal Gallery for £3,000. A James Arthur O'Connor *Recollection of the River Bray*, made a respectable £19,000, but William Leech's first-rate *The Orchard* surprisingly only went for £10,500 — somewhat below its top estimate of £12,000.

Hamilton Osborne King held an auction of silver on 1 April though no foolish prices appear to have been paid. A handsome and heavy coffee pot made by James Warren of Dublin around 1750 went for £3,600, while a plain silver salver, made by David King of Dublin c.1714 fetched £3,300. A circular and very substantial tray inscribed to Lieutenant-Colonel Blacker by the Armagh Yeomanry, which had been made by William Nowlan of West's in 1819, went for its lowest estimate of £4,000.

At Mullen's of Bray a pair of matching china cabinets in painted satinwood, made £4,000 — somewhat less than their upper estimate of £6,000, but a fair enough price. A Wooton desk, similar to that owned by Charles Stewart Parnell which was sold a few years ago, failed to find a buyer willing to pay even the lowest estimate of £4,000.

Meanwhile, Sheppard's of Durrow achieved an excellent price of £10,000 for a nineteenth century Killarneywood davenport by James Egan which carried a view of Muckross Abbey, Killarney, on its sloped writing front. Another James Egan piece, a Killarneywood and marquetry games table, again depicting Muckross Abbey, made a more modest £2,600 and a mahogany inlaid display cabinet reached £4,000. At the end of the month, Fleury's held its second auction in Cahir with mixed results. An excellent equestrian portrait by John Nost Sartorius reached its estimate of £8,000, but a bronze equestrian statuette by Pierre Jules Mène made nowhere near its top estimate of £5,000, going for just £2,000. Similarly, a pair of Jeanselme Père et Fils rosewood occasional chairs from the late nineteenth century sold for £800 (pre-sale estimate £1,200—1,500). While these prices were modest, they bore out the reality of an altogether more difficult market than existed in Ireland just a few years ago, and proved that in the salesroom, there can be no certainties.

*Robert O'Byrne*

*Robert O'Byrne is a freelance writer and critic.*

# BOOK REVIEWS

## THE SELECTED WRITINGS OF JACK B YEATS

Edited by ROBIN SKELTON
André Deutsch, 1991.
£12.99 sterling. 247pp.

## THE LITERARY WORKS OF JACK B YEATS

By JOHN W PURSER
Colin Smythe, 1991
(Princess Grace Irish Library – 5).
£25 sterling. 224 pp

Jack Yeats, besides being a painter, wrote and published several prose works during his lifetime, as well as some plays. Three of the novels were reissued about twenty years ago, shortly after the *Collected Plays* were published posthumously. Yet while interest in his pictures had been escalating during the years since his death, Yeats's writings have still not been given the attention they deserve, and for this reason alone Robin Skelton's selected edition is welcome.

In his choice Robin Skelton comes down heavily in favour of the prose, giving excerpts from *Sligo* and all the novels with the exception of *Ah Well* and allowing too much space perhaps for the sporadic articles of the early period in the *Manchester Guardian*. He edited *The Collected Plays* in 1971, now out of print. Here he confines himself to two examples of what he then so aptly called the 'plays for larger theatre', including an excerpt from *The Silencer,* and giving the greatest of the plays, *In Sand,* in full. But an example from the early miniature melodramas to fill out the picture is missing in this volume; and there is a slight drought also without a paragraph or two from that whimsical and parabolic romance, *Ah Well,* published in 1942.

Prose or drama, the examples given are teasing, charming, thought provoking; and apart from their importance as literary pieces, often described as minimalist because of their obscurity – they throw much light on Jack Yeats's paintings, and his way of painting. It was Robin Skelton who originally wrote with such insight of Yeats's writings in terms of 'unarrangeable reality' (W B's phrase) in *The World of W B Yeats* in 1965; and it is curious that he has little more to say here despite the amount of criticism and biography published in the meantime. It is misleading, if not careless, to put Yeats's illustrations willy-nilly throughout the

text without any note as to what they are, or proper attention to the new context in which they find themselves. Nevertheless, he still writes about both prose and drama with an enthusiasm and pleasure that is infectious and rewarding; and the volume should be an encouragement to those coming new to Yeats's writings to seek out the books and plays for themselves, and make sure that those out of print are republished.

John Purser, like Robin Skelton, is inclined to bypass the early miniature plays, apart from a few references, and to concentrate on the late writings. His book is of particular interest being from the hand of a great-grandnephew of Sarah Purser, artist, friend and collector of Jack Yeats, and one of the clan whom Jack Yeats's father called 'distinguished', 'intellectual' and 'infallible critics'. John Butler Yeats told another contemporary that the Pursers were critical and scornful, 'and what is called "superior". All the same they understand – no real excellence escapes them'; and his observation is still valid. Though John Purser's intellect cannot be suppressed in his approach to the writings, muffling what Yeats himself regarded as essential to any subject, 'affection' (which Purser has), he does communicate his appreciation of their real excellence. His book is a marvellous and meticulous work of literary criticism, perhaps a cornerstone of Jack Yeats studies, where no detail is ignored, and everything possible explained, with a sensitivity to Yeats's personal idiosyncrasies, and to his background in Dublin. With all of this background John Purser, by reason of his own descent, is familiar. He writes with a dry wit and perspicacious view.

In contrast to Skelton, he emphasises and enjoys the late plays. Steeped in the political tensions in Ireland during the government of De Valera in the 1930s, he reads a lot of political sentiment into them. His exegesis of *Harlequin's Positions* is fascinating in this respect; though perhaps he makes too much of Yeats's antipathy to Bernard Shaw (after all Mrs Shaw was one of Jack Yeats's patrons and had only just bought another of his pictures). Nor does he see the ironical humour in Yeats's remarks. Indeed in the analysis of the plays there is a tendency to brood on the material preludes to each work, and to neglect the investigation of the spiritual elements. (This neglect is fully compensated for in the analysis of the novels.)

Anyone who saw the performance of *In Sand* in 1964 could not fail to have been impressed by the underlying reference in the theme to the words of consecration in the Eucharist, yet while quoting Brian O'Higgins's description of it as a 'Christian play' Purser has not observed this.

One of the most valuable aspects of his study is the attention he gives to the possible dating of the writings (mainly during the 1930s). I hope a subsequent edition of the book will tell more about the manuscripts, if even to the detriment of its admirable concision. His dating concurs with Yeats's contemporaneous performance with the brush. The 1930s were lean years for Yeats's painting, the period from 1931 to 1935 being especially so, and after two quite good yields in the next two years, the paintings became fewer between 1938 and 1941, after which he entered the most prolific painting phase of his life. Purser also appreciates the paintings, and one of the pleasures of the book is the carefully chosen colour illustrations, not always correctly referred to – (for example *The Barrel Man* shown is not the version published in *Life in the West of Ireland*) – but admirable as a reminder of the breadth and internal complexities of Yeats's genius. Purser interestingly notes the tidal shape of Yeats's prose structure.

While providing a spicily argumentative and exhilarating account of Yeats's writings, with usefully slanted insights, and enough latitude to intrude his own personality entertainingly now and then, the author does not sufficiently convey the lyrical, painterly quality of Yeats's writing. Particularly when reviewing *Sligo* and *Sailing Sailing Swiftly*, both of which can be read purely for the joy of the ebb and flow of words, the author's inherited critical gift (acknowledged fully in the final chapter) comes to the fore. More too could have been made of the melodramatic origins of *Sailing Sailing Swiftly* (whose origins form the basis of the emotion and apparent inconsequentiality in other works as well); and here I felt that Purser's ignoring the importance of the early juvenile melodramas was an oversight. Yeats liked the melodrama, popular in his youth, for its entertainment value; but he recognised its wisdom as emanating from the core of life's tragedy, romance, absurdity and humour. His drama derives from that popular mould, manipulating its age-old knowledge in a pro-

# BOOK REVIEWS

vocative way which is not always successful (as Purser has noted). Similarly Yeats's novels and *Sligo* (I cannot accept that it is a novel, nor is a sufficient case made for this claim!) are, according to Yeats's own statements, rooted in his own life and thought. Their nature as creative explorations of life itself (one of the reasons for Yeats's preoccupation with death, life's completion) – which parallels Joyce's work, and, as Purser points out, Yeats's contemporary drawings in the volumes called *Lives* – has yet to be drawn out to the full. In the writings' enigmatic reflection of life's body and spirit, as John Purser has proposed and sensitively demonstrated, Yeats's real genius reveals itself. Yet at the same time, Yeats continued to maintain that painting was man's freest and noblest form of expression!

*Hilary Pyle*

## THE TIME GATHERER: EL GRECO AND THE SACRED THEME

PATRICK PYE
Dublin, Four Courts Press, 1991. £17.50

El Greco dominates the artistic panorama of late sixteenth and early seventeenth century Spain. Considered as a Spanish painter, though born a Greek on the island of Crete which was then under Venetian rule, he trained in the Byzantine tradition of the icon painters. In his early twenties he travelled to Venice, which was then in the vanguard of painting, where he absorbed the brilliant use of colour and showy brushwork of Titian and Tintoretto. He moved to Rome where he seems to have had little success in obtaining commissions, but had the good fortune to be admitted to the sophisticated and learned circle at the palace of Cardinal Farnese, where humanism and classical learning were dominant interests. There he met a young Spanish cleric, Luis de Castilla, whose father, Don Diego, was Dean of Toledo Cathedral and who invited him to Spain to undertake his first major commission, the high altarpiece and two lateral altars for the convent of Santo Domingo el Antiguo. Almost overnight El Greco, then in his late thirties, matured into a painter of genius. In Toledo, which was the ecclesiastical capital of Spain, he found patrons and a stimulating intellectual climate. He remained there until his death in 1614, painting great altarpieces for churches and convents and producing numerous small devotional works in his busy workshop.

*The Time Gatherer* has the particular interest that its author, Patrick Pye, has an established reputation as a painter, etcher and stained-glass maker of religious subjects. He is one of a number of artists – Oisin Kelly, Imogen Stuart, Patrick Pollen, Helen Maloney, Paddy McElroy – who worked on the decoration of the numerous churches which were built or renovated in Ireland during the 1960s and 1970s, a period of diocesan expansion. As Pye himself states, 'this is not a life of the artist. It is not, properly speaking, a critical study of the body of his work. It is purely speculation' (p. 15). It is, in fact, a philosophical exploration, by way of El Greco, of what it is to be a painter of Christian subjects. For Pye, El Greco is the time gatherer of European painting. 'He holds within his art the points of intersection of all Europe's diverse strands – between the mysticism and the humanism of Catholicism itself, between the historical sense and the sacred, between East and West and between Middle Ages and Modernity.' Pye gives us some interesting insights into certain concerns and anxieties, notably the isolation in which the Christian artist must work in today's materialist society in which he experiences the loss both of tradition and of a community of ideas and language. This results in a lack of meaningful exchange of ideas between artist and patron and between artists themselves. Pye sees Byzantine and Medieval art as a golden age. Subsequent periods like the Renaissance and Baroque, he interprets as somehow lacking in spirituality. He accords El Greco quasi-official status as a renovator of art in the Church according to the ideals of the Council of Trent. But the fact is that El Greco remained a unique talent – he had no true disciples – and the Church, of necessity, employed a range of artists working in a variety of styles. At the Escorial, the building that most exemplifies the spirit of the Counter-Reformation, the most orthodox of Catholic kings, Philip II, employed Italian mannerists as well as Spaniards working in a naturalist style. *The Martyrdom of Saint Maurice* which he commissioned from El Greco for the basilica was a failure, precisely because it lacked those key qualities associated with the dictates of Trent on art – decorum and a sense of piety.

El Greco ran into difficulties with other clients, usually due to his tendency to take liberties with iconography. A notable case is the *Espolio*, or *Disrobing of Christ*, for the sacrtisty of Toledo Cathedral. This is one of six paintings (*The Assumption, Two Saints John, Crucifixion, Resurrection* and *Laocoon*) which Pye has chosen to discuss in detail. The cathedral chapter criticised the painting on grounds of textual inaccuracy – (the Three Marys were not present at the disrobing) – and lack of decorum – (the heads of the mob should not be shown rising above that of Christ). El Greco took liberties, but this hardly justifies Pye's treating the *Disrobing*, commissioned appropriately for a sacristy, as an *Arrest of Christ*. El Greco has chosen the tense moment just before the executioners begin to strip off his garment prior to Crucifixion – the cross is being prepared in the foreground. The 'green-clad thug' (on the right) is not 'binding' Christ but beginning the disrobing. If scripture is to be quoted then it should relate to the scene portrayed – the cry 'Father, forgive them . . .' (Luke 23:34), was not uttered until Christ hung on the cross. That Pye can in such detail and with such conviction describe the mistaken scene underlines his deep subjectivity, and indeed the variance between the historian's emphasis on accuracy and the artist's on creativity. Mind you, it behoves the artist of scriptural subjects to encompass both values, even in these permissive days.

'Crete gave him his life, and brushes; Toledo, a better land, where he begins with Death to attain Eternity.' Thus wrote Paravicino in a funeral lament for his friend. El Greco's career is a vivid example of the importance of timing. He found a new and exciting visual language which was capable of revitalising the representation of Christian themes. His was a unique talent – he left no disciples – yet he was able to function within the normal social context of his time. His style was controversial yet he was recognised and appreciated. How very different is the situation for the painter of sacred themes today, who has to deal with ecclesiastical patrons who are rarely well versed on matters relating to art. He must struggle in an increasingly secular world to find a new and appropriate means of expression.

*Rosemarie Mulcahy*

*Dr Rosemarie Mulcahy lectures in History of Art in University College, Dublin.*

# BOOK REVIEWS

## THE COLLECTED POEMS OF JOHN HEWITT

Edited by FRANK ORMSBY
Blackstaff Press, Belfast. £25

When John Hewitt died in 1987 he left behind him a considerable body of published work and forty-seven number-ed little black notebooks containing many unpublished poems and first drafts. Much of his early work in particular had only been published in long defunct periodicals and socialist papers, so it was an immense task for Frank Ormsby to pro-duce the 540 pages of poems and the fur-ther 150 pages of annotations in this volume. For lovers of poetry and of Ulster, this book is a delight, since Hewitt was a master craftsman who dedicated much of his life to giving a sense of identity and pride in their birthplace to Ulster people of Planter stock. He accomplished this not only through his writings but also through his encouraging artists to set up a regional school. For twenty-five years John Hewitt worked in what is now the Ulster Museum, rising to be its Deputy Director and Keeper of Art. In 1953 he was passed over for the directorship because, in the eyes of the Unionist con-trolled corporation who made the ap-pointment, he was too mixed up with socialists and Roman Catholics. The last fifteen years of his working life were spent as Art Director of the Herbert Art Gallery and Museum in Coventry. On his retirement, he returned to Northern Ireland and continued to involve himself in the literary and artistic life of Belfast. As well as several volumes of verse he published monographs on the artists Col-in Middleton and John Luke. This article, then, does not set out just to review a volume of poetry but also to show the im-portance of Hewitt's position as a link be-tween poetry and art in Ulster, by linking some of the pictures in the John Hewitt Collection in the Ulster Museum with the poems written throughout his life.

One of the most valuable things that Ormsby has done for the Hewitt scholar lies in his careful annotation and dating of the early drafts as well as of the publish-ed versions of the poems. His biograph-ical chronology helps to place events in Hewitt's life with phases in his poetic and and artistic development . This is useful in tracing the growing friendship between the young graduate in English and the art-ists working in Belfast in the thirties and

W J McClughin, Portrait of John Hewitt, Ulster Museum.

forties. Thus we find that his friendship with Colin Middleton and John Luke dates from 1934, when he helped found, and acted as secretary to, the Ulster Unit, a regional progressive art group. The previously uncollected poem Roll Call is included in the appendix and gives us a lively pen picture of the two artists.

> One, the dynamic symbolist, because
> while I but half discern his nature's laws,
> he gives with lavish fist and will not stay
> content with revelation yesterday,
> still pressing out the frontiers of his mind
> and leaving me amazed to drag behind,

That was Middleton, then of Luke he wrote,

> the tall dark painter who
> no careless line or lazy contour drew,
> who sees life steadily, asserting still
> the heart-uplifting structure of a hill
> against the peevish threat and sullen whim
> that make a crazy quagmire of the time.

In these few lines we see Hewitt's personal and professional evaluation of the two men — the art critic and friend are at one. Among the previously unpublished work there is also a short poem in memory of Luke, To any dweller in Lewis Street, which praises his clear precision and 'delicate economy'.

Another friend from his early days was William McClughin. John considered that McClughin's pen and ink sketch of him caught his likeness better than other later, more considered portraits. At the same time Luke did a portrait of Roberta Hewitt, the 'vivid being' her husband describes in Clogh Oir with the

> black tossing head, the dark brows,
> as intense and definite as now.

Another portrait in the collection is McClughin's picture of Robert Hewitt,

John's father, who was the greatest in-fluence on his early life, as many of the sonnets in the autobiographical sequence Kites in Spring testify. The poet's friend-ship with McClughin did not blind him to his defects as an artist. In the poem dedicated to him he is described as

> This slow, private man, a paradigm
> of small singular disasters

Besides his physical disadvantages, his artistic abilities were choked by his ex-cessive attention to theory.

> A certain gift for colour, tone,
> offered some memorable themes,
> paper selected, brush contrived,
> the proven pigments organised,
> close-printed words, discussion, thought,
> which only eked a few filled frames
> the niggard yield of thwarted skill.

Although the art critic in Hewitt saw all too clearly what was wrong with McClughin the artist, he still valued him as a friend and treasured the works which he did produce.

William Conor (1881–1968) belonged to an older generation and was the first local artist to catch the young Hewitt's imagination with his pictures of the Belfast that both knew so well

> You, Conor, were the first of painting men
> whose art persuaded my young eyes to see
> the shapes and colours which gave quiddity
> to the strange bustling world about me then;
> and if I would recall those days again,
> yours are the shadows which companion me,
> the shawled girls linked and stepping merrily,
> the heavy-footed tread of Islandmen.

Conor's picture The Elder Sister must have appealed to Hewitt not just because of its evocation of Belfast types but also because of the relationship it shows be-tween brother and sister. John himself was a loved younger brother whose sister Eileen

> always was
> protective sister for a timid boy;
> half-roads to Mother

As ever the personal and the professional interest in art are closely linked.

In contrast to his life as a city-dwelling museum man, John Hewitt found rest and inspiration in the Glens of Antrim, where he and his wife rented a cottage for many years. The collection entitled The Day of the Corncrake is set in the glens, and this volume contains also some un-published poems celebrating the area, which well repay reading. The artist James Humbert Craig had a house in

# BOOK REVIEWS

Cushendun and painted much of the surrounding countryside. In *Glendun* Hewitt wrote

*I saw the valley patch by coloured patch,*
*potatoes, oats and grazing, flax and hay,*
*the whitewashed houses with rain-shabby*
*thatch,*
*the bigger houses, slated blue and grey,*
*the shorn sheep nibbling round the mounds*
*of gorse,*
*the red calves at the gate, the lonely horse,*
*and one man rowing slow across the bay.*

It could be a description of a Craig painting.

The last painter who influenced Hewitt was Fredrick Hull, a Belfast businessman and watercolourist. In *The Lagan in October* Hewitt described how he loved to paint on the river bank and how it was

*autumn which rinsed his vision, roused*
*his heart*
*to exaltation in the visible world*
*till his little panels, six by eight,*
*brimmed with quiet joy.*

Colour, the shape of a leaf, the felicitous matching of form with feeling, these were what appealed to Hewitt all his life. He had difficulties with the values of many later contemporary artists

*For cautious critics now define*
*a work of art as something said*
*to be just that; a coil of twine,*
*a plank with nails, a broken bed,*
*a tray of plastic gingerbread.*

In his poetry and in his art criticism he expected good workmanship, observation and fidelity to life. He clung to these values in a world where they were steadily becoming eroded, so that towards the end of his life he could look back and

*recall behind the placid verse*
*a man still stands whose attitude declares*
*his loyalty to hope, unquenched belief,*
*despite the incidence of age or grief,*
*in men's rare-hinted possibility*
*of being just, compassionate and free.*

A poet who could write this after living from 1972–1982 in Stockmans Lane in south-west Belfast must be worth reading. I can only end by urging readers to buy this splendid book and take it with them on a visit to the art collection in the Ulster Museum. Read the poems, look at the pictures and ponder with humanity and understanding on the present state of affairs in the North of Ireland.

*Geraldine Watts*

*Geraldine Watts, a native of Belfast, now long resident in Dublin, is a former teacher who has an M Litt (TCD) on the life and works of John Hewitt.*

## ART IS MY LIFE: A TRIBUTE TO JAMES WHITE

Edited by BRIAN P KENNEDY.
National Gallery of Ireland, Dublin, 1991.
IR£35, hardback.

Pulled from its Germanic roots, the *Festschrift* is a curious plant. It has traditionally provided the opportunity for pupils and colleagues of a distinguished departed professor to present a series of essays in his honour. In many cases the research contained in the resulting volume has been initiated or inspired by the person to whom it is dedicated. In one or two recent instances in the United States, the editors of these collages have insisted upon guiding principles, and have arranged the contents to demonstrate this. An example is *The Documented Image, Visions in Art History*, (1987), a series of essays in honour of Elizabeth Gilmore Holt, the pioneer revisionist art historian in North America. Elaborate dedication footnotes are common in a country where scholars are not afraid to acknowledge sources and where citation is welcomed by publishers.

It says much for the maturity of the arts in Ireland that there are figures like James White to celebrate. As Director of the National Gallery of Ireland from 1964 to 1980, art has been his avocation. As an employee of John Player and Sons, rising through the ranks to assistant manager, White was utterly atypical. Scribbling art criticism in evening and lunch-hours, he was actively involved in the Dublin art scene from the 1940s onwards. The break came in 1960 when he left Players to become Director of the Municipal Gallery of Modern Art. After a brief period of tenure when he staged exhibitions of the work of painters like Charles Lamb and Sean Keating, he moved to the National Gallery of Ireland.

Brian P Kennedy, editor of the volume of essays, *Art is my Life*, published in his honour, contributes a biographical sketch of James White, which describes the high points in his career — his building programme at the National Gallery, and the consequent dramatic rise in attendance figures which accompanied his period of office. White was ever energetic, combining management skills with the enviable ability to proselytise and provide leadership. Michael Wynne, in a lucid essay, reports upon the notable acquisitions of Irish art made during his directorship. Yet White was not confined to parochial patronage and, almost single-handed he made, in the words of Denys Sutton, 'an old fashioned gallery' into a leading European museum.

The essays now published in his honour are a mixture of scholarship and reminiscence. The volume's greatest concision lies in two poems, Seamus Heaney's *The Biretta*, from *Seeing Things* (1991), and Paul Durcan's *The Crucifixion* — both derived from celebrated National Gallery images. John Montague's paragraph on Gerard David's *The Judgement of Cambyses* reminds the reader of Auden's *Musée des Beaux Arts* in its focus upon the atrocious incidental details of Flemish painting of the late *quattrocento*. These volatile mixtures of memory and desire sharpen and cleanse the palate between courses of rambling eulogy and scholarly *politesse*. Reminiscences of White's early years are fascinating. Marian Burleigh-Motley, Louis le Brocquy and Tony Gray take us back to earlier times when White was prominent in the Living Art Exhibitions, and when he brought the International Association of Art Critics to Dublin. But perhaps the most interesting of these spotlights on White's early career is provided outside the framework of recollection by Bruce Arnold in *The Turning Point for Irish Modernism*. This charts Mainie Jellett's contribution to the Glasgow Empire Exhibition and to the New York World's Fair in 1938 and 1939. With consummate mastery, Arnold locates Jellett in time and space — the tense times which Auden summoned in the *In Memoriam for W B Yeats*, as 'the nightmare of the dark' when 'all the dogs of Europe bark.' The clarity of Jellett's voice at this time, her admiration for *Guernica* and her sympathetic understanding of Braque, were a beacon in the blackness. White's role in this was that of a bit-player who would only in later years come to occupy centre-stage.

Of the art historical contributions there are some which lead to fascinating conclusions. Eileen Kane, for instance, summarizes twenty years of her own research, in which she successfully attributes the *Avignon Annunciation*, one of White's first purchases for the National Gallery. In a similar vein, Robert Rosenblum presents the case around works by David and Bachelier. Alistair Rowan writes up the Irish Claudes — Hugh Lane's bequest of *Juno confiding Io to the care of Argus* and Lady Dunsany's loan of

# BOOK REVIEWS

*Hagar and the Angel* — pictures which, as the details indicate, are surprisingly complementary. Rowan relates these works to alternative versions and connects them, with elegant efficiency, to the pen drawings of the *Liber Veritatis*.

Both Raymond Keaveney and Brian P Kennedy select aspects of the Chester Beatty collection to discuss. Keaveney considers the little-known illustrations by Pierre Thomas Le Clerc for Desmarais' poem *Jérémie*. These, as he points out, derive from seventeenth century sources, although in several instances, in details of architecture and facial expression, they hurl the visually literate forward to D¹acroix. Kennedy's essay on the 'collecting technique' of Chester Beatty is more problematic. He cracks Beatty's codes for the qualitative grading of objects — a practice not uncommon at a time when connoisseurship aspired to science. Beatty's ambition was to better the British Museum in his chosen fields, but without the visual comparisons, and some study of taste and values in Beatty's markets, it is impossible to form a view of the critical faculty of the great collector. In this respect the stature of his impressionist paintings might provide a more accurate barometer — but to what end?

*Art is my Life* contains a group of essays related to early modernism. This sequence begins with a reprint of Denys Sutton's essay on *Degas and George Moore*, summarizing the known literature upon a fascinating relationship. There is a slight discourtesy here to the pioneering work of Anna Gruetzner who is cited as Kate Gruetzner. In this subsection Homan Potterton and Hilary Pyle provide contributions based on their specialisms in Hone and Yeats, while Julian Campbell steps momentarily out of character to consider Leech's monumental *Convent Garden*, presented to the National Gallery of Ireland by Mrs Bottrell in 1952.

The most interesting and wide-ranging essay in this group is Nicola Gordon Bowe's survey of the Friends of the National Art Collections of Ireland. This informative account should now be given depth and context, since it is so indicative of the art debate in Ireland through the dark ages of de Valera. The art community in these years was a small one, its members sustaining their interests by visiting one another's collections. In the 1970s, when the Irish Association of Art Historians was being formed in James

White's boardroom in the National Gallery, this practice was again revived. The art community at that stage still consisted of furtive *carbonari* waiting for the *risorgimento*. The Friends' contribution to cultural politics in Ireland is only accessible through a sense of the wider phenomenon of pressure groups and preservation societies active in the arts throughout western Europe. Its history is not a provincial one.

This *Festschrift* demands more mental gymnastics than most. It moves with ease from a consideration of picture frames to the poetry of suffering humanity. It is a miscellany which may irritate some readers, although each of the sections will have a particular resonance for their recipient, James White. All of the authors in the book will have directly experienced his boyish good cheer and his generous encouragement. For my part, for the record and by way of a small tribute, I recall first meeting White in Dublin in the 1970s, but the most memorable time was at the end of the decade in Leicester. I was there for a stint of external examining and was pulled into a celebrity lecture by my Hibernophile hostess, Mary Stewart. White, with customary panache, held the floor on the history of the National Gallery of Ireland and his part in adding to its collections. There were lots of good stories to tell. In the dinner which followed we two unlikely guests were engulfed by the Leicester *hoi polloi,* and James, who had sung so tunefully for his supper, was obliged to continue throughout it.

*Kenneth McConkey*

*Kenneth McConkey is Professor of Art History and Head of the Department of Historical and Critical Studies at Newcastle upon Tyne Polytechnic.*

## BERANGER'S VIEWS OF IRELAND

with text by PETER HARBISON.
The Royal Irish Academy, Dublin 1991.
IR£19.95 paperback, £30 hardback.

Gabriel Beranger (1729–1817) is the best known of the topographical artists that worked in Ireland in the second half of the eighteenth century. His activities were well documented in the last century by Sir William Wilde (Oscar's father) and collections of his watercolours are preserved in both the Royal Irish Academy and the National Library. Beranger was a Huguenot who settled in Dublin in 1750, where for a time he sold prints and kept an

artists' warehouse at number 5 South George's Street. He established a reputation as a reliable antiquarian artist, at a time when interest in Irish antiquities was in its infancy. Among his patrons were Charles Vallancey and William Burton Conyngham, two of the founder members of the Irish Antiquarian Society. The artist was a popular figure in Dublin society, with a reputation for relishing 'Irish fun'.

Sometime between 1781 and 1791, Beranger prepared two large albums of watercolours, probably with the intention of having them engraved and published. One of these albums, belonging to the Royal Irish Academy, forms the basis of the volume under review. Forty-seven of the watercolours (out of a total of ninety-one in the whole album) have been reproduced, with an introduction and commentaries by Peter Harbison. The result is an attractive and well designed book, which will bring pleasure to a wide audience. The illustrations include a variety of castles, abbeys and other monuments, many of which have either been demolished or substantially altered. Particularly memorable is a delightful picture of Swords, showing a supposed attempt to measure the height of the round tower. There is an unusual illustration of the walled town of Kilmallock, with the ghostly silhouettes of the medieval ruins spread out across the page, as well as an early view of Howth harbour. The latter was used as evidence in a planning enquiry last year, underlining the historical interest of Beranger's work. The archaeological value of the paintings is thus not in doubt, but how does Beranger rate as an artist?

Only twenty-six of the ninety-one watercolours in the album were prepared from Beranger's own sketches. Like many artists of the day, he made a practice of copying and recycling the drawings of others, which makes it difficult to assess his style. Where he follows competent topographers like Jonathan Fisher, the compositions are quite forceful, but much of his material was decidedly amateur. It is hard to disagree with Strickland's comment that Beranger was 'a painstaking draughtsman and an accurate delineator of ancient buildings; but beyond that his powers were limited and his landscapes devoid of any artistic feeling'. His buildings, which are often poorly proportioned and erratic in perspective, look rather 'toy-like', particularly when set in the bare

# BOOK REVIEWS

open landscapes which the artist favoured. As Peter Harbison observes, even the great Norman motte at Knockgraffon (Tipperary) ends up looking like a haystack. These failings are compensated by the artist's taste for fresh, bright colours, more obvious in the originals than in the reproductions (many of which have a brown/purple cast). Moreover, Beranger's figure drawing was quite accomplished and his animals are depicted with verve. There was one animal, Sir William Wilde noted, that 'he drew to perfection . . . the good old Irish pig'. While Beranger's views are enjoyable to peruse, it is important to remember the gulf that existed between his rather amateur approach and contemporary landscape artists like William Ashford, working in oils.

The Academy album was prepared at about the time that Francis Grose was embarking on his great study of Irish Antiquities. It is curious that the authors of Grose made no use of Beranger's watercolours, especially as he had travelled extensively in Ireland. Was this because they had a poor opinion of his work or was Beranger deliberately trying to keep his collection together to publish it himself, as Peter Harbison suggests? Indeed it is just possible that the Academy album was an attempt to compete with Grose.

Beranger's watercolours will remain an important source for archaeologists and architectural historians and it is a pity that finances were not available to publish all the pictures in the album. This would have had the merit of saving the originals from too much handling. The selection of views was made for a general audience, who will find Peter Harbison's commentaries an enjoyable read, though in two cases (pages 54 and 64) there is confusion over the viewpoint (north and south reversed). Nor is it quite correct to say that, whereas we have Beranger's views in colour, Grose's Antiquities will always remain in black and white. Many of the original watercolours, from which the Grose engravings were made, are in fact preserved in another volume in the Academy's library, a volume which contains a good cross section of paintings by Beranger's contemporaries. Perhaps the Academy could be persuaded to publish this as a companion volume to the Beranger?

*Roger Stalley*

*Roger Stalley is Professor of History of Art in Trinity College Dublin.*

*The Dominican Priory, Kilmallock, c. 1830, as illustrated in the new edition of Peter Harbison's* Guide to National and Historic Monuments of Ireland.

### KILMALLOCK DOMINICAN PRIORY, AN ARCHITECTURAL PERSPECTIVE 1291–1991

ARLENE HOGAN
Kilmallock Historical Society, 1991. Price £6.00.

In contrast to the informal, not to say unplanned, lay-out of the early Irish monastic sites, the orderly rectangular plan of Ireland's later medieval monasteries owes its introduction to the continental religious orders who arrived in Ireland in the twelfth and thirteenth centuries. Following the idealised St Gall plan of about 820, the new system was organised around a square or rectangular cloister, with a long church on one side (usually the north), and the 'business' buildings of the community around the other three. The Cistercian Abbey founded at Mellifont in 1142 is the country's earliest surviving example. But in the ensuing century, other orders — prime among them the Franciscans and the Dominicans, as well as the Augustinians and Benedictines — followed suit in utilising the same basic design. In his 1987 monograph, Roger Stalley made a detailed study of Ireland's Cistercian houses, and thirty years earlier the Franciscan style of architecture in Ireland was examined in a series of detailed articles by the Rev Canice Mooney, in the *Journal of the Royal Society of Antiquaries of Ireland*. But that other great order of mendicant preachers, the Dominicans, have hitherto lacked a similar champion to highlight their particular contribution.

But now Arlene Hogan has entered the lists and taken a first — and hopefully not her last — step in the right direction, with the appearance of her book on the Dominican Priory at Kilmallock, in south County Limerick, founded in 1291. It was by no means the first Dominican foundation in Ireland, but its remains can be counted among the finest to survive the ravages of time and, in its heyday, it was probably also one of the richest under the patronage of the FitzGerald White Knights. Mrs Hogan's work is certainly the most detailed and extensively illustrated discussion of any of these Irish Dominican houses, the others being usefully enumerated chronologically and mapped in colour in one of her appendices. She has painstakingly collected the scattered and scanty information on the history of the priory and, after a detailed description of the existing buildings, goes on to discuss their three main structural phases. These start with the long, halled church and the cloister dating from shortly after the foundation, followed subsequently by the constructions of the south transept for which she cogently argues a date of around 1320, and ending with the insertion of a tall, slender tower into the church during the fifteenth century. In the discussion which follows, she traces the influence from the west of England in the first two phases, rightly pointing out that, in the first phase, it took a long time for it to filter through to County Limerick. In the second, fourteenth-century, phase, that influence was more immediate and, through the illustration of a telling parallel from Frampton-on-Severn for the fine reticulated south window (surely one of the glories of the Priory), she even suggests the involvement of an English mason in the construction of the south transept. The third phase, the tower, is more typically Irish, borrowing some of its features from the Franciscans.

She reveals the same story, too, in the architecturally sculpted heads, which are more numerous and of a higher quality than in many of the Irish foundations of the Irish mendicant orders. Cashel is one of the many places cited as providing parallels, though it is perhaps a little surprising not to find mention of the rich collection of carved heads decorating the Cathedral at Cashel, of which there are many fine photographs in the archives of the Office of Public Works in Dublin.

If I have any cavil with this book, other than the occasional lapses in proofreading (e.g. the spelling 'masonary' three times, and the omission of part of a sentence in the third last paragraph on page 39), it is with the quality of repro-

# BOOK REVIEWS

duction of the numerous and very useful black-and-white photographs, one of which – Pl. XXXIII – is inserted upside down. Most of the photos suffer from that widespread Irish malaise of appearing to have had skimmed milk poured over them, a consequence – it seems to me – of many Irish printers having largely lost the art of good black-and-white reproduction after the introduction of colour printing presses which have, however, done a fine job on the striking front cover. As usual, it is only the line drawings which have managed to escape the plague – and they stand out by their quality.

Mrs Hogan is to be congratulated on a well-written and extensive exposé of the building history of the Priory, in both its architectural and sculptural aspects. But tribute should also be paid to the support which she received from her sponsors and, in particular, the Dominican order and the local Historical Society, whose small museum stands beside the bridge and path now leading to the Priory, which provide today's visitor with an easier access to the subject of this book than the earlier method of approaching it across fields, whose irate owner is said to have threatened potential trespassers with a blast from his shot-gun!

*Peter Harbison*

*Dr Peter Harbison is Editor of* Ireland of the Welcomes *and author of* Guide to National and Historic Monuments of Ireland *(3rd ed., 1992) and* The High Crosses of Ireland, *3 vols. (1992).*

### IRISH TYPE DESIGN:
### A HISTORY OF PRINTING TYPES
### IN THE IRISH CHARACTER.

DERMOT McGUINNE
Irish Academic Press, Dublin, 1992. IR£35.

Meticulous research, abundant references, and a full bibliography and index make Dermot McGuinne's study of Irish Type Design a work of scholarship. Its value is enhanced by the quality of its 150 illustrations, many of which are reproduced on a cream ground. The use of a second colour (sponsored by the printers, Colour Books Ltd) combined with the generous margins and uncluttered layout (book design by Jarlath Hayes) make it a handsome publication.

The tradition of book production in Ireland originated in the fifth century with the need of Patrick and his companions for a supply of texts for church use.

Two native writing styles emerged; one majestic and rounded with short ascenders and descenders, the other angular, compressed and with a vertical feel. The former was used as a display script and reached its perfection in the Book of Kells. The latter, less formal and used initially for notes and glosses in Irish, came to predominate after 1000 AD. The angular, spiky style is characteristic of all the surviving manuscripts in the Irish language, and when the first attempts were made in the late sixteenth century to produce a typeface for that language, it was modelled on this script. The author shows how, in the four hundred years that followed, the angular forms dominated Irish typefaces, though some designers looked back to the rounded letterforms of the Latin manuscripts as a basis for their new fonts. This study also shows how religious and, to a lesser extent, political considerations influenced the development of different printing types through the years.

The discussion of Queen Elizabeth's Irish type includes this quotation from Ware's *Annals of Ireland.* under the year 1571:

> *This year the Irish characters were first brought into this kingdom by Nicholas Walsh, chancellor of St Patrick's in Dublin ...and it was ordered that the prayers of the Church should be printed in that language and a church set apart in the chief town of every diocese, where they were to be read, and a sermon preached to the common people, which was instrumental to convert many of the ignorant sort in those days.*

In the early seventeenth century the scholarly community of Irish Franciscans, in exile at Louvain, published devotional works in Irish and it was for one such, *The Catechism of Bonaventure O'Hussey* printed in 1611, that the first truly Irish typeface was prepared. This was modelled on contemporary handwriting, most likely, the author suggests, that of O'Hussey himself. Many of the community moved to Rome where their publication work continued now linked to the Counter Reformation and the Vatican's Polyglot Press, which sponsored the design of what is called Rome Irish type.

In 1671 Robert Boyle, Earl of Cork, caused type, largely modelled on the Louvain font, to be cast in London. It was used for publications of the Reformed Church including the first edition of

William Bedell's translation of the Old Testament, published in 1685. The first font known to have been cut and cast in Ireland was produced by the Stephen Parker foundry in Dublin in 1787 and used for Charlotte Brook's *Reliques of Irish Poetry* (1789). The publication of this book and the works of Colonel Vallancey led to a surge of scholarly interest in the Irish language and, consequently, to an increased demand for type. With the passing of the Act of Union there was renewed attempt to promote the Reformed Church in Ireland. This led both the Hibernian Bible Society and the British Bible Society to commission two new fonts which are called Watts and Fry after their designers.

George Petrie (1790-1866), antiquarian, musician, scholar and artist has designed what many consider one of the finest of all Irish types. The letters he produced represented a complete break with tradition in being modelled not on mediaeval Irish hands but on the script of the eighth and ninth-century majuscule Latin gospel books. It was fitting that such a significant development should have been used for what was the Irish publication event of the century, namely John O'Donovan's seven-volume edition of the *Annals of the Four Masters.* In a most enlightening chapter, Dermot McGuinne shows how Petrie was also the designer of a traditional angular face. This, he argues, should be called Newman Irish type as the design was commissioned by John Henry Newman (later Cardinal) rector of the Catholic University of Ireland.

The author's mastery of his subject is evident in his survey of Irish printing types of the late nineteenth and early twentieth centuries. He provides many examples and proves that the Newman type provided the basic model, not only for those produced in Ireland, but also for the fonts used in Gaelic publications in the USA and Australia. Another interesting chapter follows, on Colum Cille type, wherein Dr McGuinne, using many illustrations and hitherto unpublished correspondence, shows how Colm O'Lochlainn (1892-1972), scholar, typographer and printer in the 1930s, researched, designed and contended with the Monotype Corporation to produce Colum Cille type. The hitherto little known part played by Karl Uhlemann in the origination of this elegant rounded type is also touched upon. The appearance of Colum Cille renewed the debate on spiky versus round style Irish type but soon another argument was to overshadow everything. Dermot McGuinne entitles his last chapter 'The Roman versus the Irish Character' and begins it by pointing out that the first recorded book printed in Gaelic used roman type. It was a translation of John Knox's *Forms of Prayer* published in Edinburgh in 1567 (Roman type remained predominant for printing Gaelic in Scotland). He presents the arguments of earlier times for and against and the compromises arrived at by evangelisers and scholars. He points out the tendency in the early days of the State to use Roman type for Irish on official documents and, although Mr De Valera's view is not given, it is interesting that the new constitution of 1937 was printed in Irish type. The discussion continued into the 1960s when a last attempt at compromise was made by the typographer and publisher, Liam Miller. He used Times Roman as a base replacing the lower case *t* and *f* with Gaelic style characters. Monotype produced a font which was used for some pamphlets and for the Dolmen Press edition of *An Béal Bocht* (1964).

Today the availability and use of transfer lettering, sophisticated computer design programmes and the inspired adaptations of ancient forms by lettering artists such as Michael Biggs mean that the search continues for the ideal type to print Irish. For anyone remotely interested in Gaelic texts, letter forms, or fine printing Dermot McGuinne's book is indispensable.

*Timothy O'Neill*

*Timothy O'Neill is a historian and calligrapher. His publications include a survey of the Irish manuscript tradition* The Irish Hand (1984) *and* Merchants and Mariners in Mediaeval Ireland (1987).

## DANIEL GROSE (c 1766—1838): THE ANTIQUITIES OF IRELAND: A SUPPLEMENT TO FRANCIS GROSE

Edited and introduced by ROGER STALLEY. Dublin, Irish Architectural Archive, 1992. Hardback IR£35.00, paperback IR£19.95.

On the twelfth of May 1791, Captain Francis Grose—five feet nothing, twenty-two stone, militia officer, Richmond Herald, antiquary, prodigious imbiber of food and drink in the company of like-minded topers such as Robert Burns — went to dine at his friend Horace Hone's house in Dublin and appropriately dropped dead of an apoplectic fit before reaching the table. Grose's reputation had already been made by *The Antiquities of England and Wales* (1773—6) and *The Antiquities of Scotland* (1789—91). Burns dedicated to him the comic narrative poem *Tam O'Shanter*, which combines gothic horror with heavy drinking. But Grose left unfinished the projected *Antiquities of Ireland*, on which he had been working sporadically for over ten years. While he drew and painted his own illustrations. Francis Grose also taught his servant Thomas Cooking to draw and paint. He was not alone in this practice; the Welsh antiquary and naturalist Thomas Pennant employed a self-taught artist, Moses Griffith, as his personal valet on his travels. Francis might also have instructed his nephew, Daniel Grose, a Captain in the Royal Engineers. Strickland, incidentally, calls him Daniel Charles Grose. Along with the London publisher, Samuel Hooper, Daniel took on the daunting task of completing his uncle's work, which came out in instalments beginning in 1791. Eventually, two volumes of engravings with commentaries by the Reverend Edward Ledwich were brought out in 1794 and 1796. Daniel Grose settled in Ireland, dying at Carrick-on-Shannon in 1838. Many of his antiquarian drawings were acquired by the National Library of Ireland, and that was thought to be that.

However, in July 1989 Lord Rossmore happened to walk into the Irish Architectural Archive, bringing from his library a hitherto unknown manuscript volume, written by Daniel Grose and illustrated by eighty-nine of his own watercolours. It transpired that Daniel Grose's unfulfilled intention had been to have this engraved and published as a third volume or supplement. He left it too late, for his publisher was dead, and by the 1830s his pedestrian Georgian style had been overtaken by the work of a younger generation of topographers like Petrie, Nicholl and the Geological Survey. It is much to the credit of the Directors of the Archive that they decided to celebrate the bicentenary of the Grose project by transcribing and editing Daniel Grose's text and reproducing his watercolours, all in colour, in this beautiful volume. I assume that the impressive production at a reasonable price is the result of sponsorship from Rohan Holdings, the Mark Fitch Fund, the Office of Public Works, the Kress Foundation and the Dublin School of Irish Studies. There is a preface by Nicholas Robinson, the Archive's Chairman, and a foreword by Ken Rohan. The colour separations have been excellently done by Master Photo Engraving, and Bairds' of Antrim have yet again attained their customary standard in printing.

Apart from Daniel Grose's text, for which Ann Martha Rowan deserves the credit for transcribing, Roger Stalley has provided an introduction and up-to-date commentaries on the plates. No-one can claim that Daniel Grose, or his uncle, were anything more than pleasantly naive topographical watercolourists. A rather more accomplished artist belonging to the Grose circle was the amateur, John Nixon, sometime Secretary of the Beefsteak Club, on whom no monograph has yet been written. Nixon visited Ireland many times between about 1780 and 1798. Under the influence of the equally bibulous Rowlandson, he achieved considerable success in caricature and figure-drawing, the strong point of neither of the Groses. Daniel Grose's drawings of sculpture are particularly rubbery and inaccurate. Still, his charming topographical views show us many architectural features, mainly mediaeval, which have since been lost, sometimes alarmingly recently. For instance, the tower house at Timoleague, Co. Cork (no. 9), was largely demolished by the County Council as late as 1938, on the grounds that vibration from the railway was causing stones to fall. A point is made by Professor Stalley in his introduction by juxtaposing Grose's view of Clonmel Parish Chuch (no 41) with a present-day photograph, showing the result of drastic Victorianisation completely altering the character of the building. Grose's drawings of the lost effigy of a knight from Molann, Waterford (no 2), and the late mediaeval font base (no 8) from Armagh Cathedral (taken away by the architect Cottingham for his private museum!) appear to be unique and valuable images. His view of the north elevation of Armagh Cathedral (no 74) shows Primate Robinson's restoration, before Cottingham got at it, and consequently documents the building in the same state as it appears in Cornelius Varley's very accurate pencil drawings of

# BOOK REVIEWS

1808, now in Armagh County Museum.

For an antiquary, Daniel Grose seems to have had some strange mental blocks, but frequently these were shared by his contemporaries. Before Rickman and the Pugins, knowledge of mediaeval architecture was in its infancy, and, as Stalley says, Grose 'could not recognise a latrine chute when he saw one'. More puzzling is the fact that the presence of more than one mediaeval church in a town such as Youghal could throw him into hopeless confusion. Stalley also suggests that Grose was less interested in drawing buildings than boats, proudly flying the White Ensign and the Cross of St George (Inisbofin, Longford, no 38, and Rindown, Roscommon, no 39). Conversely, his mind was not closed to prehistoric antiquities, nor indeed to fortifications and houses of the seventeenth century, and he must have been one of the earliest draughtsmen to take note of the Irish high crosses. At Tuam Cathedral (nos 28 and 29), Grose displayed antiquarian sagacity in recognising the fragmentary nature of the building, long before its remodelling by Deane in the 1860s. More remarkably, he correctly identified the elaborate romanesque arch, then on the exterior, as the original chancel arch, and appreciated its superior aesthetic quality, both in words and in an unusually careful drawing. It was not Grose's fault to call it Saxon instead of Hiberno-Romanesque, as he was limited by the terminology of his own age. One of the fascinations of Grose's text is the amount of local folklore he collected, and therefore he may be regarded as a pioneer in another field. Daniel Grose comes over as a gentle, humane character, seriously concerned with social justice both in Ireland and abroad. Well-meaningly, he supported Wilberforce's abolitionist reforms, but inevitably he found himself in his old age out of touch with hard political reality. No doubt he would have been delighted with the belated resurrection of his handiwork, in a printed form of which his own era could never have dreamed. The publication of this volume, together with the welcome appearance of Dr Peter Harbison's edition of the drawings by Gabriel Beranger from the National Library, has meant that early topographical draughtsmen in Ireland have been recently very well served.

*Martyn Anglesea*

*Martyn Anglesea is Curator of Watercolours, Prints and Drawings in the Ulster Museum.*

## FACES IN A BOOKSHOP: IRISH LITERARY PORTRAITS

Galway, Kenny's Bookshop and Art Gallery, 1990, IR£30.00

In his article 'The Possibility of Portraiture', published in *Circa*, no. 57, David Brett questions the very idea of a book of literary portraits. He asks whether 'a book of Irish fishermen, schoolmistresses, drunks or TDs' wouldn't 'do just as well': it may well do. The significance of this publication, however, is that it has been produced by Kenny's of Galway, a family bookshop which has, since its beginnings in 1940, shown a strong commitment to the visual and literary arts. (The newly named Kenny's Bookshop and Art Gallery has, since the early eighties, housed a full-time gallery on its extended premises).

A hundred and seven writers are represented by seventy-seven artists. Most of these individuals have been closely involved with Kenny's at some stage of their career.

Certain artists were invited to work with a writer of their choice and various writers were asked to nominate artists whom they might like to represent them. Some of the artists are international figures; others are hardly known outside of Galway. Many of the artists would not naturally make portraits; some would not even work with the figure. Not surprisingly, there is an immense variety of standards, media and styles in this collection and the result is ore of an 'interest show' than a high quality fine art exhibition.

There are, however, some remarkable portraits *qua* portraits/work of art in their own right. Among them are the characteristically perceptive paintings of Michael Longley and Brian Friel by Basil Blackshaw. Neil Shawcross's oil study of Michael Longley smoking and seated sideways on a high stool, is equally sensitive.

Here there are many faces — more, it would seem, than people. David Brett in the above mentioned article, asks if we might be 'expected to see in these faces some special essence of literature'. I would extend the question further and ask if the viewer of these portraits might gain any sort of real insight into the work of the individual sitter. In the poignant and perceptive portrayal of their sitters, the few fine portraits, (some of them referred to above), manage to convey a sense of the created as well as the creator.

Other artists have alluded to individual aspects or concerns of the writer in question in a more obvious way. Charles Harper's collage of John B Keane includes an image of a thatched cottage, a West of Ireland bog landscape and some sea scenes. Tom O'Reilly's large triple portrait of John Broderick is replete with references to repressed sexuality and both mutilated and authority figures.

A few writers are depicted 'at work' in the tradition of the portrait of the artist in his/her studio. Christopher Nolan, drawn by Maura Kelleher, sits by his typewriter, with a copy of his most recent novel close by. Vincent McDonnell, painted in true realistic fashion by Fergus Lyons, stares rather eerily out from the monitor of a wordprocessor, his hand and notebook resting on the keyboard.

As is so often the case with art exhibitions or publications, sculpture is quantitatively poorly represented. Marjorie Fitzgibbon's strongly modelled bronze heads of Seamus Heaney and Mary Lavin and Michael Wilkin's bust in cast cement of Pat Boran (one of the younger writers to be represented in this collection) stand out in this category.

If these works are intended to say something significant about Irish literature (which David Brett might wonder and which I doubt) there is an unrepresentative lack of humour. Exceptions are Jay Murphy's mixed media portrait of Frank McGuinness. The author, who apparently failed to make the appointment for the sitting, is depicted *in absentia* by way of a painted photograph, one of many bits of paper strewn about the room. A cat sits in the armchair in the centre of the picture while another places itself nearby.

The book is well produced on the whole, printed locally, with a high standard of photographic reproductions. The overall design, however, is deficient in its lack of definition. A concise, comprehensive biography of each artist and writer is included as well as a cross-referenced index. One significant omission is the date of each work (which I believe is mostly, although not always, 1990).

Apparently the exhibition was one of the most successful — in terms of audience, critical acclaim and sales — in the history of Kenny's Bookshop and Art Gallery, where another project is currently being planned, along similar lines.

*Sarah Finlay*

*Sarah Finlay is Visual Arts Officer in An Chomhairle Ealaíon/The Arts Council.*

# INDEX

## PICTURE CREDITS

*The numbers are those of the pages on which the photographs or plans appear.*

**(70, 71, 76, 77)** Bill Hastings; **(81)** Brendan Dempsey, TCD; **(85)** Marie Kearns, Eolas, The Irish Science and Technology Agency; **(128)** John Kellett; **(149, 150, 151)** Valerie Dowling; **(164, 165)** Courtesy Tate Gallery, London; **(179)** Arts Council of Northern Ireland; **(180, 181, 182)** Office of Public Works; **(187, 188, 189, 190)** Anthony Hobbs; **(196—207)** Mark McCall; **(238—43)** Roy Hewson.

## ACKNOWLEDGEMENTS

For permission to quote from unpublished correspondence on pp. 102—14 we are grateful to Miss Anne Yeats, Dr Michael Yeats, and the Rare Books and Manuscripts Division, The New York Public Library, Astor, Lenox and Tilden Foundations, for material from the John Quinn Collection and the Foster-Murphy Collection. Unpublished material by Lady Gregory, copyright 1992, Anne de Winton & Catherine Kennedy, with permission from Colin Smythe, representing the Estate.